WORLDS COLLIDING

For Leota John Ahdar

Worlds Colliding

Conservative Christians and the Law

REX J. AHDAR
University of Otago

Routledge
Taylor & Francis Group
LONDON AND NEW YORK

First published 2001 by Dartmouth Publishing Company and Ashgate Publishing

Reissued 2018 by Routledge
2 Park Square, Milton Park, Abingdon, Oxon OX14 4RN
711 Third Avenue, New York, NY 10017, USA

Routledge is an imprint of the Taylor & Francis Group, an informa business

A Library of Congress record exists under LC control number: 2001091527

ISBN 13: 978-1-138-72672-7 (hbk)
ISBN 13: 978-1-315-19123-2 (ebk)

Contents

List of Figures and Table

Foreword

Phillip E Johnson
Jefferson E Peyser Professor of Law, Emeritus

Not long ago, most social scientists accepted a 'secularization thesis', which assumed that modernization would inevitably lead to secularization. The thesis was not that modern people would necessarily stop being religious, but that such religion as remained would be progressively conformed to modern scientific thinking, through discarding the frankly supernatural elements. Modernist secularization would lead to a society where scientific rationalists, mainly agnostic, would rule the mind. The agnostics would be allied with liberal religionists, who would employ outmoded ideas like 'God' or 'the gospel of Jesus' to support beneficial social programmes like wealth redistribution and protection of the environment. Religious fundamentalists (that is, those who cling to the outdated belief that the old ideas describe reality) would be marginalized to a cultural backwater, and so confined could preserve their delusionary belief systems without causing trouble for the enlightened people who would rule the body politic. The secular hegemony could claim in good faith that was neutral on all religious questions—except, or course, for its insistence that those questions must be kept out of public life. Under these rules human reason would replace God as the supreme authority, and the secular rulers would have nothing to fear from religion.

The secularization hypothesis was not based only on wishful thinking, but also on objectively observable historical trends. Religion (specifically, the Christian religion) entered the nineteenth century with a dominant position in English and American society, but departed that century having lost the allegiance of the intellectuals. Many factors contributed to the change, but the most important element was the overwhelming intellectual power of Darwinism, backed by the invincible authority of science. Darwin's masterpiece, the *Origin of Species*, appeared in 1859. Before that date even religious sceptics had to acknowledge the need for a Creator, because it seemed that living organisms were too wonderfully complex to be the product of unintelligent natural forces. After 1859, the shoe was on the other foot, and theists had to scramble to find reasons for continuing the philosophical contest. Natural selection effectively took the place of God. Modernist theologians could still posit a God who created natural selection, but thinking people recognize a desperate manoeuvre when they see it. Darwinism did not prove that God does not exist, but it sufficed to persuade the brightest people that God plays no necessary role in creation.

In this philosophical environment, what Professor Ahdar calls the 'Wellington Worldview'—in the United States we would probably not call it the 'Washington Worldview', but more precisely the Harvard/*New York Times* Worldview—quite logically emerged as triumphant. If God is moribund then Man must take his place, and whatever is left of God should retire to that never-never land of 'religious belief', where Zeus and Wotan doze away the centuries. Once confined to that semi-nonexistence, God ought to be permanently incapable of repeating the kind of trouble he has caused in the past.

For better or worse, it was not to be so. Christian theism has not melted away and seems to be entering a more assertive phase. That is why the legal controversies discussed by Professor Ahdar point more to the future than to the past. The Wellington Worldview and the conservative Christian worldview are in conflict, of course. But is the outcome of that conflict in doubt? I think so. The secularizing philosophies retain the dominant position, even within the religious world. But they have not consolidated their victory, and the conservative Christian worldview now has to be regarded as a more or less permanent part of the cultural landscape, rather than something that might fade away if you give it enough time. That means that the climate of opinion might turn in another direction if events provide the opportunity.

In my opinion, Professor Ahdar succeeds admirably at approaching his subject dispassionately—while admitting that he is one of those disdained conservative Christians. Anyone who thinks that being a conservative Christian is a disqualifying bias (the unbiased people being those who could never imagine questioning the Wellington Worldview) just convicts himself of being imprisoned in an outdated rationalist mental cage. To say this is not nihilism, or even postmodernist relativism. It is merely to acknowledge that a lot of what passes for objective knowledge, at any given historical moment, probably contains a substantial measure of prejudice. If the academic world is as rational and unprejudiced as it claims to be (a mighty 'if'), it will welcome works like this one as contributing a point of view that deserves to be heard, and sympathetically understood.

The good news is that the profound differences in opinion do not necessarily lead to irreconcilable conflict. When secular rationalists learn to understand the Christian conservatives from the inside, they learn how much exaggeration there is in talk of 'culture wars', and how much accommodation and compromise is possible when people learn to treat each other with mutual respect. It is more or less comparable to what 'down-under' rationalists are learning (however reluctantly) from Maoris and Australian aborigines. Rationalists tend to be totalitarian, and to be blind to their own prejudices. When they learn to be more open to other ways of thinking it will be like a new birth. Any unborn child must yearn to stay in the womb, where things are warm and comfortable and one needs not deal with conflict. But one must go through the pain in order to meet the fullness of life.

University of California, Berkeley
November 2000

Preface

This book arises from a longstanding personal interest in the relationship between faith and law, church and state, religion and government. It is based on my Ph D thesis in law awarded by the University of Otago in 2000. I am grateful to the Faculty of Law, University of Otago for the privilege of undertaking this research and to Professor Hector MacQueen and the Faculty of Law, University of Edinburgh, for their hospitality during my sabbatical in 1998.

First and foremost I want to thank my doctoral supervisors, Professors Peter Skegg and Stuart Anderson for their expert guidance. I owe them much. I wish to credit Peter for suggesting the expression, 'Wellington worldview'.

I am grateful to many friends and colleagues who have assisted me with my research and writing, some of whom patiently read draft chapters I inflicted upon them. My thanks to, in no set order, Dr John Stenhouse, Dr Chris Gousmett, Dr Brett Knowles, Professor Jonathan Boston, Associate Professor Paul Trebilco, Professor Mark Henaghan, Associate Professor John Dawson, Associate Professor Paul Rishworth, Judge Arnold Turner CMG, Michael Robertson, Bruce Logan and Monsignor Vince Hunt. I thank Professor Patrick Parkinson and Dr Don Mathieson QC too for their valuable comments. I remember the late Reverend James Worsfold, and thank him for 'commissioning' me to undertake the project. Garth Lucas, Pastor Stan Shaw and, especially, my dear brother Gary Johnston kindly checked parts of the manuscript. I should add that the views expressed in the thesis are mine (as are any errors) and ought not to be attributed to any of the foregoing.

My appreciation to Valmai Bilsborough-York, Marianne Henderson, Fiona Masters, Kerry O'Donnell and Lucy Gray for their expert secretarial skills.

For her constant love, patience and encouragement, to mention just a few of her attributes (see Proverbs 31 for the others), I thank my beloved wife, Lidwina. *Fa'afetai lava.*

This book reflects the legal and other materials available to me up until February 2000, although I have included some significant developments since, such as the tragic *Laufau* case, the Court of Appeal's important freedom of expression judgment in *Living Word* and the progress of the Property (Relationships) Bill.

Soli Deo Gloria.

Faculty of Law, University of Otago, Dunedin
November 2000

Acknowledgements

To the extent that *Worlds Colliding* reproduces previously published work, I am grateful to the publishers and editors for permission to use and modify that material here.

Portions of Chapter 1 first appeared in the article, 'A Christian State?' (1998-1999) 13 *Journal of Law and Religion*. My thanks to Professor Marie Failinger and the *Journal*.

Parts of Chapters 6 and 7 are taken from two published essays: a chapter in Paul Beaumont and Keith Wotherspoon (eds), *Christian Perspectives on Law and Relationism*, published by Paternoster Press in 2000, and a chapter in the Peter Edge and Graham Harvey anthology, *Law and Religion in Contemporary Society*, published by Ashgate Publishing that same year.

Extracts from Chapter 8 are drawn from an article (co-written with James Allan) in the 2001 *New Zealand Law Review*. I am grateful to Neil Campbell and Grant Huscroft and the Legal Research Foundation.

Extracts from Chapter 9 will appear in Richard O'Dair and Andrew Lewis (eds), *Law and Religion*, published by Oxford University Press in 2001.

I wish to acknowledge the encouragement of John Irwin of Ashgate Publishing Limited and the opportunity he has afforded me to disseminate the work to an international audience.

List of Abbreviations

AJHR	Appendices to the Journals of the House of Representatives
BORA	New Zealand Bill of Rights Act
CC	Conservative Christian; Conservative Christianity
CRC	United Nations Convention on the Rights of the Child
CW	Challenge Weekly
CYFS	Child, Youth and Family Services
CYPFA	Children, Young Persons, and Their Families Act
FRNZ	Family Reports of New Zealand
FVPCA	Films, Videos, and Publications Classification Act
HRC	Human Rights Commission
HRNZ	Human Rights Reports of New Zealand
ICCPR	International Covenant on Civil and Political Rights
JCS	Journal of Church and State
JSSR	Journal for the Scientific Study of Religion
LJ	Law Journal
LRev	Law Review
MP	Member of Parliament
NZAR	New Zealand Administrative Reports
NZFLR	New Zealand Family Law Reports
NZPD	New Zealand Parliamentary Debates
NZJH	New Zealand Journal of History
NZLJ	New Zealand Law Journal
NZLR	New Zealand Law Reports
NZLRev	New Zealand Law Review
NZULR	New Zealand Universities Law Review
OPHM	Ordination of Openly-Practising Homosexual or Lesbian candidates for the Ministry
PCANZ	Presbyterian Church of Aotearoa New Zealand
SOP	Supplementary Order Paper
SSM	Same-Sex Marriage
UN	United Nations
VUWLR	Victoria University of Wellington Law Review

PART ONE

1 Introduction

The Aim and Scope of the Study

This is a study of a particular group and its reaction to cultural and legal change. The group is conservative Christians: theologically conservative, usually Protestant, Christians, who adhere to 'traditional' moral values. They are critical of and (to varying degrees) antagonistic to the prevailing culture and wider society, an environment which they believe is becoming increasingly hostile to traditional Christianity. They are chosen for at least three reasons.

First, they are a numerically large and visible group in New Zealand, totalling many tens of thousands, and a group which has in the last 20 years become politicized. Second, because of their attitude to the state and their occasional counter-cultural stance, they constitute a cadre of religionists likely to test the limits of liberal democratic tolerance and the law over matters of religious exercise. Third, they are a group familiar to the author. I identify with that milieu, which makes it both useful and dangerous to critique it. It is useful for I bring the insights and experiences of an insider. The danger is an undue sympathy towards the conservative Christian viewpoint resulting in a lack of criticism where this is merited. Aware of this, I have striven to be as detached and dispassionate as possible.

Within the broad rubric of conservative Christianity there are many strands. I shall unravel these later but one distinction needs mention here. The majority of conservative Christians are not active in public or political life. The 'silent majority' of 'ordinary' Christians seldom write letters to newspapers, protest in the street or lobby Parliament. They may not even be able to clearly articulate their viewpoint. Nonetheless, they form the bulk of this group. A minority are politically active and publicly vocal. This visible public subset (and its spokespeople) is the segment—of necessity—cited throughout this study. The extent to which they truly represent the rest remains, I concede, a moot point. Their attitudes may well be more polarized and their rhetoric more uncompromising than that of the majority.[1] I shall assume that they do speak for thousands of others and that they do *for the most part* accurately reflect the views of their constituency.

To explain the conservative Christian mindset I have relied upon a few leading publications. A principal one is the newspaper *Challenge Weekly*. This weekly publication captures well the typical conservative Christian view on matters of the moment. Other sources are New Zealand Christian non-denominational periodicals such as *Stimulus*, *Reality*, *Humanity*, *Cutting Edge* and *New Slant* as well as denominational newspapers such as *Crosslink* and *New Zealand Catholic*.

The reader will see frequent reference to overseas Christian writers and commentators, a practice which might initially seem strange. This is perhaps a peculiar feature of New Zealand Christianity, though it may also reflect the wider importation of culture generally. What a leading American or British evangelical extols, cautions or advocates is usually promptly disseminated and re-echoed in equivalent circles in New Zealand. For one thing, Radio Rhema, the nation-wide conservative Christian radio network, carries regular programmes of overseas Christian teachers and preachers. For instance, American psychologist, Dr James Dobson of *Focus on the Family,* is as well known, perhaps better known, in New Zealand as he is in his home country.

New Zealand conservative Christians, while they certainly have their own pressing local issues, perceive themselves to be in a common battle with believers of similar ilk in other Western countries. What happens to evangelical Christian parents in California or Pentecostal churches in Queensland is readily assimilated and extended to New Zealand. Contemporary Western Christianity forms a kind of 'seamless web' to borrow a phrase from the famous Hart/Devlin debate.[2] Lessons are to be, indeed must be, learnt from overseas: the particularities of the foreign context and the idiosyncrasies of the society from which the message originates are downplayed if not ignored.

The topics chosen in this book are largely self-selecting. The case studies—the impact of human rights laws, family and parenting issues and growing legal acceptance of homosexuality—are ones that currently loom large in certain Christian circles. They are not the only ones (abortion and sex education are others) but space permits only limited coverage. This study then is driven by conservative Christians' contemporary agenda. In the past the issues were different (battles over bible-in-schools, prohibition, divorce[3]) and in the future the issues will undoubtedly be different (cloning perhaps?).

This study is quite wide ranging and I have used somewhat broad strokes at times. The specialist philosopher, sociologist, historian and so on, may cavil at my generalizations but that is, I believe, unavoidable for the sort of 'big picture' cultural analysis and argument attempted here.

Harry Blamires in *The Christian Mind* observed: 'There is no thinking without exaggeration.'[4] Whereas scholarship cannot endure it, thinking without exaggeration is, he argued, impossible. The scholar evades decisiveness, balances conclusions against rival ones so as to negate conclusiveness, and is 'tentative, sceptical, uncommitted.' By contrast:

> The thinker hates indecision and confusion; he firmly distinguishes right from wrong, good from evil; he is at home in a world of clearly demarcated categories and proven conclusions; he is dogmatic and committed; he works towards decisive action.[5]

Now Blamires conceded these were pure types (or archetypes), for no scholar can neglect thought and no thinker is devoid of scholarship. While exaggeration, generalization and over-simplification ought to be eschewed, I am nevertheless hopeful the reader will permit me to indulge occasionally in some expansive and speculative thinking. The differences will at times be (somewhat) exaggerated, the picture portrayed as rather black and white. This strategy is deliberate and the desire is not to be polemical. Rather, I wish to reveal tensions and conflicts which a more circumspect approach might deny. Where appropriate I will re-introduce the necessary exceptions, qualifications and nuances to present a more accurate picture. One does not want to distort reality but on the other hand, dealing solely with endless shades of grey can not only be dull but less revealing.

A model which I have found most helpful is that developed by a New Zealand Presbyterian scholar, the Rev Dr Harold Turner, who devised a missiological model of cultural analysis.[6] Turner's aim is to re-orient missionary efforts to address not just the 'surface culture' (the social practices and customs, including law, which govern a people's existence) but also the 'deep culture' of a particular society. The latter refers to the 'foundational' or 'deep' level of human existence—the basic assumptions, axioms, convictions or worldview, by which people live. The visible surface clashes occurring between conservative Christians and the state may be seen, I argue, as expressions of deeper conflicts of worldview. Chapter 3 explores this in detail.

The contours of this study are as follows. Part One sets the scene. Chapter 1 describes the conservative Christian narrative, outlining the conservative reaction to cultural disestablishment. Chapter 2 examines the characteristics of conservative Christians and their distinctive worldview. Juxtaposed against this worldview is, conservative Christians argue, an opposing, supplanting *zeitgeist* or spirit of the times. Chapter 3 analyses the key tenets of the liberal, modernist state, what I call the 'Wellington worldview'. The next chapter posits a model of engagement. While peaceful coexistence between the inhabitants of the two 'worlds' is the rule, conflict also occurs. This is unsurprising, given the antithetical nature of the two worldviews and the inability of both sides always to forge an accommodation.

Part Two comprises a series of studies of substantive areas of law where the clash of worldviews is played out. Chapter 5 commences this section with an investigation of conservative Christian attitudes towards human rights theory. Conflicts with human rights advocates and enforcement agencies over the last two decades are analyzed. The next three chapters focus on a central concern of conservative Christians, the family. After contrasting Christian and liberal models of the family, Chapter 6 backgrounds the history of, and reaction of conservative Christians to, an important international treaty ratified by New Zealand in the 1990s; the United Nations Convention on the Rights of the Child 1989. Two matters of great significance to conservative Christian parents are selected—the rights of religious upbringing and corporal punishment of children. Chapters 7 and 8 respectively explore what impact, if any, the United Nations Convention will have upon these two parental prerogatives.

The next two chapters consider the conservative Christian antipathy toward homosexual practice. Will the Human Rights Act 1993 and its prohibition of discrimination based on sexual orientation curtail churches' right to ordain whom they wish? I investigate in Chapter 9 whether conservative Christian congregations will be required to ordain openly-practising gay ministers. Chapter 10 changes the focus. Instead of the defensive preservation of existing Christian freedoms, I now consider to what extent conservative Christians can influence public policy in the matter of the introduction of same-sex marriage.

Part Three contains some final thoughts.

A particular emphasis throughout is religious liberty. I am interested in ascertaining the extent to which the contrasting worldviews of my subject group and the state curtails, or potentially curtails, the religious freedoms of the former. Does the modern liberal state circumscribe the religious freedom of conservative Christians where the latter's worldview and practices challenge key tenets of liberal theory? The plight of conservative Christians is, in many ways, a test case for any minority group holding a worldview at odds with the dominant societal and governmental one.

The New Zealand Religious Landscape and Conservative Christians

The Conservative Christian Narrative

Much recent legal writing is concerned with 'story' or 'narrative'.[7] Stories are important both for the group itself and for outsiders. For the group, a story builds consensus and strengthens solidarity. For the outsider, a story is less confrontational and more insinuative than a direct plea or demand. Richard Delgado suggests the story 'invites the reader to alienate herself or himself from the events described, to enter the mental set of the teller, whose view is different from the reader's own.'[8] Furthermore, stories are a particularly effective way to challenge mindsets: they are 'useful tools for the underdog because they invite the listener to suspend judgment, listen for the story's point, and test it against his or her own version of reality.'[9] Christians claim to have a story, indeed *the* story of human existence and history. This 'historically particular story [the Gospel] is offered as an alternative to the grand stories (or metanarratives) by which our culture lives.'[10]

Conservative Christians have their own distinct story or narrative of New Zealand. My distillation of typical expressions is set out below:

> We were once a blessed, Christian nation. Not everyone was Christian but most were and the rest conceded the Christian ethic should be the rule. We are now in decline. New Zealand has lost its way and forgotten its Christian roots. The crisis is not primarily economic or political but spiritual. 'Righteousness exalteth a nation: but sin is a reproach to any people' (Proverbs 14:34). Christian ideals and morality are being supplanted by the 'spirit of the age' (a secular, humanist, pluralist worldview). A climate has developed which is increasingly antagonistic towards Christian claims of universal, public truth and higher law. The situation, while parlous, is not irredeemable. Christians can and must become active in all spheres, including politics and law, to restore and re-direct the ship of state. New Zealand can be blessed again.

Writing in *Challenge Weekly*, the Rev Arthur Gunn, for example, chronicled the divinely ordered demise of nations and empires throughout history (from Babylon to Greece and Rome and on through to twentieth century France and Germany) who sinned against God. New Zealand faced the similar prospect of failing to recognize this 'inexorable moral law' of Proverbs 14:34:

> There was a time when New Zealand, broadly speaking, could be called a righteous nation. The existence of churches throughout the land, even in remote areas, is a testimony to that. . . . In those days so many New Zealanders, Maori and Pakeha, were Christians. Churches were well attended. Bible classes and Sunday schools overflowed with young people and children. . . . In those days our nation was exalted among the nations of the world. Small though we were we were greatly admired because of our racial harmony and because of our advanced social and health services. Today all this has gone.[11]

The Christian nation story—perhaps the dominant or majority story—is, as we shall see, no longer ascendant. What was once the prevailing narrative is becoming a 'counter-story'[12] jostling with several others for control of the direction of New Zealand.

How true is the Christian nation story? Some foreign observers have viewed New Zealand as strongly religious. André Siegfried, for example, maintained that: 'No tradition has remained so strong in New Zealand as the religious one.'[13] However, the rose-coloured perception that early New Zealand was a 'golden age' for Christianity is regularly debunked today.

Hugh Jackson found that 'the churchgoing of New Zealanders was mediocre by the standards of the British at home.'[14] Indeed, usual church attendances in New South Wales, which had begun life as a penal colony, were a little higher than in New Zealand.[15] John Stenhouse offers this blunt conjecture: 'Most settlers came here to get on in life, not to worship God.'[16] Michael Hill summarizes:

> Despite some early attempts to transplant various Christian denominations to New Zealand on a regional basis—the Church of England in Canterbury, the Free Church of Scotland in Otago, vestiges of which can still be found in regional patterns of religious adherence—no denomination managed to establish claims to monopoly, and from the mid-nineteenth century there was an acceptance of pluralism and a secular stance on the part of the state. . . . While a majority of the population adopted some form of denominational label, nominalism was evident in the considerably lower proportions who engaged in regular religious activity.[17]

Whilst religious practice may have been tepid, it should be added that churches generally were held in high respect by New Zealanders.[18]

Despite Siegfried's assertion that the 'man without a religion'[19] was regarded as a pariah in New Zealand society, freethought, rationalism and non-religious profession have been viewed from the earliest days with comparative favour. Hill maintains:

> Irreligion has always been accorded a respectable status in New Zealand, and as early as 1880 the country was considered a Mecca of secularity by a group of English free-thinkers, who noted that 'there is so much greater freedom for opinions in New Zealand than [in England], that what are called heterodox, do not stand as an insuperable obstacle to high office in the Chief Council of the Country . . .'[20]

The various Freethought, Secular and Rationalist societies that survive from last century continue on today in fairly small numbers. Their modern descendants are the New Zealand Rationalist Association and the Humanist Society of New Zealand.[21]

Successive Disestablishments of Christianity

Here I adopt, and adapt to New Zealand, the sociologist José Casanova's analysis of the United States.[22] Casanova propounded three disestablishments in that country. The first (constitutional) disestablishment occurred at the founding of the Republic and culminated in the First Amendment. The second involved the secularization of American higher education after the Civil War. The third disestablishment was the disestablishment of generic Protestantism from the American way of life beginning in the 1960s. This decade saw 'the emergence of a pluralistic system of norms and forms of life.'[23]

The First Disestablishment: A de jure disestablishment (or nonestablishment) There was both an early commitment to religious freedom and religious equality and a rejection of the notion of a state church.

RELIGIOUS FREEDOM AND RELIGIOUS EQUALITY The signing of Treaty of Waitangi on 6 February 1840 saw the unexpected inclusion of an assurance concerning religious freedom. This came about due to the initiative of the Roman Catholic bishop, Bishop Jean Baptiste Francois Pompallier.[24] In response to Pompallier's request for protection of the Catholic Church by the British Government, Governor Hobson, 'with much blandness of gesture and expression', replied, 'Most certainly', and proceeded to express his regret that the Bishop had not made known his wishes earlier, as the provision 'would have been embodied in the treaty.'[25] The Rev Henry Williams, who found the task 'something of a tough morsel, requiring care,'[26] took pencil and paper and wrote: 'The Governor wishes you to understand that all the Maoris who shall join the Church of England, who shall join the Wesleyans, who shall join the Pikopo or Church of Rome, and those who retain their Maori practices, shall have the protection of the British Government.'[27] The note was relayed to the Governor, who in turn passed it on to Pompallier who read it and expressed approval ('Oh, yes, that will do very well', said the Bishop in English.[28]) Williams then read a carefully written statement to the assembly:

> E mea ana te Kawana, ko nga whakapono katoa, o Ingarani, o nga Weteriana, o Roma, me te ritenga Maori hoki, e tiakina ngatahitia e ia. ('The Governor says the several faiths [beliefs] of England, of the Wesleyans, of Rome, and also the Maori custom, shall be alike protected by him.')[29]

Claudia Orange argues that the English missionaries hoped that the Roman Catholic faith would suffer by association with *ritenga* (what

Busby termed 'heathen practices'), which they attacked as decadent and which they wished to eliminate. She adds:

> The official recognition seemingly granted Maori custom should be seen for what it was—an inclusion arising from sectarian jealousy. It ran counter to nineteenth-century Christian sensitivities, and barely accorded with Normanby's instructions to suppress, by force if necessary, the more extreme Maori usages. This promise to protect Maori custom—a verbal commitment given only by chance—amounted to very little.[30]

In the Imperial Instructions to Governor Hobson, dated 5 December 1840, religious tolerance was listed. Of the 63 clauses, one stated: 'Freedom of worship in any peaceable and orderly manner was to be permitted even if not according to the rites of the Church of England.'[31]

The principle of religious equality emerges in the first Parliamentary debates. An important background point must be first mentioned: the New Zealand Constitution Act, enacted at Westminster in 1852, was silent on the question of religion and this seemed to imply equality of religion and absence of a State church.[32]

The opening session of the first sitting day of Parliament, 26 May 1854, witnessed an unexpected debate on the question of an opening prayer.[33] James Macandrew, a Presbyterian from Dunedin, offered to fetch a nearby Anglican parish minister to ensure there should be 'an acknowledgement of dependence on the Divine Being'. It was 'clear to him that the House of Representatives, being the first embodiment of a New Zealand nationality, should be consecrated' and so he proposed a motion to that effect.[34] A counter-motion was immediately put that the House 'be not converted into a conventicle, and that prayers be not offered up.'[35] A vigorous debate ensued. Some considered such a prayer would seem 'to involve the question of a State religion, the very appearance of which ought to be avoided' by the House.[36] Edward Gibbon Wakefield tried to assuage fears by pointing out that in America 'where State religion was absolutely repudiated' the practice of opening the Legislative Houses by prayer was allowed.[37] Some members were by now becoming impatient and sought to short-circuit potentially 'fruitlessly prolonged' discussion, and so Frederic Weld suggested an amendment:

> That this House, whilst fully recognizing the importance of religious observances, will not commit itself to any act which may tend to subvert that perfect religious equality that is recognized by our Constitution, and therefore cannot consistently open this House with public prayer.[38]

Wakefield worried that 'New Zealand should be singular in this respect among the Christian countries of the earth.'[39] Dr Lee responded with doubts as to how the Jew could join with the Christian in a prayer and added: 'as the Constitution had very properly rid them of State religion, the House should take care how they voluntarily submitted to it.'[40] Weld's amendment was rejected by 20 votes to 10. The House then turned to the original motion and passed it (with no vote count recorded). It read:

> That, in proceeding to carry out the resolution of the House to open its proceedings with prayer, the House distinctly asserts the privilege of a perfect political equality in all religious denominations, and that, whoever may be called upon to perform this duty for the House, it is not thereby intended to confer or admit any pre-eminence to that Church or religious body to which he may belong.[41]

The Rev F J Lloyd was introduced, read prayers and never appeared again, the prayer being said thereafter by the Speaker.

In the Legislative Council, the upper house, a resolution on opening prayers to be read by the Speaker was passed on 27 May 1854. Dillon Bell (a Jew from Wellington) successfully opposed a motion for an Anglican to read prayers however. Bell feared this would 'interfere with the perfect religious equality which the Constitution recognized' and would be 'the thin edge of the wedge.'[42]

That same first Parliament, on 28 August 1855, also rejected a vote of £600 for Bishop Selwyn's salary despite a recommendation to this effect from the Colonial Secretary of State, Earl Gray, on 1 July 1854.[43] While the House 'fully recogniz[ed] the zeal and energy of his Lordship the Bishop of New Zealand and acknowledg[ed] the valuable services rendered by him on various occasions to the colony' the House could not vote a salary to him 'without departing from the principle of perfect civil equality of all the religious denominations—a principle this House has already affirmed and to the maintenance of which it stands pledged.'[44]

NONESTABLISHMENT New Zealand has never had an established or state church.[45] This fact was noted in 1998 by the Court of Appeal.[46] It is perhaps more accurate to describe this as 'nonestablishment' rather than disestablishment. There were, to be sure, various early regional attempts at religious establishment by the European immigrants. Otago and Southland were Free Church of Scotland settlements. The Otago settlement was begun in 1848 by the Rev Thomas Burns and Captain William Cargill, both of whom were 'fervent Free Churchmen' and who 'saw themselves as making a godly experiment after the model of the Pilgrim Fathers two centuries earlier.'[47] Unfortunately for them their dream of a Free Church theocracy, a 'Geneva of the Antipodes' was to founder.[48] Canterbury, led by John Robert Godley, was to be 'a new-world exemplar of an Anglican state.'[49] Again, hopes were not realized. One could also mention: the West Coast, a Roman Catholic stronghold; the fledging Nonconformist settlement in Albertland in Northland; and the small Scandinavian Lutheran settlements in places such as Dannevirke.[50] All this appears to support Lloyd Geering's argument that what the Europeans brought was not a homogeneous thing called Christianity.[51] Instead, the migrants saw themselves very much in denominational terms, as first Anglicans, Presbyterians, Methodists, Catholics and so on. New Zealand was less of a unified Christian nation and more of 'a Christian archipelago—a collection of denominational islands, each with its own shared set of beliefs.'[52] There was, at most, a modest preference and financial endowment for the Anglican Church leading some to describe that Church as having 'a quasi-establishment role' in the colony.[53] But as Antony Wood observes: 'The Anglican Church's pre-eminence was a shadowy affair in comparison with its position in the home country or in older established colonies of settlement.'[54] New Zealand was settled at the time when the principle of nonestablishment was gaining favour in Britain and the disestablishment of the Church of England was being seriously debated.[55]

In the nineteenth century there was a substantial formal separation of church and state. As Peter Lineham notes, the Freethinkers of the 1880s did not need to mount a constitutional campaign for the separation of church and state as 'the two were relatively separate' already.[56] Thus, Sir Robert Stout, speaking in 1879, could boast:

> It is said we are a Christian nation and the Bible is recognised by the State. I deny both propositions. As a nation we have nothing to do with religion. Every religion has equal rights before the law. None are supported by the State, and our highest offices of state can be held by men not professing the Christian religion. We have had a Jew Premier . . . We are a Christian nation in the sense that a majority of the citizens are Christian, but in no other sense.[57]

One of the few judicial pronouncements affirming nonestablishment is this one by the Supreme Court in 1910:

> There is no State Church here. The Anglican Church is in New Zealand in no sense a State Church. It is one of the numerous denominations existing in the Dominion; and, although no doubt it has a very large membership, it stands legally on no higher ground than any other of the religious denominations in New Zealand.[58]

In *Doyle* v *Whitehead*, a 1917 case, Sir Robert Stout, this time as Chief Justice of the Supreme Court, made what appears to be one of the only judicial statements pronouncing New Zealand to be a secular state. The Wellington City Council passed a by-law prohibiting playing golf on Sundays in Town Belt Reserves. Following a complaint from the Ministers' Association and clergymen of the Presbyterian Church (concerned it seems at the bad example to the young at the adjacent Presbyterian orphanage) the respondent, who breached this by-law, was charged. A Magistrate acquitted him on the grounds that the by-law was made for no other reason than to enforce Sunday observance and was thus bad in terms of the relevant legislation. The Supreme Court unanimously upheld this finding. Stout CJ declared:

> Considering that the State is neutral in religion, is secular, and that the State has provided for Sunday observance only so far as prohibiting work in public or in shops, &c, is concerned, and not prohibiting games, it cannot be said that this by-law is a reasonable by-law. It has also to be borne in mind that recreation on Sunday is not an offence even in countries where the Christian religion is established.[59]

The Second Disestablishment: A cultural, de facto disestablishment

A *DE FACTO* CHRISTIAN ESTABLISHMENT While New Zealand may not have had a state church, or an established religion, it might be argued that there was a *de facto* establishment of Christianity. Ivanica Vodanovich asserts, 'the New Zealand model . . . combine[d] separation of church and state, with recognition of the state as "Christian"'.[60] She argues that the state was committed to a 'non-specific and non-sectarian' Christianity.

The laws and institutions in New Zealand naturally reflected Christian values given the religious composition of the population. Moreover, the governing elite was also predominantly Christian. While public education was ostensibly secular, schools permitted religious, specifically Protestant, teaching on a limited basis under the so-called 'Nelson System'.[61]

This ingenious scheme was the brainchild of a Nelson clergyman, the Rev J H McKenzie and commenced in 1897. It was argued that as schools were open for five hours a day, three in the morning and two in the afternoon, a school might declare either the first or last hour of the morning as one designated for voluntary religious instruction. This was possible under the 1877 Education Act since that legislation allowed school buildings to be used on days and at hours other than those used for public school purposes.[62] This enabled religious instruction (as well as the statutory minimum four hours of secular education) to take place within the customary school hours. The Education Act 1964, which repeated the secular clause, simply formalized this long-standing arrangement: voluntary religious instructors were permitted by school boards to give religious instruction during school hours, with parents having the right to withdraw their children from such instruction.[63]

The character of this generic Christianity was Protestant and largely tolerant. Religious persecution was not absent however. Three brief instances must suffice.

New Zealand's treatment of conscientious objectors during both world wars was harsh. New Zealand was 'exceptional in the total severity of its policy'[64] towards conscientious objectors in World War II compared to other Commonwealth countries and the United States.

Next, the New Zealand government consistently suppressed certain Maori religious movements led by charismatic prophets unafraid to mix the political and religious.[65] Often these religious movements drew a parallel between themselves and the *Hurai* (Jews). Maori were viewed as antipodean Israelites, even one of the 'lost tribes of Israel'. Charismatic Maori prophets built upon this Hebrew model, casting Maori as a faithful remnant whose fortunes would be restored in a hoped-for millennium. The yoke of the Pakeha (European) oppressors would be broken and the land and *mana* (dignity) restored. Some of the better-known movements were: the *Pai Marire* (or *Hauhau*) led by Te Ua Haumene; Te Kooti, who survived the decimation of the *Hauhau* to form the Ringatu faith; Rua Kenana Hepetika, who founded a group of *Iharaira* (or Israelites) and established a theocracy at Maungapohatu in the Urewera; and, finally, Tahupotiki Wiremu Ratana, a faith healer and founder of the Ratana Church. Rua proved to be a sufficient thorn in the Government flesh that an Act was passed to combat him, and the activities generally of *tohunga* (healers, experts, priests).[66] The Tohunga Suppression Act 1907 made it a criminal offence for *tohunga* to practice on the 'superstition and credulity' of Maoris or to profess to possess supernatural healing powers.[67] Voyce, in a detailed study, concluded: 'This Act [was] typical of the response of the colonial government to the perceived threat from a traditional or revitalised tribal religion.'[68] The Act was, in Voyce's view, a failure since Maori were reluctant to inform on *tohunga* and thus invite supernatural retribution.[69]

Finally, one cannot ignore various spasms of intra-Christian sectarian conflict between Protestants and Catholics. It would be altogether surprising and wishful thinking to believe Old World suspicions, bigotries and antagonisms stayed at 'home' in Europe when the settlers came.[70] I have already noted the testiness evident at the signing of the Treaty of Waitangi.

A major battlefield was education. The churches began their own schools at first. Abolition of the provinces in 1876 meant there was a need for a national policy of education and a clarification of the roles of church and state. The debate on education in the late 1870s was conducted 'against a background of increasing sectarian tension.'[71] The passage of the Education Act 1877 is an important and fascinating story which has been well documented by historians.[72] It established a national system of education that was to be 'free, secular and compulsory'. The famous 'secular clause' read: 'The school shall be kept open five days in each week for at least four hours, two of which in the forenoon and two in the afternoon shall be consecutive, and teaching shall be entirely of a secular character.'[73] By a vote of 35 to 19, the House of Representatives deleted from the Bill the provision for religious exercises. The Legislative Council attempted to resurrect the provision but failed. Scholars emphasize that the secularity of the national education programme was not due primarily to anti-religious sentiment or the advocacy of secularism, but rather was an attempt to defuse sectarian strife.[74] Ian Breward observed:

> Careful study of the debates and divisions shows that there was very little doctrinaire secularism among members. Although [some] members of the Legislative Council . . . signed a protest against the secular provisions of the act, others saw parliament's action as a necessary way of distinguishing the sacred from the secular, or at the very least as a practical political solution to the educational tensions caused by denominationalism.[75]

THE 1960S WATERSHED: THE CRUMBLING OF THE *DE FACTO* ESTABLISHMENT The *de facto* Christian establishment seems to have been still intact in the 1960s. For example, Ivor Richardson concluded his comprehensive 1962 survey of the religious dimension of New Zealand laws by rejecting the view that Christianity was part of New Zealand law or that New Zealand was a Christian State. As he put it:

> If this means that the doctrines and principles of Christianity are legally binding on all citizens or that the political apparatus of government is subject to the mandates of the Christian religion, then the statement is patently incorrect.[76]

He continued however:

> Nevertheless, there is a certain amount of truth in the statement that Christianity is part of our law. In the first place, the Christian religion has played an important part in shaping our culture, our tradition, and our law. As Lord Sumner pointed out in *Bowman* v *Secular Society Ltd* [1917] AC 406, 464-465, the family is built on Christian ideals, and Christian ethics have made a tremendous impact on the development of our law, as is only natural considering the majority of New Zealanders come from a Christian background.[77]

The reflection of the Christian ethic and a diffuse Christianity continued, suggest some, until the 1960s.[78] At around that point there took place, as I shall call it, the second disestablishment. The first disestablishment, as we have seen, was the legal and constitutional one which occurred in the 1840s and 1850s. The second one, more difficult to pinpoint definitively, was and is the cultural or *de facto* disestablishment of generic Protestantism from its perch.

The 'cultural hegemony',[79] to adopt a sociological phrase, which Christians enjoyed (or at least believed they enjoyed) until recently has been eroded. The Rev Bruce Patrick articulates this concern:

> For many years, as long as Christendom prevailed across the Western world, the Church was comfortable in a New Zealand in which a Christian worldview largely prevailed. Since the 1960s however there has been a steady shift to a secular, now post-modern worldview, and the Church is seen as marginalized.[80]

The 1960s is usually chosen as the period ('the religiously desolate decade'[81]) in which a 'paradigm shift' or change of worldview took place in New Zealand.[82] 'From the sixties onwards things changed rapidly', suggests James Veitch.[83] A nation that was 'nominally Christian since its founding' became 'a post-Christian society', argues another.[84] Bishop Brian Carrell explains that the 1960s would prove

> to be the decade in which the form of Christianity identified with European nations for over 1300 years, and with their former colonies such as New Zealand for more than a century, began to go into rapid decline. This decade would in fact witness the demise of Christendom, arguably a more obvious end in this country than in any other Western nation.[85]

Of course the process had in fact begun at least as early as the Enlightenment.[86] Modernity has slowly but surely gathered momentum with, as Christians see it, a rapid acceleration in the late twentieth century. Christians were able to benefit from the cultural capital of centuries of Christendom, but both the structural process of secularization and the undermining effects of modernist ideas (scientific naturalism, liberal rationality, evolution and so forth) is finally coming to fruition.

The second disestablishment means the Christian worldview is no longer the prevailing one. There is a stubborn persistence among some conservative Christians, and perhaps some non-Christians, of the notion that New Zealand is a Christian nation. In terms of the history and traditions upon which people draw, the influence is, as Richardson noted earlier, unmistakably Christian. But in a formal legal sense the state is, and has been from the beginning, secular. The cultural picture is coming into alignment too. Lloyd Geering argued in 1985 that this vague public attachment to the idea of New Zealand as a Christian nation was becoming more tenuous as each year went by. He asserted:

> New Zealand is properly described today, not as a Christian state, but as a secular state. It means, on the one hand, that there is full religious freedom for all citizens. No citizen is penalized or loses any privilege because of his religious convictions. . . . To refer to New Zealand as a secular state means, on the other hand, that the state itself is not committed to or allied with any religious tradition or ideology, and therefore no religious group enjoys a privileged position.[87]

'The chief trend', wrote Geering in 1983, 'is the withdrawal of New Zealanders from active participation in any clearly recognizable religious group or institution.'[88] Geering's assessment-cum-prophecy is accurate if we measure religious conviction in terms of tangible external proxies such as church attendance and census figures for religious adherence. The levels of church attendance are low and declining. The most recent census figures show a decline for the mainline churches, growth for the 'sect-like' conservative charismatic churches, growth in non-Christian faiths (due to immigration) and a spectacular increase in the irreligious category. By 'irreligious' we should more accurately refer to: (1) the 'nones'[89]—those who stated they were in the 'No Religion' category; and possibly also (2) the 'Object to State' respondents. The largest single category in 1996 was the 'nones' (867,264).[90] If we add the 'Object to State' group (256,593) we see that around a third of all New Zealanders, 1.1 million people, are content to officially state their non-commitment to, or rejection of, religion entirely.

The assumption of an inexorable secular future for New Zealand is questionable though. Religion of a particular kind (the institutional variety) may be declining but religious revival, diversity and innovation ensure new varieties spring forth to supply people's inherent desire for the transcendent or ultimate.[91] New Zealand's large number of esoteric and innovative religious groups (its 'cultic milieu') is well documented. Moreover, whilst the 'nones' eschew traditional, organized forms of religious activity, they may often accept supernaturalism and seek spiritual guidance or solace in a variety of haphazard forms.[92] Peter Donovan suggests: 'Even if New Zealand society has become predominantly secular, then, it will not necessarily stay that way. Supernatural belief systems, far from slipping further and further out of sight, may yet come into greater prominence.'[93]

The 1999 Massey University study, 'Religion in New Zealand' (part of the International Social Survey Programme) revealed some interesting findings.[94] Some 61 per cent of New Zealanders believe in

God, or at least in 'a Higher Power of some kind'. Most (60 per cent) also believed in life after death and in heaven (55 per cent), with many further believing in religious miracles (40 per cent) and in hell (35 per cent). Superstition was not absent, with more than 40 per cent believing fortune-tellers really can foresee the future and with more than 30 per cent believing a person's star sign at birth, or horoscope, can affect the course of their future. The authors concluded:

> New Zealand is generally regarded as a very secular country, and this view is supported by the relatively low level of active involvement in religion of most New Zealanders. However, it would be wrong to conclude from this that New Zealanders are not religious or that religion is not important in New Zealand society. A sizeable minority of New Zealanders describe themselves as religious, pray regularly and regularly attend religious services. Furthermore, the majority of New Zealanders believe in God, pray at least once a year and attend a religious service at least as frequently.[95]

Manifestations of the Downgrading of Christianity: Marginalization

> In general . . . the church has lived with the politicisation resultant upon the Constantinian revolution from the fourth century until the twentieth in the way that the principal traditions of Christianity have taken for granted their right, whenever they can get it, to a position of special privilege and political power. They have seen establishment as normality, and have forgotten how late it came in Christian history.[96]

Some Christians in New Zealand think that they still live in *corpus Christianum* or Christendom. The mindset is a hard one to eradicate and is often called 'Constantinianism'—the assumption that Christians should rule. Stanley Hauerwas suggests:

> something has already gone wrong when Christians think they can ask, 'What is the best form of society or government?' This question assumes that Christians should or do have social and political power so they can determine the ethos of society. That this assumption has long been with us does nothing to confirm its truth.[97]

Many urge this mindset to be abandoned.[98] As Christians, we would be 'more relaxed and less compulsive about running the world if we made our peace with our minority situation, seeing this neither as a dirty trick of destiny nor as some great new progress but simply as the unmasking of the myth of Christendom, which wasn't true even when it was believed.'[99] Relaxing does not come easily to many Christians, however, who fear for the dire consequences to society should Christians not govern—anarchy or totalitarianism or, at the very least, the emergence of a neo-pagan culture.

The Christian viewpoint is typically treated today as just another opinion or partisan interest to put alongside others. Christians are politely (and sometimes not so politely) listened to, but their views are not automatically deferred to. One notorious instance occurred in March 1998. The Museum of New Zealand, *Te Papa*, ran a controversial exhibition which contained two works highly offensive to many Christians: the 'Virgin in a Condom' statue (a 7.5 cm statue of the Virgin Mary clad in a contraceptive) and a contemporary version of Leonardo da Vinci's, *The Last Supper*, with a topless woman at the centre of the table in place of Christ. Notwithstanding Catholic (and other religious) protests—and even an attack on the statue—the Museum refused to withdraw the exhibits.[100] In a pluralist society where the Museum acted as 'a forum within a varied social and cultural mix', the chances of one cultural or social group being offended was 'a daily risk' and so censorship would simply be inappropriate, defended senior Museum officials.[101] Compared to (what Christians perceive as) the unquestioned acceptance of conservative religious ideas in the era of cultural ascendancy, this looks like and is experienced as a downgrading of religion, a marginalization. An application to invoke the long-disused criminal prohibition against blasphemous libel was rejected by the Solicitor General. Such a prosecution, he said, would be inconsistent with the New Zealand Bill of Rights Act's protection of freedom of expression.[102]

Interestingly, the 1999 Massey Survey surveyed its sample on the *Te Papa* controversy. Opinions were fairly evenly divided, with 35 per cent supporting the Museum's decision and 45 per cent disagreeing with it. Some sympathy for Christian sensibilities was indicated:

> Half of those surveyed considered the artworks blasphemous (particularly the statue in a condom), but only a third were offended by them. Nevertheless, 75% of respondents agreed that, while they were not personally offended, they could understand how some Christians would have been, and 70% agreed that the Museum would never have displayed a Tiki or a statue of the Maori Queen in a condom.[103]

Various laws in the social, domestic and family arena implicitly reflected Christian values—or, more accurately, 'traditional' or 'conservative' Christian mores. To take some brief examples, marriage was seen as a lifelong union of two members of the opposite sex, divorce was difficult to obtain, abortion similarly, and homosexual relations between males were subject to criminal sanction. Liquor sales were restricted by time and venue, as were gambling outlets. The laws governing these areas show a declining Christian imprint. Marriage is still a union between a man and a woman but there is pressure (to be discussed at length in Chapter 10) to change the legal definition of marriage to permit same-sex couples to be legally wed. Many *de facto* couples are seeking greater equality with legally married couples in terms of state benefits and recognition. Divorce has been replaced with no-fault 'dissolution'. Abortion is easily obtained if the rising annual statistics are a reliable guide.[104] Sexual relations between same-sex adults are no longer a criminal offence and sexual orientation is a prohibited ground for discrimination along with the longer established grounds (race, religion, sex, nationality and so on). The gaming laws have been liberalized and new forms of gambling—casinos, Lotto, Keno, sports betting—have proliferated. Decriminalization of marijuana is a serious subject for debate as is the legalization of a restricted form of euthanasia.

At their core, many conservative Christians are affronted by the thought that they have become 'just another quaint subculture'.[105] A downgrading of Christianity to, at best, mere parity with other value systems and worldviews is perhaps more devastating than outright confrontation and rejection. T S Eliot once objected: 'When the Christian is treated as an enemy of the State, his course is very much harder, but it is simpler.' He continued: 'I am concerned with the dangers to the tolerated minority; and in the modern world, it may turn out that the most intolerable thing for Christians is to be tolerated.'[106]

The Response: Awakening from the Slumber The question for Christians is, 'Where to from here'?[107] One strategy is acceptance of one's minority situation and a strategic retreat into a religious enclave of holy living. The preferred response of most conservative Christians, however, is social engagement and transformation as well as the personal conversion of individuals. Transformative-minded Christians in New Zealand have belatedly realized the parlous position they are in as a minority within a post-Christian culture. The 'high ground' is to be reclaimed. They believe that New Zealand can be, in a specially defined sense, a Christian nation again. New Zealand is to be transformed by the Gospel for the glory of God.[108] How is this to be achieved however?

Theocracy is definitely not favoured.[109] Whilst there are occasional theocratic overtones in some conservative Christians' more strident utterances, few, if any, advocate a Christian theocracy. The 'Christian Reconstructionists' or 'Theonomists'—who desire Old Testament Mosaic law to be applied as a blueprint for contemporary society—have had a negligible influence in New Zealand.[110] Vehement criticism of the Reconstructionists unites Christians at divergent ends of the spectrum.

Instead, the transformatist urge is expressed in democratic form. New Zealand Christians would be quick to affirm John Stott's characterization of democracy as biblically-sound and 'the wisest and safest form of government yet devised.'[111] As 'Why Christians should be involved in politics', the statement signed by 47 prominent New Zealand evangelicals indicates, democracy is a given.[112] To the charge that they wish to theocratically impose their Christian values and beliefs upon an unwilling populace, conservative Christians disavow this claim. 'It is not', admonished one correspondent to *Challenge Weekly*, 'for humankind to usurp God's prerogative of punishing sin, and unless we admire the examples of contemporary Iran or medieval Europe, we should do better to await the Lord's return.'[113] To be sure, some conservative Christians have advocated a virtual theocracy, but the dominant strategy is attainment of a Christian nation consistent with democratic principles. A Christian nation, if it occurs at all, must come from below and not be imposed coercively from above.

Rational argument informed by Christian wisdom and directed to all citizens' innate sense of what is true and right is the favoured way. Christians of this ilk essentially retain the theocratic (or more accurately Christocratic) end, but insist on democratic means to this end. They are theonomists, small 't', in the sense that they believe in the universal application of God's law. Christian morality and ethics are applicable for everyone, not just Christians, for two reasons. First, God as Creator knows His created beings best and His laws fit the human beings He has made.[114] Second, and relatedly, is the slightly self-serving reason that a nation's obedience brings prosperity and blessing but disobedience brings cursing and divine judgment. The organizers of the 1972 Jesus March explained the permissiveness-judgment link in these terms:

> There is widespread reluctance in the community generally to affirm or accept any absolute moral standards. The increase in crime, violence, indecency, drunkenness, drug addiction, sexual permissiveness, illegitimacy, and venereal disease is alarming evidence of a moral landslide which could finally result in the decay and collapse of our society, or in the judgement of God on the nation of New Zealand.[115]

Christians themselves, along with everyone else, will suffer if God's laws are spurned and evil is tolerated. Christians for their *own* sake, let alone others, cannot be indifferent to the moral state of the nation. The oft-quoted biblical text here is, to repeat, Proverbs 14:34: 'Righteousness exalteth a nation: but sin is a reproach to any people.'[116] Some conservative Christians are quick to locate the cause for some current crisis—a drought or a power cut[117]—with flagrant public flouting of God's law such as the Hero Parade, an annual gay festivity. More sophisticated conservative Christians link social disintegration to the corrosive consequences of unrestrained liberalism—New Zealand is 'reaping the whirlwind' of high modernity.[118]

The transformatist strategy has necessitated a radical shift in attitude to culture on the part of conservative Christians. For the larger part of the twentieth century, a prominent feature of Western evangelicalism (including that in New Zealand) was disengagement from the world, especially politics, and concentration instead on personal salvation and holy living. This quietist period (from around World War I to about the 1970s) has been described as 'The Great Reversal'.[119] Abandoning the legacy of social involvement and reform of their forbears such as Wesley, Wilberforce and Finney, evangelicals retreated into a defensive fortress. Social transformation was the task for the theological liberals pursuing the 'Social Gospel'.[120] Christians of the separatist kind still maintain this 'escapist' attitude, as John Stott dubs it.[121]

However, to repeat, many conservative Christians today tend to be transformatist and socially active: 'engagement' with the world, not escape, is their preferred response. The beleaguered and inward-looking posture of earlier decades is conceded to be a mistake.[122] Jesus commended His disciples to be 'in the world' but 'not of the world'[123] which increasingly means vigorous, comprehensive engagement in the culture.

John Evans argues that in New Zealand the Jesus Marches in 1972 were a significant turning point. From about this point, conservative Christians 'were prepared to be like their more liberal counterparts and be more political in the pursuit of their aims.'[124] The movement from quietism to activism was to be accelerated by the homosexual law reform issue in 1985 (to be explored in detail in Chapter 9).

The Vision New Zealand Congresses of the 1990s are an important crystallization and significant furthering of this trend. Influenced by 'Kingdom theology' (which rejected the dualistic sacred/secular compartmentalism in favour of the extension of the Kingdom of God over every area of life[125]) Vision New Zealand was founded on 27 September 1990. Three Congresses, the inaugural one in 1993 and those in 1997 and 1999, have seen hundreds of Christian activists, lay and clerical, gather to discuss mission strategy for a post-Christian New Zealand.[126] The Congress motto is: 'Calling the Whole Church to take the Whole Gospel to the Whole Nation to the Whole World.' The formal distillation of the Congress, *The Waikanae Declaration 1993* (and its revision in 1997) state: 'God calls the Church to be agent for change in society'. It acknowledged 'the tendency to retreat into a comfortable ghetto. We confess we have failed to present adequately the whole gospel to New Zealanders . . ..' There is stress upon 'transforming every aspect of life' and an acknowledgement that 'too often we have proclaimed a truncated gospel.'[127]

Many conservative Christians then have forsaken their political quietism and launched forth into the public square. The homosexual law reform debate was the final straw which led, in time, to a conservative Christian political consciousness and the formation of conservative Christian political parties. José Casanova refers to the 'deprivatization' of religion, namely, 'the process whereby religion abandons its assigned place in the private sphere and enters the undifferentiated public sphere of civil society to take part in the ongoing process of contestation, discursive legitimation, and redrawing of the boundaries.'[128] The emergence of a conservative Christian presence in New Zealand public life in the last decade is unmistakable.

Notes

1 I note here the cautionary words of Rhys H Williams writing about America's so-called 'culture war': see 'Is America in a culture war? Yes-no-sort of,' *Christian Century*, 12 November 1997, 1038 at 1041.

2 See Basil Mitchell, *Law, Morality and Religion in a Secular Society* (1970) ch 1 at 15.

3 See Brett Knowles, 'Some Aspects of the History of the New Life Churches of New Zealand 1960-1990', Ph D thesis, University of Otago, 1994, chs 5 and 6 for an account of earlier decades' 'moral issues'. A version of his thesis (without footnotes) was published recently: Knowles, *New Life: A History of the New Life Churches of New Zealand 1942-1979* (1999).

4 Harry Blamires, *The Christian Mind* (1963) at 51.

5 Ibid.

6 See Harold Turner, 'The Three Levels of Mission in New Zealand' in Patrick (ed), *New Vision: New Zealand* (1993) ch 4 and Turner, 'Deep Mission to Deep Culture' in Flett (ed), *Collision Crossroads: The Intersection of Modern Western Culture with the Christian Gospel* (1998) ch 2.

7 See Richard Delgado, 'Storytelling for oppositionists and others: a plea for narrative' (1989) 87 *Mich L Rev* 2411; Robert M Cover, 'The Supreme Court: Foreword: *Nomos* and Narrative' (1983) 97 *Harv L Rev* 4.

8 Delgado, 'Storytelling for Oppositonists', at 2434-2435.

9 Ibid at 2440.

10 Lawrence Osborn, 'The Gospel and Culture' in Flett (ed), *Collision Crossroads* (1998) ch 3 at 35.

11 A Gunn, 'Righteousness exalts a nation', *Challenge Weekly* ('*CW*'), 25 May 1994, at 16. See also Mike Riddell, 'The Divine Right', *New Outlook*, September/October 1985, 24 at 24; Gordon Vick, 'New Zealand's Government founded upon Christianity', *CW*, 15 July 1988, at 10.

12 Osborn, 'The Gospel and Culture', at 38.

13 André Siegfried, *Democracy in New Zealand* (1914; 2nd edn and reprint, 1982) ch 24 at 310.

14 Jackson, 'Churchgoing in Nineteenth-Century New Zealand' (1983) 17 *NZJH* 43 at 51.

15 Ibid at 55-56.

[16] Stenhouse, 'The History of the Christian Movement in New Zealand' in Patrick (ed), *New Vision: New Zealand* (1993) ch 2 at 36.

[17] Hill, 'Religion' in Spoonley et al (eds), *New Zealand Society: A Sociological Introduction*, 2nd edn (1994) ch 18 at 295.

[18] See H Mol and MTV Reidy, 'Religion in New Zealand' in Webb and Collette (eds), *New Zealand Society: Contemporary Perspectives* (1973) ch 27 at 275.

[19] Siegfried, *Democracy in New Zealand*, at 311.

[20] Michael Hill, 'Ennobled Savages: New Zealand's Manipulationist Milieu' in Barker et al (eds), *Secularization, Rationalism and Sectarianism: Essays in Honour of Bryan R Wilson* (1993) ch 9 at 150. The passage in quotations is from Lineham, 'Freethinkers,' below fn 55 at 62-63.

[21] See Beverley Eales, 'Humanism' in Donovan (ed), *Religions of New Zealanders*, 2nd edn (1996) ch 13 and Bill Cooke, *Heathen in Godzone* (1998).

[22] José Casanova, *Public Religions in the Modern World* (1994) ch 6. For a similar analysis detailing the decline of Protestantism's 'cultural hegemony' in America, see James Davison Hunter, *Evangelicalism: The Coming Generation* (1987) ch 7. I developed this analysis in Ahdar, 'New Zealand and the Idea of a Christian State' in Ahdar and Stenhouse (eds), *God and Government: The New Zealand Experience* (2000) ch 3 and Ahdar, 'A Christian State?' (1998-1999) 13 *J L Religion* 101.

[23] Casanova, *Public Religions*, at 145.

[24] J B F Pompallier, *Early History of the Catholic Church in Oceania* (1888) at 63.

[25] T Lindsay Buick, *The Treaty of Waitangi : How New Zealand Became a British Colony*, 3rd ed (1936) at 152. See also Hugh Carleton, *The Life of Henry Williams*, rev edn (1948) at 314.

[26] Carleton, ibid, at 314-315.

[27] Buick, *The Treaty of Waitangi*, at 153; Carleton, *Henry Williams*, at 315.

[28] Buick, ibid, at 153.

[29] William Colenso, *The Authentic and Genuine History of the Signing of the Treaty of Waitangi* (1890) at 32.

[30] Claudia Orange, *The Treaty of Waitangi* (1987) at 53.

[31] A N D Foden, *The Constitutional Development of New Zealand in the First Decade (1839-1849)* (1938) at 86.

[32] G A Wood, 'Church and State in New Zealand in the 1850s' (1975) 8 *J Religious History* 255 at 258.

[33] For a detailed discussion, see Wood, ibid and Allan Davidson and Peter Lineham, *Transplanted Christianity*, 2nd edn (1989) at 80 et seq.

[34] (1854) *NZPD* 4.

[35] Ibid per Dr Lee; seconded by Revans.

[36] Ibid at 4 per James Edward Fitzgerald.

[37] Ibid at 5.

[38] Ibid at 5.

[39] Ibid at 6.

[40] Ibid.

[41] (1854) *NZPD* 6.

[42] Ibid at 14.

43 The dispatch is reproduced in Davidson and Lineham, *Transplanted Christianity* (above n 33), at 88.

44 (1855) *NZPD* 512-513. The Bishop's salary was reconsidered on 12 September 1855 and the vote against was won by only eight votes to seven: (1855) *NZPD* 544.

45 J D Hight and H D Bamford, *The Constitutional History of New Zealand* (1914) at 378.

46 *Mabon* v *Conference of the Church of New Zealand* [1998] 3 NZLR 513 at 523 per Richardson P.

47 H R Jackson, *Churches and People in Australia and New Zealand 1860-1930* (1987) at 17. See further Peter Mathieson, '1840-1870: The Settler Church' in McEldowney (ed), *Presbyterians in Aotearoa 1840-1990* (1990) at 15 et seq.

48 Allan K Davidson, *Christianity in Aotearoa: A History of Church and Society in New Zealand* (1991) at 34.

49 Jackson, *Churches and People*, at 17.

50 See Davidson *Christianity in Aotearoa*, at 54; Jackson, ibid at 17-18.

51 Geering, *2100: A Faith Odyssey—The Changing Face of New Zealand Religion* (1995) at 8.

52 Ibid at 13. See also Geering, 'Pluralism and the Future of Religion in New Zealand' in Colless and Donovan (eds), *Religion in New Zealand Society*, 2nd edn (1985) at 218.

53 Davidson and Lineham, *Transplanted Christianity* (above n 33), at 74.

54 Wood, 'Church and State . . . in the 1850s'(above n 32), at 267.

55 Peter Lineham, 'Freethinkers in Nineteenth-Century New Zealand' (1985) 19 *NZJH* 61 at 71.

56 Ibid at 76.

57 Presidential address to the Otago Education Institute in 1879. Quoted by D V MacDonald, 'The New Zealand Bible in Schools League', MA thesis, Victoria University of Wellington, 1964, at 9; quoted in turn in John Adsett Evans, 'Church State Relations in New Zealand 1940-1990, with particular reference to the Presbyterian and Methodist Churches', Ph D thesis, University of Otago, 1992, at 3 fn 10.

58 *Carrigan* v *Redwood* (1910) 30 NZLR 244 at 252 per Cooper J. See also *Public Trustee* v *Commissioner of Stamps* (1907) 26 NZLR 773 at 779 (Sup Ct) per Cooper J again for his earlier statement. The Court of Appeal affirmed this judgment: ibid.

59 [1917] NZLR 308 at 314.

60 Vodanovich, 'Religion and legitimation in New Zealand: redefining the relationship between church and state' (1990) 3 *Brit Rev of NZ Studies* 52 at 52.

61 See Colin McGeorge, 'On the Origins of the Nelson System of Religious Education' in Gilling (ed), *Godly Schools? Some Approaches to Christian Education in New Zealand* (1993) at 1. The following account draws from this as well as chapter 3 of Ian Breward, *Godless Schools? A Study of Protestant Reactions to Secular Education in New Zealand* (1967).

62 Section 84(3).

63 Sections 77 to 79. The 'Nelson system' provision was first enacted in the Religious Instruction and Observances in Public Schools Act 1962.

[64] J E Cookson, 'Illiberal New Zealand: The Formation of Government Policy on Conscientious Objection, 1940-1' (1983) 17 *NZJH* 120 at 120.

[65] The following account is drawn from Hill, 'Religion', at 296-298; Geering, *Faith Odyssey*(above n 51), at 7-8; Manuka Henare, 'Christianity: Maori Churches' in Donovan (ed), *Religions of New Zealanders*, ch 9, at 124-125; John Garrett, *Footsteps in the Sea: Christianity in Oceania to World War II* (1992) ch 5, at 123-125; Davidson, *Christianity in Aotearoa* (above n 48), ch 13, at 128-129.

[66] Davidson, ibid, at 128.

[67] Section 2. The penalty for a first offence was a maximum fine of £25, or imprisonment up to six months.

[68] Malcolm Voyce, 'Maori Healers in New Zealand: The Tohunga Suppression Act 1907' (1989) 60 *Oceania* 99 at 116.

[69] Ibid at 98. The Act was denigrated by Sir Geoffrey Palmer recently in his *New Zealand's Constitution in Crisis* (1992) at 66-67.

[70] See Davidson, *Christianity in Aotearoa* (above n 48), at 85. See also Michael King, *God's Farthest Outpost* (1997).

[71] Davidson, ibid, at 65.

[72] Ian Breward, *Godless Schools?*(above n 61); Davidson, ibid, ch 7 and John Mackey, *The Making of a State Education System* (1967).

[73] Section 84 (2) of the Education Act 1877.

[74] Geering, *Faith Odyssey* (above n 51) at 10; Davidson, *Christianity in Aotearoa* (above n 48), at 65.

[75] Breward, *Godless Schools?* at 18. See also ibid at 102.

[76] I L M Richardson, *Religion and the Law* (1962) at 61.

[77] Ibid.

[78] See Vodanovich, 'Religion and legitimation' (above n 60), at 52.

[79] See Casanova, *Public Religions in the Modern World* (above n 22), at 137; Hunter, *Evangelicalism* (above n 22), ch 7 at 187 et seq, for discussions of the decline in a Protestant cultural hegemony in America in the twentieth century. By 'hegemony' is meant rule by ideas not force alone. Cooperation is secured by the consent of the led, 'a consent that is secured by the diffusion and polarisation of the world view of the ruling class.': Thomas R Bates, 'Gramsci and the Theory of Hegemony' (1975) 36 *J History of Ideas* 351 at 352.

[80] Patrick, 'After the 1997 Congress' in Patrick (ed), *The Vision New Zealand Congress 1997* (1997) ch 1 at 32-33.

[81] Brian Carrell, *Moving Between Times—Modernity and Postmodernity: A Christian View* (1998) at 15.

[82] Murray Robertson, 'New Zealand as a Mission Field: The Paradigm Shift' in Patrick (ed), *The Vision New Zealand Congress* (1993) ch 3. A New Zealand sociologist, Ivanica Vodanovich, 'Religion and Legitimation' (above n 60), at 52 and 58 confirms this. She argues that the values and ethical ideals of denominational Christianity which provided the basis of the 'normative consensus' predominated 'until the late 1960s.' The term 'paradigm shift' is of course drawn from Thomas Kuhn, *The Structure of Scientific Revolutions*, 2nd edn (1970). Casanova, *Public*

Religions (above n 22), at 145, identifies the 1960s as the decade of the disestablishment of Protestantism from the American way of life.

83 James Veitch, 'Christianity: Protestants Since the 1960s' in Donovan (ed), *Religions of New Zealanders*, ch 7, at 90.

84 Robertson, 'The Paradigm Shift', at 46.

85 Brian Carrell, 'New Culture, New Challenge' in Patrick (ed), *New Vision New Zealand* (1993) ch 3 at 49.

86 See Carrell, ibid at 49-50: The 'acids of modernity' are to be traced to the Enlightenment which 'subtly shifted the centre of European spirituality from heaven to earth, from God to nature, from revelation to reason, from hope in the future to life in the present, from an aspiration to become divine to a preoccupation with becoming more human, from worship of the transcendent to obsession with the transient.'

87 Geering, 'Pluralism and the Future of Religion' (above n 52), at 218.

88 Geering, 'New Zealand enters the Secular Age' in Nichol and Veitch (eds), *Religion in New Zealand*, 2nd edn (1983) 161 at 173.

89 See Michael Hill and Wiebe Zwaga, 'The 'Nones' Story: A Comparative Analysis of Religious Nonalignment' (1989) 4 *NZ Sociology* 164.

90 1996 Census: see Statistics New Zealand, *New Zealand Official Yearbook 1998*, 101st edn (1998) at 121.

91 See Peter L Berger, 'Secularism in Retreat', *National Interest*, Winter 1996-1997, at 3.

92 Donovan, 'Zeal and Apathy: The Future' in Donovan (ed), *Religions of New Zealanders*, ch 18.

93 Donovan, ibid at 267.

94 'Religion in New Zealand', Department of Marketing, Massey University, January 1999. The survey was conducted in 1998 with 996 respondents and had a margin of error of 3 per cent.

95 Ibid at 4.

96 Adrian Hastings, *Church and State—The English Experience* (1991) at 8.

97 Hauerwas, 'A Christian Critique of Christian America' in Pennock and Chapman (eds), *Religion, Morality and the Law: NOMOS XXX* (1988) ch 5 at 121.

98 See also Francis Schaeffer, *A Christian Manifesto* (1981) at 121: 'The whole "Constantine mentality" from the fourth century up to our day was a mistake. . . . Making Christianity the official state religion opened the way for confusion up till our own day.'

99 Hauerwas, 'A Christian Critique', at 124 (quoting John Howard Yoder, *The Priestly Kingdom: Social Ethics as Gospel* (1984) at 158).

100 See 'Virgin statue on show despite attack', *Sunday Star-Times*, 8 March 1998, at A2; 'Violent and personal threats to museum staff over 'Virgin'', *Otago Daily Times*, 10 March 1998, at 2; 'Virgin statue stays—Protests ignored', *Sunday Star-Times*, 15 March 1998, at A1; 'Te Papa's fingers burnt in outrage over condom art', ibid, at A5. The statue was by British artist, Tania Kovats, while the painting, entitled *Wrecked*, was by Sam Taylor Woods; both works appearing in the exhibition, *Pictura Britannica*.

[101] 'Virgin statue on show despite attack', *Sunday Star-Times*, 8 March 1998, at A2; 'Museum refuses to remove exhibit', *Otago Daily Times*, 9 March 1998, at 2.

[102] See 'No prosecution over exhibits', *Otago Daily Times*, 28 March 1998, at 35. National Party MP, John Banks, and Fr P Denzil Meuli had sought permission to prosecute under s 123 of the Crimes Act. Solicitor-General, John McGrath, refused the Crown's consent saying the principle of freedom of expression was the main factor against allowing prosecutions to proceed.

[103] Massey Survey, 'Religion in New Zealand', at 3.

[104] In 1996 there were 14,805 abortions performed in New Zealand, whereas in 1990 there were 11,173 abortions and in 1994, 12,835. See *Report of the Abortion Supervisory Committee* (for the year ended 30 June 1997) at 20. In 1998 the abortion total dropped very slightly from the previous year (15,208 in 1997) to 15,029. In 1999 the total rose once more (to 15,501).

[105] Casanova, *Public Religions* (above n 22), at 156.

[106] T S Eliot, *The Idea of a Christian Society* (1939) at 23.

[107] Andrew Howie, 'Orthodoxy and Ethics in a Pluralist Society' in Trebilco (ed), *Considering Orthodoxy* (1995) ch 7 at 168, posits four Christian responses: (1) Accommodation (the liberal response); (2) Domination (the Constantinan impulse); (3) Separation and; (4) Interactive Distinctiveness.

[108] See, for example, 'Waikanae Declaration' in Patrick (ed), *The Vision New Zealand Congress 1997* (1997) at 20.

[109] For overseas disavowals, see John Stott, *New Issues Facing Christians Today*, 3rd edn (1999) at 55-57; Schaeffer, *A Christian Manifesto* (above n 98), at 120-121; Carl F H Henry, *The Christian Mindset in a Secular Society* (1984) at 106-107 and 114-115.

[110] This despite the visit of two leading theonomists, Gary North and R J Rushdoony, to the Coalition of Concerned Citizens in 1986: see Craig Young, 'The New Zealand Religious Right and Armageddon Theology', *New Zealand Monthly Review*, March 1987, 9 at 10.

[111] Stott, *New Issues Facing Christians*, at 47. See further Henry, *Christian Mindset*, at 97-128.

[112] *Reality*, October-November 1996, at 33.

[113] Letter by J W Early, Christchurch, 'Living in a pagan world', *CW*, 23 August 1985, at 16.

[114] John Hitchen, 'Involved in politics . . . why?' in Patrick (ed), *The Vision New Zealand Congress 1997* (1997) ch 10 at 191; 'Why Christians should be involved in politics', *Reality*, October/November 1996, 33 at 36.

[115] Quoted in John Adsett Evans, 'The New Christian Right in New Zealand' in Gilling (ed), *'Be Ye Separate': Fundamentalism and the New Zealand Experience* (1992) 69 at 75.

[116] Evans, 'New Christian Right,' at 98 fn 46 notes this scriptural text 'provided a biblical warrant for the law to be used in support of Christian moral principles.'

[117] The Auckland Hero Parade of 1995 was linked to the drought that summer: See I J Thrower, Mangere East, (letter), 'God is warning us', *CW*, 3 May 1995, at 2. The

crippling Auckland central city power-cuts in February/March 1998 were likewise linked to that year's Hero Parade.

[118] Brian Carrell, 'Reaping the whirlwind' (1986) 6 *Stimulus* 31.

[119] See Stott, *New Issues Facing Christians* (above n 109), at 8.

[120] This is associated with Walter Rauschenbusch, an American theologian. See Stott ibid at 8-9.

[121] Stott, ibid, at 18.

[122] See Brian Hathaway et al, 'Thy Kingdom come,' *CW*, 1 June 1989, at 7-8; Mike McMillan, 'A Bigger Ghetto or a Brighter Bride?' *Reality*, October-November 1998, 23 at 28.

[123] John 17:11-19.

[124] Evans, 'New Christian Right' (above n 115), at 75.

[125] See Brian Hathaway et al, 'Thy Kingdom Come,' *CW*, 1 June 1989, at 7-8.

[126] The inaugural Vision New Zealand Congress was held at Waikanae on 25-28 January 1993. Some 300 Christians attended including heads of denominations, ministers, pastors, lay leaders, theologians, educationalists, service agency leaders and people from many other spheres of life and Christian service. Nearly every denomination was represented: *The Waikanae Declaration* 1993. Its proceedings are published: Patrick (ed), *The Vision Congress 1993* (1993) as well as preliminary papers: Patrick (ed), *New Vision New Zealand* (1993). The second New Zealand Congress also saw around 300 Christians meet at Waikanae on 20-24 January 1997, including for the first time, a 'strong Catholic delegation': *Vision Congress 1997*, at 26-27. Its preparatory papers are published (Patrick (ed), *New Vision New Zealand Volume II* (1997)) as well as the Conference papers, Patrick (ed), *The Vision New Zealand Congress 1997* (1997). The third congress involved around 300 people again at Waikanae on 17-22 January 1999.

[127] The 1993 *Declaration* is found in *Vision Congress 1993*, at 14-18. The 1997 *Declaration* (reproduced in *Vision Congress 1997*, at 16-24) repeats these statements.

[128] Casanova, *Public Religions* (above n 22), at 65-66.

2 Conservative Christianity

Defining the 'Conservative Christian'

To describe the conservative Christian (hereafter 'CC'[1]) I must first explain a divide which has occurred in modern Western Christianity.

The Great Divide: Christian 'Conservatives' versus 'Liberals'

Within Christianity scholars discern a split between two broad groups variously defined as 'conservatives', 'orthodox', 'traditionalists', on the one hand, and 'liberals', 'progressives', 'radicals', on the other. In the leading empirical study, sociologist Robert Wuthnow surveyed American Christianity since the 1940s and found a 'religious restructuring' or 'realignment' taking place.[2] Believers were being polarized into 'conservatives' and 'liberals', a split that transcended denominational barriers.[3] The two groups could be seen within particular denominations and not just between denominations.[4] This restructuring into a conservative/liberal divide has, to some extent, largely replaced the old historic divides and hostilities between Protestant and Catholic, Christian and Jew, even believers and non-believers.[5] James Davison Hunter's analysis is helpful. There is, he maintains, a deep cleavage in American culture based on fundamentally differing worldviews. These antagonistic moral visions take expression as 'polarizing impulses or tendencies', one toward 'orthodoxy', the other toward 'progressivism'.[6] The 'orthodox' are committed to:

> *an external, definable, and transcendent authority*. Such objective and transcendent authority defines, at least in the abstract, a consistent, unchangeable measure of value, purpose, goodness, and identity, both personal and collective. It tells us what is good, what is true, how we should live, and who we are. It is an authority that is sufficient for all time.[7]

The 'progressivists', by contrast, view truth 'as a process, as a reality that is ever unfolding.'[8] They have:

> a strong tendency to translate the moral ideas of a religious tradition so that they conform to and legitimate the contemporary *zeitgeist.* In other words, what all *progressivist* world views share in common *is the tendency to resymbolize historic faiths according to the prevailing assumptions of contemporary life.*[9]

Like many dichotomies there is the problem of blurring and the reality of intermediate situations.[10] Some deny the claim that there is a clear divide between conservatives and progressives: the imagery of 'two monolithic camps' has been fanned by the media and some political leaders, but is 'overdrawn', if not 'simply false'.[11] Moreover, there may be more than one axis or continuum to consider. Those who are 'liberal' on one set of issues may not necessarily be 'liberal' on other issues.[12] This complicates the analysis considerably.

The conservative/liberal (or orthodox/progessivist) split is really a polarization into 'pure' or 'ideal' types. There is, and always will remain, a large 'middle' group, greater in size probably than the sum of either extreme, which refuses to be identified with either polarized 'camp'. As Wuthnow stressed again recently: 'the liberal-conservative continuum is, in fact, a continuum. People in the middle may lean slightly to the left or to the right. But they are nevertheless in the middle.'[13]

A similar restructuring of Christianity has occurred in New Zealand. The conservative/liberal split is readily apparent but the subject of relatively little published research.[14] Certainly the schism is not a novel one. As Peter Matheson notes: 'The dialogue of the deaf in contemporary, post-modernist New Zealand between "liberals" and "evangelicals" would appear to have deep roots in our history.'[15] He details the 'battle royal' that raged within New Zealand Presbyterianism in the late nineteenth century. 'From an extraordinarily early period', he recounts, 'dialogue between "liberal" and "conservative" broke down within Presbyterianism, and was replaced by fierce polemics and a string of heresy trials which were to culminate in that of Lloyd Geering in our century.'[16] The point about this phenomenon being a continuum is borne out as well: 'Many of course, not least in the laity, sought to maintain a middle course, but the tendency to polarisation is clear enough.'[17] The Rev Stuart Lange, explained the third, middle group within contemporary New Zealand Presbyterianism this way:

> The third perspective is the so-called 'middle of the road' perspective. These middle of the road people are *neither* thorough-going liberals *nor* card-carrying evangelicals and they would [not] want to be labelled as *either* . . .

> The middle of the road people are influenced by *both* orthodox and liberal approaches. On the core doctrines of the faith the middle of the road people may in themselves be essentially 'orthodox'. But they are often 'liberal' in their understanding of scriptural authority, and 'liberal' to the extent that they would not want to insist on orthodoxy in anyone else . . . this middle perspective is quite happy to live in a theologically pluralistic church, in fact they may really *believe* in a broad church, they really *value* people being able to choose from a *range* of convictions.[18]

The fracturing is of course not confined to Presbyterians. For instance, the monthly newspaper, *Crosslink,* has a regular 'Crossfire' feature where liberal and conservative Methodists debate controversial issues of the day in an effort to convince the uncommitted 'middle' Methodist reader.

What is the reason for this split? One explanation for the divide is the difference between 'centrifugal' and 'centripetal' forces in the reading of religious texts.[19] Liberals tend to emphasize the former (the truth and its meaning is more complex than first thought; meanings open out in new ways), whereas conservatives emphasize the latter (in the face of the increasing complexities of life a return to simple core answers is better). Perhaps the split is better seen in terms of engagement with the contemporary culture and its prevailing worldview. Peter Berger pinpoints what I regard as the key here:

> Some [religious people] have defined modernity as the enemy, to be fought whenever possible. Others have, on the contrary, seen modernity as an invincible worldview to which religious beliefs and practices should adapt themselves. In other words, *rejection* and *adaptation* are two strategies open to religious communities in a world understood to be secularized.[20]

Religious conservatives typically prefer to confront the world 'head-on'.

Defining the Conservative Christian

General The term 'conservative Christian' is by no means a novel designation.[21] It has been used in various senses and with different connotations, the epithet 'conservative' referring to the theological, political, economic or cultural stance of the adherent. My use of the expression CC then may not correspond with the way others use the term. The epithet 'conservative', small 'c', is used not because such persons are politically right-wing or conservative (although they often are) but because it aptly describes a certain mindset or attitude of these persons toward their faith and its relationship with culture. Theologically, they are certainly conservative insofar as they wish to conserve (what is for them) the best, most authentic, pure or orthodox version of the faith. The 'conservative' label is superior to 'evangelical' or 'orthodox' since it is sufficiently broad to embrace a number of diverse movements and denominations within Christianity. The defining and essential characteristics of CC can be broken down into four interrelated convictions.

SUBMISSIVENESS TO AUTHORITY First, CCs defer to and endeavour to faithfully obey 'authority', so defined. For the Protestant CC, the ultimate authority is Scripture (*sola scriptura*), for the Roman Catholic CC it is Scripture and Tradition.[22] Wuthnow summarizes the dichotomy between the orthodox and the progressives this way:

> In simplest terms, orthodox believers hold to the view that God exists, that the Bible is an authoritative source of divine truth, and that there are absolute standards of right and wrong that apply to everyone, whereas progressives are less sure of the existence of God, convinced that they must seek their own truth from a variety of sources, and persuaded that moral questions must be decided on situational and relativistic grounds.[23]

CCs, particularly Protestant ones, typically take the Bible literally and view it as, in a very real sense, the infallible or inerrant Word of God.[24] When CCs insist that the Bible is taken literally they do not mean that all passages are taken at face value as eye-witness, newspaper accounts.[25] This would be better described as 'literalism', something Evangelicals (a term to be explained shortly) reject.[26] Rather, CCs are alert to the use of symbolism, allegory and figurative and poetic forms of expression where the context so indicates. James Packer explains that interpreting Scripture literally means that 'the proper, natural sense of each passage (i.e., the intended sense of the writer) is to be taken as fundamental; the meaning of texts in their own contexts, and for their original readers, is the necessary starting-point for enquiry into their wider significance.'[27] The analogy in law would be the 'plain meaning' approach to words in statutory interpretation. This too is commonly referred to as the literal rule.[28]

CCs will depart from the literalist interpretation when the context so requires. The point about the preference for a literal approach to sacred texts is that it best displays, to CCs, an attitude of obedience or faithfulness to authority. God's Word is just that, the Word of God, and so it is to be taken literally—unless indications are clearly to the contrary. Scripture is taken literally since to do so is, in their view, to take it reverently and seriously.[29]

MORAL ABSOLUTIST Second, CCs are moral and ethical absolutists.[30] Recall Wuthnow's observation quoted earlier: CCs hold 'that there are absolute standards of right and wrong that apply to everyone'.[31] David Arrowsmith in his New Zealand study observed that CCs 'invoked a tradition of personal morality which upheld an unchallengeable set of ethical precepts.'[32] The women's editor of *Challenge Weekly*, the weekly New Zealand CC newspaper, expresses a typical CC view:

> God has left us no doubt about his standards, for his Word is full of instructions from Exodus with the giving of the Ten Commandments to the last letter in the New Testament. His commands are positive and have not changed nor deviated from their first pronouncement. There are no degrees of right and wrong. God expects his children to be holy for he is holy, and he does not allow for excuses for wrong behaviour.[33]

RESTORATIONIST Third, CCs are restorationists. Sometimes this takes a nostalgic turn. They do not want to merely retain or conserve the best of tradition but they desire a return to a purer, atavistic form of Christianity.[34] Some CCs see this as only occurring within a separated enclave. For others, the Christendom model beckons; there is overt yearning for a return to some 'Golden Age' where society was ordered in accordance with God's will assisted by believers in positions of influence. Increasingly, however, as we saw in the previous chapter, CCs seek a fresh approach in what is perceived as an entirely new era. Rejecting the Christendom model they seek to transform or restore society.

OPPOSITIONAL Fourth, CCs are reactionary and oppose the prevailing ethos or 'the spirit of the age'. They are antagonistic, in varying degrees, to this unredeemed and rebellious sector of God's creation and the miscreant spirit is described variously as modernism, secularism, humanism or simply 'permissiveness'. Basil Mitchell, for instance, notes: 'Traditionalists will often be suspicious of what passes as "modern knowledge" and determined not to assimilate Christianity to the prevailing secular worldview.'[35]

There are further, *secondary* characteristics of CC which I shall list separately. These traits or convictions are often associated with CC but, in my view, are not necessary elements of CC. They are instead better viewed as frequent correlates with CC—prevalent but not intrinsic to all

CCs. First, to reiterate from Chapter 1, CCs exhibit much international comity with overseas CCs. The transnational flavour of CC is pronounced (and similar to international socialism). Second, there is an uncompromising 'either/or', 'black or white' attitude to many social and ethical issues. Third, many CCs display a siege mentality. There is often an embattled, defensive, even paranoid quality to their rhetoric. As we shall see, there is frequent recourse to 'domino theories' and 'ratchet' effects. Things are inexorably changing for the worse, yet disaster typically comes in small insidious increments, not in one grand stroke. Allowing one step will lead, if unchecked, to others unless CCs nip the ruinous process in the bud. This attitude resonates with a particular eschatological position held. Many CCs see these as literally the 'last days' prior to the second coming of Christ whereupon the divine millennium of God's Kingdom will commence. Under this apocalyptic and pessimistic view, society is on a slippery slope to inevitable decline. Fourth, many CCs take an anti-globalization stance, one which is often vented against the United Nations. Again, this has an eschatological root: the apocalyptic fear of a demonic totalitarian world government is traceable to the anti-Christian world oppressor or 'beast' described in chapter 13 of the book of Revelation.

There is, further, the observable link between CC and political conservatism. In recent times many CCs have found more affinity with right-of-centre political interests. But CCs have not always, historically, supported right-wing politics. The link is a common modern one but by no means a necessary one. Second, CCs are typically economic individualists and supporters of free enterprise capitalism.[36] But again, the connection is not a necessary one.

Cultural Interaction Within the broad rubric CC there appear to be two distinct strains in terms of cultural engagement. First, there is a separatist or counter-cultural strain that seeks to maintain a religious and social enclave against the corruptive forces of secular society. Second, there is a transformative strain that seeks not disengagement, but rather conversion of society to bring it into harmony with God's will. In terms of Richard Niebuhr's renowned typology of Christian responses to culture,[37] these two strains correspond to Niebuhr's 'Christ Against Culture'[38] and 'Christ The Transformer of Culture'[39] respectively.

CCs have traditionally been preoccupied with issues of personal morality (parental rights, abortion and contraception, homosexuality, pornography, sex education and so on) in the private sphere (the home, school and church). These are the issues closest to their heart, quintessentially arenas where the CC should be free to practise the faith unhindered by an intrusive state. 'I will preach about *Playboy* because that is a moral issue, but not about starvation for that is a political issue'[40] is a graphic and extreme example of this mindset. This personal, private versus socio-political, public morality division still remains but has been rapidly closing. Some CCs have recently rekindled their social concern and have come to denounce structural injustices as well.

Denominational Profile The CC is usually Protestant but not exclusively so. The defining characteristics—deference to authority, moral absolutism, anti-modernist stance and so on—which single out the CC can embrace Roman Catholics as well. As noted earlier, the religious realignment transcends the old denominational boundaries. Both in attitude and in respect of particular issues (preservation of the family, pro-life issues, homosexuality) some (conservative) sectors of Catholicism overlap with Protestant conservatives.[41]

The overlap has begun to take visible form in the last two decades. There are various terms to describe the new public coalition of CCs. Some refer to it as the 'new ecumenism', a fresh dialogue and a mobilization of activists rather than the old-style ecumenism which sought denominational unification.[42] Others prefer the term suggested by Francis Schaeffer: 'co-belligerence'.[43] Commonalities are more readily perceived than differences, 'especially when the fury of anti-Christian forces around us deprives us of leisure for intra-Christian polemics.'[44] As Charles Colson colourfully put it: 'When the barbarians are scaling the walls, there is no time for petty quarrelling in the camp.'[45] Whether or not the historic doctrinal differences (ones which saw much blood spilled) can simply be dismissed as 'petty', the basic strategy is nevertheless considered sound. Bishop Brian Carrell endorsed the approach for New Zealand in 1993:

> When Christianity is more or less accepted as the faith of the nation, a society can afford the luxury of competing denominations. But when the grey cloud of secularism descends upon a people, Christians have to stand together (or at least respect with integrity the differences between them) and affirm one another publicly and sincerely as brothers and sisters in Christ.[46]

The second Vision New Zealand Conference in 1997 saw the welcoming of a Catholic delegation. To the organizers this was a signal that 'the Berlin Wall of New Zealand Christendom' was weakening and relationships were being 'built on common ground, of which there is much.'[47]

My focus is conservative *Christianity* not religious conservatives generally. Nonetheless, it is worth noting that orthodox, traditional or conservative adherents of other faiths—Orthodox Jews, devout Muslims, Jehovah's Witnesses and the Church of Latter Day Saints of Jesus Christ

(Mormons)—share many of the same concerns with CCs. The emergence of the so-called 'Religious Right' is, of course, just an extension of the principle of collaboration against the common enemy; a wider circle of anti-modernist religionists is now included. What are in one sense unnatural alliances become sensible and pragmatic collaborations which need no more justification than 'the dictum that "an enemy of an enemy is a friend of mine."'[48] Figure 2.1 endeavours to capture the group CC:

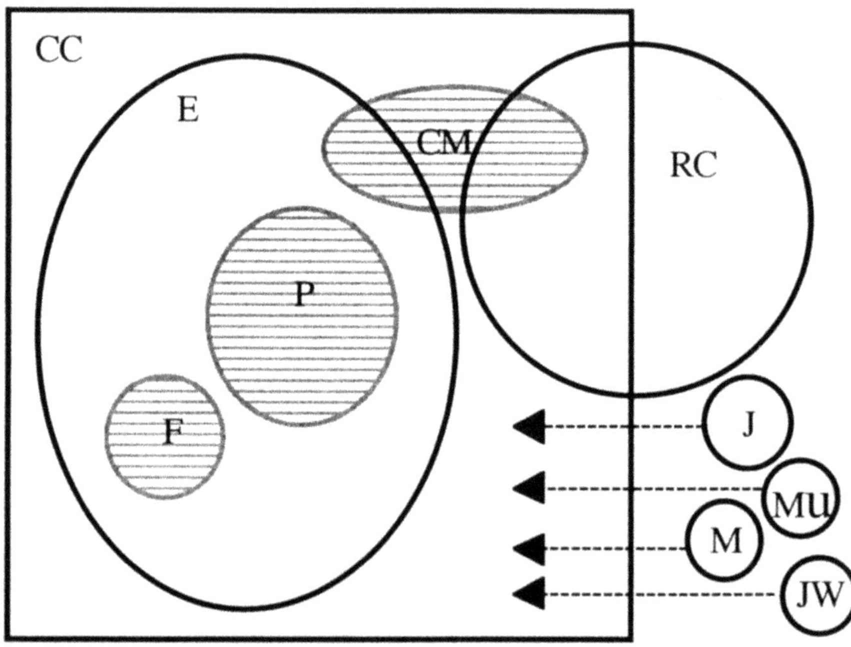

Figure 2.1 Conservative Christianity

CC comprises, principally, Evangelicals (E). Indeed, when the reader sees the term 'CC' the initial mental image should be that of an Evangelical. Conservative Roman Catholics (RC) also are included. Within Evangelicalism are: Fundamentalists (F), Pentecostals (P) and Protestant Charismatics (CM representing the Charismatic Movement). Charismatics are also to be found in Catholicism, hence the overlap there. Sharing many of the CC concerns, but not within Christianity, are conservative Jews (J), Muslims (Mu), and (from a CC perspective) heterodox sects such as Jehovah's Witnesses (JW) and Mormons (M).[49] The circles are not to scale, but do give a very rough indication of relative significance and influence of each group.

CC can be thought of as a fast flowing river which has various tributaries.[50] The mingling of the streams can produce eddies and vortices which are the debates and disagreements within CC. Nonetheless, there is a central flow the source of which is the trinitarian God of the Nicene creed.

Regarding Christian churches and denominations we see the conservative/liberal split is not along denominational lines. There are some denominations which are virtually wholly made up of CCs. All the Pentecostal denominations (Assembly of God, New Life, Elim, Apostolic Churches, to mention the major ones) are CC, as are the Open Brethren, Salvation Army, Reformed and Seventh Day Adventist Churches. Of the more traditional or 'mainstream' churches, there are significant 'wings' or sub-groupings of conservative Christians in each. Anglicans, Presbyterians, Methodists and Roman Catholics all have sizeable, identifiable numbers of members of conservative temper, as does (particularly) the Baptist Church. In some churches the conservatives have their own formal conservative associations: Anglican AFFIRM,[51] Presbyterian AFFIRM and the Presbyterian Westminster Fellowship[52] and Methodist AFFIRM are examples. Whilst there are conservative elements within all denominations, the 'reverse is however not true: liberal Christians are not drawn from all denominations.'[53] Liberal Christians simply would not fit into many of the avowedly conservative or fundamentalist fellowships. Again, the caveat must be repeated that while it is correct to talk of a 'divide', the extremes of conservative and liberal are just that; the majority of members of the mainstream churches are grouped in the middle of the continuum and eschew any self-identifying label. The polemics and activism of both conservative and liberal camps is not for them.

A mark of evangelicals (and perhaps CCs generally) is their propensity to form interdenominational, parachurch organizations. Reflecting foreign influences, the transdenominational institutions of CC in New Zealand are as much transplants as the churches were themselves. Early organizations such as SPCS (Society for the Promotion of Community Standards) and SPUC (Society for the Protection of the Unborn Child) are of British origin. Later movements and organizations reflect an American ancestry, the homeschooling movement and 'Promise Keepers', a men's spiritual revitalization movement, being two recent examples.

Evangelicalism The largest group within conservative Christianity is evangelicalism.[54] This is a diverse coalition which includes 'any

Christians traditional enough to affirm the basic beliefs of the old nineteenth-century evangelical consensus.'[55] What are these basic beliefs? George Marsden argues they include:

> (1) the Reformation doctrine of the final authority of the Bible, (2) the real historical character of God's saving work recorded in Scripture, (3) salvation to eternal life based on the redemptive work of Christ, (4) the importance of evangelism and missions, and (5) the importance of the spiritually transformed life.[56]

Alister McGrath's list is similar. He discerns six 'fundamental convictions':

> (1) The supreme authority of Scripture as a source of the knowledge of God, and a guide to Christian living; (2) The majesty of Jesus Christ, both as incarnate God and Lord, and as the saviour of sinful humanity; (3) The lordship of the Holy Spirit; (4) The need for personal conversion; (5) The priority of evangelism for both individual Christians and the church as a whole; (6) The importance of the Christian community for spiritual nourishment, fellowship and growth.[57]

Evangelicalism is seen by its proponents as nothing more than pure or true historic Christianity under a modern label.[58] James Packer explains:

> It [evangelicalism] is, we maintain, the oldest version of Christianity; theologically regarded, it is just apostolic Christianity itself. Ideally, the Evangelical would choose no title for himself but 'Christian'. He holds that he alone is entitled to call his faith 'Christian' without qualification. If, however, he must use a further label to differentiate himself from other groups within the Church, he accepts 'Evangelical' as being the historically established term for his position . . .[59]

Evangelicalism is the label preferred by most conservative Protestants today. They usually reject the term 'fundamentalism' because of its odious connotations. Because of the widespread use of 'fundamentalism' it is necessary to examine this term closely.

Fundamentalism Despite the tendency to indiscriminately call all conservative Christians 'fundamentalists',[60] the temptation ought to be resisted. Scholars explain that fundamentalism is a 'sub-species'[61] of evangelicalism: 'all fundamentalists are evangelicals but not all evangelicals are fundamentalists.'[62] Most British and New Zealand evangelicals are quick to distinguish themselves from the fundamentalists.[63]

Defining this pilloried sub-group of evangelicalism has proved difficult. Fundamentalism is not coterminous with a particular church, sect or denomination, but is better described as a religious mass movement.[64] The origins of the term are quite modern. The appearance of 'fundamentalism' as a distinct label in the religious lexicon occurs at the early part of the twentieth century.[65] Conservative American Protestants were concerned at the rise of liberal theology during the latter part of the nineteenth century. These American evangelicals responded to the 'liberal' or 'modernist' challenge with a series of 12 booklets, the first of which was published in 1909. Around three million copies of *The Fundamentals: A Testimony to the Truth* were circulated. In 1910 the General Assembly of the (American) Northern Presbyterian Church pronounced five items as 'the fundamentals of faith and of evangelical Christianity.' The list, which varies slightly,[66] was: (1) the inspiration and infallibility of Scripture (also referred to as the inerrancy of Scripture), (2) the deity of Christ, (3) His virgin birth and miracles, (4) His penal death for our sins, and (5) His physical resurrection and personal return.[67] The actual term 'fundamentalist' was coined in 1920 by Curtis Lee Laws, the editor of the Baptist *Watchman Examiner*. Then it carried no pejorative connotations but rather was a badge of pride denoting those who defended 'the fundamentals of the faith'.

Today, of course, the word fundamentalism has acquired an ineradicable negative connotation. It has become a by-word for extremist, rigid, unthinking, fanaticism of any kind, a generic put-down of not just fervent religious groups but fanatics of other persuasions too.[68] William Shepard submits that whatever label the face of conservative and confrontational religion is given it will incur a pejorative flavour, since what it opposes (modernity) is typically what many in Western academic and journalistic circles hold dear.[69]

One characteristic of fundamentalism (of the transformative kind) marking it out from evangelicalism generally is its militancy. 'A fundamentalist is an evangelical who is angry about something', suggests Marsden.[70] Bridget Carr in her study of a rural fundamentalist community in New Zealand found this very much in evidence.[71] This militancy is directed at an enemy that goes by various names, as we shall see shortly. To the fundamentalist, an active confrontational response is needed. Fundamentalism associates modernism with multifarious social evils.[72] It is also typically restorationist in seeking to restore society to a golden age which existed (in fundamentalists' eyes) in the past.[73] There is, as with evangelicals, a high view of scripture, but it is pushed to an extreme. Scripture is infallible or 'inerrant' (without error) in a sense which is unflinching. Evidence that would contradict biblical factual accounts or depictions of reality is simply wrong: 'When the Word of God says one thing, and scholarship says another, scholarship can go to hell', as Billy Sunday, a fundamentalist preacher, once put it.[74] Fundamentalists customarily adopt the excessively literalistic style which is often attributed to evangelicals. For example, the seven days of creation in Genesis are just that, seven 24-hour days, so the earth cannot be more than a few thousand years old.[75] The literalistic reading of scripture by creationists is something evangelicals have major trouble with. Packer claims evangelicals know symbolism when they see it.[76] Moreover, evangelicals vigorously draw a distinction between the infallibility or inerrancy of scripture versus the often all-too-fallible interpretations of scripture[77] by those who would invoke it in their anti-modernist agendas.

Another characteristic of fundamentalists is an excessive dogmatism and certainty about the truth. The truth is non-negotiable; it is not a matter for debate or discussion. The fundamentalist moreover knows the truth.[78] There are 'no grey areas', as Carr entitled her New Zealand study: 'There are no "ifs" or "buts", no "perhaps" or "maybes", instructions for a life everlasting as one of God's children is explicit in its simplicity. This black and white, dualistic philosophy of good and evil, leaves nothing to chance.'[79]

An anti-intellectualism or 'obscurantism', which was not a mark of the early 'classical' fundamentalists, became an unfortunate feature of later fundamentalism as it 'withdrew more and more into [its] shell'.[80] As we have already seen with the Billy Sunday quotation, sometimes the anti-intellectualism was perversely worn as a badge of orthodoxy. Evangelicals, by contrast, are at pains to emphasize that evangelicalism is not afraid of facts ('all truth is God's truth' is a favourite refrain[81]) and that 'obscurantism in all its forms is wholly out of keeping with true Evangelicalism.'[82]

Fundamentalism contains both separatist and transformatist strains. There is a broad correlation here with the particular eschatological position held. Premillennial fundamentalists see these as the 'last days' prior to the second coming of Christ whereupon the divine millennium will commence.[83] Large-scale cultural involvement and transformation is thus pointless; rather one must do one's utmost to 'rescue the perishing'. Premillennialism was usually combined with 'dispensationalism', a doctrine of seven great ages or 'dispensations' in which God unfolded His plan of history.[84] Dispensationalists saw this as the penultimate sixth era, or church age, an era culminating in imminent catastrophe, perhaps through nuclear holocaust.[85] The disintegration of secular society and the decline of morals are evidence aplenty to the fundamentalists that their views are correct.

The transformative fundamentalists, a much smaller group, are postmillennialists. The second coming will occur after the millennium of God's rule through His Church. Christians have a large job ahead to transform or 'reconstruct' the world in accordance with God's law.

The two strains of fundamentalism are mirrored in the political sphere. Some fundamentalism is quietist, content to live out its life in its own enclave away from the fallen and corrupt world of politics. Separatist fundamentalists, if they vote at all, most certainly do not stand for public office, nor support and lead political parties. In contrast, the transformatist fundamentalists are political activists. The Moral Majority had self-avowed fundamentalists such as the Rev Jerry Falwell at its helm.[86] In New Zealand, fundamentalists from the Reformed churches were at forefront of the establishment of the Christian Heritage Party.

Pentecostals and Charismatics The fastest growing elements of modern Christianity are the Pentecostals and the Charismatics.

Pentecostals are a diverse group whose origins date from the 1890s to the 1920s.[87] Mainstream Protestant denominations rejected the supernatural outward manifestations of the Spirit experienced by certain believers. Pentecostalism 'insisted that true heart religion be evidenced by unmistakable signs of the Spirit's radical transforming power, especially the Pentecostal signs of faith healing and speaking in tongues.'[88] This contemporary dramatic outpouring of the Holy Spirit was likened to the day of Pentecost in the book of Acts, hence the name. Pentecostal growth was sparked by revivals such as the Azuza Street revival in Los Angeles in 1906 and the Welsh revival. These vibrant groups, marked by their exuberance and experience of the 'full gospel', eventually crystallized into denominations such as the Assemblies of God, the Apostolic Church and the Elim Church. Theologically, Pentecostals are not fundamentalists and indeed were targets of the classical fundamentalists of the early twentieth century.[89] The latter were 'cessationists' insisting that the 'charismata' or supernatural spiritual gifts (speaking in tongues, divine healing, prophecy) ceased with the passing of the first-century apostles.[90] However, while not fundamentalists *stricto sensu*, Pentecostals are 'fundamentalistic'[91] in that they affirm the fundamentals (virgin birth, substitutory atonement, second coming of Christ and so on). The trouble was they were fundamentalists 'plus'—they believed more and it was the supernatural additions which were the sticking point. Pentecostalism was to align itself with mainstream evangelicalism.[92]

Charismatics are believers who adopt a Pentecostal style of worship but remain in their own Catholic or Protestant churches. Russell Spittler explains:

> The word *charismatic* . . . functions as an adjective describing mainline folk who have adopted Pentecostal beliefs, values and practices. Hence, charismatic Catholics, charismatic Presbyterians, charismatic Lutherans, and so on. . . . Charismatics, who could be described as Pentecostals in mainstream garb, can be found today in virtually every sector of Christendom—including the Roman Catholic and Eastern Orthodox traditions.[93]

'Liberal' Christianity Although my subject group is CC, liberal Christianity deserves brief examination. First, it gives a fuller picture of Christian attitudes and thought. Second, this interpretation of Christianity is the one which, I suspect, has the most influence upon public life and policy. This is because those in the 'knowledge sector' who profess Christianity tend to be of a liberal temper. Indeed, the more highly-educated and those within the upper sociocultural and economic strata of society tend to be the core of liberal Christianity. Finally, and relatedly, one sees an affinity or easiness of cooperation between 'liberal' Christianity and liberal or modernist thought generally.

The roots of liberal Christianity, especially liberal Protestantism, can be traced to the nineteenth century. The enemy again was modernity but, whereas conservatives sought to stiffen their resolve by a vigorous reaffirmation of traditional beliefs, liberal Christians determined the path of wisdom was not rejection but accommodation of the faith to what was perceived as a formidable, secular, scientific worldview. Christianity needed to be refashioned to meet the Enlightenment challenge. In Protestant Christianity the term for this reworking was called 'liberalism' and in Catholic Christianity it was called 'modernism'.[94] Whichever label one prefers, the sincere motive was to save Christianity.[95] At the forefront of the liberal defence of the faith were those who most keenly felt the onslaught—the well-educated, the intellectual, the sophisticated elite. If they were going to retain their integrity Christianity must either be abandoned or modified. For many, the latter was the preferred course. In Niebuhr's *Christ and Culture* typology this is 'The Christ of Culture' type.[96] Their apologetic strategy is primarily directed to powers-that-be.[97] A good distillation of liberal/modernist theological thought is provided by James Veitch:

> In [liberalism/modernism], religion was considered a human phenomenon; the Bible, the record of the human experience of God's presence;

> Christianity the crown of all the searching for God and, therefore, not the only way to God, nor the only expression of the word of God; Jesus was a human in and through whom God was present; but he was not divine, not born of a virgin, nor did he have miraculous power; his death was a profound example of the love of God, and his resurrection was spiritual and not physical. All humans are, nevertheless, precious in God's sight, and none is ever finally divorced from the love of God and acceptance by an all-compassionate God.[98]

Liberal Christians have, historically, been strong advocates of the so-called 'Social Gospel'. Under this approach the Kingdom of God is realizable on earth and, moreover, this social transformation can be brought about by *human* means.[99] The last aspect is telling for—and this drew the scorn of CCs—it implied that human beings could establish the Divine Kingdom by themselves.[100] Liberal Christians have frequently been at odds with the state on matters of socio-political and economic morality. For them, addressing 'structural' injustice is the foremost religious concern. Ivanica Vodanovich describes the New Zealand situation this way: 'Within the established churches, a small group of liberal clergy and parishioners arguing government policy should embody the social gospel had, throughout the seventies, become increasingly involved in secular humanitarian issues, such as race relations, anti-nuclear protests, poverty, Maori land rights and the Treaty of Waitangi.'[101]

The liberal Christian approach has not gone without criticism: some CCs 'see in them the seeds of apostasy.'[102] This is not the place to traverse such conservative criticisms of liberal Christianity. Suffice to note that the subjectivist and anti-supernaturalist tendencies of liberal Christianity are considered by the conservatives to have had tragically unproductive and frustratingly spoiling consequences for the entire Christian enterprise.[103]

The Worldview of Conservative Christians: Defining Attitudes, Beliefs and Values

The Idea of a 'Worldview'

Conservative Christians have, I suggest, a distinctive 'worldview'. First, we must define what we mean by a 'worldview', for it is a term seldom used in legal discourse, and when it is, it is invariably left undefined.[104] The term is a translation from the German word *weltanschauung*[105] (hence I write 'worldview' instead of 'world view' or 'world-view').

Alternative expressions are 'fundamental, unspoken assumptions'[106] and 'underlying axiomatic unconsciously-assumed convictions'.[107] I shall stay with 'worldview'. Giesler and Watkins provide a helpful definition:

> A world view is a way one views the whole world. . . . A world view is a way of viewing or interpreting all of reality. It is an interpretive framework through which or by which one makes sense out of the data of life and the world. . . . [It] is the structure with which one molds the stuff of experience. It is the mold into which the clay of reality is cast. A world view is like a plot that holds the play of life together. It is a pattern superimposed on the cloth of the world by which one knows where to cut the fabric of experience.[108]

Some characteristics of a worldview are as follows. First, it is comprehensive, a '*macro*-model', designed to explain all of reality not merely some aspect of it.[109] Second, it is enduring, not a fickle, easily changeable thing. If worldviews are like spectacles, they are spectacles worn continuously and seldom changed. A change in worldview is a major event which might be dubbed a 'paradigm shift' (in science) or a 'conversion' (in religion).[110] Third, worldviews inform and guide life; one lives by a worldview.[111] A worldview that did not guide life would not be a worldview at all.[112] Fourth, worldviews, while possessed by an individual, do not belong just to an individual: 'Worldviews are always shared; they are communal.'[113] Fifth, worldviews are, suggest Walsh and Middleton, 'intensely spiritual [and] are a religious phenomenon.'[114] Their argument is that: 'Faith is an essential part of life. Humans are confessing, believing and trusting creatures.'[115] If this is so, then where, or in whom, we place our faith determines the worldview which we adopt—'our ultimate faith commitment sets the contours of our world view.'[116] In this sense believing is seeing. What one believes in (or has faith in, given the impossibility of convincing empirical proof of many things believed in) shapes what our vision for life is (our worldview) and thereafter what we value and how we act.[117] If worldviews do rest upon 'faith commitments' then what are these? Walsh and Middleton argue faith commitments refer to the way we answer four basic questions:

(1) *Who am I?* Or, what is the nature, task and purpose of human beings?
(2) *Where am I?* Or, what is the nature of the world and universe I live in?

(3) *What's wrong?* Or, what is the basic problem or obstacle that keeps me from attaining fulfillment? In other words, how do I understand evil?
(4) *What is the remedy?* Or, how is it possible to overcome this hindrance to my fulfillment? In other words, how do I find salvation?[118]

The answers to these sorts of basic questions (formulations of the questions vary[119]) reveal our foundation beliefs—in other words, faith commitments. It seems justifiable to call these faith commitments 'religious' since they comprise 'ultimate concerns' (or answers), which is at least one major attempt at defining religion.[120] Ronald Nash argues:

> Religion is an inescapable given in life. All humans have something that concerns them ultimately and whatever it is, that object of ultimate concern is that person's God. Whatever a person's *ultimate* concern may be, it will have an enormous influence on everything else the person does or believes; that, after all, is one of things *ultimate* concerns are like.[121]

Yet another term for the basic answers we give are 'presuppositions'.[122] People presuppose answers to the basic questions.[123] The presupposed answers or presuppositions often remain unconscious. They can be brought to consciousness and explicitly articulated, but seldom are.[124] The basic answers, faith commitments, or presuppositions (brought to the surface or not, and whether one wishes to characterize them as 'religious') set the contours of a person's worldview.

Sixth, and finally, just as basic beliefs or presuppositions can be held unconsciously, so too can a worldview. Middleton and Walsh argue:

> It is indeed paradoxical that worldviews best provide orientation to life when we are not aware of them. They best provide a secure world and home for human activity when they are so internalized that we simply assume that we experience reality the way it truly is, that we picture the world 'the way things in sheer actuality are.'[125]

A similar comment was once made about metaphysics and its relationship with the hard-headed, down-to-earth lawyer: 'Judges and non-judges who denounce metaphysics do not thereby escape from metaphysics. Nor do they establish the truth of their own metaphysical assumptions. All they establish is their unawareness of their own basic assumptions.'[126]

Some Worldviews

There are many worldviews on offer but I will very briefly refer to just two.

Maori It is difficult to generalize and posit *a* Maori worldview, for modern Maori may be Christian, Marxist, atheist and so on. I shall focus upon the traditional, pre-Western Maori view of reality. A convenient summary is that by the Waitangi Tribunal in its 1985 report on the Manukau claim:

> It might be considered that Western society, although espousing a religion, is predominantly secular and individualistic in its world-view. Although there is a religious premise for the presumption that human-kind has authority over nature, that view probably springs from the secular and rational characteristics of our society. Maori society on the other hand is predominantly spiritual and communal. The Maori world view emphasises the primacy of nature and the need for man to tread carefully when interfering with natural laws, and processes.[127]

Maori have their own 'indigenous discourse'[128] or *teo reo Maori*. Naturally, the Maori story of New Zealand would read differently from the European (Pakeha) one. Nigel Jamieson has helpfully explicated some 'archetypal forms' of Maori thought and feeling pattern. Some of these dimensions of *Te Ao Maori* are:

> Te ao Maori is essentially all one. Common bonds running through the universe count for more than specific differences. This means that the three areas of action—physical, intellectual, and spiritual—are intimately related as one.
> The essential oneness of te ao Maori gives rise to a cosmic or whole-world view. The many are one. Reality is united and absolute, and only appearances are fragmented and relative.
> Because te ao Maori is essentially all one, then, as in gestalt psychology, the whole counts for more than the sum of its constituent parts. Although one is outnumbered by the many, the many are outweighed by the one.
> Te ao Maori seeks simplicity. If the world is one, then truth is simple.
> Te ao Maori is alive—tihe mauri ora! Even trees and stones have a spiritual life force. The world is vital and dynamic, being in a process of either growth or decay. The life sciences come first—physics tags along behind.
> The oneness of te ao Maori is spiritual. What happens on this world is explicable only in terms of what happens in the other world.[129]

In terms of the classical problem of the One and the Many (of explaining unity and diversity), the traditional Maori worldview says all is ultimately One and the diversity (Many) is only apparent or temporary.[130] This is Monism, in philosophy, or Pantheism, in religion. Harold Turner has a simple metaphor for this, which he calls, 'The Ocean View':

> life's phenomena and the relationships between them [are] ephemeral and of no permanent significance, like an ocean where each of us is but a passing wave, a temporary ripple on the surface, or a momentary jet of spray[] . . . The Ocean View says there is no problem about a One and a Many, since there is only the One; so no answer is needed.[131]

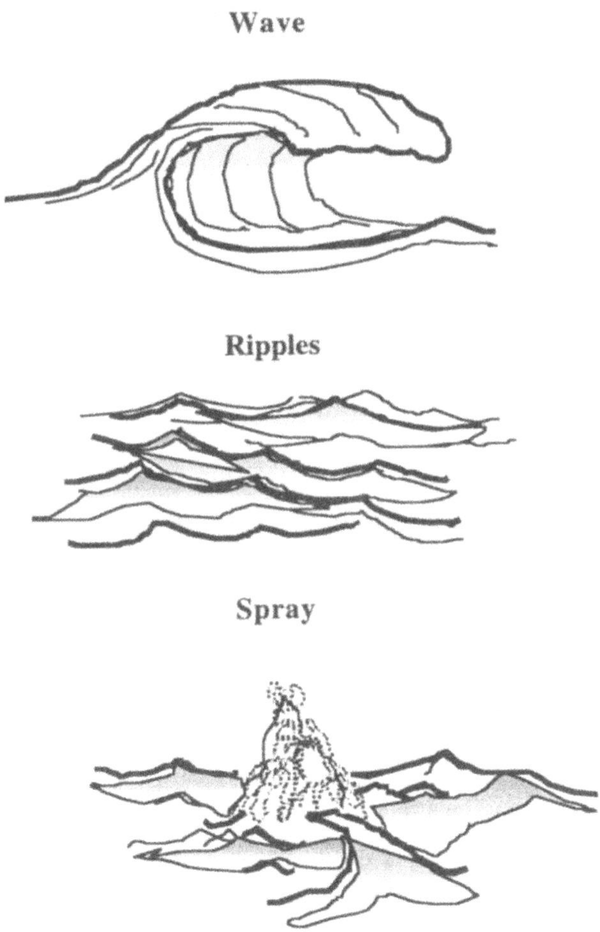

Figure 2.2 The Ocean View

Postmodern The present Western era is increasingly described as a 'postmodern' one. 'Postmodernism' is difficult to define and reflects more an attitude than a coherent philosophy or 'ism'.[132] Stanley Grenz argues there is in fact no postmodern 'worldview' as such:

> postmodernism defies definitive description . . . .the postmodern era spells the end of the 'universe'—the end of the all-encompassing worldview. In a sense, postmoderns have no worldview. A denial of the reality of a unified world as the object of our perception is at the heart of postmodernism. Postmoderns reject the possibility of constructing a single correct worldview and are content simply to speak of many views and, by extension, many worlds.[133]

Grand stories and narratives are eschewed: 'I define postmodernism as incredulity toward metanarratives', summarized Jean-François Lyotard, a leading postmodernist.[134]

At its simplest, postmodernity represents a profound disillusionment with modernity and all it stood for—the ideal of progress and the myth of mastery of nature by science and technology. Modernity's grand narrative, the so-called 'Enlightenment project' ('the human intellectual quest to unlock the secrets of the universe in order to master nature for human benefit and create a better world.'[135]) has run aground. The optimism and idealism of modernity is replaced with 'a gnawing pessimism'[136] and a radical sense of anxiety. Middleton and Walsh call the latter, *anomie*, 'the loss of a *nomos*—the loss of any secure sense of a meaningful order to the world.'[137]

Postmodernism embraces the following interrelated cluster of concepts:

> (1) The self is not, and cannot be, an autonomous, self-generating entity; it is purely a social, cultural, historical, and linguistic creation. (2) There are no foundational principles from which other assertions can be derived; hence, certainty as the result of either empirical verification or deductive reasoning is impossible. (3) There can be no such thing as knowledge of reality; what we think is knowledge is always belief and can apply only to the context within which it is asserted. (4) Because language is socially and culturally constructed, it is inherently incapable of representing or corresponding to reality; hence all propositions and all interpretations, even texts, are themselves social constructions.[138]

Postmodernists are sceptical of Truth, capital 't', as a fixed notion[139]: 'there is no absolute truth; rather, truth is relative to the community in which we participate.'[140]

In terms of the problem of the One and the Many, postmodernism answers there is only the Many, the diversity. The notion of a One, the 'uni'-verse is a chimera. Turner invokes the 'pebbles' metaphor here. Reality here is 'like a beach of pebbles jumbled accidentally together, but each separate and self-contained without any necessary connection with the others.' Under this view, 'there is nothing to hold the pebbles together, there is no universe; any one pebble might as well be anywhere. We must put up with the meaningless jumble.'[141] His illustration is Figure 2.3 below:

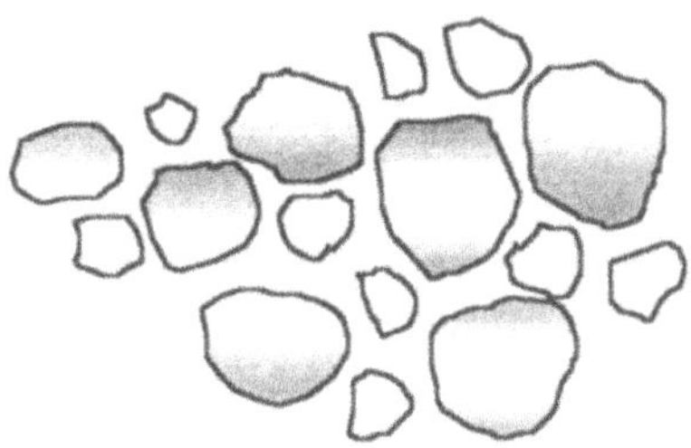

Figure 2.3 The Pebbles View

The Conservative Christian Worldview

Harry Blamires once tried to explain the definitive characteristics of 'the Christian mind.'[142] His study was not with reference to a particular kind of Christian, viz., the 'conservative' one, but most of the attributes he expounds fit nicely into my model of CC. In describing the Christian mind, Blamires was throughout using the term 'mind' to mean view of life (worldview).[143] He identified six features: (1) its supernatural orientation; (2) its awareness of evil; (3) its conception of truth; (4) its acceptance of authority; (5) its concern for the person, and; (6) its sacramental cast.

A 'prime mark', said Blamires, of the Christian mind is its supernatural orientation: 'it cultivates the eternal perspective . . . it looks beyond this life to another one.'[144] This other-worldly mindset cannot for a moment escape a frame of reference which reaches out to the supernatural.[145] By a similar token, 'the breaking-in of the greater supernatural order upon our more limited finite world'[146] is a given. Second, the Christian mind thinks in terms of the fact of Heaven and Hell. These are real places and the Christian is 'conscious of the universe as a battlefield between the forces of good and evil.'[147] The CC is firmly located in this battleground. Other doctrines are relevant here—the doctrine of Original Sin explains mankind's tendency toward evil, while the Fall underscores man's fallen nature. (John Stott suggests the Christian mind is best viewed as one which has absorbed and now thinks in terms of the fourfold scheme of biblical history—the Creation, the Fall, the Redemption and the End (or Restoration)).[148] Third, the Christian mind has a distinct notion of the truth centred upon the divine revelation. Blamires observes:

> The marks of truth as christianly conceived, then, are: that it is supernaturally grounded, not developed within nature; that it is objective and not subjective; that is a revelation and not a construction; that it is discovered by inquiry and not elected by a majority vote; that it is authoritative and not a matter of personal choice.[149]

This describes the CC to a tee. Fourth, the Christian mind accepts and defers to authority. This was the first and primary characteristic of the CC noted earlier. The Christian mind has 'an attitude to authority which modern secularism cannot even understand, let alone tolerate.'[150] CCs correspond to those 'who accept the revelation and the Church for what they are, the visible vehicles of God's action in the world.'[151] Fifth, the Christian mind is concerned for the person ahead of the impersonal, mechanical contrivances which reduce man's life to a sub-human level.[152] This characteristic is not one so far associated especially with the CC. However, to the extent Blamires emphasizes the sacredness of the human person, made in the image of God, we find a resonance with the CC attitude to such issues as abortion and euthanasia.

Ontologically, and returning to the issue of the One and the Many, CCs believe it is a case of the One *and* the Many: 'reality is structured in some intermediate way that says both the One (the unity) and the Many (the plurality) are equally real and possess some permanent relationship.'[153] Turner evokes the 'web' or 'network' metaphor here:

> The Web-Network View says both the problem and the answer are real, since there really is both a richness of diversity (the Many) and an order that governs this diversity systematically (the One). Reality consists of a system of interdependent, interrelated, levels of being, structuring everything that exists in a hierarchy which is itself part of the order or system. There is a universe and it has a system which can be investigated and understood, and a meaning we can appreciate.[154]

Turner's depiction of this 'unitive, integrative plurality' is depicted below in Figure 2.4:[155]

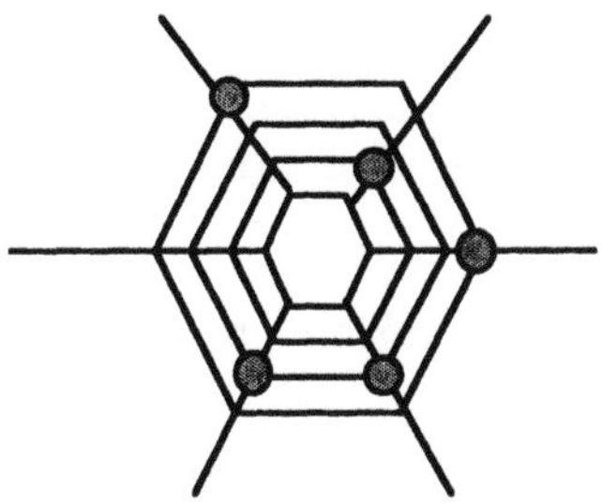

Figure 2.4 The Web-Network View

If we return to Walsh and Middleton's four basic worldview shaping questions and ask how the CC would answer them, the CC might respond with something like this:

(1) *Who am I?* I am a creature of God, special in that I am made in God's image (*imago Dei*). My purpose is to do God's will on earth by (a) living a holy separate life untainted by the world (the separatist response) or (b) living a holy life engaged with and transforming 'culture'[156] (the transformatist response).

(2) *Where am I?* I am in a world created by God, a world that has a physical, visible, temporal aspect as well as a spiritual, unseen, eternal dimension. God sustains and 'speaks' (intervenes) into this world today.

(3) *What is wrong?* The entire creation is fallen; mankind rebelled and sin is a present fact. Satan is a leader of this rebellion and evil is sin's fruit. The *zeitgeist*, or spirit of this age, is antagonistic to God; it denies His existence and His absolute, unchanging moral and ethical standards.

(4) *What's the remedy?* The solution and salvation is found exclusively in the person of Jesus Christ who redeemed all creation and mankind. Restoration, however, is not yet complete, nor will it be completed until the Second Coming of Christ.

Whilst I have tried to crystallize the CC worldview and delineate its broad contours, it is again important to note that this is a generalization. Some would say it is more accurate to speak of Christian worldviews plural.[157] Certainly, CCs (like other broad groupings such as marxists or feminists) will not necessarily agree on *every* issue. Nash wisely reminds us that:

> Any account of world-views that implied this would be gravely mistaken. Even Christians who share beliefs on all essential issues may disagree on other important points . . . They may disagree over how some revealed law of God applies to a twentieth-century situation. They may squabble publicly over complex issues like national defence, capital punishment, and the welfare state, to say nothing about the issues that divide the Church into different denominations.[158]

Despite the sharp differences in certain respects there are, I believe, sufficient 'family resemblances'[159] shared between CCs to speak sensibly of them, as a group, possessing a distinctive worldview.

Stance toward the State

Conservative Christians respect the state and consider it important to be exemplary law-abiding citizens.[160] The state is a necessary institution, ordained by God, to restrain the exercise of evil and sin, punish wrongdoers, and promote social peace and well being. Rulers 'are sent by him [the Lord] to punish those who do wrong and to commend those who do right.'[161]

The precise role of the state and its limits differ within the various Christian traditions. The Reformed, Calvinist view of government's proper role is restricted: 'The state has the practical, specific task of maintaining the law and upholding public justice. . . . To go further and to seek the direct and control human action and motives is to go too far into totalitarian control.'[162] Catholicism has a more positive view seeing it as 'the role of the state to defend and promote the common good of civil society'[163] as well as exercising the juridical function.

CCs of whatever persuasion see the state as a servant of God having only delegated authority.[164] All authority or sovereignty is ultimately grounded in God alone; all authorities exist at God's behest: 'for there is no authority except that which God has established. The authorities that exist have been established by God.'[165] The concept of a totalitarian state, or even a state which intrudes into and pervades a large number of areas of life, is rejected. Whether described as 'subsidiarity'[166] (in Roman Catholicism) or 'sphere sovereignty'[167] (in neo-Calvinism), the state's proper sphere of operation is divinely limited. Other groups, institutions or communities—schools, families, churches, business corporations and so on—have their own integrity and sphere of activity before God and are not to be interfered with unnecessarily.[168] A state which tries to intrude into these communities or institutions by taking them over has gone too far.

The limits to the state are mostly clearly seen when the question of unjust or immoral law is raised. Civil disobedience is never a first resort but it remains a necessary route for the CC in certain circumstances. As Colson puts it: 'where a state either demands what God prohibits or prohibits what God demands, the believer is to obey God and graciously accept the state's imposed consequences.'[169] Catholics need turn no further than to Aquinas and his dictum *lex injusta non est lex* ('An unjust law is no law at all.')[170] Protestant CCs have any number of Reformation dissenters to draw from.[171] Francis Schaeffer, one of the most influential theologians for modern American Protestant CCs (whose influence was felt in New Zealand) re-echoed the duty of civil disobedience in his *A Christian Manifesto*:

> It was, is, and it always will be:
>
> GOD
>
> and
>
> CAESAR
>
> The civil government, as all of life, stands under the Law of God. In this fallen world God has given us certain offices to protect us from the chaos which is the natural result of that fallenness. But when *any office* commands that which is contrary to the Word of God, those who hold that office abrogate their authority and they are not to be obeyed. And that includes the state. . . . God has ordained the state as a *delegated* authority; it is not autonomous. The state is to be an agent of justice, to restrain evil by punishing the wrongdoer, and to protect the good in society. When it does the reverse, *it has no proper authority*. . . . The *bottom line* is that at a certain point there is not only the right, but the duty, to disobey the state.[172]

A Christian who is forced to choose God over Caesar must, as noted before, willingly accept the penalty. This is, 'in reality expressing the very highest respect for law.'[173]

The CC attitude to religious freedom is somewhat ambivalent. CCs claim religious liberty for themselves, of course, but historically have not always been magnanimous to non-Christian faiths.[174] The modern realization that religious liberty must be extended to all religions has come belatedly (and perhaps due in part to a pragmatic recognition of their loss of cultural dominance), but is now reasonably well established.[175]

'The Spirit of the Age'

One of the four distinctive characteristics of CC is its opposition to the prevailing ethos, values, or *zeitgeist*, 'the spirit of the age'. Many CCs see themselves as always in a deadly spiritual battle against the prevailing rebellious, God-denying spirits of the age. St Paul's warning in Ephesians is taken seriously: 'For our struggle is not against flesh and blood, but against the rulers, against the authorities, against the powers of this dark world and against the spiritual forces of evil in the heavenly realms.'[176] Some CCs are quick to invoke military metaphors: 'We face the challenge of arming and especially of organizing ourselves to be better engaged in the battle for our nation's spiritual and social future.'[177]

Christians are increasingly reminded that they are 'in the world' (and so engaged with and transforming the culture) but are 'not of the world'.[178] The latter admonition means not succumbing to, and being moulded by, its unregenerate, rebellious, fallen way of thinking. As Bishop Brian Carrell exhorts:

> Our calling as Christians is not to succumb to the spirit of the times and the outlook of a world that has come to ignore God, but in an attitude of gracious defiance to show that there is another way of looking, another way of living—a way found and focussed in the person of Jesus Christ.[179]

The CC sees a clear chasm between good and evil, not in terms of areas of creation being redeemed or unredeemed (dualism), but in terms of two opposing spiritual forces—either divine or satanic—which endeavour to shape and direct culture and claim mankind's allegiance. Schaeffer put it this way: 'It is not too strong to say that we are at war, and there are no neutral parties in the struggle. One either confesses that God is the final authority, or one confesses that Caesar is Lord.'[180] C S Lewis similarly warned: 'There is no neutral ground in the universe: every square inch, every split second, is claimed by God and counterclaimed by Satan.'[181] Mankind's response is either obedience or disobedience to God: 'Christian anthropology cannot avoid seeing the duality of obedience or rebellion as the basic conflict in human life.'[182] Many CCs adhere to a binary, bipolar 'either/or' approach in this regard. There is a pivotal and unavoidable 'directional question'[183] to be answered. There is no middle ground, people must choose. 'He who is not with me is against me',[184] is the scriptural warrant here. Rather than call this 'dualism' (where areas or spheres of life are God's and others are not), it is better to describe it as 'duality', as Walsh and Middleton do:

> Now there is a world of difference between *dualism* and *duality*. Christian discipleship forces us to recognize duality in life: *either* we serve the Lord *or* we follow idols. Dualism blurs the valid duality between obedience and disobedience because dualism identifies obedience, redemption and the kingdom of God with only *one* area of life. It sees the rest of life as either unrelated to redemption (or the sacred), or worse—under the power of disobedience, sin and the kingdom of darkness.[185]

Dualism is a distortion since it superimposes upon the structure of creation the 'directional' question of obedience or disobedience. 'Dualism . . . confuses structure and direction. Rather than seeing how the directional question runs through *all of life*, it identifies the direction with *particular parts* of the structure.'[186] Creation is diverse and there is a plurality of structures which exist—schools, families, churches, teams, orchestras, governments, and so on. This 'associational' or 'structural' pluralism is normative. The plurality of directional responses or 'confessional' pluralism is, by contrast, not normative. Confessional pluralism is a fact of a fallen rebellious world.[187]

Naming 'The Enemy'

CCs believe there has been a steady rise in, indeed a shift to, another supplanting worldview. There are various names for it among CCs.

Traditionally, it was called by the name historians prefer, 'modernity'. The roots of modernity lie in the Enlightenment (the Age of Reason).[188] 'Modernism', the expression of the ideas and values of modernity (a period), is marked by a faith in reason, science and technology and the conception of man as an autonomous individual,[189] able to conquer nature and improve the human condition. Following Kant, external authority, or 'tutelage of others'[190] is rejected, the Church or God especially.[191] Emancipated from past superstitions and traditions, modernism is confident and optimistic: 'the spirit of modernity is the spirit of progress.'[192] Lucien Goldmann comments: 'all the writers of the Enlightenment [were] united in their hostility to traditional

Christianity and the Church.'[193] Modernity is by nature antagonistic to religion which it sees as having an irrevocable 'dark side'.[194]

Another term often used interchangeably with modernity, is 'secularism'. This is derived from the Latin, *saeculum*, meaning 'generation, age or world'. Ruth Smithies explains:

> Secularism is that aspect of our post-Christian culture which denies the existence of a transcendent dimension to both human existence and the world or universe itself. We are self-reliant: God is superfluous and the pursuit of happiness is limited to this world and age.[195]

Secularism is not to be confused with 'secularization'. The latter is a particular process of structural change in society, a 'process by which religious thinking, practice and institutions lose social significance and become marginal to the operation of the social system.'[196] Many social institutions have ceased to be under religious control. Nonetheless, there is an intimate symbiotic relationship between the two concepts, one reinforcing the other. Secularism (the internal, ideological) is reflected in secularization (the external, sociological), and vice versa. Secularism may have promoted secularization but equally (and perhaps more so) the secularity of modern society may be a consequence of structural changes pursuant to the secularization process.[197] The process that creates the largely religion-free public environment generates a mindset that thinks typically of this-worldly things and not of God.[198]

In the last 30 years many American evangelicals and fundamentalists preferred to describe the enemy as 'secular humanism'. Schaeffer identified humanism as the antithetical worldview usurping the Judeo-Christian one. To him, humanism was pervasive and powerful:

> the humanist world view includes many thousands of adherents and today controls the consensus in society, much of the media, much of what is taught in our schools, and much of the arbitrary law being produced . . . The term humanism used in this wider, more prevalent way means Man beginning from himself, with no knowledge except what he can discover and no standards outside of himself. In this view Man is the measure of all things, as the Enlightenment expressed it.[199]

Timothy La Haye's influential book, *The Battle for the Mind,* (dedicated to Schaeffer) distilled and simplified Schaeffer's critique, whilst reformulating it in popularized, inflammatory form:

> Most people today do not realize what humanism really is and how it is destroying our culture, families, country—and one day, the entire world. Most of the evils in the world today can be traced to humanism, which has taken over our government, the UN, education, TV, and most of the other influential things of life. The church of Jesus Christ is the last obstacle for the humanists to conquer.[200]

Both Schaeffer and, to a lesser extent, La Haye, were widely read by many CCs in New Zealand. Schaeffer drew directly from the largely obscure *Humanist Manifestos I* and *II* which contain the doctrinal tenets of Humanism.[201]

Humanist Manifesto I (1933) was designed to be a comprehensive statement of *religious* humanism and outlined 15 theses regarding 'the means and purposes' of religious humanism, a religion described as 'a vital, fearless, and frank' one.[202] Thesis 6 noted that the time for theism had passed. Thesis 13 maintained that 'all associations and institutions exist for the fulfilment of human life' and, somewhat ominously for some CCs, concluded: 'Certainly religious institutions, their ritualistic forms, ecclesiastical methods, and communal activities must be *reconstituted* as rapidly as experience allows, in order to function effectively in the modern world.'[203]

By the time of the publication of *Humanist Manifesto II* in 1973, humanism had moved away from being an avowedly religious belief system. *Manifesto II* explained that this form of humanism (religious humanism) was but a variety and emphasis within *naturalistic* humanism, the latter being, by implication, the principal expression of humanist thought now.[204] The opposition to traditional theism and the supernatural was reaffirmed, although it cautioned that views that merely rejected theism were not equivalent to humanism. Humanism constitutes, in a positive sense, the 'belief in the possibilities of human progress and to the values central to it'. *Manifesto II* outlines 17 common principles which provide 'a design for a secular society on a planetary scale.' Principle 1 notes that religion 'in the best sense' may inspire and foster human progress. Yet there is religion and religion:

> We believe, however, that traditional dogmatic or authoritarian religions that place revelation, God, ritual, or creed above human needs and experience do a disservice to the human species. . . . As nontheists, we begin with humans not God, nature not deity . . . . No deity can save us; we must save ourselves.[205]

Corliss Lamont, author of the leading text on the subject, describes Humanism as follows:

> This philosophy can be more explicitly characterized as scientific Humanism, secular Humanism, naturalistic Humanism, or democratic Humanism, depending on the emphasis that one wishes to give. Whatever it be called, Humanism is the viewpoint that men have but one life to lead and should make the most of it in terms of creative work and happiness; that human happiness is its own justification and requires no sanction or support from supernatural sources; that in any case the supernatural, usually conceived of in the form of heavenly gods or immortal heavens, does not exist; and that human beings, using their own intelligence and cooperating liberally with one another, can build an enduring citadel of peace and beauty upon this earth.[206]

Schaeffer and his fellow American CCs objected to the founding anthropocentric premise of humanism—'Man is the measure of all things' (as Protagoras, the fifth century BC Greek philosopher, put it[207]). To them this was pure idolatry, the deification of humankind. For these CCs: 'Secular Humanism is a religion whose doctrine worships Man as the source of all knowledge and truth, whereas theism worships God as the source of all knowledge and truth.'[208] There was, to be sure, a strain of humanism, Christian humanism,[209] which was not objectionable to these critics,[210] but that variety of humanism was decidedly not the ascendant one in the late twentieth century.

The attack upon secular humanism was strident and alarmist. Moreover, it fed the paranoid fears of some CCs ever alert for apocalyptic, Satanic-controlled, one-world government, conspiracies.[211] The secular humanist thesis has not gone without criticism from American evangelical scholars. David Wells, for example, identifies the loss of cultural hegemony with long-term structural processes (secularization) as much as with the growth of secular humanism.[212] Sophisticated CC theorists invoke Peter Berger's concept of 'plausibility structures'.[213] Any religious (or other) worldview needs external, social reinforcement. The social structures that reinforce a particular worldview, that give it credibility, are 'plausibility structures'. Berger spoke of a 'plausibility crisis' for religion generally: 'secularization has resulted in a widespread collapse of the plausibility of traditional religious definitions of reality.'[214] Christianity is not immune from this problem.[215]

The American anti-secular humanism critique was imported into New Zealand in the mid-1980s. While the Moral Majority's political agenda was viewed with some suspicion by many New Zealand CCs (there were 'no direct linkages between the New Zealand and American movements and their constituencies were also significantly different'[216]), the identification of the bête noire as 'secular humanism' was gratefully received by many: it served as a convenient shorthand label for the enemy, and as a seemingly compelling socio-philosophical explanation of why permissiveness was increasing. In the 1980s, New Zealand CCs were convinced that 'more and more the very fabric of the nation was called into question. No longer was New Zealand a Christian nation. The concern was now with "secular humanism" and the godlessness of the body politic.'[217] For example, in 1987 the Coalition of Concerned Citizens published articles on 'Humanism in the Media', 'Humanism in the Classroom', 'Declaring Victory over Secular Humanism' and 'Humanism . . . a Global Plan'.[218] This humanist exposé edition ran to 105,000 copies and was distributed throughout New Zealand.[219]

In the late 1990s the humanist critique was less prominent, but still lived on. The Rev Brian Brandon, a CC minister, stated in his Internet critique of humanism that 'revival is imperative, and no more than in New Zealand where humanism has taken its toll perhaps more than anywhere'; humanism is a dominating Western worldview that 'grips the church and society'.[220]

The Postmodern Worldview

If we take postmodernity to be a period of transition in Western culture, one marked by 'a growing sense that all knowledge is conditioned by a variety of human factors and that any pretension to objectivity and absoluteness in knowledge is misplaced',[221] then this period seems to offer CCs little more than modernity did. Opinions amongst Christians differ.

In theory, postmodernism might be more tolerant of religion than modernity. It advocates pluralism so perhaps religious viewpoints will be more freely welcomed in public discourse. The Rev Rob Yule is one such New Zealand optimist:

> The 1990s is a pluralistic post-secular era, in which cultural diversity and religious belief are much more welcome than in the secular age preceding it, which dated from the European Enlightenment. Religious conservatives, lamenting the loss of the privileges they enjoyed in the Christendom era, have not always recognised the significant opportunities that the new pluralistic situation provides.[222]

The openness of postmodernity, its receptivity to diverse stories of all stripes, might spell an opportunity for Christians to proffer their story with renewed vigour, suggests another commentator.[223]

But some doubt postmodernity will benefit conservative religions. Most CCs believe in absolutes based on the known revealed Truth (capital 't'). If postmodernism does become the dominant worldview there may remain, as Robert Jenson calls it, an 'asymmetry' between the way the 'Abrahamic' religions (Christianity, Islam and Judaism) are treated and the manner other, less dogmatic, religions are. The Semitic faiths (in their conservative form) insist upon absolute values and standards for all[224] and reject the desirability of pluralism as a good in itself.[225] Arguably, postmodernism will reveal itself to be just another 'secularist creed', with its own metanarrative of tolerance suppressing those with 'intolerant' narratives at odds with its own.[226] Far from eschewing metanarratives, CCs insist 'there *is* a single metanarrative encompassing all peoples and all times.'[227] This being so, they may well remain as equally unwelcome participants in the public arena as they were under modernity.[228]

Notes

1 The abbreviation 'CC' is used instead of 'cC' for the sake of elegance. I use CC to refer to 'conservative Christianity' or 'conservative Christian', the context indicating which is meant.

2 *The Restructuring of American Religion: Society and Faith Since World War II* (1988). Wuthnow's update is *Christianity and Civil Society: The Contemporary Debate* (1996) at 48 et seq.

3 For a recent attempt to bridge the gap, see Richard G Hutcheson and Peggy L Shriver, *The Divided Church: Moving Liberals and Conservatives from Diatribe to Dialogue* (1999).

4 See Basil Mitchell, *Faith and Criticism* (1994) at 1.

5 See James Davison Hunter, *Culture Wars: The Struggle to Define America* (1991) at 132 and Douglas Laycock, 'Continuity and Change in the Threat to Religious Liberty: The Reformation Era and the Late Twentieth Century' (1996) 80 *Minn L Rev* 1047 at 1088.

6 Hunter, *Culture Wars*, at 43.

7 Ibid at 44 (original emphasis).

8 Ibid at 44.

9 Ibid at 44-45 (original emphasis).

10 Ibid at 105.

11 Nancy J Davis and Robert V Robinson, 'Religious Orthodoxy in American Society: The Myth of a Monolithic Camp' (1996) 35 *JSSR* 229 at 231 and 243. They found the religiously orthodox to be 'conservative' on social issues of sexuality, reproduction and schooling of children but 'moderate' or 'liberal' on gender, racial

and economic issues. There was not the coherence around a single ideological position that Wuthnow and Hunter suggest.

[12] Rhys H Williams, 'Is America in a culture war? Yes—no—sort of', *Christian Century*, 12 November 1997, 1038 at 1041.

[13] Wuthnow, *Contemporary Debate* (above n 2), at 59.

[14] But see John Adsett Evans, 'The New Christian Right in New Zealand' in Gilling (ed), *'Be Ye Separate': Fundamentalism and the New Zealand Experience* (1992) at 69-106.

[15] Peter C Matheson, *'A Time of Sifting': Evangelicals and Liberals at the Genesis of New Zealand Theology* (1991) at 1.

[16] Ibid at 8.

[17] Ibid at 1.

[18] Transcript of a lecture by Stuart Lange reprinted in *Presbyterian AFFIRM Newsletter*, September 1998, at 11 (emphasis in original).

[19] Wuthnow, *Contemporary Debate* (above n 2), at 63 (drawing upon work by Northrup Frye).

[20] Peter L Berger, 'Secularism in Retreat', *National Interest*, Winter 1996/1997, 3 at 4 (original emphasis). Berger is not posing these two strategies as exhaustive alternatives. In his influential work, *The Social Reality of Religion* (1969) Berger points out (at 152-153): 'Obviously there are various intermediate possibilities between these two ideal-typical options, with varying degrees of accommodation and intransigence.'

[21] See, for example, Mitchell, *Faith and Criticism* (above n 4), at 2; Evans, 'New Christian Right'(above n 14); David Arrowsmith, 'Christian Attitudes Towards Public Questions in New Zealand in 1975', MA thesis, Political Studies, University of Auckland, 1978; Brett Knowles, 'Some Aspects of the History of the New Life Churches of New Zealand 1960-1990', Ph D thesis, University of Otago, 1994.

[22] See *Catechism of the Catholic Church* (Liberia Editrice Vaticana) (1994) at para 82.

[23] Wuthnow, *Contemporary Debate* (above n 2), at 55.

[24] Evans, 'New Christian Right' (above n 14), at 95 fn 11. See James Barr, *Fundamentalism* (1977) ch 3 at 40 et seq for helpful explanation.

[25] James I Packer, *'Fundamentalism' and the Word of God* (1958) at 104.

[26] Ibid at 104.

[27] Ibid at 102.

[28] See, for example, Sir Rupert Cross, *Statutory Interpretation* (1976) at 1 and 13.

[29] William Shepard in an essay about both Islamic and Christian 'fundamentalism', makes a valuable observation in this regard: 'More important—and this may be the "truth behind" the charges of literalism—both groups of "fundamentalists" want to take literally, or at least very seriously, elements in the Scriptures and traditions that their modernist opponents would either reject or reinterpret. Examples in the

Christian case would be supernaturalism, original sin, and blood atonement'. W Shepard, '"Fundamentalism" Christian and Islamic' (1987) 17 *Religion* 355 at 362.

30 See generally, Oliver Barclay, 'The nature of Christian morality' in Kaye and Wenham (eds), *Law, Morality and the Bible* (1978) pt 1, ch 1, at 130.

31 Wuthnow, *Contemporary Debate* (above n 2), at 55.

32 Arrowsmith, 'Christian Attitudes' (above n 21), Introduction, at viii.

33 Betty Scott, 'Observance of Right and Wrong', *Challenge Weekly ('CW')*, 28 February 1991, at 9.

34 See, for example, Arrowsmith, 'Christian Attitudes' (above n 21), at viii.

35 Mitchell, *Faith and Criticism* (above n 4), at 3.

36 Arrowsmith, 'Christian Attitudes' (above n 21), at ix and 116.

37 H Richard Niebuhr, *Christ and Culture* (1951).

38 Ibid at ch 2.

39 Ibid at ch 6.

40 Quoted (and strongly denounced) in David Bronnert, 'Social Ethics' in Kaye and Wenham (eds), *Law, Morality and the Bible*, ch 5, at 216.

41 See John Stenhouse, 'Fundamentalism and New Zealand Culture' in Gilling (ed), *Be Ye Separate,* at 5: 'Roman Catholic Christians could adopt strikingly similar positions to Protestant fundamentalists, and for many of the same reasons.'

42 See Hunter, *Culture Wars* (above n 5), at 97-104.

43 See Alister McGrath, *Evangelicalism and the Future of Christianity* (1993) at 176.

44 Harold O J Brown, 'Unhelpful Antagonism and Unhealthy Courtesy' in Armstrong (gen ed), *Roman Catholicism: Evangelical Protestants Analyze What Unites and Divides Us* (1994) at 177.

45 Quoted in Armstrong, ibid, at 241 fn 22.

46 Brian Carrell, 'New Culture, New Challenge' in Patrick (ed), *New Vision, New Zealand* (1993) ch 3 at 57.

47 Patrick, 'After the 1997 Congress' in Patrick (ed), *The Vision New Zealand Congress 1997* (1997) ch 1 at 30.

48 Hunter, *Culture Wars* (above n 5), at 104. Lesslie Newbigin puts a more principled case for co-operation between Christians and people of other faiths and ideologies in his, *The Gospel in a Pluralist Society* (1989) ch 14 at 180-181.

49 Mormonism, or more properly the Church of Jesus Christ of Latter Day Saints, is classified here as a non-Christian faith, although I acknowledge that Mormons themselves vigorously seek inclusion in the Christian fold.

50 Here I borrow from and adapt McGrath's description of the streams with Evangelicalism: see *Evangelicalism,* at 17.

51 AFFIRM stands for Anglicans For Faith, Intercession, Renewal and Mission. It is a partnership of Church Army, Anglican Renewal Ministries, Church Missionary

Society, Latimer Fellowship, South American Missionary Society. Presbyterians have borrowed the AFFIRM label for their own conservative sub-group.

52 The Westminster Fellowship was formed in 1950 declaring its belief in the 'infallible truth and divine authority of Holy Scripture' and the acceptance of the Westminster Confession and Catechisms. See Allan Davidson, *Christianity in Aotearoa* (1990) at 164.

53 Evans, 'New Christian Right' (above n 14), at 106, fn 132.

54 On the history of evangelicalism, see McGrath, *Evangelicalism* (above n 43), ch 2. For a recent common statement of evangelical beliefs and affirmatives—endorsed by most prominent Anglo-American evangelical leaders and theologians—see 'A Call to Evangelical Unity', *Christianity Today*, 14 June 1999, at 49-56.

55 George M Marsden, *Understanding Fundamentalism and Evangelicalism* (1991) at 4.

56 Ibid at 4-5.

57 McGrath, *Evangelicalism* (above n 43), at 51.

58 See McGrath, *Evangelicalism* (above n 43), at 94 and John Stott in David L Edwards/ John Stott, *Essentials: A Liberal-Evangelical Exchange* (1988) at 39: 'the Evangelical faith is historic, mainline, trinitarian Christianity, not an eccentric deviation from it. For we do not see ourselves as offering a new Christianity, but as recalling the Church to original Christianity.'

59 Packer, *'Fundamentalism' and the Word of God* (above n 25), at 38.

60 Or else, 'born again Christians', 'evangelicals', 'Pentecostals' or 'Charismatics'.

61 James Veitch, 'Fundamentalism and the Presbyterian Experience' in Gilling (ed), *Be Ye Separate*, at 30 and Colin Brown, 'Where have all the fundamentalists gone?' ibid, at 143.

62 Lyman Kellstedt and Corwin Smidt, 'Measuring Fundamentalism: An Analysis of Different Operational Strategies' (1991) 30 *JSSR* 259 at 260.

63 Packer's monograph, *'Fundamentalism' and the Word of God*, attempts to explain precisely how (British) evangelicalism differs from classic American fundamentalism. For a recent detailed treatment of this and many other points, see Harriet A Harris, *Fundamentalism and Evangelicals* (1998). I regret that my eleventh-hour discovery of this excellent treatise precluded its fuller integration into this book.

64 Kellstedt and Smidt, 'Measuring Fundamentalism', at 261; James Barr, 'Fundamentalism—A Challenge to the Church' (1991) 11 *Quarterly Review* 30 at 34.

65 The following account is drawn from Packer, *Fundamentalism*, ch 2; Tom W Smith, 'Classifying Protestant Denominations' (1990) 31 *Rev Relig Res* 225 at 226; McGrath, *Evangelicalism*, at 18-27; Shepard, '"Fundamentalism" Christian and

Islamic' (above n 29), at 356; Veitch, 'Fundamentalism and the Presbyterian Experience,' at 28-30.

66 See Shepard '"Fundamentalism" Christian and Islamic', at 356 and fn 5; Veitch, 'Fundamentalism and the Presbyterian Experience' (above n 61), at 29.

67 Packer, *Fundamentalism* (above n 25), at 28.

68 The term fundamentalist is of course applied to Muslims and other religious groups. There can be economic fundamentalism and even agricultural fundamentalism: see Shepard, '"Fundamentalism"; Christian and Islamic' (above n 29), at 355.

69 Shepard, ibid at 367.

70 Marsden, *Understanding Fundamentalism* (above n 55), at 1.

71 Bridget Carr, 'No Grey Areas: A Rural Fundamentalist Christian Perspective,' MA thesis, Religious Studies, University of Canterbury, 1992, at 24.

72 Carr, 'No Grey Areas,' at 24 records: 'The rural Fellowship central to this investigation is extremely fearful of the consequences of "Modernism" seen in the cities. Materialism, corruption and degenerating morals, to them, are associated with a secular, sick society.'

73 Barr, 'Fundamentalism—A Challenge' (above n 64), at 33.

74 Quoted in John Stenhouse, 'The Rev Dr James Copland and the Mind of New Zealand "Fundamentalism"' (1993) 17 *J Relig Hist* 475 at 475.

75 Marsden, *Understanding Fundamentalism* (above n 55), at 154.

76 Packer, *Fundamentalism* (above n 25), at 98-99.

77 Ibid at 96.

78 Barr, 'Fundamentalism—A Challenge' (above n 64), at 32-33.

79 Carr, 'No Grey Areas' (above n 71), at 39.

80 Packer, *Fundamentalism* (above n 25), at 32.

81 See, for example, Stott, *Essentials* (above n 58), at 96.

82 Packer, *Fundamentalism* (above n 25), at 34.

83 McGrath, *Evangelicalism* (above n 43), at 21; Stott, *Essentials* (above n 58), at 91.

84 Marsden, *Understanding Fundamentalism* (above n 55), at 39-41.

85 The best-selling book in America in the 1970s was a dispensationalist apocalyptic potboiler by Hal Lindsey, *The Late Great Planet Earth* (1970).

86 See generally Walter H Capps, *The New Religious Right* (1994) ch 2, for an in-depth profile of Falwell.

87 Russell P Spittler, 'Are Pentecostals and Charismatics Fundamentalists?' in Poewe (ed), *Charismatic Christianity as a Global Culture* (1994) ch 5 at 104-105. For an account of New Zealand Pentecostalism, see Brett Knowles, 'Some Aspects of the History of the New Life Churches' (above n 21).

88 Marsden, *Understanding Fundamentalism* (above n 55), at 43.

89 Spittler, 'Are Pentecostals?', at 108-110.

90 Spittler, ibid at 113.

91 Spittler, ibid at 114.

[92] Spittler, ibid at 112. Spittler refers to the 'Pentecostalization of evangelicalism' since the 1970s.

[93] Spittler, 'Are Pentecostals?', at 105 (original emphasis).

[94] Veitch, 'Fundamentalism and the Presbyterian Experience' (above n 61), at 29. Marsden comments that 'liberalism' stressed freedom from tradition, while 'modernism' emphasized adjustment to the modern world: *Understanding Fundamentalism* (above n 55), at 33.

[95] Marsden, ibid, at 32. See generally Packer, *Fundamentalism* (above n 25), ch 7.

[96] Niebuhr, *Christ and Culture* (above n 37), at 85 et seq.

[97] Niebuhr, ibid at 104 comments: 'The cultural Christians tend to address themselves to the leading groups in a society; they speak to the cultured among the despisers of religion; they use the language of the more sophisticated circles, of those who are acquainted with the science, the philosophy, and the political and economic movements of their time. They are missionaries to the aristocracy and the middle class, or to the groups rising to power in a civilization.'

[98] Veitch, 'Fundamentalism and the Presbyterian Experience' (above n 61), at 29.

[99] For a brief discussion, see John Stott, *New Issues Facing Christians Today*, 3rd edn (1999) at 8-9.

[100] Stott, ibid, at 7. As Stott adds: 'But the Kingdom of God is not Christianized society. It is the divine rule in the lives of those who acknowledge Christ.'

[101] 'Religion and Legitimation in New Zealand: Redefining the Relationship Between Church and State' (1990) 3 *Brit Rev of NZ Stud* 52 at 60.

[102] Mitchell, *Faith and Criticism* (above n 4), at 123.

[103] See Packer, *Fundamentalism* (above n 25), at 160-168. Packer casts liberalism as an entirely sincere but thoroughly misguided apologetic strategy, as does Carl F H Henry: see Henry, *Gods of This Age or God of The Ages?* (1994) ch 20 at 280. See J Gresham Machen, *Christianity and Liberalism* (1923) for the classic critique.

[104] For cases where the term has been used, see *King-Ansell* v *Police* [1979] 2 NZLR 531 at 535 and 543; *Barton-Prescott* v *Director-General of Social Welfare* [1997] 3 NZLR 179 at 185; *Re SDG* [1997] NZFLR 375 at 377 and *M* v *H* [1999] NZFLR 439 at 446.

[105] James H Olthuis, 'On Worldviews' (1985) 14 *Christian Scholar's Review* 153 at 153 explains that the German *weltanschauung*, or 'worldview' in English, is traceable to Kant's *Kritik der Urteilskraft* (1790). See also Gregory Clark, 'The Nature of Conversion: How the Rhetoric of Worldview Philosophy Can Betray Evangelicals' in Phillips et al (eds), *The Nature of Confession: Evangelicals and Postliberals in Conversation* (1996) ch 14 at 205-206.

[106] Hunter, *Culture Wars* (above n 5), at 119.

[107] Harold Turner, 'The Three Levels of Mission in New Zealand' in Patrick (ed) *New Vision New Zealand* (1993) ch 4 at 67.

[108] Norman L Giesler and William D Watkins, *Worlds Apart: A Handbook on Worldviews,* 2nd edn (1989) at 11 and 15. See also James W Sire, *The Universe Next Door*, 2nd edn (1988) at 16-18; Arthur F Holmes, *Contours of a World View* (1983) at 31-34; Olthuis, 'On Worldviews,' at 155; Ronald H Nash, 'The missing link in Christian evangelism: the importance of worldviews' (1998) 6 *Stimulus* 41 at 41. For criticism of the merits of Christians utilizing worldview analysis, see Clark, 'How the Rhetoric of Worldview Philosophy' (above n 105).

[109] Gielser and Waktins, *Worlds Apart*, at 14 (original italics).

[110] Ibid at 12.

[111] Ibid. See also Nash, 'Missing link' (above n 108), at 46.

[112] Brian J Walsh and J Richard Middleton, *The Transforming Vision: Shaping a Christian World View* (1984) at 32.

[113] Walsh and Middleton, ibid, at 32.

[114] Ibid at 34. See also Holmes, *Contours of a World View* (above n 108), at 32.

[115] Ibid at 35. See also Nash, 'Missing link,' at 44.

[116] Ibid.

[117] See Olthuis, 'On worldviews' (above n 105), at 156: 'a worldview functions both descriptively and normatively. . . . A worldview is both a sketch of and a blueprint for reality; it both describes what we see and stipulates what we should see.'

[118] Walsh and Middleton, *Transforming Vision*, at 35 (original emphasis).

[119] See, for example, Sire, *Universe Next Door* (above n 105), at 18 (posing seven questions); Nash, 'Missing link', at 42-43 (five questions); Charles Colson and Nancy Pearcey, *How Now Shall We Live*? (1999) at 14 (three questions).

[120] The allusion to 'ultimate concerns' here is to Paul Tillich's renowned definition: Tillich *Systematic Theology* (1951) vol 1 at 11-55. For a critique, see Roy A Clouser, *The Myth of Religious Neutrality* (1991) at 12-13.

[121] Nash, 'Missing link', at 44 (emphasis in original).

[122] See Clouser, *Religious Neutrality*, at 101-107; Sire, *Universe Next Door*, at 17.

[123] Clouser, ibid, at 104; Walsh and Middleton, *Transforming Vision* (above n 112), at 35.

[124] Walsh and Middleton, ibid at 35.

[125] J Richard Middleton and Brian J Walsh, *Truth is Stranger Than It Used to Be* (1995) at 36-37 (quoting Clifford Gertz, *The Interpretation of Cultures* (1973) at 89).

[126] Felix Cohen, 'Field theory and judicial logic' (1950) 59 *Yale L J* 232 at 260. See also Phillip E Johnson, *Reason in the Balance* (1995) at 67: 'Most people . . . go about day-to-day life without thinking about metaphysics, but their thinking is nonetheless influenced by metaphysical assumptions. In fact, metaphysical assumptions are most powerful when they are unconscious and do not come to the surface because everyone in the relevant community takes them for granted.'

[127] Waitangi Tribunal, *Report of the Waitangi Tribunal on the Manukau Claim*, 2nd edn (1989) at para 9.3.5. This passage is quoted in *Huakina Development Trust* v *Waikato Valley Authority* [1987] 2 NZLR 188 at 222 per Chilwell J.

[128] J G A Pocock, 'Law, Sovereignty and History in a Divided Culture: The Case of New Zealand and the Treaty of Waitangi' (1998) 43 *McGill L J* 481 at 487.

[129] Nigel Jamieson, 'The Maori Magna Carta' [1992] *NZLJ* 101 at 108-109. Jamieson's list contains 23 points of difference between *Te Ao Maori* and *Te Ao Pakeha*. See also Ulrich Klein, 'Belief-Views on Nature — Western Environmental Ethics and Maori World Views' (2000) 4 *NZ J Environmental Law* 81 at 104-119.

[130] See generally Norman L Geisler and Paul D Feinberg, *Introduction to Philosophy: A Christian Perspective* (1980) ch 11.

[131] Harold Turner, 'Deep Mission to Deep Culture' in Flett (ed), *Collision Crossroads* (1998) ch 2 at 28-29. See also Dr Turner's forthcoming book, *Frames of Mind: A Public Philosophy for Religion and Cultures* (2001) ch 10.

[132] Michael W McConnell observes: 'Post-modernism is more a congeries of attitudes and ideologies than it is a single, coherent philosophical position': McConnell, '"God is Dead and We Have Killed Him!": Freedom of Religion in the Post-modern Age' [1993] *Brigham Young U L Rev* 163 at 181.

[133] Stanley J Grenz, *A Primer on Postmodernism* (1996) at 40.

[134] Lyotard, *The Postmodern Condition: A Report on Knowledge*, (trans by G Bennington and B Massumi) (1984) at xxiv. See Douglas E Litowitz, *Postmodern Philosophy and Law* (1997) at 9-10.

[135] Grenz, *Primer on Postmodernism*, at 3. Litowitz, *Postmodern Philosophy and Law*, at 9, summarizes it 'broadly as the project of bringing reason and science to bear on social and political beliefs, thereby freeing humanity from superstition and slavish tradition.'

[136] Grenz, ibid at 7.

[137] Middleton and Walsh, *Truth is Stranger* (above n 125), at 36.

[138] Peter C Schanck, 'Understanding Postmodern Thought and Its Implications for Statutory Interpretation' (1992) 65 *S Cal L Rev* 2505 at 2508-2509. For another discussion of the principal beliefs of postmodernism, see Litowitz, *Postmodern Philosophy and Law*, at 10-17.

[139] Litowitz, *Postmodern Philosophy and Law*, at 13.

[140] Grenz, *Primer on Postmodernism* (above n 133), at 8.

[141] Turner, 'Deep Mission to Deep Culture', at 28-29.

[142] Harry Blamires, *The Christian Mind: How Should a Christian Think?* (1963).

[143] See Blamires, ibid at 44 and 67, where he equates the Christian mind with the religious view of life which is its constant frame of reference.

[144] Blamires at 67.

[145] Ibid at 69.

[146] Ibid at 68.
[147] Ibid at 86.
[148] Stott, *New Issues Facing Christians Today* (above n 99), at 39-41. Colson and Pearcey, *How Now Shall We Live*? (above 119) at xiii and 14, identify Creation, Fall and Redemption as the three key stages.
[149] Blamires, *The Christian Mind*, at 107.
[150] Ibid at 132.
[151] Ibid.
[152] See ibid at 156 et seq.
[153] Turner, 'Deep Mission to Deep Culture' (above n 131), at 28.
[154] Ibid at 30.
[155] Ibid at 32.
[156] 'Culture' is used here in its broadest theological sense. As Walsh and Middleton explain, culture refers to what human beings have cultivated of our world. It does not refer to just intellectual and aesthetic pursuits (as in 'high culture' or a 'cultured' person) but 'covers the whole range of human society.' So not merely art, music and scholarship but also economics and politics, religion, education, technology, the media, marriage, family life, advertising and entertainment are culture. Walsh and Middleton, *Transforming Vision* (above n 112), at 55. See also Lesslie Newbigin, *Foolishness to the Greeks* (1986) at 3: 'By the word culture we have to understand the sum total of ways of living developed by a group of human beings and handed on from generation to generation.'
[157] See Holmes, *Contours of a World View* (above n 108), at 35.
[158] Nash, 'Missing link' (above n 108), at 43.
[159] See Robert Song, *Christianity and Liberal Society* (1997) at 14 explaining the family resemblances shared by 'liberals' and hence the justification for the label 'liberalism'.
[160] See, for example, *Catechism of the Catholic Church* (1994) at para 2240.
[161] 1 Peter 2:14 (New International Version). See generally Alan Storkey, *A Christian Social Perspective* (1979) ch 12.
[162] Storkey, ibid, at 299-300. See also Gordon Spykman, 'The Principled Pluralist Position' in Gary Scott Smith (ed), *God and Politics: Four Views on the Reformation of Civil Government* (1989) ch 5 at 86: 'Principled pluralism teaches that the primary task of the state is to promote justice in society.'
[163] *Catechism*, at para 1927. 'The common good' is defined in para 1906 to be 'the sum total of social conditions which allow people, either as groups or as individuals, to reach their fulfilment more fully and more easily.'
[164] See *Catechism*, ibid, at para 1899 (quoting Romans 13:1-2).
[165] Romans 13:1-2.
[166] See *Catechism*, at para 1883: 'Excessive intervention by the state can threaten personal freedom and initiative'.

[167] 'The concept of sphere sovereignty teaches that each sphere in society has its own independent authority; no one sphere should dominate or usurp the role of the others.' Spkyman, 'Principled Pluralist Position,' at 79-80.

[168] See Storkey, *A Christian Social Perspective*, at 309; Herman Dooyeweerd, *The Christian Idea of the State* (trans by J Kraay) (1968) at 28-29.

[169] Charles W Colson, 'Kingdoms in Conflict,' *First Things*, November 1996, 34 at 35.

[170] See John Finnis, *Natural Law and Natural Rights* (1980) ch 12 for a discussion of this doctrine. The modern reaffirmation is found in the *Catechism*, at para 2242.

[171] The Scottish Covenantor, Samuel Rutherford, and his work *Lex Rex* (1644) is a favourite of some, especially Schaeffer and John Whitehead.

[172] Francis A Schaeffer, *A Christian Manifesto* (1981) at 90-93 (original emphasis).

[173] Martin Luther King Jr, *Letter from Birmingham City Jail* (1963): quoted in Colson, 'Kingdoms in Conflict' (above n 169), at 38.

[174] A point conceded by Carl F H Henry, *The Christian Mindset in a Secular Society* (1984) at 66-67.

[175] See the multi-authored statement, 'Why Christians should be involved in politics,' *Reality*, October-November 1996, 33 at 35. The authors agree with Sir Norman Anderson's dictum that Christians 'must accord to others the liberty of conscience which they claim for themselves' (quoting J N D Anderson, *Into the World: the Need and Limits of Christian Involvement* (1968) at 48).

[176] Ephesians 6: 12. The *King James Version* uses the phrase 'against principalities, against powers.' See Lesslie Newbigin, *The Gospel in a Pluralist Society* (1989) at 207-208: 'The principalities and powers are real. They are invisible and we cannot locate them in space. They do not exist as disembodied entities floating above the world, or lurking within it. They meet us as embodied in visible and tangible realities—people, nations and institutions. . . . The language is pictorial, mythological if you like, because we have no other language. But the things described are real and are contemporary.'

[177] Bruce Patrick, 'After the 1997 Congress' in Patrick (ed), *The Vision Congress 1997'*, ch 1 at 32.

[178] John 17.

[179] Carrell, 'Reaping the Whirlwind' (1996) 6 *Stimulus* 31 at 35.

[180] Schaffer, *Christian Manifesto* (above n 172), at 116.

[181] C S Lewis, 'Peace Proposals for Brother Every and Mr Bethell' in Hooper (ed), *Christian Reflections* (1981) at 52: quoted in Walsh and Middleton, *Transforming Vision* (above n 112), at 71.

[182] Richard J Mouw and Sander Griffioen, *Pluralisms and Horizons* (1993) at 89.

[183] Walsh and Middleton, *Transforming Vision* (above n 112), at 96.

[184] Matthew 12:30; Luke 11:23 (NIV).

[185] Walsh and Middleton, *Transforming Vision* (above n 122), at 95 (original emphasis).

[186] Walsh and Middleton, ibid, at 96 (original emphasis).

[187] See Scott Smith (ed), *God and Politics*, at 75.

[188] See Immanuel Kant, *An Answer to the Question: What is Enlightenment?:* 'Enlightenment is man's emergence from his self-imposed minority. This minority is the inability to use one's own understanding without the guidance of another. It is self-imposed if its cause lies not in a lack of understanding, but in the lack of courage and determination to rely on one's own understanding and not another's guidance. Thus the motto of the Enlightenment is "Sapere aude! Have the courage to use one's own understanding!"': quoted in Lucien Goldmann, *The Philosophy of the Enlightenment: The Christian Burgess and the Enlightenment* (1968) at 3.

[189] Walsh and Middleton, *Transforming Vision* (above n 112), at 119, believe this element, human autonomy, to be 'the core of modern secularism . . . In the modern world view, man becomes a law *(nomos)* unto himself *(autos).*' Thus, they coin the phrase, *homo autonomous.*

[190] Kant in Goldmann, *Philosophy of the Enlightenment,* at 3.

[191] To quote Kant again: 'I see the central achievement of Enlightenment—that is, of man's emergence from his self-imposed minority—above all in matters of religion. . . . this religious dependence is both the most damaging and the most humiliating of all.' Goldmann, ibid at 4.

[192] Middleton and Walsh, *Truth is Stranger* (above n 125), at 15.

[193] Goldmann, *Philosophy of the Enlightenment* (above n 188), at 31-32.

[194] See William P Marshall, 'The Other Side of Religion' (1993) 44 *Hastings L J* 843 at 854.

[195] Ruth Smithies, 'Gospel and Culture' in Patrick (ed), *The Vision New Zealand Congress 1997* (1997) ch 6 at 99.

[196] Bryan Wilson, 'Secularisation': Religion in the Modern World' in Sutherland et at (eds), *The World's Religions* (1988) ch 58 at 954.

[197] Wilson, ibid.

[198] 'Secularization and secularism are related to one another as the glove is to the hand or as the body is to the soul. The former is the public environment created by the modernizing process that produces a conscious counterpart that is its echo and in which the sound of God and of the transcendent order are never heard; the latter is the psychological reflex to our reshaped society.' David F Wells, *No Place For Truth or Whatever Happened to Evangelical Theology?* (1993) at 87.

[199] Schaeffer, *Christian Manifesto* (above n 172), at 24.

[200] Timothy La Haye, *The Battle for the Mind* (1980) at 9.

[201] The *Humanist Manifesto I* (1933) and the *Humanist Manifesto II* (1973). These are reproduced in the appendix to Corliss Lamont, *The Philosophy of Humanism*, 7th edn (1990).

[202] Lamont, ibid at 286.

[203] Ibid at 288 (emphasis added).

[204] Ibid at 291.

[205] Ibid at 292-293. 'Reason and critical intelligence' were reaffirmed as the most effective instruments for human progress (principle 4) as were: the belief in 'maximum individual autonomy consonant with social responsibility' (principle 5); the commitment to democracy (principle 8); the separation of church and state (principle 9); and the principle of moral equality (principle 11).

[206] Lamont, ibid at 14.

[207] Lamont, *Philosophy of Humanism*, at 31.

[208] John W Whitehead and John Conlan, 'The Establishment of the Religion of Secular Humanism and its First Amendment Implications' (1978) 10 *Texas Tech L Rev* 1 at 30-31.

[209] Lamont describes Catholic Humanism in his book (at 21-22) and traces in detail the religious roots of humanism at 48 et seq. The ethical teachings of a non-divine Jesus ('a great good man') are 'an inspiration for the human race.'(at 51)

[210] See Schaeffer, *Christian Manifesto* (above n 172), at 23, who endorses Christian humanism.

[211] To quote La Haye again: 'It is all very simple, if you face the fact that we are being controlled by a small but very influential cadre of committed humanists, who are determined to turn traditionally moral-minded America into an amoral, humanistic country. Oh, they don't call it humanist. They label it *democracy*, but they mean humanism, in all its atheistic, amoral depravity.' La Haye, *Battle for the Mind*, at 142 (original emphasis).

[212] Wells, *No Place for Truth* (above n 198), at 79.

[213] See Berger, *Social Reality of Religion* (above n 20), ch 6.

[214] Ibid at 126.

[215] See ibid at 47: 'The reality of the Christian world depends upon the presence of social structures within which this reality is taken for granted and within which successive generations of individuals are socialized in such a way that this world will be real to *them*. When this plausibility structure loses its intactness or conformity, the Christian world begins to totter and its reality ceases to impose itself as self-evident truth.' (original emphasis)

[216] Knowles, 'History of New Life Churches' (above n 21), at 303.

[217] Evans, 'New Christian Right' (above n 21), at 80-81.

[218] *Coalition Courier*, vol 3, no 2, March 1987: reproduced as a supplement in *CW*, 13 March 1987.

[219] *Coalition Report*: reproduced as a supplement to *CW*, 17 April 1987.

[220] Brandon, 'Freedom from Humanism', a six-part study series on the Internet website of St Martin's Presbyterian Church, Papatoetoe, found at: http://homepages.ihug.co.nz/~brandon1/resources/study.htm#freedom

[221] Smithies, 'Gospel and Culture' (above n 195) at 104, fn 3.

[222] Rob Yule, 'I've been thinking too—about MMP,' *CW*, 9 October 1996, at 5.

[223] 'In contrast to the modern, scientific perspective, postmodernity is open to the transcendent, to the mysterious, to spirituality and even to the Spirit.' Jeff Fountain, 'Postmodernity', *Reality*, April/May 1997, 13 at 14.

[224] See Sir Norman Anderson, 'Public law and legislation' in Kaye and Wenham (eds), *Law, Morality and the Bible* (1978) pt 2, ch 6, at 235.

[225] See Newbigin, *Gospel in a Pluralist Society* (above n 176), at 244.

[226] Diogenes Allen, 'Christianity and the Creed of Postmodernism' (1993) 23 *Christian Scholar's Rev* 117 at 124.

[227] Grenz, *Primer on Postmodernism* (above n 133), at 164 (emphasis in original).

[228] Robert W Jenson, 'The God-Wars' in Braaten and Jenson (eds), *Either/Or: The Gospel or Neopaganism* (1995) at 23-26.

3 Liberalism and the 'Wellington Worldview'

Law is naturally influenced greatly by 'the spirit of the age'. New Zealand is commonly described as a liberal democracy.[1] In this chapter, based on the premise that New Zealand law and government reflects liberal democratic beliefs, values and principles, I describe the salient characteristics of the philosophy undergirding the New Zealand legal system. I shall argue that: (1) liberal democracies in general reflect a distinctive philosophy or worldview, and that; (2) New Zealand law and government in particular evinces a similar worldview—what I shall call the 'Wellington worldview'.

The Liberal Model

Liberal democracies subscribe, in varying degrees, to liberalism. A preliminary cautionary comment is appropriate here. As Lovejoy has noted, doctrines ending in 'ism' are best thought of as 'compounds' or 'complexes', not 'simples':

> They stand, as a rule, not for one doctrine, but for several distinct and often conflicting doctrines held by different individuals or groups to whose way of thinking these appellations have been applied . . . and each of these doctrines, in turn, is likely to be resolvable into simpler elements, often very strangely combined and derivative from a variety of dissimilar motives and historical influences.[2]

I take liberalism to be the principal philosophical tradition that underlies the Western concept of a liberal democracy.[3] There are, to be sure, other philosophies of relevance, especially the political philosophy and tradition of conservatism, and, in New Zealand, socialism. I shall nevertheless, concentrate upon liberalism on the premise it constitutes the *dominant* contemporary political philosophy. This view is not without support. For instance, Roy Perrett argues:

> The dominant Pakeha [European] conception of justice is liberal and individualistic. This is not, of course, to say there are no differences between Pakeha liberals. . . . But what egalitarian and libertarian liberals have in common is the assumption that we are all separate, individual persons with our own goals and values, and that the function of a system of justice is to promote a neutral framework of rights which will further our own individual interests to a degree maximally consistent with similar liberty for other individuals.[4]

Sir Ivor Richardson refers to rights being 'at the heart of liberalism' and adds that for anyone 'to question the prevailing philosophy, to put limits on rights and their protection through the Courts, is easily represented as an attack on liberal values.'[5] Liberalism may be the ascendant ideology but it is leavened by conservative and socialist strains and echoes. I shall mention the differences between liberalism and other 'isms' where appropriate.

The Characteristics of Liberalism: General

> Liberalism has been the hope that, despite [the] tendency toward disagreement about matters of ultimate significance, we can find some way of living together that avoids the rule of force. It has been the conviction that we can agree on a core morality while continuing to disagree about what makes life worth living.[6]

Liberalism is, as the theorist John Gray puts it, 'the political theory of modernity.'[7] Notoriously, it comes in many different forms, which makes it 'foolish to attempt a univocal definition of such a historically and conceptually complex phenomenon'.[8] The task of isolating its core characteristics is difficult. There is, for example, classic liberalism and social or new liberalism.[9] John Rawls[10] delineates three general types—liberalism based upon moral scepticism, one based upon pragmatic or prudential considerations or, thirdly, a moral conception of liberalism.[11] Rawls calls his 'anti-perfectionist' version of liberalism 'political liberalism' to distinguish it from 'perfectionist' or 'thick' versions—such as Immanuel Kant's and John Stuart Mill's—which presuppose some general and comprehensive philosophical or moral doctrine, some comprehensive view of the good life.[12] William Galston's *Liberal Purposes* is a recent example of this latter strain of liberal theory, the author putting forward a definite programme of liberal values and virtues, a liberalism 'committed to a distinctive conception of the human good.'[13] Rawls' liberalism, by contrast, (a 'thin' form or 'procedural liberalism'[14]) is something less, a 'partially comprehensive view'[15], albeit still a 'moral' conception of justice in that it is 'distinct from a consensus, inevitably fragile, founded solely on self- or group-interest'.[16]

What are the principal characteristics of liberalism? Naturally, different scholars have different lists.[17] Gray pinpoints four:

> Common to all variants of the liberal tradition is a definite conception, distinctly modern in character, of man and society. What are the several elements of this conception? It is [1] *individualist*, in that it asserts the moral primacy of the person against the claim of any social collectivity; [2] *egalitarian*, in as much as it confers on all men the same moral status and denies the relevance to legal or political order of differences in moral worth among human beings; [3] *universalist*, affirming the moral unity of the human species and according a secondary importance to specific historic associations and cultural forms; and [4] *meliorist* in its affirmation of the corrigibility and improvability of all social institutions and political arrangements. It is this conception of man and society which gives liberalism a definite identity which transcends its vast internal variety and complexity.[18]

Robert Sharpe identifies three central premises: in addition to individualism, he adds: [5] *freedom*—the state's role involves 'maximizing human dignity, self-fulfilment and autonomy, while minimizing interferences with individual moral choice'; and [6] *neutrality*—the belief that 'the state and the law should be neutral as to particular conceptions of the good life.'[19] To this growing list one could add liberalism is typically [7] *rationalistic*—favouring reason over affect, emotion and so on.[20] Finally, and contentiously, it might be argued liberalism is [8] *humanistic*—concerned solely with human aspirations and interests divorced from theistic or other transcendent interests.

From this brief sketch I wish to focus upon certain characteristics in more detail.

Individualism

Individual Choice; Autonomy Liberalism draws upon the philosophy of individualism to a significant degree. Indeed, liberals are, assert some, 'formally committed to individualism'.[21] Under individualism the individual human being is the central focus, the basic unit of society. As Bhikhu Parekh explains:

> Unlike the Greeks, and indeed all the premodern societies which took the community as their starting point and defined the individual in terms of it, liberalism takes the individual as the ultimate and irreducible unit of society and explains the latter in terms of it. Society 'consists' or is 'made up' of individuals and is at bottom nothing but the totality of its members and their relationships.[22]

Liberalism defines the individual in 'austere and minimalistic terms', argues Parekh, by abstracting the person from all of his or her 'contingent' and 'external' relations with other people and nature.[23] For liberals: 'The self is fundamentally detached from contingencies, being related to them (if at all) through choice or consent.'[24] Michael

Sandel has dubbed this conception of the person, 'the unencumbered self'. He argues:

> rights-based liberalism begins with the claim we are separate, individual persons, each with our own aims, interests and conceptions of the good, and seeks a framework of rights that will able us to realize our capacity as free moral agents consistent with a similar liberty for others. . . . The priority of the self over its ends means I am never defined by my aims and attachments, but always capable of standing back to survey and assess and possibly revise them. This is what it means to be a free and independent self, capable of choice.[25]

The freedom to control one's destiny, to retain self-direction or mastery, has been described by others as 'autonomy'.[26] The idea of the completely self-enclosed individual, always able to run his or her own life and make his or her own choices ('the individual as its own god', as one critic puts it[27]) is not the only conception of personhood on offer. Sandel, along with other communitarian critics of modern liberalism, points to a different conception:

> Following Aristotle, [the communitarian critics] argue that we cannot justify political arrangements without reference to common purposes and ends, and that we cannot conceive our personhood without reference to our role as citizens, and as participants in a common life. . . . Communitarian critics of rights-based liberalism say we cannot conceive ourselves as independent in this way [where the self is prior to its ends], as bearers of selves wholly detached from our aims and attachments. They say that certain of our roles are partly constitutive of the persons we are—as citizens of a country, or members of a movement, or partisans of a cause.[28]

Sandel points instead to the 'situated self', the person whose life is always embedded or situated in those communities from which the individual draws his or her identity—whether family, tribe, party, religion or cause.[29]

A Weak Concept of Community If liberalism views society as simply an aggregation of individuals, then *a fortiori* it views groups or communities likewise. So, many argue, liberalism has a weak or under-developed concept of community.[30] Groups are of value only to the extent they represent the aggregation of individual choices and desires. They are a sort of collecting house or 'matrix within which private preferences are formed.'[31] The modern liberal state is content with a bilateral relationship between the state, on the one hand, and the individual, on the other. So-called 'intermediate institutions' standing between the individual and the state, such as the family, the church, the voluntary society, are accorded little worth.[32]

The liberal themes of autonomy and voluntary choice have, some argue, a destabilizing effect upon communities and communal life.

Paul Marshall suggests that the liberal insistence upon the informed right to exit at any time can undercut any community's integrity and solidarity, for the religious community

> must inform its members that they can quit at any time and thus it must inform its members that believing along with the rest of the community is not the most fundamental thing of all. Communities thus become half-minded and thus half-hearted. . . . they become communities founded on prior respect for individual choice and thus they become mirror images of the larger liberal society. In this liberal society, communities are not left free: rather they are constrained to become liberal associations.[33]

The liberal view of community can be contrasted with the conservative conception, a more 'organic', communitarian one.[34] Conservatism has a 'care for institutions', a concern to foster corporations, firms, schools, universities, theatres, clubs, teams, as well as the family and the church. Society—the term 'civil society' is usually preferred—is made up of 'the totality of free institutions.'[35]

Neutrality

Neutrality Explained A central tenet of liberalism, perhaps the defining feature,[36] is its claim to be neutral concerning questions of the good life and ideas of the good. In Ronald Dworkin's words, a liberal theory of equality

> supposes that government must be neutral on what might be called the question of the good life. . . . political decisions must be, so far as is possible, independent of any particular conception of the good life, or of what gives value to life. Since the citizens of a society differ in their conceptions, the government does not treat them as equals if it prefers one conception to another, either because the officials believe that one is intrinsically superior, or because one is held by the more numerous or more powerful group.[37]

New Zealand Prime Minister, Sir Robert Stout, said much the same thing in 1914:

> To say that the State has a right to select one religion and teach its creed because it is the religion of the majority, is to declare it to be the duty of the State to propagate the religious experiences of only one section of the people. That would not be 'the Government of the people for the people,' but a Government for part of the people. . . . Hitherto those who have been what are called liberals and progressivists have recognised that there are varieties of religious experiences, and that whatever the beliefs of citizens may be, all must have equal rights and equal privileges 'before the law'. Make one class outcasts because of their race or religion, and you banish freedom and liberty from the State. . . . If a State is to be fair and just to

> all and human liberty preserved, the State must be neutral to all phases of religious experience.[38]

The concept of neutrality is, as Jeremy Waldron observes, 'far from a straightforward concept',[39] and Rawls similarly refers to the term as 'unfortunate'.[40] Of the versions of neutrality on offer there seem to be two general types.[41]

First, there is neutrality of aim—the basic institutions of public policy must not aim to bring about a particular conception of the good. The policy must not be motivated by, and designed to favour, some particular comprehensive doctrine, religion and so on. Some dub this 'procedural' neutrality.[42]

Second, there is neutrality of effects—the institutions of public policy must take care to ensure that the effects of the policies upon different conceptions of the good life are even-handed. On this view a policy ought not to increase the chance of one way of life flourishing and another diminishing, a position described by some as 'unimpaired flourishing'.[43] This second 'substantive' version of neutrality is, however, unsustainable in many theorists' eyes.[44] Deborah Fitzmaurice argues, for example, that: 'Whatever principles a state embodies, whether based on a particular conception of the good or not, it is an inescapable feature of a set of political institutions that it constrain the modes of life lived within it.'[45] Similarly, Rawls comments: 'it is surely impossible for the basic structure of a just constitutional regime not to have important effects and influences as to which comprehensive doctrines endure and gain adherents over time; and it is futile to try to counteract these effects and influences, or even to ascertain for political purposes how deep and pervasive they are.'[46]

What is the justification for neutrality? Unless we have some idea of *why* neutrality is important, then our conception will, argues Waldron, be in danger of being incoherent.[47] He suggests various possible arguments for neutrality: one based upon moral scepticism; a commitment to diversity; a faith in moral progress; the importance of autonomy and the evil of coercion; equal respect, or the danger of entrusting legislators with the moral authority perfectionism would involve. Galston proffers three explanations. Neutrality may be justified because:

> First, it may be argued there is in fact no rational basis for choosing among ways of life. Assertions about the good are personal and incorrigible. State neutrality is desirable because it is the only nonarbitrary response to this state of affairs. Second, it may be argued that even if knowledge about the good life is available, it is a breach of individual freedom—the highest value—for the state to impose this knowledge on its citizens. Of course, the best outcome occurs when individuals freely choose to pursue the good. But freely chosen error is preferable to the coerced pursuit of the good. . . . Third, it may be argued the diversity is a basic fact of modern social life and

> that the practical costs of public efforts to constrain it would be unacceptably high.[48]

Non-neutrality: Concession and Defence Some liberal theorists have been prepared to abandon the claim to neutrality.[49] Galston, for example, concedes that liberalism 'cannot, as many contemporary theorists suppose, be understood as broadly neutral concerning the human good. It is rather committed to a distinctive conception of the human good, a conception that undergirds the liberal conception of social justice.'[50] If a liberal society is individualistic, rationalistic, one placing emphasis upon autonomy and so on, the liberal's response might be: 'But so what?'[51]

However, the obvious implication is that conceptions of the good life which do not conform with the liberal model nor share its tenets are destined to struggle. At worst, these non-liberal ways of life or communities may disappear. Recall that neutrality of effects or outcome is ruled out by many liberals as an attainable state of affairs. Certain ways of life will inevitably suffer. Rawls concedes this:

> The principles of any reasonable political conception must impose restrictions on permissible comprehensive views, and the basic institutions those principles require inevitably encourage some ways of life and discourage others, or even exclude them altogether.[52]

The discouragement of certain ways of life might, says Rawls, occur for two reasons. The way of life might directly conflict with the principles of justice, for example, by advocating racial discrimination or even slavery. Second, the way of life may be admissible but simply fail to gain adherents under the liberal social order. Interestingly, Rawls cites 'certain forms of religion'[53] as examples of this second situation. He continues:

> Suppose that a particular religion, and the conception of the good belonging to it, can survive only if it controls the machinery of state and is able to practice effective intolerance. This religion will cease to exist in the well-ordered society of political liberalism.[54]

Is this unfair? Given a social world of limited space ('No society can include within itself all forms of life.'[55]), if any ways of life must make way it would seem logical to expunge the illiberal ones:

> But if a comprehensive conception of the good is unable to endure in a society securing the familiar equal basic liberties and mutual toleration, there is no way to preserve it consistent with democratic values as expressed by the idea of society as a fair system of cooperation among citizens as free and equal. This raises, but does not of course settle, the question of

> whether the corresponding way of life is viable under other historical conditions, and whether its passing is to be regretted.[56]

Privatization

The well-recognized strategy of liberalism is to confine religion to the private realm. As Basil Mitchell notes: 'Religion, says the new liberalism, is a private matter. It belongs to the realm of ideals, not to that of interests. It follows that religious considerations, as they affect morality, should have no place in law making.'[57] Stanley Fish adds: 'the liberal feels obliged to quarantine religious pronouncements, to confine them to contexts (the home, the Church) that present the least risk of general infection.'[58] As a New Zealand Christian commentator noted recently:

> Church is now generally regarded as something you do in private—like Rotary or stamp collecting—which shouldn't be allowed to have an impact on public or even professional life.[59]

The view of conservative political theory is markedly different. Religion is an indispensable device to foster public morality and preserve social order. Religion, or at least traditional, incumbent religious institutions, are important *public* institutions. Roger Scruton, for example, notes:

> If conservatism deserves our attention for nothing else, it is at least for having recognised these difficulties [concerning the interface of politics and religion], and for having refused to consign to the private realm (the realm of 'consenting adults') a phenomenon that is manifestly public both in its content and in its effects. For the conservative, as for the socialist, the public and the private are far more intricately intertwined than the liberal tends to acknowledge.[60]

For some liberals privatization is a benign strategy. Religion is consigned to the private realm out of respect for and solicitude towards it. Liberalism tends 'to relegate that which is most important to the private sphere'[61] and religion is one of these cherished institutions. Under this view religion is being left alone and is protected from invasive public regulation.

Privatization of religion is achieved through a careful drawing of the boundary between public and private life (obviously itself a contentious dichotomy). Frederick Gedicks' exposition is particularly lucid:

> one of the key tasks of contemporary liberal politics is to police the boundary between public and private life by distinguishing value from fact and desire from reason. Beliefs or values that reside in private life are suspect as a basis for government action unless they can be relocated in public life as facts or reasons. Only when confirmed by widely shared

human experience, scientific investigation, or reasoning from premises that can be verified by experience or investigation does a belief qualify as knowledge upon which government legitimately can act.[62]

Having drawn a dichotomy whereby one category (public life) is reserved for scientific facts, empirical evidence and reason, and another category (private life) is set aside for values, beliefs and personal preferences, the fate of religion is sealed. Gedicks continues:

> As one of the purest contemporary expressions of subjective, impossible-to-confirm values, religious beliefs need not (and, indeed, cannot) be considered by those who act in public life. Liberal government thus treats religious beliefs neutrally—as a subjective value preference restricted to private life, rather than as objective knowledge proper to public life.[63]

Why is religion privatized? Liberalism gives at least three answers. First, the neutrality argument again. The liberal state cannot espouse any one particular controversial conception of the good, cannot 'impose' beliefs, religious or otherwise, upon others.[64] (This position is however, as we have seen, under-cut by some liberal theorists' admission that liberalism does promote a substantive conception of the good.) Second, there is the epistemological objection. Religion is viewed as an inferior source of knowledge, being private, inaccessible, speculative and irrational. However, the liberal overlooks or exaggerates the rationality of science and underestimates the rationality or reasonableness of religion. Third, there is the recurrent fear that religion, when introduced into the public sphere, is simply too divisive.

The last reason requires further comment: the 'contemporary liberal nightmare'[65] of religious and sectarian conflict is a powerful and persistent (and understandable) one. The sixteenth and seventeenth century wars of religion are 'the relevant historical memory'[66] for liberal theorists, such as Rawls, when they consider the public role of religion today. Bosnia and Northern Ireland provide contemporary reminders, if one was needed. Privatization attempts to dampen religious fervour. William Marshall suggests:

> If religion is seen as private and not universal, there is less imperative to conquer the religious beliefs of others. Instead of viewing the religious beliefs of others as a challenge to an individual's belief structure, the individual who accepts privatization sees others' beliefs as routine and non-threatening. The only threat occurs when others violate the privatization norm by seeking to use the public square for their own religious purpose.[67]

The question remains, however, whether religious fervour compared to secular, ideological, ethnic or any other enthusiastic, mass promotion of a cause is *especially* dangerous and deserving of restraint. For those insisting on a strict separation of church and state and the exclusion of religion from public life, the Enlightenment nightmare of incessant religious conflict and division may well have 'assumed the character of an unquestioned assumption of eternal validity.'[68] But others see religion as no more a threat to social cohesion and political stability than rival ideologies or 'isms' of various kinds.[69] Indeed, as Schwarzchild counters:

> Religion seems an odd choice as prime threat to liberalism at the end of a century that has been so greatly dominated by struggles over Communism, fascism, and extreme nationalism . . . For most of the twentieth century, at least outside the Islamic world, illiberal politics have overwhelmingly been Communist politics, or the politics of essentially secular forms of fascism, nationalism, or Third World socialism: the politics, one might say, of the Enlightenment's illegitimate heirs, liberalism's bastard siblings. These movements, in our time, loosed the demons that the Enlightenment was supposed to exorcise: dogma, intolerance, mass enthusiasm, and total war.[70]

Rationality

Liberalism is a child of the Enlightenment[71] and so it would be unsurprising if liberalism did not give primacy to reason. The autonomous individual makes choices on rational grounds. Such persons, in the liberal conception, are 'suspicious of, and feel nervous in the presence of, feelings and emotions, especially those that are deep and powerful and not fully comprehensible to reason or easily brought under control.'[72] The legacy of the Enlightenment and its antipathy to tradition, mystery, awe and superstition as ordering principles cannot be underestimated.

In superstition's place was put reason—everything has to answer, as Waldron puts it, at 'the tribunal of reason.'[73] Here, religion is typically found wanting. It is usually associated by liberals with subjectivism and emotion, with superstition. Liberals are concerned with sterner stuff. Anthony Cook criticizes the liberal attitude:

> Conceptually, liberalism—given its emphasis on the rational, empirical, and factual—sees questions of religious faith as a set of speculative assertions incapable of rational verification or disproof. Liberalism has, then, a structural bias against religious knowledge. The empirical orientation of the former has deemed the transempirical faith of the latter irrational from the start.[74]

Again, we might pause to contrast the liberal with the conservative political view. The latter is committed to defending tradition, the 'tacit understanding of social forms'.[75] There is what Scruton refers to as 'the conservative defence of prejudice—of the instinctive moral sense whereby people come to act with understanding, even though they have no understanding of why they act.'[76] Prejudice is not blind or irrational behaviour but 'is "pre-judgment", a distillation of experience over generations.'[77] Conservatism has a much more benign view of religion, or at least traditional, institutional religion. Edmund Burke, for example, saw religion as 'the basis of civil society and the source of all good and of all comfort.'[78] Scruton submits:

> Conservatism has seen religion as a necessary bulwark to morality, and morality as a *sine qua non* of social order. Religion, however, when it breaks free from institutions, and elects the individual conscience as its sovereign, is as much a danger to the social order as a support to it. It can never be a matter of indifference when the institutions of religion decline, or impetuously discard their inheritance. The conservative vision of a stable establishment has therefore always made room for churches, and sought to protect them with the legal privileges suited to their spiritual task. . . . recognising that values are more easily destroyed than engendered, the conservative will naturally sympathise with the religious worldview.[79]

Progress

A core characteristic of liberalism is, as Gray posited earlier in this chapter, that it is *meliorist*, 'in that it asserts the open-ended improvablity, by the use of critical reason, of human life.'[80] Liberals thus have a doctrine of progress, 'some notion of improvement in moral and political understanding and behaviour is fundamental to any form of liberalism.'[81] Modernity's belief in progress is, suggest some, but a secularized substitute for the Christian eschatological hope: 'The providence of God guiding the historical process toward eschatological fulfillment is replaced by a philosophy of progress guided by the predictive power of science and technology and promising a future of worldly happiness.'[82]

The 'Wellington Worldview'

Most of the political and bureaucratic elite have never heard of John Rawls or Ronald Dworkin nor read abstruse books on liberal political theory. Very few, if any, of the governing elite subscribe to secular humanism *per se* (the bogey man of many conservative Christians, as we saw in the previous chapter) in the sense that they are 'card-carrying' members, consciously adhering to humanism's tenets, advocating its goals, attending meetings and so on. Rather, it would be more accurate to say there subsists, among the powerful and influential, a prevailing, and largely unconscious, worldview.

Secular liberal thought and values operate by way of subconscious absorption or 'osmosis'.[83] For all practical purposes, for 'getting things done' in public life, there is, as James Davison Hunter suggests (when speaking of the American scene), a 'latent moral ideology' or a 'tacit faith', held by the so-called 'knowledge sector'—professors, journalists, media elites, lawyers and educators.[84]

Secularism, he argues, has become 'the dominant moral ideology of American public culture and now plays much the same role as the pan-Protestant ideology played in the nineteenth century.'[85] For Hunter:

> Secular humanism in American public life is neither an all-embracing and self-aggrandizing religion conspiring to control American institutions, nor is it a fiction manufactured by the religious right as a scapegoat for all the problems they see. Where secular humanism can be described accurately as a sectarian religion, it has almost no impact on American institutions. Yet where it does have an impact (as the latent moral ideology of the intellectual classes, of the media of mass communications and of public education, and the like) it does so as a relatively diffuse moral ethos rather than as a religion.[86]

In the United Kingdom, Ninian Smart similarly suggests: 'The most influential world view in the ruling echelons of British life is scientific humanism, which lives unreflectively together with various forms of more or less liberal Christianity.'[87]

In New Zealand it would be surprising if the prevailing 'Wellington worldview'—the mindset of the vast majority of parliamentarians, bureaucrats, consultants, academics, business leaders, company directors, news media editors and journalists, medical specialists and doctors, judges and lawyers, and so on—were not a modernist or scientific humanist one. It is difficult, I concede, to substantiate this claim for, *ex hypothesis*, a worldview is the taken-for-granted way of conceiving reality, the 'unarticulated premises' (à la Oliver Wendell Holmes) which require no articulation.

To reiterate, few belong to humanist or rationalist societies—in New Zealand these are small, peripheral groups with low memberships. But the modernist worldview nonetheless remains the ascendant one, the 'diffuse moral ethos' and 'latent ideology' of those in positions of influence, especially among those responsible for shaping public policy. The prevailing 'plausibility structure'[88] is one shaped by modernist ideals. Faith, the spiritual realm, God, these are matters for private taste. John Stenhouse observes:

> There are not many modern intellectuals whose basic intellectual outlook is not fundamentally antithetical to that of such fundamentalists. Nowadays the basic intellectual assumptions of most are shaped and informed by scientific naturalism with its implicit anti-supernaturalism and the pervasive agnosticism of post-Kantian philosophy. . . . fundamentalists appear rather like beings from another planet, and invite caricature and dismissal rather than understanding.[89]

Trevor de Cleene, a former New Zealand Minister of Revenue, expressed (in a newspaper article on euthanasia) what is a common secularist view: 'Frankly, it is my personal view that if a medical practitioner lets his or her view of religion come into a professional judgment, then such a person should not be practising medicine in the first place.'[90] An incident in April 1997 illustrates this secularist attitude. A doctor was censured by the Heath and Disabilities Commissioner after he suggested prayer as a form of treatment to a patient. The patient declined this suggestion. The doctor, a Christian, nonetheless prayed for his patient and told him that all science pointed to religion and God as the truth. Following a complaint, the Commissioner ruled that he must apologize to the patient, his actions having breached the latter's right to freedom from exploitation and the patient's right to give informed consent to the treatment.[91]

To describe the prevailing New Zealand secular worldview of the elite in terms of Walsh and Middleton's four worldview questions (Chapter 2) yields something along the following lines:

> *Who am I?* I am an autonomous individual *(homo autonomous)*, master of my own destiny.
> *Where am I?* I stand in a world of natural potential and my task is to utilize that potential for society's betterment.
> *What's wrong?* I am hindered by ignorance of nature and a lack of tools for controlling it.
> *What's the remedy?* My hope rests in the good life of progress wherein nature yields its bounty for human benefit. Only then will people find happiness in a life of material affluence, with no needs nor dependence. There is no God to help me, no supernatural intervention can assist me. I must help myself through my own creative intelligence.[92]

Three characteristics of this mindset are worth brief elaboration.

The Wellington worldview assumes a specific ontology—a particular picture of reality, or what is ultimately real. Phillip Johnson refers to the contemporary Western metaphysical or ontological position as scientific naturalism or simply naturalism for short. This is 'the doctrine that nature is "all there is".'[93] Although many of the initial founders of liberalism (for example, Locke) were theists, the modern liberal accepts, usually implicitly, the naturalistic account of the world.[94] Johnson explains:

> Modernism's metaphysical foundation rests firmly on scientific naturalism, which is 'the way things really are'. Through science we now know that nature, of which we are a recently evolved part, really *is* a closed system of material causes and effects, whether we like it or not. Any other system—particularly one based on the supposed commandments of a supernatural being—would therefore be founded on illusion rather than reality. God is a product of the human imagination, not the Creator of us all . . . Modernist naturalism is equivalent to rationality because it excludes consideration of miracles, defined as arbitrary breaks in the chain of material causes and effects. . . . Most modernists' identification of naturalism with rationality is so complete that they do not think of naturalism as a distinct

> and controversial metaphysical doctrine, but simply assume it as part of the definition of *reason*.[95]

Closely related to its ontology is its epistemology, what counts as knowledge. Knowledge is that which is empirical, factual, discoverable by reason—it is data which is, in principle, available to every citizen.[96] Again one is driven back to the Enlightenment. According to Waldron, for liberals:

> the social order must be one that can be justified to the people who have to live under it. We have seen that the Enlightenment impulse on which this is based is the demand of the individual mind for the intelligibility of the social world. Society should be a *transparent* order, in the sense that its workings and principles should be well-known and available for public apprehension and scrutiny.[97]

Under this view, religion and religious knowledge appears to be an 'epistemologically inferior' system of belief or values from which to conduct public debate and make public decisions.[98] Take this anecdotal illustration. In the parliamentary debate on the Death with Dignity Bill 1995, a voluntary euthanasia measure, Bill English, a National MP, noted that nonreligious arguments carried much more weight than theological ones: 'As a Catholic politician I regret that a key part of defeating the bill was to show that the arguments against it were procedural, practical and political, not just moral. However the moral arguments are in the end the strongest.'[99]

Decisions based upon faith and divine revelation appear inherently undemocratic, coming as they do from a source of knowledge not available or readily accessible to others.[100] Moreover, not only are religious grounds lacking in accessibility they also are dangerous: they have the potential to re-ignite old sectarian or religious passions long thought to be buried following the rise of the liberal secular state.[101] The epistemological attack upon religion is criticized in trenchant terms by Cook:

> The increasing secularism of the modern age, founded on a faith in the capacity of human reason and rooted in empiricism, rejects systems of knowledge grounded in faith as superstitious nonsense on stilts, unreceptive to human verification or disproof. Liberalism marginalizes religious epistemologies, sequestering them within the narrow confines of private life in the hope that the havoc they might engender, if let loose in the public side of democratic deliberation, will be prevented.[102]

To the liberal, to accuse liberalism of bias or hostility to religion is to make a 'category mistake'.[103] Gedicks explains:

> The liberal argument is that because the claims of religion are not amenable to empirical or rational proof, they are fundamentally different from the

> claims of secular ideologies and disciplines and that can be proven rationally or empirically and thus need not be dealt with in the same way. Secular enterprises yield knowledge, which the liberal state is bound to accept; religion only yields unprovable beliefs about the good, as to which the liberal state must remain neutral.[104]

Once the dichotomy between 'science, reason and knowledge' versus 'religion, faith and belief' is accepted, the former is readily found to trump the latter.[105] In terms of the split between public and private life, it becomes immediately obvious that (to remain rational, ordered and accessible), public life must be secular, with religion confined to private life.[106]

The prevailing worldview refuses to be tied to a timeless, absolute moral code such as that provided by some religions. Ethics are relativistic and anthropocentric. Ethical relativism 'claims there is no way to justify a single morality as the *correct* one and others as *mistaken*.'[107] As one MP put it in the debate on homosexual discrimination law, 'one person's belief is another person's heresy.'[108] Those who insist on a single version of morality are entitled to their opinion but they cannot expect to have it imposed on others nor translated into law. Michael Cullen MP, during the same debate, tersely reminded the ethical absolutist lobbyists:

> I say to those people who have a moral abhorrence of homosexual acts that nothing in the Bill prevents them holding the view that they hold . . . that they are welcome to live according to the lights of their own morality. The legislation says their rights stop at the end of their nose, that they cannot impose their views on other people . . .[109]

The modernist worldview may be the ascendant one but it is not the exclusive one. Other worldviews compete for ascendancy. New Zealand is really in a period of transition. As I argued in Chapter 1, the Christian worldview, once dominant culturally, is waning and is being supplanted by a secularist liberal one. But the demise of the former is not total and the triumph of the latter is not complete. At least one major complicating factor is the acknowledgement in the last two decades in New Zealand of a traditional Maori worldview.

The renaissance in Maoridom in the last two decades is reflected in many ways. In public ceremonial occasions a prominent place is given to Maori. Peter Donovan argues:

> We in New Zealand do not have an established church, but we do have an increasingly accepted civil religion. With growing public recognition of biculturalism and Treaty partnership ideals, Maori ceremonial has come to take on much of the role of official public and community spirituality. It is Maori tradition, after all, that nowadays provides the means for appropriately laying to rest public figures, dealing with the shock and grief

> of tragedies, solemnising the opening of buildings, the commencement of conferences and cultural festivals, the launching of frigates, and so on.[110]

In law, the Maori resurgence is abundantly documented, the prime example being the resurrection of the Treaty of Waitangi to a quasi founding-document status. Recognition of Maori cultural values, which inescapability include spiritual concerns, is virtually *de rigeur* in recent social (and other) legislation. I will simply take two brief examples.

The family law statute which most explicitly acknowledges Maori interests is the Children, Young Persons and Their Families Act 1989.[111] The Director-General of Social Welfare is required in all policies adopted and all services provided by the Department to 'have particular regard for the values, culture, and beliefs of the Maori people'.[112] The Act recognizes and supports the role of the distinctive Maori forms of collective life, namely, the whanau (extended family), hapu (tribe) and iwi (sub-tribe). Policies ought to 'avoid the alienation of children and young persons from their family, whanau, hapu, iwi and family group.'[113] Similarly, numerous custody cases reveal Family Court judges are sensitive to the cultural and spiritual benefits a traditional Maori upbringing can give to a child.[114]

In environmental law, the acknowledgement of a Maori worldview is perhaps clearest of all. The Resource Management Act 1991 provides:

> **6. Matters of national importance**—In achieving the purpose of this Act, all persons exercising functions and powers under it . . . shall recognise and provide for the following matters of national importance . . .
> (e) The relationship of Maori and their culture and traditions with their ancestral lands, water, sites, waahi tapu [sacred places], and other taonga [treasures].
>
> **7. Other matters**—In achieving the purpose of this Act, all persons exercising functions and powers under it . . . shall have particular regard to—
> (a) Kaitiakitanga: [and, pursuant to section 2] 'Kaitiakitanga' means the exercise of guardianship by the tangata whenua [indigenous people of the land] of an area in accordance with tikanga Maori [Maori ways and customs] in relation to natural and physical resources; and includes the ethic of stewardship . . .

Regarding 'kaitiakitanga', this 'refers to the act of applying the celestial and terrestrial curricula to guard the mauri (life-force) of the resource and the wairua (ordained spirit) of the relationship of the people with resource as a creation from God.'[115]

Quite how local authorities and the Environment Court practically take into account Maori spiritual values is an interesting question (and another study in itself).[116] Certainly, some commentators are irritated at the requirement to entertain such metaphysical concerns. As one mocked:

> If my Maori neighbour claims that I am polluting the stream which runs through both our properties with dairy waste we can analyse the water before and after it flows through my property and present the evidence to a hearings committee or a Court. The evidence should carry the day. But if my Maori neighbour claims that my developments are upsetting the mauri or life force of the water then I can mount no evidence to refute the claim. Similarly I should have no power to insist that my neighbours plant their crops according to the signs of the zodiac . . . In reality all manner of races, groups and cultures have spiritual values and we should have learned to keep them out of the legislative arena as much as we can. By definition such values are subjective and yet strongly shape our perceptions. But a Court or hearing is a poor venue in which to debate competing perceptions. We do not live in a theocracy.[117]

The Wellington worldview may in fact be a heterogeneous one comprising a fluid, plurality of worldviews. Anti-modernist counter examples can be pointed to. The (then) Prime Minister, Jenny Shipley, for instance, ruffled secularist sensitivities in a March 1998 speech criticizing 'political correctness'. She referred to the pressure in education to 'try and be so neutral to the point that we have created almost an amoral environment' for children to learn in:

> We also know that where a child is spiritually nurtured, whether it's Christian faith, the Bhuddist [sic] faith or any other faith in the world . . . it gives that individual a greater level of confidence, to stand tall knowing who they are . . . Many people would argue that [secular education] was an important development when it was passed into law in New Zealand. Some would argue now that in fact it is an idea whose time has gone . . . with a modern education system where boards of trustees are in place, we should trust parents to decide what flavour and tone their school seeks to articulate in the charter and the law should be silent on this issue . . . when I hear people then argue that it is the fact that we are a secular society that is justification for us not to allow the traditions, whether they are cultural traditions or religious traditions to be practised in our learning institutions, again I can't help but wonder whether it's time we asked some of these fundamental questions.[118]

In a subsequent interview, the Prime Minister made it clear that a return to Christian schooling was not what she had in mind. In postmodernist language, she explained: 'I want the visiting vicar, the visiting monk and the visiting Buddhist. I want children to be subjected to a wide range of spiritual experiences so that they can make a judgement of their own as to where their needs can be best met.'[119] The Prime Minister's kite-flying initiative drew predictable criticism. Mrs

Shipley had simply 'succoured the religious right'[120] wrote one journalist, while the editor of the *Sunday Star-Times* was dismayed:

> Many New Zealanders have a more jaundiced view of the powers of religion [than the Prime Minister]. They can point to conflicts between Moslem and Jew, Christian and Christian, Christian and Jew, Hindu and Moslem, to illustrate what happens when that confidence of knowing who they are that Mrs Shipley speaks of, goes awry . . . This is an issue which will divide not enrich our lives. Mrs Shipley should back off now.[121]

Notwithstanding such counter-currents, I maintain that the New Zealand elite, while not without some who hold to conservative Christian and other worldviews, *by and large* is comprised of those who unconsciously adopt, and practically operate upon, secular, liberal, modernist premises.

The Justification for a Secular Public Sphere

> Religious conviction is all very well when we come to private behaviour, what we might do behind closed doors, but it can have nothing to do with public policy because it has, by its very nature, an inbuilt prejudice. For example, judge or teachers should not allow their personal beliefs to intrude into their professionalism. This view of life and politics has been accepted as normative in New Zealand for most of my lifetime.[122]

Judges and legislators (and lawyers) who are Christians must in practice operate upon modernist premises. Liberal democratic principle constrains them to do so. The basis for a judicial decision cannot be religious; the justification for why the defendant should be excused or why the law should prohibit *X* must not be a solely religious one. Stephen Carter characterizes the notion that it is wrong for any government official to take conscious account of his or her religious understanding in performing his or her duties as a 'liberal axiom':

> The liberal ideal is an objective judge . . . In order to fit the objective model, she must in effect promise that she will strive to put aside *all* of her prejudices and preconceptions. Her religious preconceptions are simply one part of this personal moral knowledge that she must promise to ignore. If her personal religious convictions should somehow leak into her reasoning process, she will have failed . . .[123]

Case law bears this out. Thus, for example, in *C* v *C*, an English custody case, Balcombe LJ observed:

> in making a decision on welfare the judge should not be influenced by subjective considerations. To take an example: the issue may be whether the child is to be brought up in the faith of religion A or in that of religion

B. The judge may be a member of religion A, and a firm believer in its tenets: nevertheless, he must try to ensure that his personal beliefs do not affect his judicial function in deciding where the child's welfare lies.[124]

The secular, liberal environment constrains public officials from invoking their religion directly. Religion must be 'bracketed', to use the term favoured by some political and legal theorists.[125]

There is an unwitting capitulation on the part of many Christians themselves. The charge of some Christian scholars is that Christians who do hold positions of influence too readily accept a secular framework of reference, a modernist worldview. Blamires, in *The Christian Mind*, lamented the fact that: 'Except over a very narrow field of thinking, chiefly touching questions of strictly personal conduct, we Christians in the modern world accept, for the purpose of mental activity, a frame of reference constructed by the secular mind and a set of criteria reflecting secular evaluations.'[126] Johnson re-echoed this recently:

> The domination of naturalism over intellectual life is not affected by the fact that some religious believers and active churchgoers hold prestigious academic appointments. With very few exceptions, these believers maintain their respectability by tacitly accepting the naturalistic rules that define rationality in the universities. They explicitly or implicitly concede that their theism is a matter of 'faith' and agree to leave the realm of 'reason' to the agnostics.[127]

Why are Religious Reasons or Justifications Impermissible?

There is a voluminous and sophisticated debate among (mainly American) political philosophers on the propriety of religious argument and justification in public debate. The basic issue is not so much the fact of participation by religionists in public debate (this is conceded), but the reasons they give for their arguments and, to a lesser extent, the language they use.

Although the writing is often equivocal and opaque, few, if any, liberal theorists can be found who would bar religionists from the public arena. This would contradict liberalism's claims to neutrality and tolerance. Religionists can participate but they must have a 'secular', 'public', 'non-religious', 'pragmatic' (terms vary) reason for the change they seek. Reliance upon religion *alone*, what the Bible or the Pope says, is insufficient and impermissible. This observation by Kent Greenawalt is typical:

> I assume that in a liberal democratic society neither officials nor citizens should seek legal prohibitions of actions simply because they are regarded as sins. Such prohibitions . . . lie too close to imposing religious views themselves on people to be proper. Thus, someone should not urge that consenting homosexual acts be penalized solely because she believes they are sins in the eyes of God or will bring bad consequences in an afterlife.

> The decision on prohibition should depend on harms and benefits that are comprehensible in nonreligious terms in this life.[128]

A religious reason can still be proffered but it must be accompanied by an adequate 'secular'[129] or 'public' reason for the advocacy. John Rawls has aptly dubbed this, 'the proviso'. Clarifying his central concept of 'public reason' recently, he submits that:

> reasonable comprehensive doctrines, religious or nonreligious, may be introduced in public political discussion at any time, *provided* that in due course proper political reasons—and not reasons given solely by comprehensive doctrines—are presented that are sufficient to support whatever the comprehensive doctrines introduced are said to support.[130]

When making important decisions, legislators and citizens, argues Rawls, cannot invoke reasons drawn from their comprehensive moral, religious or philosophical doctrines, but only from the concept of 'public reason'. This is 'the reason of [a democracy's] citizens, of those sharing the status of equal citizenship.'[131] Reliance upon one's particular religious faith or knowledge is impermissible. In Rawls' words:

> on matters of constitutional essentials and basic justice, the basic structure and its public policies are to be justifiable to all citizens, as the principle of political legitimacy requires. We add to this that in making these justifications we are to appeal only to presently accepted general beliefs and forms of reasoning found in common sense, and the methods and conclusions of science when these are not controversial. . . . This means that in discussing constitutional essentials and matters of basic justice we are not to appeal to comprehensive religious and philosophical doctrines—to what we as individuals or members of associations see as the whole truth . . . As far as possible, the knowledge and ways of reasoning that ground our affirming the principles of justice . . . are to rest on the plain truths now widely accepted, or available, to citizens generally. Otherwise, the political conception would not provide a public basis of justification.[132]

It can be seen that 'common sense', 'science', the 'accepted general beliefs' or 'plain truths' are associated with secular knowledge and thinking, whereas the controversial and inaccessible are associated with religion. There is an initial and pivotal categorization of knowledge and reasoning.

Supporters of religion may load the dice against religion by acceding to this crucial compartmentalization whereby religion is deemed to be in the realm of faith (subjective, unprovable, speculative) as opposed to reason (empirical, objective, rational).[133] Carter unwittingly does this: 'The effect of privileging rationality', he complains, 'is to skew the public dialogue that liberalism demands, so that everyone has a voice except those whose epistemology rests on faith.'[134] A brief example from the New Zealand euthanasia debate again. The Christian Democrat MP, Graeme Lee, began his attack upon the Death with Dignity Bill 1995 by emphasizing the sanctity of life. However, a change of tack was called for: 'But it is appropriate to continue to argue this Bill on a rational basis, the argument being that the Bill cannot be seen to be sustainable for any rational reason at all.'[135]

For Rawls, 'fundamentalists' (lumped in with 'autocrats and dictatorial rulers') are unable to make such public justifications.[136] Furthermore, they are excluded from his notion of an 'overlapping consensus'[137] since their commitment to the idea of public reason and deliberative democracy is purely contingent and pragmatic.[138] Those then who 'assert that the religiously true . . . overrides the politically reasonable'[139] have reached the boundary of liberal, democratic tolerance.

Is liberal theory reflected in the New Zealand public square? This is again a difficult question to evaluate. It is hard to find public policies or Acts of Parliament that are justified simply upon a religious basis today. Legislators do demand a secular rationale for their policies. In matters of obvious 'moral' sensitivity—abortion, capital punishment, homosexual law reform, and so on—a conscience vote usually applies. Understandably, freed from the dictates of the party whip, religious and theological arguments are frequently invoked on these occasions.[140] Even so, as I argued using the euthanasia debate as an example, secular arguments are still favoured by religiously-minded parliamentarians in convincing their colleagues.

The Limits of Tolerance

> Liberalism may be said to have originated in an effort to disentangle politics and religion. It has culminated in what I see as a characteristic liberal incapacity to understand religion. This incapacity has theoretical implications, for it prevents liberals from fully comprehending what is distinctive (and partisan) in their creed. Nor is it devoid of political consequences: Policies that liberals typically defend as neutral are experienced by many religious communities as hostile. Liberals see themselves as defenders of our constitutional faith, while many of the religiously faithful see themselves as the victims of secularist aggression.[141]

The Problem of 'Foreign Policy'

Liberal states are tolerant of religion. Indeed, religious liberty is 'a defining feature of liberal democracy.'[142] People appear relatively free to follow their religious aspirations—to pray, worship, spread their message, and so on. It is a truism of constitutional discourse, however, that freedoms are seldom if ever unlimited: 'rights are never absolute'.[143] Religious freedom is no exception. So, while liberal states grant religionists a large measure of freedom—indeed, it should be acknowledged, greater freedom than in any other stage in recent world history, and more freedom than that afforded religion in other 'non-liberal' nations—there are still, necessarily, limits.

This illustrates the broader problem of 'foreign policy' in political theory: any comprehensive philosophy or ideology must deal with those who oppose its basic tenets. Larry Alexander observes:

> Any comprehensive normative theory must deal with the problem of how to regard and deal with those who reject the theory itself . . . Liberalism as a normative theory is not exempt from the problem of 'foreign policy,' the problem of how to treat nonliberal views and their proponents.[144]

Galston agrees: 'A liberal democracy must have the capacity to articulate and defend its core principles, with coercive force if needed.'[145] The legislative expression of this self-defence principle is contained in s. 5 of the New Zealand Bill of Rights Act 1990, which denotes the broad basis upon which rights may be curtailed:

> **5. Justified limitations**— . . . the rights and freedoms contained in this Bill of Rights may be subject only to such reasonable limits prescribed by law as can be demonstrably justified in a free and democratic society.

If liberalism is a distinctive, partisan ideology with particular bedrock tenets (an argument developed in Chapter 4), we would expect it to tolerate and accord favour to those belief systems, ideologies and religions which reflect liberal thinking, and not otherwise. A 'liberal' religion, a 'religion that emphasizes rationality and individual discovery of truth and downgrades emotional commitment, scriptural revelation, and hierachical control'[146] would fit comfortably into a liberal framework. For example, in the debate on the abolition of the ban on shop trading at Easter, Katherine O'Regan MP commented:

> I will not go into the religious aspect today, although I must admit that the Mount Maunganui [retailers] brought to the select committee a minister of the church who supported the Bill. He hoped people would do both: he hoped they would go to church in the morning and go shopping in the afternoon. I thought he was a particularly enlightened vicar or minister.[147]

At its crudest, liberalism favours liberal religions and disfavours and suppresses illiberal ones. Edward Foley argues:

> the political philosophy of liberalism necessarily divides religions into two categories: (1) liberal religions, which are those philosophically reasonable religions that accept the liberal position that the government must be impartial among all philosophically reasonable religions; and (2) illiberal

> religions, which are those that deny this liberal position and insist, instead, that the government endorse or favor their particular creed as the one true faith. While the government can maintain a position of neutrality among liberal religions, liberalism itself necessitates that the government must disfavor and discriminate against illiberal religions.[148]

For example, Rawls discusses the problem of those religions which insist that certain issues are so fundamental (in the sense that their or society's salvation depends upon it) that their right resolution justifies civil disorder.[149] Rawls' reluctant answer to the foreign policy problem is suppression:

> in affirming a political conception of justice we may eventually have to assert at least certain aspects of our own comprehensive religious or philosophical doctrine (by no means necessarily fully comprehensive). This will happen whenever someone insists, for example, that certain questions are so fundamental that to insure their being settled justifies civil strife. . . . At this point we may have no alternative but to deny this, or to imply its denial and hence to maintain the kind of thing we had hoped to avoid.[150]

There comes a certain point where liberalism, if it is to remain intact as the governing ideology, must defend itself. Rawls explains that all religions respecting liberalism's conception of justice are welcomed (and liberalism is indifferent towards them) but, otherwise, beware:

> These opposing [religious, philosophical or moral] doctrines we assume to involve conflicting and indeed incommensurable comprehensive conceptions of the meaning, value and purpose of human life (or conceptions of the good) . . . They are equally permissible provided they respect the limits imposed by the principles of political justice.[151]

Commenting upon this passage, Stephen Macedo cautions: 'Underline "provided": All religions compatible with liberalism will be respected; those not compatible will be opposed. The liberal *must* in this way imply that religious convictions incompatible with liberalism are insupportable.'[152]

What is Liberalism's Limit?

It might be thought that liberalism's tolerance for religion ceases at the point when religion advocates civil disorder. Certainly, any religion promoting civil strife would deserve close scrutiny and, if need be, direct curtailment. The liberal simply points to the standard Millian justification for restriction upon liberty, 'harm to others'.

But liberalism is likely to be offended by less blunt, more intellectual challenges to its authority. 'Tolerance is,' according to one vocal liberal critic, 'exercised in an inverse proportion to there being anything at stake.'[153] Liberalism will defend itself when any of its fundamental premises are directly challenged. Religions that conform their beliefs and practices to liberal ways avoid trouble, but ones that do not court it. Jay Newman describes the liberal attitude in these terms:

> 'We will tolerate your religious actions and beliefs only as long as they do not come into conflict with any of our major institutions; when they do, it is you people who will have to do the accommodating.' . . . even in a liberal society, the member of a religious minority must 'know his place' in order to survive, and he must be constantly mindful of the fact his liberal neighbours will only tolerate so much.[154]

Newman suggests that limit of tolerance is reached at the point of conflict with liberalism's 'major institutions'. One of these major institutions is the primacy of reason as the adjudicative criterion for public order. Stanley Fish sees religious conservatives' attack upon reason—where (as liberals define it) reason is 'a faculty that operates independently of any particular world view'[155]—as a central challenge:

> 'Tolerance' may be what liberalism claims for itself in contradistinction to other, supposedly more authoritarian, views; but liberalism is tolerant only *within* the space demarcated by the operations of reason; any one who steps outside that space will not be tolerated, will not be regarded as a fully enfranchised participant in the marketplace (of ideas) over which reason presides.[156]

This would not be so devastating if reason was prepared to treat religious knowledge as rational. But, as we have seen, for liberalism, operating under naturalistic premises, such forms of knowledge have been ruled out in advance as subjective speculations suitable only for the private realm. As Johnson charges: 'modernist tolerance stops at the point where the religious people start demanding that public institutions treat their subjective beliefs as if they might possibly be objectively true.'[157] To acknowledge truth claims based upon divine knowledge is to risk destabilizing the entire liberal edifice. Again, Fish articulates this more eloquently than most:

> In this liberalism does not differ from fundamentalism or from any other system of thought; for any ideology—and an ideology is what liberalism is—must be founded on some basic conception of what the world is like (it is the creation of God; it is a collection of atoms), and while the conception may admit of differences within its boundaries (and thus be, relatively, tolerant) it cannot legitimize differences that would blur its boundaries, for that would be to delegitimize itself. A liberalism that did not 'insist on reason as the only legitimate path to knowledge about the world' would not be liberalism; the principle of a rationality that is above the partisan fray (and therefore can assure its 'fairness') is not incidental to liberal thought; it *is* liberal thought . . .[158]

The problem is conservative religionists' 'obdurate refusal to "listen to reason"'[159](as that term is defined by secular liberals). They insist upon their concept of the good for all. They commit the cardinal liberal 'sin' of 'imposing one's beliefs upon others'[160], or at least trying to do so. Conservative Christians reject ideological or confessional pluralism. New Zealand today may be a pluralistic, multi-ethnic, multi-religious society, where 'tolerance' is the ultimate virtue. Conservative Christians, however, stubbornly challenge the goodness of an ethical or moral pluralism and scorn the supposed worth of a diversity of views of the good life for its own sake.[161] There is *one* way revealed (through the Bible or the Church) for people to follow. A pluralism in fact is inescapable but a pluralism of beliefs is not. Conservative Christians who applauded the Prime Minister's 1998 attack upon a purely secular education were decidedly uneasy at the prospect of other religionists having equal opportunity to propagate their faith in the nation's classrooms. Robert Jenson explains the root of the concern thus:

> The *ideology* of pluralism is, however, [for conservative Christians], quite another matter—though it too is old, as old as late antique civilization. Pluralism as ideology is a rule for deciding what ideas or practices, besides pluralism itself, are to be approved. Tolerable ideas and practices are those that lead us unreservedly to applaud the fact of pluralism, and good ones are those that actively promote the proliferation of pluralism both factual and ideological.[162]

Conservative religionists decline to play along and refuse to take their place quietly in the pantheon. Truth has a public, universal character and must be proclaimed. Such views, when expressed, typically evoke a chorus of criticism. Advocates of this anti-pluralist thesis are typically called 'fundamentalists', 'intolerant', 'bigoted', 'fascist', 'illiberal' and so on. Jenson believes an 'asymmetry' is at work here. Whilst in theory all views are welcome, in reality, conservative religious ones are not. 'This asymmetry', he suggests, 'has a simple explanation: Judaism, Christianity, and Islam are in fact disruptive of the discourse shaped by pluralist ideology and so will naturally be ejected if possible.'[163] In a telling passage, he comments:

> when we go on to ask *who* in fact is silenced and *when*, and what sorts of speech are offensive within the discourse of ideological pluralism . . . the silenced are almost always those who if they spoke would say something characteristically Jewish or Christian or Islamic. Try, for example, arguing that unrestricted permission to abort the unborn is a social and political evil at a party in Manhattan or a college town in Minnesota. Your arguments will not be rebutted: heads will merely be turned as from one who has audibly broken wind. If, on the other hand, you argue what is in fact the *conventional* opinion, you will be praised for courage and compassion.[164]

This is an American observation but many New Zealand conservative Christians would concur. Bruce Logan complains: 'The religious view of life, and in our culture that means the Christian Faith, is by definition likely to turn people into bigots at worst or flat-earthers at best.'[165] The Rev Bruce Patrick at the 1996 Vision New Zealand Conference likewise observed:

> This postmodern era is seen as a new age of tolerance, where all views are valid and equally true. There is however one important proviso: tolerance is extended as long as views are accepted by a majority, or are so promoted by a vocal minority that they are seen to be politically correct. In the last ten or possibly twenty years it has become distinctly politically incorrect to represent Christianity or a Christian view in any sphere apart from the purely religious.[166]

Notes

1. See, for example, Richard Mulgan, *Politics in New Zealand* (1994) at 17.
2. Arthur O Lovejoy, *The Great Chain of Being: A Study of the History of an Idea* (1936) at 5-6: quoted in Steven Lukes, *Individualism* (1973) at 43.
3. See Stephen Carter, *The Culture of Disbelief* (1993) at 55: 'I use the term *liberalism* to denote the philosophical tradition that undergirds the Western ideal of political democracy and individual liberty—a tradition that such conservatives as Robert Bork claim to represent no less than many prominent liberal intellectuals.' See also Robert J Sharpe, 'New Ways of Thinking—Liberalism' in McArdle (ed), *The Cambridge Lectures 1991* (1991) 265 at 297: 'For the past two hundred years, since the French and American revolutions, [liberalism] has been the dominant political philosophy of western society.' On the basic tenets of liberal democracy, see Kent Greenawalt, *Religious Convictions and Political Choice* (1988) ch 2.
4. Roy W Perrett, ' Individualism, Justice and the Maori View of the Self' in Oddie and Perrett (eds), *Justice, Ethics and New Zealand Society* (1992) 27 at 27.
5. Ivor Richardson, 'Rights Jurisprudence—Justice for All?' in Joseph (ed), *Essays on the Constitution* (1995) 60 at 60.
6. Charles Larmore, 'Political Liberalism' (1990) 18 *Political Theory* 339 at 357.
7. John Gray, *Liberalism*, 2nd edn (1995) at ix.
8. Robert Song, *Christianity and Liberal Society* (1997) at 9.
9. See Andrew Vincent, *Modern Political Ideologies* (1992) at 27.
10. John Rawls, *Political Liberalism* (1993).
11. See Paul F Campos, 'Secular Fundamentalism' (1994) 94 *Colum L Rev* 1814 at 1822-1824.
12. Rawls, 'The Idea of an Overlapping Consensus' (1987) 7 *OJLS* 1 at 5-6.
13. William Galston, *Liberal Purposes: Goods, Virtues, and Diversity in the Liberal State* (1991) at 18.
14. See Charles Taylor, *Philosophical Arguments* (1995) at 186 and Paul Horwitz, 'The Sources and Limits of Freedom of Religion in a Liberal Democracy: Section 2(a) and Beyond' (1996) 54 *U Toronto Fac L Rev* 1 at 14.
15. Rawls, 'Overlapping Consensus', at 16.
16. Ibid at 2.

[17] See Song, *Christianity and Liberal Society*, at 40 et seq for a helpful discussion.

[18] Gray, *Liberalism* (above n 7), at xii (italics in original).

[19] Robert J Sharpe, 'New Ways of Thinking—Liberalism', at 265-266.

[20] Nomi Maya Stolzenberg, '"He Drew a Circle that Shut Me Out": Assimilation, Indoctrination, and the Paradox of a Liberal Education' (1993) 106 *Harv L Rev* 581 at 612-613.

[21] Vincent, *Modern Political Ideologies*, at 32 (italics omitted).

[22] Bhikhu Parekh, 'The Cultural Particularity of Liberal Democracy' in Held (ed), *Prospects for Democracy* (1993) at 157.

[23] Ibid at 158.

[24] Song, *Christianity and Liberal Society*, at 40.

[25] Michael J Sandel (ed), *Liberalism and its Critics* (1984) at 4-5.

[26] Lukes, *Individualism* (above n 2), ch 8.

[27] Anthony E Cook, 'God-Talk in a Secular World' (1994) 6 *Yale J Law and Hum* 435 at 442.

[28] Sandel, *Liberalism and its Critics*, at 5-6.

[29] Ibid at 6. Sandel's criticism echoes the view of human personhood to be found in British political Conservatism. That political philosophy posits a rival conception of the person where 'human freedom and human personality are social artefacts, and the human person emerges already encumbered by obligations to those who have gone before.': Roger Scruton, 'What is conservatism?' in Scruton (ed), *Conservative Texts: An Anthology* (1991) at 8.

[30] See Parekh, 'Cultural Particularity of Liberal Democracy', at 162.

[31] Mark Tushnet, *Red, White and Blue: A Critical Analysis of Constitutional Law* (1988) at 271.

[32] Ibid.

[33] Paul Marshall, 'Liberalism, Pluralism and Christianity: A Reconceptualization' (1989) 21 *Fides et Historia* 3 at 9.

[34] Vincent, *Modern Political Ideologies*, at 74.

[35] Scruton, 'What is Conservatism?' (above n 29)', at 10.

[36] Peter Jones, 'The ideal of the neutral state' in Goodwin and Reeve (eds), *Liberal Neutrality* (1989) ch 2 at 11: 'Several of the advocates of neutralism regard it as the defining feature of liberalism: a liberal state *is* a state which imposes no conception of the good upon its citizens but which allows individuals to pursue their own good in their own way.' (original emphasis)

[37] Ronald Dworkin, 'Liberalism' in Hampshire (ed), *Public and Private Morality* (1978) 113 at 127. See also the formulation by Bruce A Ackerman, *Social Justice in the Liberal State* (1980) at 11.

[38] Robert Stout, 'Religion and the State', A New Year's address delivered at the Unitarian Free Church, 4 January 1914, at 4-5 (on file with author).

[39] Jeremy Waldron, 'Legislation and Moral Neutrality,' in his *Liberal Rights* (1993) ch 7 at 145.

[40] Rawls, *Political Liberalism* (above n 10), at 191.

[41] See Waldron, 'Legislation and Moral Neutrality' (above n 39), at 149-150; Galston, *Liberal Purposes*, at 100-101; Rawls, *Political Liberalism*, at 190-194 and Eric Mack, 'Liberalism, Neutralism and Rights' in Pennock and Chapman (eds), *Religion, Morality and the Law: NOMOS XXX* (1988) ch 2 at 46-49.

42 But note that Rawls distinguishes between neutrality of aim and procedural neutrality: see *Political Liberalism* (above n 10), at 191-192.

43 Christopher Eisgruber and Lawrence Sager, 'The Vulnerability of Conscience: The Constitutional Basis for Protecting Religious Conduct' (1994) 61 *U Chicago L Rev* 1245 at 1254.

44 See Rawls, *Political Liberalism*, at 194: 'Neutrality of effect or influence political liberalism abandons as impracticable . . .'; Larmore, 'Political Liberalism' (above n 6) at 358, fn 4: 'Liberal neutrality . . . is thus a procedural idea. It also usually involves a "neutrality of aim" in virtue of which political principles are not intended to favor any controversial view of the good life . . . But it does not include the additional requirement ("neutrality of effect") that political principles have an equal influence on all permissible ways of life, for this is likely to be impossible.'

45 Deborah Fitzmaurice, 'Liberal Neutrality, Traditional Minorities and Education' in Horton (ed), *Liberalism, Multiculturalism and Toleration* (1993) at 193.

46 Rawls, *Political Liberalism* (above n 10), at 193.

47 Waldron, 'Legislation and moral neutrality' (above n 39), at 152-153.

48 Galston, *Liberal Purposes* (above n 13), at 82.

49 See Stephen Macedo, 'The Politics of Justification' (1990) 18 *Political Theory* 280 at 298: 'The liberal must, in the end, defend his partisanship and not evade it.'

50 Galston, *Liberal Purposes* (above n 13), at 18.

51 I am quoting Waldron: see 'Legislation and moral neutrality' (above n 39), at 166.

52 Rawls, *Political Liberalism* (above n 10), at 195.

53 Ibid at 196.

54 Ibid at 196-197.

55 Ibid at 197.

56 Ibid at 198.

57 Basil Mitchell, *Law, Morality, and Religion in a Secular Society* (1970) at 100.

58 Stanley Fish, 'Liberalism Doesn't Exist' [1987] *Duke L J* 997 at 999.

59 Mike McMillan, 'A Bigger Ghetto or a Brighter Bride?', *Reality*, October/November 1998, 23 at 25.

60 Scruton, 'What is conservatism?'(above n 29), at 28.

61 Theodore Y Blumoff, 'The New Religionists' Newest Social Gospel: On the Rhetoric and Reality of Religions' "Marginalization" in Public Life' (1996) 51 *U Miami L Rev* 1 at 5.

62 Frederick M Gedicks, 'Public Life and Hostility to Religion' (1992) 78 *Virg L Rev* 617 at 678.

63 Ibid at 679.

64 See Rawls, *Political Liberalism* (above n 10), at 179-180: 'The difficulty is that the government can no more act to maximize the fulfillment of citizens' rational preferences, or wants (as in utilitarianism), or to advance human excellence, or the values of perfection (as in perfectionism), than it can act to advance Catholicism or Protestantism, or any other religion.'

65 Gedicks, 'Public Life', at 684.

66 Bernard G Prusak, 'Politics, Religion and the Common Good,' *Commonweal*, 25 September 1998, 12 at 17 (quoting US Catholic political theorist, David Hollenbach).

67 William P Marshall, 'The Other Side of Religion' (1993) 44 *Hastings L J* 843 at 861-862.

68 James Hitchcock, 'Church, State and Moral Values: The Limits of American Pluralism' (1981) 44 *Law and Contem Prob* 3 at 8. See also, Gerard V Bradley, 'Dogmatomachy—A "Privatization" Theory of the Religion Clause Cases' (1986) 30 *St Louis U L J* 275.

69 See Douglas Laycock, 'Continuity and Change in the Threat to Religious Liberty: The Reformation Era and the Late Twentieth Century' (1996) 80 *Minn L Rev* 1047 at 1094-1095.

70 Maimon Schwarzschild, 'Religion and Public Debate in a Liberal Society: Always Oil and Water or Sometimes More Like Rum and Coca-Cola?' (1993) 30 *San Diego L Rev* 903 at 911.

71 And, some would argue, it is equally a child of the Protestant tradition, especially Puritanism: Stephen Mott, *A Christian Perspective on Political Thought* (1993) ch 9 at 131.

72 Parekh, 'Cultural Particularity' (above n 22), at 158.

73 Jeremy Waldron, 'Theoretical Foundations of Liberalism' (1987) 37 *Phil Q* 127 at 134.

74 Cook, 'God-Talk' (above n 27), at 436.

75 Scruton, 'What is conservatism?' (above n 29), at 6.

76 Ibid at 3.

77 Vincent, *Modern Political Ideologies* (above n 9), at 73.

78 T Mahoney (ed), *Reflections on the Revolution in France* (1790)(1955 edn) at 102: quoted in Mott, *A Christian Perspective* (above n 71), at 117.

79 Scruton, 'What is conservatism?' at 27-28.

80 Gray, *Liberalism* (above n 7), at 86.

81 Song, *Christianity and Liberal Society* (above n 17), at 43.

82 Wolfhart Pannenberg, 'How to Think about Secularism', *First Things*, June/July 1996, 27 at 29.

83 The absorption of culture and foundational values by 'osmosis' is discussed by Ruth Smithies, 'Gospel and Culture' in Patrick (ed), *The Vision New Zealand Congress 1997* (1997) ch 6 at 100.

84 James D Hunter, 'Religious Freedom and the Challenge of Modern Pluralism' in Hunter and Guinness (eds), *Articles of Faith, Articles of Peace* (1990) ch 4 at 66-67.

85 Ibid at 57.

86 Ibid at 71.

87 Ninian Smart, 'Church, Party, and State,' in Badham (ed), *Religion, State and Society in Modern Britain* (1989) ch 20 at 386. Muslim scholar, Tariq Modood, 'Establishment, Multiculturalism and British Citizenship' (1994) 65 *Political Q* 53 at 60-61, likewise argues: 'secularism in its various forms is *the* dominant ideology; and one which is more dominant in London than in the regions, more amongst "the chattering classes" than outside it, more at the political and cultural centre then at the periphery. Indeed, it is no exaggeration to say that secularism is one of the principal "-isms" which define the political and cultural centre of this country.' (original italics).

88 See Peter L Berger, *The Social Reality of Religion* (1969) ch 6.

89 Stenhouse, 'Fundamentalism and New Zealand Culture', in Gilling (ed), *'Be Ye Separate': Fundamentalism and the New Zealand Experience* (1992) 1 at 7.

90 T De Cleene, 'Thou shalt die with dignity and mercy', *NZ Herald*, 30 October 1992: quoted in McMillan, 'A Bigger Ghetto', at 25.

[91] 'Praying doctor must apologise', *Otago Daily Times*, 5 December 1998, at 7. See Heath and Disability Commissioner, Report on Opinion—Case 97HDC7400 (3 April 1998).

[92] I adapt this from Walsh and Middleton's description of the (unarticulated) worldview of typical North Americans. See their *Transforming Vision*, at 36.

[93] Phillip E Johnson, *Reason in the Balance: The Case Against Naturalism in Science, Law and Education* (1995) at 7.

[94] Ibid at 40.

[95] Ibid at 46 (original emphasis).

[96] Johnson, *Reason in the Balance*, at 47.

[97] Waldron, 'Theoretical Foundations' (above n 73), at 146 (original emphasis). See also Greenawalt, *Religious Convictions and Political Choice* (above n 3), at 55-56: 'the thesis that political decisions should be made on naturalistic, nonreligious, publicly accessible grounds is a claim about the ethical import of liberal democracy. . . . The common theme of the [liberal] writers is that the grounds of decision should have an interpersonal validity that extends to all, or almost all, members of society; decisions should be based either on commonly shared premises or on modes of reasoning that are accessible to everyone.'

[98] William Marshall, 'The Other Side of Religion' (above n 67), at 845-846 notes: 'The response to this attack [by religionists against exclusion from public decision making] has rested primarily on epistemological grounds. It has been contended that because religious principles are based on faith rather than reason, they are not commonly accessible to the polity and, therefore, cannot serve as a basis for political discretion making. According to this view, religion is an epistemologically inferior belief system from which to construct norms of public behavior and morality.'

[99] 'Euthanasia debate: 'politics working well',' *The Tablet*, 10 September 1995, at 11. For a full discussion, see Ahdar, 'Religious Parliamentarians and Euthanasia: A Window into Church and State in New Zealand' (1996) 38 *JCS* 569.

[100] Johnson, *Reason in the Balance* (above n 93), at 47.

[101] Kathleen M Sullivan, 'Religion and Liberal Democracy' (1992) 59 *U Chicago L Rev* 195 at 197-198.

[102] Cook, 'God-Talk' (above n 27), at 437-438.

[103] Gedicks, 'Public Life and Hostility to Religion' (above n 62), at 693.

[104] Ibid at 693-694.

[105] Johnson, *Reason in the Balance* (above n 93), at 10.

[106] Gedicks, 'Public Life (above n 62),' at 695-696: 'Liberalism politically privileges secularism over religion by naming public life (the realm of secularism) rational and orderly and private life (the realm of religion) irrational and chaotic.'

[107] Victor Grassian, *Moral Reasoning* (1981) at 28 (emphasis in original).

[108] (1993) 537 *NZPD* 16976.

[109] (1993) 537 *NZPD* 16974.

[110] Peter Donovan, 'Civic Responsibilities of the Churches to People of Other Faiths' in Ahdar and Stenhouse (eds), *God and Government: The New Zealand Experience* (2000) ch 4 at 81-82.

[111] See generally William Atkin and Graeme Austin, 'Cross-cultural Challenges to Family Law in Aotearoa/New Zealand' in Lowe and Douglas (eds), *Families Across Frontiers* (1996) ch 22 at 331 and Joan Metge and Donna Durie-Hall, 'Kua Tutu Te

Puehu, Kia Mau: Maori Aspirations and Family Law' in Henaghan and Atkin (eds), *Family Law Policy in New Zealand* (1992) ch 2 at 74 et seq.

112 Section 7(2)(c)(ii) of the Act.

113 Section 7(2)(c)(iii). See also s 13 and s 4(a)(i) and (c), as well as the Long Title.

114 See, for example, *Rikahana* v *Parson* (1986) 4 NZFLR 289; *Makiri* v *Roxburgh* (1988) 4 NZFLR 673.

115 W M Karaitiana, 'Core Values and Water Resources' [1999] *NZLJ* 337 at 340.

116 For a helpful overview (by a non-lawyer), see Mason H Durie, *Te Mana Te Kawanatanga: The Politics of Maori Self-Determination* (1998) ch 2.

117 Owen McShane, 'Maori Issues and the RMA' [1999] *NZLJ* 346 at 346-347.

118 Jenny Shipley, speech to the UNESCO 'Values in Education' Summit, Wellington, 26 March 1998.

119 Remarks reported in 'Spiritual element "needed"', *Otago Daily Times*, 27 March 1998, at 1.

120 Bruce Ansley, 'That old-school religion', *NZ Listener*, 11 April 1998, 23 at 23.

121 'Keep state out of spirituality', *Sunday Star-Times*, 29 March 1998, at A12.

122 Bruce Logan, 'Public policy and religious conviction' (1995) 3 *Stimulus* 20 at 20 (italics omitted).

123 Stephen L Carter, 'The Religiously Devout Judge' (1989) 64 *Notre Dame L Rev* 932 at 934 (original emphasis). See also Scott Idelman, 'The Role of Religious Values in Judicial Decision Making' (1993) 68 *Indiana L J* 433.

124 [1991] 1 FLR 223 at 230.

125 See, for example, Carter, *The Culture of Disbelief* (1993) at 56.

126 Blamires, *The Christian Mind* (1963) at 4.

127 Johnson, *Reason in the Balance* (above n 93), at 8.

128 Kent Greenawalt, *Private Consciences and Public Reasons* (1995) at 6.

129 Robert Audi dubs this 'the principle of secular rationale': see his 'The Place of Religious Argument in a Free and Democratic Society' (1993) 30 *San Diego L Rev* 677 at 691, and Robert Audi and Nicholas Wolterstorff, *Religion in the Public Square* (1997) at 25-28.

130 Rawls, 'The Idea of Public Reason Revisited' (1997) 64 *U Chicago L Rev* 765 at 783-784 (italics supplied). Or, as he explains in plainer terms in an interview: 'People can make arguments from the Bible if they want to. But I want them to see that they should also give arguments that all reasonable citizens might agree to.': Prusak, 'Politics, Religion and the Common Good' (above n 66), at 15.

131 Rawls, *Political Liberalism* (above n 10), at 213.

132 Ibid at 224-225.

133 Larry Alexander, 'Liberalism, Religion and the Unity of Epistemology' (1993) 30 *San Diego L Rev* 763 at 770 fn 20.

134 Carter, 'Religiously devout judge' (above n 123), at 939.

135 (1995) 549 *NZPD* 8421.

136 'Idea of Public Reason', (above n 130), at 805-806.

137 See Rawls, 'The Idea of an Overlapping Consensus' (above n 12), at 14.

138 'Idea of Public Reason,' at 806. He adds (ibid): 'Unreasonable doctrines are a threat to democratic institutions, since it is impossible for them to abide by a constitutional regime except as a *modus vivendi*.'

139 Ibid.

140 See Ahdar, 'Religious Parliamentarians' (above n 99), at 583-584.

[141] William Galston, *Liberal Purposes* (1991) at 13.
[142] Kent Greenawalt, *Religious Convictions and Political Choice* (above n 3), at 18.
[143] Richardson J in *R* v *Jefferies* (1993) 10 CRNZ 202 at 217 (CA).
[144] Alexander, 'Liberalism, Religion, and the Unity of Epistemology', at 763-764.
[145] William Galston, 'Expressive Liberty, Moral Pluralism, Political Pluralism: Three Sources of Liberal Theory' (1999) 40 *Wm and Mary L Rev* 869 at 904.
[146] Greenawalt, *Religious Convictions and Political Choice*, at 21.
[147] Hon Katherine O'Regan, Report back of the Commerce Committee on the Shop Trading Hours Act Repeal (Easter) Amendment Bill 1997: (1997) 562 *NZPD* 3470.
[148] Edward B Foley, 'Political Liberalism and Establishment Clause Jurisprudence' (1993) 43 *Case Wes Res L Rev* 963 at 973-974.
[149] *Political Liberalism* (above n 10) at 152.
[150] Ibid at 152.
[151] Rawls, 'The Idea of an Overlapping Consensus' (above n 12), at 9.
[152] Stephen Macedo, 'The Politics of Justification' (1990) 18 *Political Theory* 280 at 289 (original emphasis).
[153] Stanley Fish, 'Almost Pragmatism: Richard Posner's Jurisprudence' (1990) 57 *U Chicago L Rev* 1447 at 1466.
[154] Jay Newman, 'The Idea of Religious Tolerance' (1978) 15 *Am Phil Q* 187 at 191.
[155] Stanley Fish, 'Liberalism Doesn't Exist' [1987] *Duke LJ* 997 at 997.
[156] Ibid at 1000 (italics in original).
[157] Johnson, *Reason in the Balance* (above n 93), at 48.
[158] Fish, 'Liberalism Doesn't Exist', at 1000 (original emphasis)(the passage in quotation marks is from Stephen Carter).
[159] Stanley Fish, 'Mission Impossible: Settling the Just Bounds between Church and State' (1997) 97 *Colum L Rev* 2255 at 2283.
[160] Paul Marshall refers to 'the common liberal piety that "you can't impose your beliefs on others"': 'Liberalism, Pluralism and Christianity: A Reconceptualization' (above n 33), at 6.
[161] See, for example, Daniel Taylor, 'Deconstructing the gospel of tolerance', *Christianity Today*, 11 January 1999, 43.
[162] Robert W Jenson, 'The God-Wars.' in Braaten and Jenson (eds), *Either/Or: The Gospel or Neopaganism* (1995) 23 at 25 (original emphasis).
[163] Ibid at 26.
[164] Ibid at 25 (italics in original).
[165] Bruce Logan, 'Eve, Red Liberal Apples and Human Rights', *Cutting Edge*, June/July 1996, 1 at 4.
[166] Patrick, 'Introduction: Envisioning the Kiwi Church', in Patrick (ed), *New Vision New Zealand Volume II* (1997) ch 1 at 22-23.

4 A Model of Engagement

In this chapter I sketch a model of engagement. Having detailed the conservative Christian worldview (Chapter 2) followed by the prevailing Wellington worldview (Chapter 3) I am now concerned with how these two worlds (or rather the participants in them) interact.

Ira Lupu's legal model of church-state interaction is a useful one.[1] So far as the law is concerned there are, he argued, really only two basic models of church-state interaction to consider. The first is the model of *conflict*.[2] The believer and the state may clash over the application of secular law to religious conduct. The second relevant model is church-state *alignment*.[3] This in turn may take two forms, either (a) the state co-opting religion for its purposes (Erastianism) or, (b) religion co-opting the state for its purposes (theocracy).[4] Complete co-opting of one by the other is most unlikely to occur in the West today. Instead of an entire take-over of one institution by the other, there are a variety of intermediate positions that are likely to prevail. Religious communities and the state typically coexist amicably and co-operate together in advancing societal goals.

The pattern of interaction between conservative Christians (CCs) and the New Zealand state can be broadly divided into two. The first and predominant paradigm is peaceful coexistence. Although there are tensions, the two worlds, by and large, live together harmoniously, with mutual adjustment being the lubricant. Second, there is a model of conflict. Occasionally, the tensions between the two worlds spill over into open confrontation. I shall elaborate upon each model now.

Peaceful Coexistence

Conservative Christians seldom experience repression or curtailment in a liberal democracy. Peaceful coexistence best describes the relationship between the majority of CCs and the state for the majority of the time. The reasons for this are undoubtedly many. There is a sensitivity by the state to the claims of religious conscience, certainly where the religionists concerned are numerous and reasonably powerful, as CCs are. The state does, for example, grant exemptions from legal duties for believers in certain circumstances.[5] Equally, I suggest, there is willingness on the part of many CCs to accommodate themselves to the spirit of the times. Conservative Christians have largely become accustomed to their privatized status. When they do transgress the boundary between public and private realms and assert themselves in the public arena, they have learnt to use a new language.

The Translation Strategy

Conservative Christians internationally have come to the sober realization that explicitly religious arguments cut increasingly little ice in society. Appeals to authority, such as 'the Bible says', or 'the Church teaches', fail to convince secular citizens (and probably many Christians also). In a postmodern, relativist, post-Christian society, many CCs recognize that the path of progress requires a different strategy. They ought still to 'think Christianly', and let the Scriptures or Church guide them, but the eternal divine truths need to be translated into 'rational', 'secular', 'prudential' arguments palatable for *homo autonomous*.[6] Thus, although, as 'a matter of principle', Christians are 'not precluded from adducing religious considerations in advocating a political choice, it would in practice be useless for [them] to do so.'[7] Hence, a translation process is wise (quite apart from being 'good manners'[8]). As John Stott urges:

> In social action . . . we should neither try to impose Christian standards by force on an unwilling public, nor remain silent and inactive before the contemporary landslide, nor rely exclusively on the dogmatic assertion of biblical values, but rather reason with people about the benefits of Christian morality, commending God's law to them by rational arguments.[9]

Similarly, Charles Colson reminds American evangelicals that modern culture is a mission field in much of need of translation of the message as any other. Instead of simply 'brandishing [our] Bible . . . let's find ways to translate biblical truth into prudential principles that nonbelievers understand and find persuasive.'[10]

Non-Christians are able to understand and be persuaded by such suitably-translated arguments. Humankind is made in the image of God and has an in-built conscience or 'inkling'[11] of the Truth. Whether this in-built recognition is grounded in 'natural law' (in the Catholic tradition) or 'common grace' and 'general revelation' (the Reformed), it is real.[12] We should not be surprised, argues the Christian, that Scriptural truth resonates with people's own sense of justice since 'God has written his law in two places, on stone tablets and on the tablets of the human heart (Romans 2:14 f). The moral law is not alien to human beings, therefore.'[13] Postmodernist confusion is 'overstated', for 'the claims of faith' (properly translated into contemporary language) can 'be understood, assessed and debated publicly—including by those who do not share them. Indeed, this is what makes serious [political] theology possible and necessary.'[14]

The 47 prominent evangelical New Zealand Christians who signed, 'Why Christians should be involved in politics', endorse this optimistic view. People's 'inborn awareness of right and wrong' is accompanied by the eminent 'reasonableness of God's moral principles for people.' Thus, a 'wide spectrum of thinking women and men endorse the Biblical values because they make common sense.'[15]

Is appealing to people's self-interest, extolling the benefits of God's law rather than the truth of it, an unworthy strategy?[16] No, answer its defenders, for one has 'to be realistic.'[17] Prudential appeals to self-maximization of welfare 'may not save souls',[18] but they still contribute to a moral ecology containing laws which facilitate that prime directive. Part of the entire Gospel is the cultural mandate to redeem and transform, as far as humanly possible, the world. Christians, then, are instruments of God's common grace or providence, obedient to the divine command 'to promote righteousness and hold back the forces of evil in society.'[19] The law ought not to be used to secure mankind's salvation, but there are still other important ends it may contribute to.

Conflict

The differences in worldview between CCs and the political and bureaucratic elite may produce conflict. There are 'pressure points' and, despite self-restraint by both sides, disputes sometimes occur. It is important to stress that the instances of conflict are few, even tiny, in relative terms, compared to the examples of cooperation. Nonetheless, they do exist.

A source for the increasing tension recently has come from the realization by many CCs that the tide has turned against them and that the state can no longer be assumed to be 'Christian'. Christians have no *a priori* right to govern, nor to expect public policies to reflect their values. Two core tenets of liberalism are the target for CCs: privatization and neutrality.

Privatization Challenged

Some CCs question liberal theory's dividing line—a secular, rational public sphere must be quarantined from speculative passions such as religion. The private realm is the home for the latter. Criticism by CCs is twofold. Liberalism is unconvincing in (1) its claim that their religion is an epistemologically inferior source of knowledge and, relatedly, (2) its claim that the Christian religion is irrational.

First, some critics of liberalism have endeavoured to show that both liberalism and religion operate on the same epistemological level. Both the sceptic and the believer know the world the same way—through a mixture of experience, testimony, evidence, reason and belief.[20] Christians' beliefs in the existence of God, miracles, the divinity of Christ and so on, are based on such a thing as the number of witnesses, their independently-tested reliability and the number of intelligent people who accept these things as true. A Christian's religious epistemology may be quite consonant with her epistemology in general and all of that person's beliefs, criteria of evidence and methods of reasoning may cohere. To adapt Larry Alexander's hypothetical example,[21] Jane's religious beliefs are supported in exactly the same way that her beliefs that Abel Tasman 'discovered' New Zealand, that Apia is the capital of Samoa, that cricketer Sir Richard Hadlee took 431 test wickets and that the speed of light is constant. She 'does not believe any of these things based on first-hand observation, and the last item she finds counter-intuitive and impossible to conceptualize, though she believes it to be true, nonetheless.' [22] Thus, continues Alexander:

> There are not two ways of 'knowing', religious and secular/liberal; there are not both sectarian and secular/liberal 'truths'. As a consequence of epistemological unity, liberalism must establish its tenets by rejecting conflicting religious ones, not by the illusion of 'neutrally' banishing them to the 'private realm', where they can somehow remain 'true' but impotent, but by meeting them head on and showing them to be false or unjustified. Liberalism is, as many critics claim it to be, the 'religion' of secularism . . . both liberalism and antiliberal religious views inhabit the same realm and make conflicting claims within it. Liberalism is not at a different level . . .[23]

Others question the supposed inaccessibility of religious knowledge.[24] David Smolin, for instance, argues that religious reasons are just as 'publicly accessible', even 'reasonable', as abstruse, philosophical, or scientific ones: 'I would . . . deny the premise that Biblical Christianity is less understandable to the public than is, for example, the often obscure and pedantic language of modern secular moral philosophy. I doubt that the people of America understand the language of Kant better than the language of the Bible.'[25]

Second, it might be that religious claims are rational and secular claims are irrational.[26] If a key premise of liberalism—the naturalistic view that 'nature is all there is'—is wrong, then it would be decidedly irrational to ignore spiritual or other-worldly claims. Not all secular theories depend on reason, and not all religions eschew reason or rational proofs for the existence of God. Charles Curran notes, for example, that: 'Epistemologically, Roman Catholicism has insisted that the word and work of God are mediated in and through reason and human nature. Reason and reason's ability to know the truth have been stressed in Catholicism.'[27] Moreover, reason is susceptible to the same sort of epistemological attack that faith is. Reason might itself rest upon belief. Perhaps, as liberal theorist Jean Hampton discerns, liberalism is a kind of 'secular political faith', where liberals share a common 'faith' in 'the unifying power of reason'.[28] Robert George maintains that 'secularism itself is based on a nonrational faith [and] secularism must, in the end, also rest on metaphysical and moral claims that cannot be proved.'[29] Stanley Fish has developed this critique most eloquently:

> liberalism is informed by a faith (a word deliberately chosen) in reason as a faculty that operates independently of any particular world view. . . . liberalism depends on not inquiring into the status of reason, depends, that is, on the assumption that reason's status is obvious: it is that which enables us to assess the claims of competing perspectives and beliefs. Once this assumption is in place, it produces an opposition between reason and belief, and that opposition is already a hierarchy in which every belief is required to pass muster at the bar of reason. But what if reason or rationality itself rests on belief? Then it would be the case that the opposition between reason and belief is a false one, and that every situation of contest should be recharacterized as a quarrel between two sets of belief with no possibility of recourse to a mode of deliberation that was not itself an extension of belief.[30]

Fish's argument is that reasons do not hang in mid-air or come from nowhere, but rather come from 'the realm of particular (angled, partisan, biased) assumptions and agendas.'[31] The attempt by liberals to assign to reason some overarching, transcendent status, whereby reason can stand 'above the fray' and adjudicate between belief systems but not be drawn into the fray and have to compete itself, is unconvincing. Reason is no Archimedean point, for reason is immanent, this-worldly—if we want a lever to move the world, it must be a lever outside the world.[32] Invoking reason as a sort of 'God term' or 'master concept' does not dispense with the problem of providing particular reasons.[33] For some liberals, argues Paul Campos, '*invoking* "reason" becomes equivalent to *giving* reasons.'[34] But this will not do. Anthony Cook maintains:

> For liberalism, the arbiter of clashing desires is human reason rather than God's will. Human reasoning, however, only has instrumental capacity. That is, it is no more than a tool for elaborating our value commitments. It might permit us to explain the implications of certain values or conceptions of the Good, but it cannot determine what that Good should be.[35]

Rather, 'what is and is not a reason will always be a matter of faith, that is, of the assumptions that are bedrock within a discursive system'.[36] Reason then is just the vehicle that leads liberals to the fundamental assumptions or values in their belief system or 'faith', namely, the priority of the individual and the primacy of individual choice and autonomy.[37]

Neutrality Challenged

A central tenet of liberalism, as we have seen, is its claim to be neutral concerning questions of the good life and ideas of the Good. But is the state neutral?

Conservative Christians belatedly realize that there is always a 'particular conception of the good life', orthodoxy or worldview which is *de facto,* if not *de jure,* established. Lesslie Newbigin argues: 'No state can be completely secular in the sense that those who exercise power have no beliefs about what is true and no commitments to what they believe to be right.'[38] The state may be 'religiously neutral', in the sense that it 'does not establish any of the world's religions'[39], but, continues Newbigin, 'the state is not neutral in respect of world-views, meta-narratives or whatever term one may use for the framework which gives overall coherence to our understanding of what it is to be human.'[40] The liberal state's worldview 'embodies truth-claims which Christians cannot accept and which must be brought out into the open and challenged.'[41]

Non-neutrality went unnoticed and uncriticized for a long period while the state favoured CC interests. Bias exercised in one's favour is usually invisible. With their cultural establishment eroded, however, Christian theorists now question the alleged neutrality of the state. The privatization of religion is now being experienced with full vigour. A cultural Christian establishment had shielded Christians from the full effects of privatization. In this sense the thoroughgoing privatization of religion was never achieved for the *de jure* disestablishment was offset by a continued *de facto* establishment of a cultural Christianity. This cultural hegemony has now gone leaving many CCs feeling bewildered and vulnerable. Their religion really is privatized now, in law and in fact. Liberal tolerance is now castigated by some as a fraud and liberalism is typically equated with secularism. Robert Wilken charges:

> Secularism wants religious practice, especially Christian practice, banished to a private world of feelings and attitudes, at the same time it expands the realm of the public to include every aspect of life. The earlier secularist appearance of tolerance toward religion is now seen to have been a sham.[42]

Robert George likewise maintains that conservative Christians and other conservative religionists:

> quite reasonably reject secularism's claim to constitute nothing more than a neutral playing field on which other worldviews may fairly and civilly compete for the allegiance of the people. . . . secularism is itself one of the competing worldviews. We should credit its claims to neutrality no more than we would accept the claims of a baseball pitcher who in the course of a game declares himself to be umpire and begins calling his own balls and strikes. . . . [For conservative religionists] secularism itself is a sectarian doctrine with its own metaphysical and moral presuppositions and

> foundations, with its own myths, and, one might even argue, its own rituals. It is a pseudo-religion.[43]

Patrick Neal argues that even if liberalism is neutral with regard to conceptions of the good, it is not neutral in its *conceptualization* of what it means for someone to have a conception of the good. Rather, liberalism has a distinctive individualistic way it requires the good life to be conceived and pursued. This conceptualization or 'meta-theory', as Neal calls it, requires that individuals define for themselves, separately and individually, their own ends.[44] So liberalism prevents the person from saying he or she cannot know and understand the good apart from others. The individual cannot say: 'I can only know the good to the extent I share the good with others.' Persons can share the ends with others but only once they have first separately worked out their own ends. Individuals must be 'the primary bearers of conceptions of the good.'[45] In Neal's words:

> this liberal theory of neutrality regarding the good presupposes a meta-theory of the good which is not neutral. That meta-theory holds that conceptions of the good are properly understood as the individually defined and possessed ends which separate selves pursue. . . . This meta-theory is non-neutral because it necessarily rules out any alternative meta-theory which denies that a 'conception of the good' can be properly understood as the ends which separate selves define and pursue. One such alternative is [the person] who maintains that 'conceptions of the good' are properly understood as essentially, and not just contingently, shared relations which are primarily definitive of, and not primarily defined by, individual selves.[46]

Christian theorists share a similar critique of liberal neutrality to that of many postmodernists. The credit for the 'deconstruction' of liberalism and its supposed neutrality is often given to the latter,[47] but, as we noted earlier, some liberal theorists themselves concede that liberalism is not neutral. The postmodernist critique is, in essence, that liberalism is just another ideology reflecting a partisan belief system, moreover, one grounded upon a particular historical culture.[48] I return to Fish:

> liberalism doesn't have the content it believes it has. That is, it does not have at its center an adjudicative mechanism that stands apart from any particular moral and political agenda. Rather it is a very particular moral agenda (privileging the individual over the community, the cognitive over the affective, the abstract over the particular) that has managed, by the very partisan means it claims to transcend, to grab the moral high ground, and to grab it from a discourse—the discourse of religion—that had held it for centuries.[49]

Defenders of a secular liberal state explain that it is 'not hostile to religion, [but] can be defined as a state that is uncommitted to any religious institution or institutions or to religious beliefs and practices.'[50] The secular state is simply concerned with temporal matters leaving religion alone,[51] even, suggest some, out of respect for religion.[52] Moreover, it is said, there is a clear difference between 'nonreligion' and 'irreligion',[53] the secular state adopting the former position.

However, the notion of secular as purely nonreligious (indifferent to religion) and not irreligious (opposed to religion) is rejected by many CCs. Any attempt at pure neutrality is transitory at best. The nonreligious can easily, and does eventually, degenerate into the irreligious state and into a kind of 'practical atheism'.[54] For example, if the state teaches that all religious references are to be excluded from public life and proceeds on the assumption that society can be ordered as if God did not exist, this sends a negative anti-religious message to citizens. Some, in more strident fashion, dub liberalism as little more than 'secular fundamentalism'.[55]

Pluralism is also challenged. Behind its façade of tolerance and openness there lurks intolerance.[56] Don Carson argues:

> But if any religion claims that in some measure other religions are wrong, a line has been crossed and resentment is stirred up. . . . Exclusiveness is the one religious idea that cannot be tolerated. Correspondingly, proselytism is a dirty word. One cannot fail to observe a crushing irony: the gospel of relativistic tolerance is perhaps the most 'evangelistic' movement in Western culture at the moment, demanding assent and brooking no rivals.[57]

Ian Leigh likewise refers to a form of 'liberal fundamentalism' at work:

> Liberals view any attempt to practice or express religious belief outside the confines of subjective thought and experience with suspicion and hostility. Claims that religious truth is objective or universal are, paradoxically, the one type of religious expression which Liberals cannot tolerate.[58]

Conservative Christians concede there have existed hybrid or synthesized belief systems and worldviews which mixed Christian and other values together. 'There has never been a time when society was completely Christian; Christianity has never been more than a leaven working in the world, and its work is never finished.'[59] Christendom itself was never purely Christian—Hellenistic influences, for instance, remained; the wheat and the tares lived together.[60] Nonetheless, most CCs were sure that the Christian worldview was the dominant partner in the synthesis that was Western Christendom. Following the Enlightenment, the mixture changed: the dominant partner became reason not revelation. As Christopher Dawson puts it: 'The one merit of a *relatively* Christian age or culture—and it is no small one—is that it recognises its spiritual indigence and stands open to God and the spiritual world; while the age or culture that is thoroughly non-Christian is closed to God and prides itself on its own progress to perfection.'[61] It has taken a long time (for Christendom had a great deal of momentum) but inexorably, the secularist corrosion has done its work. The dominant partner in the Western worldview finally emerges in the late twentieth century, one that is, for CCs, patently a secularist or humanist one.

The differences between the worldviews (which generate the potential 'pressure points') are catalogued below in Table 4.1:

Table 4.1 A Catalogue of Worldview Differences

Wellington worldview	CC worldview
the individual emphasized	the individual-in-community stressed
mankind is autonomous	mankind is heteronomous
naturalism is assumed	supernaturalism is assumed
truth is relative, contingent	truth is universal, transcendental
there are many paths	there is one path
ethical relativism	ethical absolutism
mankind has evolved	mankind was created
mankind is basically good	mankind is fallen
mankind is progressing	mankind is rebelling and faces judgment
heterosexuality is not uniquely normative	heterosexuality alone is normative
reason is final	revelation/tradition is final
religion is private	religion is also public
the state is neutral	the state is, in practice, non-neutral

Predictions

I shall leave aside the peaceful coexistence model. The conflict model is of greater interest. One possibility is that CCs will simply lose out in cases of conflict between the Wellington and CC worldviews. The Reformed Churches of New Zealand in their submission to Parliament concerning the proposed Bill of Rights 1985, a supreme, entrenched constitutional document, expressed this concern eloquently and a lengthy quotation is merited:

> The potential for abuse and judicial persecution and restriction upon Christianity is made all the more likely because of the religious climate of our day. Whether religious practices will be accepted[sic] to the courts will be determined by the prevailing religious values—in this case, secular humanism. The courts will be most likely to look with favour upon those religions which show some accord with humanism. Certain religions will be favoured. In particular, those religions which accept the ideal of a pluralistic society, which are not universal in their claims and principles; those religions which emphasize personal choice, the ultimacy of human rights, the tolerance of other views, proclaim a non-discriminating 'love', promote social egalitarianism, have a libertine ethical system and do not discriminate ethically or sexually; those religions which propage [sic] against the traditional nuclear family with its 'stereotyped sex roles' will be seen to be most consistent with the values of the secular state. On the other hand, those religions such as Christianity which implicitly deny the pluralistic society by declaring all other beliefs erroneous or false, which reject human self-determination in any ultimate sense, have an authoritative revelation to which they are subject, uphold an authoritative social structure in church, society, and family, and which will not tolerate or encourage evil ethical practices are almost certainly to be viewed as anti-democratic and contrary to the ultimate values of a democratic society. It has become increasingly common in the past ten years for officials of the State, whether they be psychologists or judges in family courts, or elected representatives, to portray Christianity and Christians, even when they have used the normal democratic channels and responsible and lawful means to advocate their positions, as being intolerant, bigoted, irrational, unthinking, socially destructive, harmful, and at times positively dangerous. It is only a small step to declare particular practices and beliefs intrinsic to such religions as not in the best interests of a 'free' and 'democratic' society.[62]

Another possibility is that where conflict occurs, CCs and the state will reach an accommodation. Compromise may go at least part of the way to assuage CC concerns. The ultimate form of the accommodation is hard to predict. In the next part I will consider several areas of engagement to see what has transpired in practice.

Notes

1 Ira C Lupu, 'Models of Church-State Interaction and the Strategy of the Religion Clauses' (1992) 42 *De Paul L Rev* 223.

2 Lupu, 'Models', at 224.

3 Ibid at 225.

4 On models of church-state relationship see, for example, Francis Lyall, *Of Presbyters and Kings* (1980) ch 1; Leo Pfeffer, *Church, State and Freedom*, rev edn (1967) ch 1.

5 See, for instance, two examples mentioned by Keith J in *Mendelssohn* v *Attorney-General* [1999] 2 NZLR 268 at 274: the right to refuse on the grounds of conscience to belong to district law societies and to refuse to answer census questions about religious affiliation (s 24 of the Law Practitioners Act 1982 and s 43 of the Statistics Act 1975 respectively).

6 See, for example, John Coffey, 'How Should Evangelicals Think about Politics? Roger Williams and the Case for Principled Pluralism' (1997) 69 *Evangelical Q* 39 at 59.

7 Patrick Hannon, 'On Using Religious Arguments in Public Policy Debates' in Treacy and Whyte (eds), *Religion, Morality and Public Policy* (1995) 68 at 70.

8 Phillip E Johnson, 'Nihilism and the End of Law', *First Things*, March 1993, 19 at 25.

9 John Stott, *New Issues Facing Christians Today*, 3rd edn (1999) at 61.

10 Charles Colson and Nancy Pearcey, 'Quoting the Bible Isn't Enough', *Christianity Today*, 11 August 1997, at 72.

11 Stott, *New Issues Facing Christians*, at 62.

12 See, for example, Richard John Neuhaus, 'Why We Can Get Along', *First Things*, February 1996, 27 at 30 et seq.

13 Stott, *New Issues Facing Christians*, at 64.

14 Max L Stackhouse, 'Theo-cons and neo-cons on theology and law', *Christian Century*, 27 August-3 September 1997, 758 at 760.

15 'Why Christians should be involved in politics', *Reality*, October/November 1996, 33 at 35.

16 See T S Eliot, *The Idea of a Christian Society* (1939) at 59: 'To justify Christianity because it provides a foundation of morality, instead of showing the necessity of Christian morality from the truth of Christianity, is a very dangerous inversion . . .'

17 Stott, *New Issues Facing Christians*, at 66.

18 Colson and Pearcey, 'Quoting the Bible isn't enough' (above n 10), at 72.

19 Ibid.

20 Larry Alexander, 'Liberalism, Religion, and the Unity of Epistemology' (1993) 30 *San Diego L Rev* 763 at 768-770.

21 Ibid at 769.

22 Ibid.

23 Ibid at 790.

24 See, for example, Patrick Neal, 'Religion within the Limits of Liberalism Alone?' (1997) 39 *JCS* 697 at 717 -718.

[25] David M Smolin, 'Regulating Religious and Cultural Conflict in Postmodern America: A Response to Professor Perry' (1991) 76 *Iowa L Rev* 1067 at 1085. See also Jeremy Waldron, 'Religious Contributions in Public Deliberation' (1993) 30 *San Diego L Rev* 817 at 846: 'what is striking about foundational writing in modern secular liberal thought is its dryness and relative inarticulacy.'

[26] Frederick M Gedicks, 'Public Life and Hostility to Religion' (1992) 78 *Virg L Rev* 671 at 694.

[27] Curran, 'Religious freedom and human rights in the World and the Church: a Christian perspective' in Swidler (ed), *Religious Liberty and Human Rights in Nations and in Religions* (1986) at 147.

[28] Jean Hampton, 'The Common Faith of Liberalism' (1994) 75 *Pacific Phil Q* 186 at 191 and 214.

[29] Robert P George, 'A Clash of Orthodoxies', *First Things*, August/September 1999, 33 at 34.

[30] Stanley Fish, 'Liberalism Doesn't Exist' [1987] *Duke L J* 997 at 997-998. For a fuller treatment see his 'Mission Impossible: Settling the Just Bounds Between Church and State' (1997) 97 *Colum L Rev* 2255.

[31] Fish, 'Liberalism', at 998.

[32] See Fish, 'Mission Impossible', at 2274; Charles Fried, 'Perfect Freedom, Perfect Justice' (1998) 78 *Boston U L Rev* 717 at 719; John Warwick Montgomery, 'Law and Christian Theology: Some Foundational Principles' in Cranfield, Kilgour and Montgomery (eds), *Christians in the Public Square* (1996) 117 at 127 (no Archimedean lever or fulcrum exists).

[33] See Paul F Campos, 'Secular Fundamentalism' (1994) 94 *Colum L Rev* 1814 at 1820-1821: 'It seems that, for Rawls, "reason" and "reasonable" fill the lexical space that in many discourses would be filled by "God," or "the Scriptures," or "moral insight." The concept of the reasonable becomes for Rawls what Kenneth Burke calls a "God term"; and the characteristics of this god remain, as perhaps befits its metaphysical status, somewhat mysterious.'

[34] Ibid at 1821 (emphasis in original).

[35] Anthony E Cook, 'God-Talk in a Secular World' (1994) 6 *Yale J Law and Hum* 435 at 443.

[36] Fish, 'Liberalism Doesn't Exist' (above n 30), at 998.

[37] Cook, 'God-Talk', at 443.

[38] Lesslie Newbigin, *Foolishness to the Greeks* (1986) at 132.

[39] Lesslie Newbigin, 'Activating the Christian Vision' in Lesslie Newbigin, Lamin Sanneh and Jenny Taylor, *Faith and Power: Christianity and Islam in 'Secular' Britain* (1998) ch 18 at 152.

[40] Ibid at 151.

[41] Ibid at 152.

[42] Robert Wilken, 'Serving the One True God', in Braaten and Jenson (eds), *Either/Or: The Gospel or Neopaganism* (1995) 49 at 50.

[43] George, 'Clash of Orthodoxies' (above n 29), at 34-35. See also Michael W McConnell, 'Equal Treatment and Religious Discrimination' in Monsma and Soper (eds), *Equal Treatment of Religion in a Pluralistic Society* (1998) ch 2 at 33.

[44] Patrick Neal, 'A Liberal Theory of the Good?' (1987) 17 *Canadian J Phil* 567.

[45] Ibid at 573.

[46] Ibid at 578.

[47] See Michael W McConnell, '"God is Dead and We Have Killed Him!": Freedom of Religion in the Post-Modern Age' [1993] *Brigham Young U L Rev* 163 at 182: 'the

central insight of post-modernism is the exposure of liberalism as just another ideology. What post-modernists have taught us is that the supposed neutrality often claimed for liberalism is really only a mask for a system and a way of life that now seems to post-modernists to be based upon patriarchal, white, male, European, and bourgeois interests and values.'

48 See Cook, 'God Talk' (above n 35), at 443.

49 Fish, 'Liberalism Doesn't Exist' (above n 30), at 1000.

50 John Swomley, *Religious Liberty and the Secular State* (1987) at 7.

51 Muldoon J in *O'Sullivan* v *Canada* (1991) 84 DLR (4th) 124 at 134.

52 See James E Wood, 'An Apologia for Religious Human Rights' in Witte and van der Vyver (eds), *Religious Human Rights in Global Perspective* (1996) 455 at 470.

53 See Stanley Ingber, 'Religion or Ideology: A Needed Clarification of the Religion Clauses' (1989) 41 *Stanford L Rev* 233 at 310-312.

54 Wilken, 'Serving the One True God' (above n 42), at 50.

55 See Campos, 'Secular Fundamentalism' (above n 33).

56 See also Peter Donovan, 'The Intolerance of Religious Pluralism' (1993) 29 *Rel Stud* 217.

57 Don A Carson, *The Gagging of God: Christianity Confronts Pluralism* (1996) at 32-33 (italics omitted).

58 Ian Leigh, 'Towards a Christian Approach to Religious Liberty' in Beaumont (ed), *Christian Perspectives on Human Rights and Legal Philosophy* (1998) ch 2 at 35.

59 Christopher Dawson, *Religion and the Modern State* (1935) at 146.

60 Matthew 13:24-30 and 36-43.

61 Dawson, *Religion and the Modern State*, at 120. The italics are mine. As Dawson notes (ibid): 'In reality no age has the right to call itself Christian in an absolute sense . . ..'

62 Submission No 62 to the White Paper 1985, *A Bill of Rights for New Zealand (1985)* at 8 (para 4.2)(on file with author).

PART TWO

5 Human Rights

In this chapter I examine the conservative Christian concerns with human rights laws. In general, conservative Christians (CCs) are disturbed at the individualistic and intolerant tendencies of modern human rights laws. For CCs the root cause is the humanistic foundation of these laws.

An Ambivalent Attitude

CCs have, historically, maintained a lukewarm 'cautious'[1] attitude to human rights theory. Contemporary Christian scholars admit this. A leading American evangelical theologian, and founder of *Christianity Today* magazine, Carl F H Henry observed: 'It is only fair to concede that evangelical Christians have not in the recent past been the active vanguard of human rights concerns, including religious liberty issues.'[2] Likewise, Fr John Langan conceded:

> The [Catholic] Church, especially in France, experienced the proclamation of human rights in 1789 as a very cold and hostile wind, and it cannot claim for itself a significant place in either the theoretical or the practical struggle for human rights in the eighteenth and nineteenth centuries. Human-rights theory in an explicit and politically dynamic form confronted Catholicism as an alien force, and it has taken Catholicism a long time to appropriate it.[3]

Notwithstanding their apologetic tone, CCs still believe 'a critical attitude towards dominant ideologies on human rights'[4] is warranted. There are three inter-related reasons for this attitude.

The Non-Theistic Foundation of Human Rights

CCs are ready and willing to defend people's human rights: 'It is not intrinsically wrong for Christians to participate in the human rights movement as a means of service to others.'[5] Christians are enjoined by Scripture to vindicate the rights of the poor, the weak, the fatherless, the alien, the disadvantaged. Opposition is not directed to human rights as such but to their foundation. The basis of human rights is perceived by many CCs as being human-centred not God-centred, anthropocentric instead of theocentric. Such a grounding is, as they see it, unstable and is likely to lead to arbitrary and oppressive outcomes.

In ethics and in legal theory questions of right and wrong, of what one ought to do—for example, one should not steal or commit adultery—will have some ultimate basis. The curious, if not impertinent, will at some point, when presented with a rule or command, ask 'the grand sez who?', as Arthur Leff once put it.[6] At rock bottom, there is someone or something which is 'the unjudged judge, the unruled legislator, the premise maker who rests on no premises, the uncreated creator of values.'[7] Leff continued, 'Now, what would you call such a thing if it existed? You would call it Him.'[8] The ultimate source of law is God or some God analogue. Rushdoony explained it in these terms:

> Law is in every culture *religious in origin*. Because law governs man and society, because it establishes and declares the meaning of justice and righteousness, law is inescapably religious, in that it establishes in practical fashion the ultimate concerns of a culture. . . . Second, it must be recognized that in any culture *the source of law is the god of that society*. If law has its source in man's reason, then reason is the god of that society. If the source is an oligarchy, or in a court, senate, or ruler, then that source is the god of that system. . . . Modern humanism, the religion of the state, locates law in the state and thus makes the state, or the people as they find expression in the state, the god of that system.[9]

The location of the ultimate source of authority in a legal system (the 'god' of that system) would seem to be, at its simplest, either divine and transcendent, on the one hand, or temporal and earthly, on the other. The choice is between God (or gods) and humankind. Jesus was questioned by the chief priests and elders on one occasion about His authority ('by what authority are you doing these things?', 'And who gave you this authority?'). The stark alternatives posited in Jesus' reply (in the form of a question) were: did John's and His own authority come 'from heaven, or from men?'[10] Law is either 'what God requires' or 'what man wills.'[11] Leff submits: 'Put briefly, if the law is "not a brooding omnipresence in the sky", then it can be only one place: in us.'[12] The answer to the crucial question 'sez who?' is humankind in the form of: each autonomous, rational individual; some outstandingly wise or noble individual or individuals (the king, the highest court); or some abstract collective (the people, the state). Identifying the foundation of the legal system in an abstract principle—the principle of 'utility' (Bentham), the 'rule of recognition' (HLA Hart) or the 'grundnorm' (Hans Kelsen)—simply begs the question as to *who* promulgated the principle.[13]

The choice between either God or humankind as the foundation of law reflects the dualist mindset of CCs explored in Chapter 2. To recap, CCs believe people must respond in either obedience or disobedience to God; 'either we serve the Lord or we follow idols.'[14] For the CC, the dominant worldview in contemporary Western societies such as New Zealand is a modernist, humanistic one. 'Man is the measure of all things', including law and human rights. Under humanism there is no God to save us nor to promulgate fundamental norms or a 'higher law'. As the Humanist Manifesto II (1973) puts it: 'Ethics is autonomous and situational, needing no theological or ideological sanction.'[15] Humanists are strong supporters of human rights, such rights having their foundation in human experience, needs and interest. The 'preciousness and dignity of the individual person is a central humanist value.'[16]

CCs object to the purely human foundation of human rights. Christopher Marshall observes:

> Within the church, many conservative Christians look with great suspicion on any talk of rights, deeming it to be humanistic, egotistical and overly optimistic about human nature. Human beings are sinners; they have no rights before God, least of all absolute and inalienable rights. The fact that most human rights declarations make no mention of God, and that people appeal to rights to justify licentious lifestyles, simply confirms that rights have nothing to do with divine revelation. They are an expression of human rebellion against the law of God, a law which makes demands, not issues rights.[17]

If human beings have rights they can only, given the sovereignty of God, be granted by God. Human rights are not innate but are gifts from the Creator.[18] Everything in creation belongs to God. Thus, 'the idea that human beings, because of their own reason, might be able to establish rights for themselves, to decide these on the basis of their own authority and to ground these in their own humanity,'[19] is wholly repudiated. If people have dignity it is because God has graciously caused it to be so, having made humankind in His own image (*imago Dei*). While human rights *per se* are laudable, the idea or *theory* of human rights (as a purely human construct) is eschewed. A Reformed theologian comments:

> The so-called Calvinistic rejection of 'human rights' appears to be far from simple: it is due to their origin within a humanist frame of thought in which humankind itself sovereignly allocates these rights to itself. As far as rights themselves are concerned, as opposed to the question of their

foundation, Calvinists have no objection. Rather, they oppose the idea of human rights for sake of human rights.[20]

The human-centred character of rights theory is criticized by CCs for at least two reasons. First, being based upon 'the will of changeable men' they are likely to be arbitrary.[21] A humanistic foundation is unstable, whereas God's commandments and ordinances are not. Second, to repose the power to formulate rights in sinful men is dangerous.[22] If the people or the state (simply a collective of sinners) acknowledge no other authority than itself, it may lead to absolutism and tyranny.[23] 'Law comes to represent', warns Harold Brown, 'not the will of the creator but the will of the strongest creatures.' Thus, 'Oliver Wendell Holmes Jr, thought no differently in this respect from the great dictator, Adolf Hitler. Both of them believed that laws simply represent the will of the dominant majority.'[24]

CCs differ on the wisdom of basing human rights on the inherent dignity of man, a divergence reflecting the different strands of Christian theological thought.[25] Catholic scholars, in the natural law tradition, are readier than Protestants to ground human rights in this way. This is attributable in part to a desire for 'a foundation for human rights which would be universally accessible',[26] not one simply amenable to Christians. Protestant scholars are more chary. The naturalistic and evolutionary premises of humanism seem to undercut humanist arguments for human rights based upon human dignity. Carl Henry, for example, argues:

> humanism as a philosophy provides no metaphysical basis adequate to preserve [human] rights in distinction from other principles that humanism relegates to a sociocultural by-product of a particular period of history. Universal and permanent human rights are logically inconsistent with the humanist theses that personality is an accident in the universe and that human nature is evolving. We cannot empirically extrapolate unchanging values and final truths either from a world of impersonal processes or merely from the human situation.[27]

Several Christian scholars argue that secular theory is 'most vulnerable'[28] at this key point of providing a justification for human dignity. It is here, they argue, that a theistic, biblical account of human dignity and rights is strongest.[29]

The belief that the foundation of rights must be in God rather than in humankind reflects fundamental CC notions about religion, law and the state. As we saw in Chapter 2, CCs are adamant that the state is the servant of God possessing delegated and limited authority. The state stands under God and God's law. The state cannot grant rights for two reasons.

First, only God can bestow rights. As Marshall observes: 'Paradoxically it is their gift-character that guarantees them as rights. If they were of human origin, humans could unmake them. As grants from a faithful God, their inalienablity is secure.'[30] Second, people already have God-endowed rights prior to society and the state. 'Rights are prior to society and must be recognized by it.'[31] The purpose of government then is to acknowledge and protect these antecedent God-given rights.[32] There can be no question of the state subsequently entitling its citizens to exercise their human rights. This understanding of rights accords with the view of some CCs that 'true law is never *made*, but *found*.'[33] Brown observes:

> It is self-evident that we cannot make the laws of nature, the laws of physics and chemistry . . . But there is a specific kind of law that we *can* make—or at least we think we can make. We can pass resolutions, enact statutes, and write them in the law books. The great question remains: Can we make whatever laws we please, or are we bound to respect a higher order in human affairs as we must in physics and chemistry?. . . the most dangerous revolution in history was when men discovered that they can *make* laws. The older term *legislation*—derived from the Latin, *lex, legis* (law), and *latus* (moved, as in 'translate')—corresponds to the view that laws are 'found', as it were in heaven, and 'moved' into our human law codes and statute books.[34]

When governments in their arrogance purport to make law with disregard for the higher law (of God), CCs believe arbitrary and often repressive law is the outcome.

In the international sphere, the United Nations Universal Declaration of Human Rights (UDHR) is criticized for not clarifying its foundation. The UDHR, adopted by the United Nations in 1948,[35] has been described as the 'spiritual parent of and inspiration for many human rights treaties.'[36] If it is the spiritual parent then its ancestry was left frustratingly opaque. Carl Henry cautions:

> A major weakness of the United Nations Universal Declaration of Human Rights adopted in 1948 was and is its failure to clarify the source and sanction of human rights . . . the UN Declaration does not identify the transcendent source of rights. It leaves unstated whether or not a *super*state—perhaps the United Nations itself—might ultimately be viewed as the source and stipulator of human rights. Were Marxist or other totalitarian powers to dominate the United Nations, could they then

> manipulate the content of human rights on the premise that all particular nations are answerable to the catalogue of rights that the international or supernational body imposes?[37]

Christians were, in fact, intimately involved in the birth of the Declaration. René Cassin, one of its principal architects, viewed it as a worthy extension of the Ten Commandments.[38] The decision not to identify the philosophical or religious foundation of the UDHR was a deliberate, pragmatic one designed to 'present the image of universality'[39] and thus ensure maximum acceptability to signatory nations. One result is that the philosophical foundations of human rights still remain contested today.[40]

The Individualistic Bias of Human Rights

Human rights laws strike CCs (or, to be precise, CC theorists and commentators) as excessively individualistic documents. This is, of course, not a sentiment unique to CCs. The President of the New Zealand Court of Appeal, Sir Ivor Richardson, for instance, recently promulgated a tripartite schema of individual, group and community rights and responsibilities, with a proper balance required between them being the goal.[41] The undeniable liberal tenor of human rights theory carries with it the concomitant liberal emphasis upon personal autonomy and individual freedom. CCs discern the ugly face of *homo autonomous*[42] in the background. Modernism, as we saw in Chapter 3, conceives of man as an autonomous individual, emancipated, as Kant put it, from the 'tutelage of others', the Church and God included. Modernism's anthropological conception of man as answerable to no one but himself (*homo autonomous*) is deeply disturbing. CCs are reminded of the damning *leitmotif* in the book of Judges: 'In those days there was no king in Israel: everyone did what was right in his own eyes.'[43] Many 'see behind the use of rights a society of isolated, self-contained units. Each relates to others primarily for purposes of his or her own benefit. The community becomes fragmented and secondary.'[44] Catholic voices echo this concern:

> liberalism errs in giving too much room to individual freedom at the expense of the common good and the needs of the disadvantaged, that its doctrine of rights lends to a neglect of duties, that liberal societies have lapsed into a resentful and self-protective consumerism, and that liberalism involves both the denial of a normative structure of goods for human beings in society and serious errors in anthropology.[45]

Instead of the selfish assertion of rights by the unencumbered individual, CCs prefer to think in terms of the sacrificial non-assertion of one's rights, of doing one's duty and carrying out responsibilities to others.[46] Marshall reminds that freedom 'can never mean absolute autonomy . . . [it] is not a lordless anarchy in which isolated individuals are free to do whatever their vanity dictates.'[47] There is, rather, another classic Christian paradox at work here—true freedom comes with submission to rightful authority: 'Freedom is not freedom from subjection to all restrictions, but freedom in subjection to God's will.'[48]

In the Reformed tradition, persons have particular 'offices' or 'callings' (mother, child, labourer, pastor, artist, Prime Minister) with responsibilities attached. Rights are necessary to fulfil one's office and discharge one's duties to God and man: they are never rights in the abstract or rights for rights' sake.[49] Rights in the CC lexicon are always duty-rights.[50] As Paul Marshall expounds: 'Human beings have the right to do what God calls them to do. Their rights relate to their God-given human duties and responsibilities.'[51]

The Intolerant, Totalitarian Dimension of Human Rights

Some CCs perceive human rights theory as having coercive, even totalitarian tendencies. The human rights corpus is not as neutral or universalist as it pretends to be, but rather is based on a particular ideology. This observation is common fare among critics of human rights.[52] This ideological foundation is liberalism, the political philosophy of modernism which, as Chapter 2 explored, is the 'enemy', the supplanting worldview of this age. There is a clear link between human rights laws (especially the 'International Bill of Rights'[53]) and Western liberal democratic theory.[54] Mutua argues: 'human rights and Western liberal democracy are virtually tautological. . . . one is in fact the universalized version of the other; human rights represent the attempted diffusion and further development at the international level of the liberal political tradition.'[55] The human rights corpus is simply 'a proxy'[56] or 'the moralized expression'[57] of a political ideology. Mutua continues:

> it was presumptuous and shamelessly ethnocentric for the UDHR to refer to itself as the 'common standard of achievement for all peoples and all nations.' A closer examination of the rights listed in both the UDHR and the International Covenant on Civil and Political Rights (ICCPR) leaves no doubt that both documents—which are regarded as the two most important human rights instruments—are attempts to universalize civil and political rights accepted or aspired to in Western liberal democracies.[58]

The animating spirit behind human rights theory is the very one CCs discern to be the God-opposing *zeitgeist*. 'Human rights' is but an expression or alter ego for modernism, secularism and humanism.

If law is fundamentally religious in origin (as Rushdoony postulated), then CCs' concerns are exacerbated when they hear human rights norms being referred to in quasi-religious terms. Human rights advocates characterize human rights standards as constituting 'a large normative canon'[59] or 'a set of secular ethics'.[60] Mutua opines that the UDHR has become 'the "gospel" of the human rights movement'[61] with many human rights advocates appearing to share 'an unequivocal belief in the redemptive quality and power of human rights law.'[62] Mary Ann Glendon too notes how, in its fiftieth year, the UDHR is 'showing signs of having achieved the status of holy writ within the human rights movement.'[63] When human rights scholars refer to this being 'the age of rights' and 'human rights being the idea of our time',[64] they effectively elevate human rights (universal, omnipotent) 'to a near-mythical, almost biblical plateau.'[65]

For CCs there can be only one canon, one gospel, one set of ethics. 'The good news of Jesus Christ is not found in the Universal Declaration of Human Rights.'[66] Surrogate normative codes, even promulgated by the United Nations, are pale substitutes. The UDHR and its progeny, moreover, can, if one is not careful, become false idols, another ill-fated tower of Babel.[67] People may worship abstract ideals of liberty, equality and tolerance instead of gold or bronze statutes, but worship they must. Matthijs de Blois sounds the alarm here:

> [There is] a tendency which disturbs me, namely that human rights have for many people almost the significance of a religious belief . . . Human rights seem to have become the basis of a new creed. Similarly, a Dutch humanist philosopher, Paul Cliteur, recently wrote that the human rights tradition has since the Second World War become the first real world religion, albeit without God, church or rituals.[68]

If human rights theory is but the universalized expression of a political ideology (liberalism), then we would expect it to be concerned with self-preservation. Liberalism will not tolerate challenges to its fundamental tenets. So, as we saw in Chapter 3, religion in the liberal democratic state is relegated to the private realm and 'tolerated' to the extent it 'knows its place'. Its place is not to challenge essential liberal tenets (expressed in human rights discourse) such as maximum individual choice, freedom of sexual expression, equality of the sexes, avoidance of exclusivist or dogmatic claims, and so on. Interestingly, with privatization and atomization there comes statism. Christopher Marshall comments:

> privatism goes hand in hand with a kind of statism inasmuch as there is almost exclusive focus on State action to secure rights. Government is seen as the primary duty-bearer, responsible to remove as many impediments to personal freedom as possible. Individuals have rights; government has duties.[69]

David Smolin, an American evangelical legal scholar, puts the case against human rights in the strongest terms (perhaps to shock the reader): 'Will International Human Rights be used as a Tool of Cultural Genocide?' is the provocative title of his essay.[70] If totalitarianism comprises 'an attempt to place all aspects of life of a people under the control of a centralized political authority'[71] then mediating groups, such as families and religious organizations, pose a threat. They provide a different locus for citizens' affections, a different loyalty. Ironically, argues Smolin, human rights evolved out of efforts to curb the horrendous abuses of totalitarian governments, both left and right, but is itself in danger of falling into the same trap: 'the modern human rights movement . . . mistook the establishment of human rights as an ultimate good, and thus yearned (however comically, given its impotence) to constitute a new form of totalism.'[72] Smolin illustrates his thesis by exploring the potentially devastating effect the impact of the United Nations Convention on the Elimination of All Forms of Discrimination Against Women[73] would have upon a traditional religious community, such as Hasidic Jews, if coercively implemented. Groups such as these perpetuate 'stereotyped roles for men and women' (Article 5) in violation of the Convention's norm of sexual equality. It is ironic, he argues, that nations that do not accept certain norms (such as feminist ones) as a matter of domestic law, may be made to accept them as a matter of international law. Smolin concludes:

> It is certainly too soon for the religious community to give up on international human rights law. . . . At the same time, many religious communities have probably been far too sanguine, and even naive, about international human rights law. They have failed to perceive its potential totalism, or appreciate the way in which secular ideologies have come to color its goals, language, and processes. . . . practitioners of traditionalist religions, and all who endorse religious and familial liberty, cannot wholeheartedly support the strengthening of the enforcement of international human rights norms. Support for an expansion of enforcement of human rights law must be nuanced and selective, or risk creating a totalitarian force upon religious communities and families across the globe.[74]

Conservative Christian concern with human rights theory is, unsurprisingly, echoed by Muslim theorists. For example, in 1981 the Islamic Council for Europe promulgated its own 'Islamic Declaration on Human Rights'.[75]

The clash of human rights theory with traditionalist religions again exposes the familiar paradox of liberalism—how to treat those who reject its theory (the 'foreign policy' problem discussed in Chapter 3). There are limits to tolerance, even for liberalism.[76] Human rights theory, the alter ego of liberalism, confronts the same issue. Toleration, rights, cannot be extended to the intolerant. To the extent that CCs violate liberal axioms, intolerance can be expected. And in the modern era, governments will have the weight of international human rights treaties to press home the point. Malcolm Evans argues that the UN's emphasis upon a 'culture of tolerance' implies that:

> freedom of religion does not include the right to adhere to a religion which is intolerant of the beliefs of others. On this view 'Human Rights' has itself become a 'religion or belief' which is itself as intolerant of other forms of value systems which may stand in opposition to its own central tenets as any of those it seeks to address. ... In seeking to assert itself in this fashion, the international community risks becoming the oppressor of the believer, rather than the protector of the persecuted. . . . [There exists] the reluctance of the international community to accept that in the religious beliefs of others the dogmas of human rights are met with an equally powerful force which must be respected, not overcome.[77]

Specific Concerns

Conservative Christian unease regarding human rights theory may be divided into two distinct areas. First, there is an internal, defensive posture: Is human rights law going to significantly affect the life of the believer and the faith community? Are traditional religious liberties under threat? Second, there is an external, societal focus: Do human rights laws restrict believers in witnessing to the truth in public life? Is the ability to influence public policy and retain (or reform) public institutions likely to be curtailed?

Internal and Defensive

As we saw in Chapter 3, liberalism 'privatizes' religion, confining religion to the private realm where it can enjoy relatively unrestricted freedom. The concept of religious liberty preferred by the modern liberal state is what Sir Isaiah Berlin termed an example of 'negative freedom': 'I am normally said to be free to the degree to which no man or body of men interferes with my activity. Political liberty in this sense is simply the area within which a man can act unobstructed by others.'[78] The Court of Appeal noted recently that most of the rights and freedoms under the New Zealand Bill of Rights Act 1990, including freedom of religion, are 'negative freedoms, to use one part of Isaiah Berlin's famous categorisation.'[79] They are primarily protections against state interference. Yet, this is not to say, the Court added, that there are no circumstances in which the state may be required to take positive steps to ensure the effective enjoyment of negative freedoms.[80] A right to liberty points to the need for positive state interventions such as prohibitions against kidnapping; likewise an offence of disturbing congregations protects worship. As the Court reiterated, 'the "negative" and "positive" labels may mislead. Negative freedoms require a supportive state environment with the establishment or recognition of positive rights . . . buttressed by available and effective policing and Court process.'[81]

To many CCs the area of non-interference from the state appears to be diminishing. Encroachment upon CCs' negative freedom is being felt in cherished spheres such as the family and the church. The Human Rights Act 1993 (NZ) received only cautious approval:

> Christians should . . . support the general objective of the Act because it reminds all citizens of their duty to act fairly toward one another. However, Christians have concerns that some of the provisions of the Act go too far. . . . The experiences which some Christians have had over the way the Act is working have caused them to ask: do some of the requirements of the Act mean that Christians must sometimes act in a manner which conflicts with conscience? Do some of those requirements conflict with the doctrines and practices of churches and Christian organizations?[82]

Bishop Brian Carrell summarized some of these 'flashpoints' in his 1998 book:

> A car salesman is successfully prosecuted because he advertises for a Christian staff member . . . A Christian bookbinder is taken to court by an outspoken rationalist for declining to bind a set of papers denying the existence of God (even though the accused had offered to arrange an alternative bookbinder to do the work at no extra charge). A kindergarten diligently removes the pastry crosses from Easter buns so as not to offend any under-fives who may come from non-Christian homes, or who may perchance belong to another faith—while feeling no compunction about initiating the same little children in the mumbo-jumbo of Americanised

> Halloween with its 'tricks or treats'. Strangely, in these and other cases like them, there is no sense of the law protecting the personal position and convictions of any Christians involved.[83]

As the CC sees it, certain behaviour it would castigate as sinful has now become endorsed by the state as lawful and even worthy of protection as a human right. 'We are all sinners. But we all do not demand that our sins be recognized as civil rights.'[84] Some Christians may thus be required to act against conscience in the wake of recent state-enforced human rights norms. The 'dark-side' of humanistic human rights theory is being revealed. Thus, for example, there is an anxiety among some CCs that their churches (after the prohibition of sexual orientation discrimination) might be required to: ordain gay ministers or pastors; hire gay staff such as secretaries or counsellors; conduct same-sex marriages and even stop preaching against homosexuality. Parachurch organizations such as Christian bookshops, camps, or Radio Rhema will be under similar strictures. With discrimination based on marital status being banned, churches and church schools may be required to employ persons living in *de facto* relationships.[85] Outside of churches and related entities, the CC businessperson or landlord may be forced to act against his or her conscience by hiring someone at odds with the spiritual ethos cultivated at the workplace, or be forced to let a flat to an unmarried or same-sex couple. I take two important 'pressure points'—parental rights and ordination of gay clergy—as case studies in later chapters.

External and Assertive

As Chapter 2 noted, a mark of conservative Christianity is that it is restorationist. As CCs see it New Zealand can still be a Christian nation and the dire consequences if humanistic ideology is given further rein do not bear thinking about. The preferred strategy of the majority of CCs is social engagement and transformation. To recap, Christian morality and ethics are applicable for everyone not just Christians. God as Creator knows what is best for His creations, human beings. In utilitarian terms, God has already done the cost-benefit calculations and His perfect laws are the result.[86] Second, spurning God's requirements and commands renders believer and non-believer alike subject to judgment.

The desire to influence the character and path of society in the public sphere corresponds to Berlin's second concept of liberty, 'positive freedom'. For Berlin, this notion of freedom derived from the wish of a person to be his or her own master: 'I wish my life and decisions to depend on myself, not on external forces of whatever kind.'[87] For CCs, purely negative religious freedoms—non-interference with faith-directed activity in the family, church, school and so on—are certainly important, but more is claimed. Christians are called to publicly proclaim the Truth. Liberalism may want religion to stay privatized but Christianity (of this transformatist variety) will not oblige. Vatican II in its *Declaration on Religious Freedom* 1965 espouses this concept of positive religious freedom:

> it comes within the meaning of religious freedom that religious bodies should not be prohibited from freely undertaking to show the special value of their doctrine in what concerns the organization of society and the inspiration of the whole of human activity.[88]

Fr John Courtney Murray's explanatory footnote to this passage is helpful:

> Implicitly rejected here is the outmoded notion that 'religion is a purely private affair' or that 'the Church belongs in the sacristy.' Religion is relevant to the life and action of society. Therefore religious freedom includes the right to point out this social relevance of religious belief.[89]

CCs wish to fully participate in the public square and influence public policy. CCs cannot be indifferent to what they regard as sinful, immoral behaviour in society, even where this takes place between consenting adults in private. 'No man is an island' is their attitude. Millian liberalism that would permit government interference with individual liberty only where it was necessary to prevent 'harm to others'[90] is rejected, at least where harm is viewed in narrow, individualistic terms. There is, in the intricate web of relationships that comprise society (recall the Web-Network View, Figure 2.4 in Chapter 2), no such thing as 'self-regarding' behaviour. 'The consequences of human actions can rarely, if ever, be isolated to one person',[91] is a proposition most CCs would completely endorse. Sinful actions do have ramifications, sometimes invisible but always real, upon others. At a personal level, offence is caused and at a broader, societal level, the 'moral ecology' of the society is adversely affected. Everyone ultimately suffers and the raising of children in particular becomes most difficult. Victor Grassian, taking the question of homosexual conduct as an illustration, nicely articulates the CC position:

> While Mill, no doubt, would have said that consenting adult homosexual behavior does not 'affect the interests' of disapproving heterosexuals, and consequently should not be the subject of legal sanction, the fact is that many disapproving heterosexuals do indeed 'take an interest' in such behavior—behavior which many of them see as a 'moral abomination,'

> contrary to the will of God. For such individuals, the presence in their community of homosexuals may cause greater pain than a physical blow. Furthermore, they will certainly consider the possibly corrupting influence of homosexuals as affecting their own vital interest in their community and especially in the bringing up of their own children.[92]

Many CCs are disturbed at the way the state is undermining institutions necessary for a healthy society. Again their list of specific concerns is a long one. There is trepidation at: the abolition of Sunday observance; liberal censorship laws permitting pornography and other obscenity to proliferate; introduction of virtual abortion-on-demand; increasing legal recognition of cohabitation outside of marriage (fornication to CCs); increasing recognition of homosexuality as a legitimate lifestyle. One contemporary contentious issue—legal recognition of same-sex marriages and its consequences—is selected later as a case study to assess to what extent CCs' positive religious freedom is restricted.

The Legacy of Distrust

Conservative Christians have a legacy of distrust and antagonism towards human rights theory (and, in New Zealand, the Human Rights Commission). Certain CCs have, over the last 20 years, found themselves at odds with rights proponents, whether law reformers or the Commission. In this section I shall chronicle and analyze several of the principal instances of conflict.

The Eric Sides Saga[93]

The first 'flashpoint' remains perhaps the most significant. In 1979, Eric Sides, a Christchurch garage proprietor and devout Brethren, placed advertisements for a service station attendant in the local newspapers. *The Press* advertisement read: 'SERVICE STATION ATTENDANT—We have a vacancy for a keen Christian person, 16-18, who is not afraid of work, to assist on our Forecourt, only permanents need apply.' Ian Robinson, an unemployed youth aged 16, telephoned Sides. Sides asked about Robinson's age and work history. Robinson had had some experience operating petrol pumps and had shortly before lost his job with another station. Sides asked Robinson whether he was a Christian and Robinson said he was. Sides probed further to inquire whether Robinson went to church on Sundays. Robinson said he did not. At that point Sides indicated there would be little chance of his being offered the post. Robinson told his mother,[94] who was sufficiently upset to lodge a complaint about her son's treatment with the Human Rights Commission (HRC). Sides himself took umbrage with the Commission's taking up of the complaint. On 12 October 1979 he was quoted in a newspaper article as saying that he was willing to go to court to defend his right to advertise for committed Christian staff and he criticized the Chief Human Rights Commissioner for inconsistency.[95] In August of that year, the HRC had issued a public statement declaring that freezing works were lawfully entitled to specify Muslim slaughtermen as mutton slaughterers for Iranian-bound carcasses.[96] Halal killing was an essential requirement for this job and only Muslim slaughtermen were qualified to perform it. The matter had, by now, become one of considerable public interest. Efforts at conciliation between the parties (required under the legislation) proved fruitless, leading the HRC to institute proceedings before the Equal Opportunities Tribunal. The plaintiff Commission sought declarations that the defendant, Eric Sides Motors, had breached s. 15(1) of the Human Rights Commission Act 1977 (refusal to employ a person because of his or her religious or ethical belief) and s. 32(1) (lodging a discriminatory advertisement).

The declaration sought under s. 15(1) was refused. The evidence did not establish that the refusal by Sides to employ Robinson had been 'by reason of [his] religious or ethical belief.' The Tribunal could not rule out the likelihood that Sides may have declined to employ Robinson because of secular, business reasons such as Robinson's poor work record. The Tribunal did, however, find there had been a violation of s. 32(1). The defendants had advertised a position as being available only to Christians and had thereby indicated an intention to breach s. 15(1) of the Act. An order was made restraining Eric Sides Motors from placing any similar advertisements and costs were awarded against it.

The Tribunal's reasoning contains much of interest, especially as its opinion stands as one of the very few substantial judicial examinations of religious discrimination in New Zealand law. Indeed, *Eric Sides* stands as one of New Zealand's few modern religion and state cases.[97] The Tribunal was fully aware of the significance of the case. It prefaced its opinion by noting that:

> the questions [raised] are not trivial nor are the answers obvious. In fact the proceedings raise age-old questions of morality and enter areas where the law and the State have often found difficulty in drawing an appropriate line between individual freedom on the one hard and unfair discrimination on the other: in modern terminology, the issues concern the interface between freedom of religion and the right to employment.[98]

The opening paragraphs of the Tribunal's opinion are revealing and reflect a modernist worldview. The Tribunal begin: 'In our view the questions raised are ones to which there are as a matter of morality no absolute answers. Rather it is a matter of where the line is to be drawn between competing rights.'[99] Further, that line is one drawn by the state in the guise of the Act.[100] Recall that CCs are ethical absolutists who reject that notion that morality is what the state says it should be.

Next, the Tribunal cast Eric Sides, and his CC fellow-travellers, as hypocritical and intolerant. Much of the defence evidence expounded the rights of Christians, yet it was the Tribunal's 'understanding that the teachings of Christ require care and compassion for others.'[101] Defence witnesses had little to say about the rights of employees or the need to help the unemployed. Despite its desire 'not to become involved in moral and theological arguments'[102] the Tribunal continued to allude to the intolerant attitude of certain Christians. Oliver Wendell Holmes' maxim was invoked: 'Particularly in the field of human rights the life of the law is not logic but experience. History is replete with examples where the strict and apparently logical application of moral or religious views has led to great intolerance and injustice.' The outcome was effectively decided once the Tribunal had characterized the defendant as lacking consciousness of the rights of others. It was irritated by the combative stance taken by Sides to the original complaint. Certain intolerant religionists were mounting an open attack on human rights theory. They needed to be taught that all rights were qualified, 'all freedom is governed by the law', in this case, 'by the terms of the Act.'[103]

Sides defended that his case was on an equal footing with the Muslim slaughterman situation. Being a committed Christian, he argued, was a 'qualification' for this work, in terms of s. 15(1). Sides testified that his company 'was set up as a totally Christian enterprise, the true purpose of the business being not the selling and repair of motorcars or the pumping of petrol but rather the serving of the Lord, with the business merely being a platform for giving witness to the Lord's work, and for the drawing of people together in Christian fellowship.'[104] Sides was attempting to collapse the dualistic compartmentalization of life into sacred and secular spheres. As we saw in Chapter 2, CCs, influenced by 'Kingdom theology', argue all areas of life are under the Lordship of Christ and that there is no 'secular' work that is not Christian work as well. A local minister gave evidence on behalf of Sides to this effect. The Tribunal commented: 'we pay full regard to the passages in the evidence of the Reverend Yule in which he pointed out that the separation of life into sacred and secular, or spiritual and material, reflects a distinctly modern outlook lacking justification in Christian tradition and Christian morality.'[105] Nonetheless, the Tribunal found it impossible to accept that Christian belief could be an essential qualification for the job of a forecourt attendant. Such a contention was 'simply too extreme'[106] for a number of reasons. First, it would mean that the employee's tenure would be tied to his continuance in the faith, so that if the employee lost his faith his services could be dispensed with. Second, 'looked at in a reasonable and objective way'[107] it was plain a non-Christian forecourt attendant could do virtually all that was required. Third, the employer's ability to place such an idiosyncratic meaning upon 'qualified' may lead to 'very grave problems.'[108] The Tribunal gave the unflattering analogy of an employer with a sincere belief in the supremacy of a certain racial group. Such a person could hardly be allowed to say membership of that race was an essential qualification for employment since he or she was running a business devoted to extolling the racial superiority of that group.[109] Finally, the Tribunal was sceptical that the whole purpose of Sides' operation was to serve God and propagate the faith. An examination of Sides' accounts revealed a normal family business. In the modernist understanding the operation was a secular enterprise and no superimposition of spiritual motives could alter that.

Sides' parallel submission—that he satisfied the exemption under s. 15(7)(b) of the Act (permitting preferential treatment in employment based on religious belief where the sole or principal duties of the position were substantially the same as those of a clergyman, pastor or priest)—was similarly rejected. A forecourt attendant could hardly be said to undertake duties akin to those of a clergyman.[110] Filling petrol tanks is very far from propagating the faith. The Tribunal was fortified by a (Christian) witness for the plaintiff who observed: 'It is not imperative to pray before pouring petrol.'[111] The witness believed Sides could still maintain the Christian character of his operation by beginning each day with a prayer for his employees; indeed, in her view, employing a non-Christian may itself be an evangelistic opportunity. Her closing remark raised the historic nightmare of liberalism: 'If Mr Sides and all other employers were legally able to discriminate on the basis of religion, this could lead to sectarianism and strife.'[112] The liberal state was of course created to defuse these very tensions. The Tribunal cautioned: 'It is not difficult to foresee difficulties in New Zealand if there were such discrimination, for example in the case of a large employer who desired to employ only members of one religion or denomination.'[113] The Tribunal was adamant that the Act did not place a Christian employer 'in an impossible or devious situation' nor did it 'cut[] across Christian principles or interfere[] with the ability of a Christian to devote his whole life to the service of Christ.'[114] In its opinion there were still opportunities open to Sides to evangelize and serve God. It refused to defer to Sides' own subjective assessment of what serving God meant and of how a Christian business ought to be run. The matter had to be looked at in 'a reasonable and objective way'.[115] Rationality is the modernist benchmark.

The aftermath of the *Eric Sides* decision was interesting.[116] Public reaction to it was mostly unfavourable. The Prime Minister, Robert Muldoon, described the judgment as 'a farce' and levelled the oft-heard cry 'the law is an ass.'[117] Sides claimed to have a large 'fighting fund' to pursue the matter further but ultimately decided otherwise.[118] *Challenge Weekly* predictably portrayed the decision as religious persecution.[119] Secular newspapers joined the chorus of criticism.[120] A bill was introduced to amend the Human Rights Commission Act. However, support for the bill was decidedly lukewarm. The majority of the 45 submissions to the Select Committee supported the HRC's actions and the retention of the Act without any amendment.[121] The Jewish Council opposed the amendment, as did certain church leaders. The latter insisted that the teachings of Christ called for tolerance.[122] Nonetheless, the bill was passed and a new section was inserted into the 1977 Act to accommodate the Eric Sides problem.[123] The victory for CCs was to be one of the few however.

A 1990s sequel to *Eric Sides* attracted no public controversy. In *Proceedings Commissioner* v *Boakes*[124] the Complaints Review Tribunal found a similar case of religious discrimination had been made out. Neville Boakes, a member of the Exclusive Brethren Fellowship in Dargaville, purchased an auto-electrical business. With this purchase came a Mrs Mary McLean, the sole-charge office administrator. Mrs McLean was a fine worker but, in the ensuing years, Boakes began to have serious reservations about her continued employment. He admitted in evidence that he said words to the effect: 'it's been worrying my conscience for three years—we don't believe married women should work. My wife stopped working as soon as she got married.'[125] He referred with approval to remarks made by the Catholic Archbishop of Melbourne that married women in the workplace was a major reason for the decline of moral standards since World War II. Boakes testified that 'while he did not say that his church did not believe that married women should work, he did say that it was his belief before God that they should not.'[126]

Following her dismissal, an upset Mrs McLean lodged a complaint with the Human Rights Commission. The Complaints Review Tribunal held that the defendant had committed a breach of s. 15(1)(c) of the Human Rights Commission Act 1977. Boakes had dismissed his employee by reason of her sex and marital status. The remedies awarded were extensive. Aside from a declaration that the Act had been breached, Boakes was enjoined from committing further similar breaches. Damages for pecuniary loss in the form of wages lost and for humiliation were awarded. Furthermore, it issued an order pursuant to s. 38(6)(g), requiring the defendant to supply the complainant with a written apology within a fortnight. This last order seemed unnecessarily heavy-handed.[127]

Criticism of the Proposed Bill of Rights

The present New Zealand Bill of Rights Act 1990 is a diluted version of an entrenched, supreme-law, Bill of Rights proposed in 1985. The Fourth Labour Government in its 'White Paper' outlined an entrenched Bill of Rights, one substantially modelled on the Canadian Charter of Rights and Freedoms 1982 and the ICCPR 1966.[128] The White Paper proposal attracted much criticism from a diverse range of groups, including CCs.

On 22-23 November 1985, 200 people attended a conference at Willow Park Convention Centre, Auckland, to analyze the proposed Bill of Rights. It was organized by the Coalition of Concerned Citizens (the newly-formed political voice of CCs following the homosexual law reform debate) at the suggestion of *Challenge Weekly*.[129] The tone was set prior to the meeting after a visiting Canadian minister had warned of the devastating effect on churches that the Canadian Charter had had in that nation (the international seamless web at work here again).[130] The Willow Park delegates expressed 'grave concern' with the White Paper.[131] While opponents of the Bill were many and varied (including, for instance, the New Zealand Law Society), Sir Geoffrey Palmer, the architect of the White Paper, recently singled out CCs for special mention. Reflecting upon the events of the time, he observed that 'extensive submissions from fundamentalist Christian groups did not help' the cause.[132] In the Parliamentary debates some MPs pilloried CCs as 'the looney Right'.[133]

Many CC concerns coincided with those raised by others lodging submissions upon the Bill. They also harboured, however, some distinctive reservations.

Transfer of Power to the Judiciary The principal reason for opposition to the Bill of Rights proposal from the entirety of the submissions was the transfer of power from the elected representatives to the judiciary.[134] (Widespread concern at the incorporation of the Treaty of Waitangi into the Bill was another major concern.[135]) The grant of wide-ranging power to determine social and political matters to a select few (namely judges) and the resultant politicization of the judiciary were concerns for CCs too. There was a special danger for CCs here however. Many doubted that judges would be appointed that held, or were sympathetic to, the CC worldview. The Reformed Churches of New Zealand, in a comprehensive submission on the Bill, argued:

> It is clear that the Bill of Rights will involve the courts in determining matters of social policy . . . If we may posit for the moment that there is a liberal humanist world-and-life-view, and a traditional-conservative world-and-life-view it is reasonable to expect that the Cabinet and Parliament, insofar as it has jurisdiction, will appoint judges that reflect the dominant social consensus of the Government of the Day. This is exactly the situation in the United States.

Unnecessary Some CCs resented the idea that the government could somehow belatedly bestow rights which New Zealanders already possessed. The Coalition of Concerned Citizens remonstrated:

> This pernicious Bill is a thinly disguised attempt by the State to define and therefore to delimit [common law] rights enjoyed by an individual; it seeks to arrogate to itself the right to bestow upon New Zealanders those things which we, at present, already legitimately have. . . . The late Sir Robert Menzies once said that when a government was given the power to confer rights upon the people, the implied power was also given for the government or its successors to remove those rights.[136]

Sir Geoffrey Palmer conceded that the rights in the Bill were, generally speaking, already part of New Zealand law, their ancestry dating back to the Magna Carta 1215 and the Bill of Rights 1689.[137] The original proposal (and the eventual Act) recognizes this, for its Long Title states that it is an Act 'to *affirm* . . . human rights and fundamental freedoms in New Zealand'.

Foreign Intrusion and Loss of Sovereignty[138] CCs could take no comfort from the fact that one of the reasons for the Bill was a desire to ensure New Zealand more closely complied with its international obligations.[139] Although the Government had ratified the ICCPR in 1978, reference to the International Covenant in the Preamble of the Bill (and paraphrased or refined versions of its articles in its main body) would help demonstrate to the UN Human Rights Committee that the New Zealand Government was well and truly meeting its obligations.

For many CCs, however, the imprimatur of the UN carried all the wrong connotations. That global organization had been tainted by input from too many totalitarian, 'godless' regimes. Secular humanism had infiltrated the UN. Some CCs even drew links here between the feared one-world, anti-Christ government spoken of in the book of Revelation and the global structures of the UN. Concerned Citizens, considered that 'many of [the Bill's] provisions [had] been made in high-sounding but rubbery language which [was] so common in Communist countries.'

Secular Humanistic Foundation Many CCs were dismayed that the Preamble contained no explicit acknowledgement of God as the source of rights. For them, New Zealand still was a Christian nation; they sought to thwart any further erosion of the *de facto* Christian establishment (as I have called it). The Concerned Citizens' submission was typical:

> For the last 2000 years . . . the law has been based on the Bible and, being founded on God's law, has had far more authority than would a set of rules arbitrarily thought up by a government in power . . . Since the Queen is titled a Christian monarch, is head of the Church of England, and over 70% of New Zealanders consider themselves Christian, it is clear that the presuppositions for a Bill of Rights must be Christian rather than secular humanist ones.

Instead, the New Zealand public had been presented with a 'humanist' document. 'The preamble to the Bill of Rights', charged the Mount Maunganui Baptist Church, 'sets up as the supreme standard, not the God based values on which our society is founded, but those of a "democratic society" (i.e. humanist) based on the rule of law and on principles of freedom, equality and the dignity and worth of the human person.' Once more the Reformed Churches' submission provided the fullest theological critique:

> we believe that the Bill fails because it does not acknowledge Almighty God as the Source and Bestower of human rights. We believe that as soon as fundamental rights are decreed from an immanent source, immanent in creation, the work of interpreting, administering, applying, or defining those laws must be given to some institution or body which will hold awesome powers. This means that any fundamental law to protect freedoms and rights, which is grounded in the creation, will inevitably remove freedoms and take away rights, for it will concentrate infallible power in one or some governmental institutions. They will function as the supreme authority, and will have absolutist prerogatives over the community.

This was, it continued, 'a true irony' given that one of the avowed aims of the Bill of Rights was to restrain governmental power.[140] The only real check upon tyranny was the divine one: 'Only by acknowledging Almighty God, to whom all human courts are subject, can effective limits be placed upon courts and parliaments alike.' An historical analogy was drawn:

> the Bill of Rights actually makes the political expression of secular humanism—Statism—the established religion, and supreme value of our nation. In doing so, the Bill reincarnates the principles of religious liberty that operated in the Roman Empire. What is not often understood is that the Empire was perfectly ready to tolerate all religions and beliefs, provided each acknowledged the Supremacy of Caesar and the State. The Bill of Rights is a secularized form of the same principle. Christianity would have been tolerated in the Empire if the church had burnt incense to the Emperors from time to time. Under the Bill of Rights, Christianity will be tolerated in our society only if it conforms to the mores of the ultimate and established religion—the values of the democratic State.[141]

CCs noted the conspicuous absence in the New Zealand Bill of the theistic acknowledgement found in the Canadian Charter, the model for the Bill. (The Charter Preamble begins: 'Whereas Canada is founded upon principles that recognize the supremacy of God and the Rule of Law'). The non-reference to the Deity in the White Paper was in stark contrast to such a reference in the ill-fated Bill of Rights 1963 introduced by Ralph Hanan, the National Government's Minister of Justice, a generation earlier.[142] This point underscores the changed environment CCs now felt themselves to be in—the *de facto* Christian establishment (see Chapter 1) had crumbled.

The Select Committee's response to the Preamble issue was to say that a theistic or Christian reference would be unfair to non-Christians: 'In our view it would be inconsistent with Articles 6 and 8 of the bill [to eventually become ss 13 and 15 respectively of the 1990 Act] to acknowledge the supremacy of God. These two Articles would protect the beliefs and practices of those who reject the Christian God.'[143] To the Committee, a lack of reference to God was neutral; to CCs, it was a rejection of a theocentric foundation and its substitution with a humanist one.

A Downgrading of Christianity The corollary of a failure to give God His due was the relegation of Christianity to mere equality with all other religions. The Mount Maunganui Baptist Church, for example, decried the fact that 'not only does the Bill ignore Christian values but gives equal pre-eminence to values which may be totally foreign to our society. To be extreme, the values of a Satanic cult or mindbending group are given equal status to those of a Christian group.' Others believed the religious freedom article would lead to 'pluralistic excess' and even 'moral anarchy'. Under the guise of manifestation of religious or ethic belief, a litany of immoral and unethical practices ('pornography, obscenity, immorality, idolatry, the use of drugs, prostitution, homosexuality') might be forced upon the public. It was 'preposterous to put unethical views on the same level as ethical ones.' Society ought not to allow persons espousing immoral or ethical views 'equal privileges in the public arena'. The Christian majority, in their view, needed protection from 'aggressive and disruptive minorities'.

Disestablishment Ramifications Some predicted that the religious freedom provisions of the proposed Bill of Rights might be given an anti-establishment reading. Now the Bill contained no express anti-establishment provision—such as the opening clause in the First Amendment of the US Constitution (which stipulates that: 'Congress shall make no law respecting an establishment of religion, or prohibiting the free exercise thereof'). The omission of an anti-establishment provision was a deliberate one. The White Paper pointed out that Article 8 of the draft Bill (to become s. 15 of the Act) was different from the First Amendment:

> That provision [the First Amendment] was designed to prevent the creation of a state or official religion. That does not appear to be a real question to address in New Zealand. The American provision moreover has been used to deny state aid to religious schools—a practice long followed in New Zealand—and even voluntary prayers or bible readings in schools. The Covenant [International Covenant on Civil and Political Rights 1966] and the Canadian Charter contain no such provision. Accordingly it has not been included in the above text.[144]

Some were highly critical of the absence of a non-establishment clause. Two academic lawyers, Elkind and Shaw, argued that, while the question of a state religion was not a question at the present time, it might become one in the future and was it 'not the very purpose of the Bill of Rights to attempt to foresee and prevent future abuses?' They suggested the insertion of an explicit unambiguous provision worded: 'There shall be no official State religion in New Zealand.' Without such a provision they considered religious freedom was not really protected.[145] The Auckland Ethnic Council, New Zealand Jewish Council, Society for the Protection of Public Education and the New Zealand Rationalist Association shared this view.[146]

In its Interim Report two years later, the Select Committee reaffirmed the view expressed in the White Paper that the establishment of a state religion did not loom as a 'real question' adding, somewhat curtly, that inclusion of an anti-establishment provision would be 'inappropriate'. Further, there was no need either for an express recognition that freedom from religion was protected since the Bill did 'not give any greater protection to persons holding a religious belief than it gives to those who do not.'[147]

Threats to the Family and Parental Authority With the primacy accorded to individual rights, many CCs feared this would have serious adverse repercussions for family life and parental rights. The individual rights of the child would have to be accorded due weight and the state would consider itself obliged to vindicate the child's rights in any parental-child conflict. Parental religious upbringing especially would be threatened. 'The enormity of the suffering that this Bill could bring to Christian parents weighs on my mind,' was the lament of one CC commentator.[148] In response, some CC submissions advocated the inclusion of 'family rights' in the Bill. Concerned Christians, for example, contended:

> We note that some family rights have been included in the International Covenant on Political and Civil Rights, Article 23. The state should recognise the particular rights, authority and dignity of the family as a divine institution, pre-dating the state and indeed the very foundation of it. . . . Parental authority should also be reaffirmed in that no contraceptive or sex education or similar manipulation of values be taught without parental consent.[149]

Insufficient Protection for the Unborn Child Anti-abortion activists were convinced that the 'right to life' guarantee (in Article 14 of the proposed Bill) would do little or nothing to stem the rising abortion rate in New Zealand. *Humanity,* the newspaper for the Society for the Protection of the Unborn Child, ran the headline, 'Bill is unsafe for unborn', quoting leader Marilyn Pryor as saying the Bill would leave unborn children 'about as safe as a grass hut in a hurricane.'[150] CC anxiety was exacerbated by the reference in the White Paper to Canadian authority which had held that the corresponding guarantee in the Charter did not extend to giving rights to the foetus.[151]

Following the widespread opposition to an entrenched, supreme-law Bill of Rights, its architect, Geoffrey Palmer, by now Prime Minister, was forced to set his sights lower. As Sir Geoffrey (as he now is) noted in his introductory speech in Parliament: 'the select committee concluded New Zealand was not ready for a fully-fledged Bill of Rights. However, it did consider that there was considerable merit in a Bill of Rights of some kind.'[152] An interpretative Bill of Rights, having the status of an ordinary statute, was the result. Judges would be required to interpret the law so as to protect citizens' rights and freedoms, but there would be no power to strike down contravening legislation.

With the notion of a supreme law abandoned, most CCs lost interest. The fears of an unsympathetic judicial elite instigating humanistic social engineering had dissipated. Few Christian individuals or organizations issued submissions on the diluted Bill that was now proposed.[153]

There were still some concerns from pro-life advocates. The Seventh-Day Adventist Church alluded in its submission to the danger of the Bill being easily altered to become entrenched by later Parliaments. In parliamentary debate, CC MP Graeme Lee emphasized this point: 'It will just be a matter of time until the Bill will move from being ordinary law—albeit *de facto* supreme law—to being the benchmark for all New Zealand law: the original objective.'[154] The submission of the Social Responsibility Commission of the Anglican Church of New Zealand opposed the revised Bill for its undue emphasis upon individual as opposed to group rights, and for its failure to acknowledge the Treaty of Waitangi. It expressed concern at the prospect of sinister cults having a right to religious liberty. It even suggested an exclusion be drafted to ensure 'religions or beliefs which [were] fraudulent and not bona fide or which involve devil worship, voodoo, black magic or bondage' not receive legal protection. On the other hand, it did not support any 'tightening up' of the right to life provision and most CCs would not have agreed with its recommendation to add sexual orientation discrimination to the other grounds of prohibited discrimination. This last issue is examined in Chapter 9.

The Christian Bookbinder Complaint

In 1995 a Christian bookbinder complained publicly about his treatment at the hands of the Human Rights Commission.[155] He was asked by a customer to bind a book containing material which was, in the bookbinder's opinion, blasphemous. He completed the job for the customer, a rationalist, but asked him not to bring any similar books in to be bound. It made no difference to the customer that the bookbinder had offered to supply another binder with matching binding material so that the customer could get the job done elsewhere. The customer complained to the HRC. The complaint went through the initial stages of consideration prescribed by the Human Rights Act 1993: the complainant, the bookbinder and Commission staff attended a compulsory conciliation meeting. The complainant ultimately decided to withdraw his complaint and the matter did not proceed to a hearing. The bookbinder was, however, warned by the Commission by letter, not to refuse any subsequent orders of this kind. The letter concluded: 'It should be made clear that the reason for closing the matter is because the complaint was withdrawn. The Complaints Division has asked me to remind you that discriminating against people because of their religious beliefs (or lack of them) is unlawful under the Human Rights Act 1993.'[156] Arguably, the Commission was incorrect in that the bookbinder was not discriminating against the customer or his beliefs, but against the particular offensive material being provided[157] (the bookbinder, it appears, did not refuse to bind other material for the customer). No matter, the bookbinder (whose identity and particular religious affiliation were kept private by him) took issue with his treatment by the Commission. He complained in a *Sunday Star-Times* article that it was unconscionable for the law to force him to handle material he found offensive: 'This is something that is really against mankind. Christianity governs the way we (Christians) live, but the law says it can be overridden.'[158] Legal commentary questioned whether there ought not to be some exemption for this type of religiously-motivated discrimination, since without such an accommodation sincere religious persons might be hindered from operating in a commercial marketplace.[159]

Some CCs took up the issue and launched a petition to amend the Act to allow an exemption on the grounds of religious conscience for businesspeople such as the bookbinder.[160] They could gain succour from the secular media on this occasion. The *Dominion,* in an editorial entitled, 'Rights druids need sacking', attacked the HRC as a bureaucratic, meddling entity which needed scrapping. It scolded:

> The implications [of the bookbinding ruling] are outrageous. The commission is saying, in effect, that people's religious convictions must not influence their business decisions. Presumably a doctor who opposes abortions on religious grounds may not decline to perform them; a Christian builder must not refuse to build a house for satanists. It is apparently of no consequence that other bookbinders, doctors and builders are readily available, so that no customer is deprived of the desired service. It is bizarre that the very institution set up to protect and promote human rights should be prepared to violate an individual's conscience in this way. The Christian bookbinder might have wished for the same consideration which the commission showed a Muslim boy when it told his school it must set aside its uniform rules and let him wear long trousers on religious grounds.[161]

No CC could have put the case more pungently.

Human Rights Commission Criticism of the Christian Coalition

On 20 August 1996, prior to the General Election, the Chief Commissioner for the Human Rights Commission, Pamela Jefferies, sent an open letter to Graeme Lee, co-leader of the Christian Coalition. (The Coalition was formed by the Christian Heritage Party and the Christian Democrats to contest the 1996 election.) The Commission was 'particularly concerned' with certain aspects of the Coalition's policies.

The latter's family policy was viewed by the HRC as being inconsistent with the Human Rights Act 1993. The Coalition had floated a new 'home carers allowance' designed to give additional welfare assistance to married, but not unmarried, couples with dependent children.[162] To assist only those families of a particular marital status was, said the HRC, 'inconsistent . . . with concepts of equity, fairness and tolerance' and sat uneasily with s. 74 of the Act. The Coalition responded in a press release by condemning the Commission letter as 'laughable'.

The media largely ignored the exchange, but this graphic and unusual intervention by a governmental agency into electoral politics disturbed at least one legal commentator. Grant Huscroft, an Auckland University law lecturer, criticized the action in a guest editorial for the *New Zealand Law Journal*. He expressed disquiet that the Commission's interference with the election campaign had passed without comment. The reason, he surmized, was that the Christian Coalition was an 'easy target'—a small, struggling party advocating unfashionable policies well outside mainstream opinion. Even though few, he continued, 'will be upset at criticism of its policies, but that is beside the point. The Chief Commissioner's letter was wrong not because of the position she took, but simply because she took a position.'[163] The HRC responded in a subsequent issue. Mrs Jefferies pointed out that s. 5(1)(c) allowed the Commission 'to make public statements in relation to any matter affecting human rights' and there was nothing to suggest this power did not apply during pre-election periods.[164] The incident was yet another example of the antagonism that had developed over the years between CCs and successive Commissions.

The Hero Parade Advertisement

A final illustration is the *New Zealand Herald* advertisement on 10 February 1999. A group calling itself 'Stop Promoting Homosexuality International (NZ)' placed a full-page advertisement pointing out that 'real heroes' affirmed lifelong marriage and the family and demonstrated public modesty avoiding indecent displays. Depicted in support were Mother Teresa, Dame Whina Cooper, Mahatma Ghandi and Martin Luther King Jr. The advertisement was a pre-emptive attack upon the 'Hero Parade', the annual Auckland celebration of the homosexual and lesbian way of life. A spokesman for the group, the Rev Bruce Patrick of the Auckland Baptist Tabernacle (and, it will be recalled from Chapter 1, an organizer of the Vision New Zealand Congresses) explained the need for the notice given the media's 'politically correct' silencing of the 'silent majority' opposed to the promotion of homosexuality.[165] The following day, the Chief Human Rights Commissioner criticized it as a destructive attempt 'to stir up ill-feeling' against such groups, one 'inconsistent with the spirit of a tolerant and inclusive society.'[166]

The response was another advertisement a week later from 'The Campaign for Human Rights' entitled, 'It takes real heroes to stand up to hate'. It castigated the Stop Promoting group for 'spreading bigotry', 'breeding intolerance' and 'homophobia'. Significantly, the long list of names of those who 'proudly supported' the latter advertisement included 'Chris Lawrence, Proceedings Commissioner, Human Rights Commission'.[167] A complaint that the HRC had now compromized itself was rejected by the Chief Commissioner.[168] Bruce Logan was one of several CCs who were displeased: 'How can the public have confidence in the HRC when it considers complaints on the ground of sexual orientation when its own Proceedings Commissioner subscribes to intemperate and even inflammatory language in a newspaper advertisement.'[169] The Chief Human Rights Commissioner's accusation that the original advertisement was an attempt to stir up ill-feeling 'looked very much like intimidation'. But, continued Logan, a 'tolerant and inclusive society allows all of us to state, without fear, what we believe to be right and wrong.'[170] CCs would not be cowed.

Conclusion

Conservative Christians have, historically, been somewhat wary of human rights. While CCs believe in vindicating the rights of the weak and powerless, the ideology of human rights is viewed with some suspicion. The humanistic foundation of human rights is, as CCs see it, unstable. It can lead to oppressive outcomes for persons (such as CCs) who are perceived as 'intolerant' or 'bigoted'. Human rights theory is but the alter ego of liberalism, and so groups which test the limits of liberal tolerance can expect to be rebuffed. The secular supplanting 'spirit of the age' is behind human rights laws for many CCs. Whether, to take one key objection, the recognition of God as the source of rights would make as significant a difference as CCs believe is debatable. Mere lip service might be paid to theistic preambles in a social and legal environment where the recognition of a divine or higher law is not prevalent.

Many CCs are uneasy at the prospect of contemporary human rights law working against them. Specifically, their negative religious freedoms (religious exercise in the private realm) and positive religious liberty (capacity to influence society and public policy) may be restricted.

To better understand this anxiety I traced several of the significant 'flashpoints' between CCs and rights proponents over the last two decades. The prosecution of a Brethren garage proprietor, Eric Sides, by the Human Rights Commission in the early 1980s set the tone for frosty relations ever since. Spats between the two have recurred during the 1990s.

At one level, the continued antipathy of CCs to human rights law is puzzling—there have been only a few cases where their conduct has been impugned. Are not CCs unnecessarily alarmist and given to over-reaction? This, I suggest, is to fail to see the importance of these cases at the socio-cultural and symbolic level. They are 'surface culture' indicators of 'deep culture' movements. In the 'culture war', the struggle for the control of the 'narrative' of New Zealand, public rebukes from the Human Rights Commission or Parliamentary select committees remind CC activists that their concept of the good, of what counts as a 'right', is no longer dominant. Rights reversals underscore the cultural disestablishment of CCs and elicit from them an immediate, powerful and sometimes strident counter-reaction.

Notes

1 Christopher Marshall, '"A Little Lower than the Angels": Human Rights in the Biblical Tradition' in Atkin and Evans (eds), *Human Rights and the Common Good: Christian Perspectives* (1999) 14 at 15: 'Historically Christian churches have been cautious, if not overtly hostile, to any assertion of "natural rights" or "the rights of man", fearing its non-theistic tone and its potential to weaken the traditional Christian emphasis on obligation.'

2 Carl F H Henry, *The Christian Mindset in a Secular Society* (1984) at 67.

3 John Langan, 'Human Rights in Roman Catholicism' in Swidler (ed), *Human Rights in Religious Traditions* (1982) ch 3 at 32.

4 Matthijs de Blois, 'The Foundation of Human Rights: A Christian Perspective' in Beaumont (ed), *Christian Perspectives on Human Rights and Legal Philosophy* (1998) ch 1 at 27.

5 David M Smolin, 'Church, State and International Human Rights: A Theological Appraisal' (1998) 73 *Notre Dame L Rev* 1515 at 1538.

6 Arthur Allen Leff, 'Unspeakable Ethics, Unnatural Law' [1979] *Duke L J* 1229 at 1230.

7 Ibid at 1230.

8 Ibid.

9 Rousas John Rushdoony, *The Institutes of Biblical Law* (1973) at 4-5 (original emphasis).

10 Matthew 21: 23-27.

11 Harold O J Brown, *The Sensate Culture: Western Civilization Between Chaos and Transformation* (1996) at 79.

12 Leff, 'Unspeakable Ethics', at 1233. The 'brooding omnipresence in the sky' is the phrase coined by American Supreme Court Justice, Oliver Wendell Holmes, in

Southern Pac Co v *Jensen*, 244 US 205, 222 (1916). For a powerful critique of Holmes' 'omnipresence' thesis and a clarification of the metaphysical dimension of law, see Steven D Smith, 'Believing like a Lawyer' (1999) 40 *Boston College L Rev* 1041.

[13] See further Phillip E Johnson, 'Nihilism and the End of Law', *First Things*, March 1993, 19-25.

[14] Walsh and Middleton, *The Transforming Vision* (1984) at 95.

[15] Third principle of the Manifesto. The Manifesto is reproduced in full in Corliss Lamont, *The Philosophy of Humanism*, 7th edn (1990) 290 at seq.

[16] Fifth principle. See ibid, at 294.

[17] Marshall, 'Little Lower than the Angels' (above n 1), at 25.

[18] Aad van Egmond, 'Calvinist Thought and Human Rights' in An-Na'im et al (eds), *Human Rights and Religious Values: An Uneasy Relationship?* (1995) ch 14 at 194-195.

[19] Ibid at 194.

[20] Ibid at 197.

[21] Ibid at 196 (quoting Groen van Prinsterer, *Unbelief and Revolution* (1847)). See also Brown, *Sensate Culture* (above n 11), at 82.

[22] See van Egmond, 'Calvinist Thought', at 195.

[23] See ibid at 196. That is not to ignore the history of rulers claiming divine authority acting as despots also.

[24] Brown, *Sensate Culture* (above n 11), at 88.

[25] As Marshall, 'Little Lower than the Angels' (above n 1), at 28 explains: 'There is . . . no such thing as a single Christian perspective on human rights.'

[26] Langan, 'Human Rights in Roman Catholicism' (above n 3), at 26.

[27] Henry, *Christian Mindset* (above n 2), at 65.

[28] Marshall, 'Little Lower than the Angels' (above n 1) at 33. See also Lesslie Newbigin, 'The Secular Myth' in Lesslie Newbigin, Lamin Sanneh and Jenny Taylor, *Faith and Power*: *Christianity and Islam in 'Secular' Britian* (1998) ch 2; Stephen Layman, 'God, Human Rights, and Justice' (1987) 17 *Christian Scholar's Review* 189; John W Montgomery, *Human Rights and Human Dignity* (1995); Michael J Perry, *The Idea of Human Rights: Four Inquiries* (1998) at 11: 'There is no intelligible (much less persuasive) secular version of the conviction that every human being is sacred; the only intelligible versions are religious.'

[29] Marshall, ibid; Montgomery, ibid.

[30] Marshall, 'Little Lower than the Angels' (above n 1), at 37.

[31] *Catechism of the Catholic Church* (1994) at para 1930.

[32] See John W Whitehead, *The Stealing of America* (1983) at 32.

[33] Roy Clements, *Practising Faith in a Pagan World* (1997) at 120 (original emphasis).

[34] Brown, *Sensate Culture* (above n 11), at 84 and 89 (original emphasis).

[35] GA Res 217 A (III), UN Dec A/810 (1948). The UDHR was adopted without opposition by 48 votes to zero with 8 abstentions.

[36] Henry J Steiner, 'Political Participation as a Human Right' (1988) 1 *Harvard Human Rights Year Book* 77 at 79: quoted in Makau wa Mutua, 'The Ideology of Human Rights' (1996) 36 *Virg J Int'l L* 589 at 605.

[37] Henry, *Christian Mindset* (above n 2), at 67-68.

[38] René Cassin, 'From the Ten Commandments to the Rights of Man' in Shoham (ed), *Of Law and Man: Essays in Honor of Haim H Cohn* (1971) 13-25. See Marshall, 'Little Lower than the Angels' (above n 1), at 44. For an excellent comprehensive account, see Johannes Morsink, *The Universal Declaration of Human Rights: Origins, Drafting, and Intent* (1999) ch 8.

[39] Mutua, 'The Ideology of Human Rights' (above n 36), at 629; Karin Mickelson, 'How Universal is the Universal Declaration?' (1998) 47 *UNBLJ* 19 at 22. See Montgomery, *Human Rights and Human Dignity*, 275 n 23: 'The Commission on Human Rights which drafted the declaration . . . and the Third Committee which revised it . . . avoided for political and pragmatic reasons the question of the ultimate origin of human rights—leaving each signatory and reader to supply the lacuna (hopefully with transcendence as Cassin and [Lebanese Christian, Charles] Malik surely did).'

[40] See Michael Freeman, 'The Philosophical Foundations of Human Rights' (1994) 16 *Human Rights Q* 491; Tom Campbell, 'Human Rights: A Culture of Controversy' (1999) 26 *J Law and Soc* 6; Mary Ann Glendon, 'Foundations of Human Rights: The Unfinished Business' (1999) 44 *Am J Juris* 1.

[41] Ivor Richardson, 'Rights Jurisprudence—Justice for All?' in Joseph (ed), *Essays on the Constitution* (1995) at 61-83.

[42] Walsh and Middleton's term for modern secularism's concept of man. See Chapter 2.

[43] Judges 21: 25.

[44] Stephen Mott, 'Human Rights and Christian Thought', *Reformed Journal*, June 1989, 9 at 9.

[45] Langan, 'Human Rights in Roman Catholicism' (above n 3), at 35.

[46] Mott, 'Human Rights and Christian Thought', at 9.

[47] Marshall, 'Little Lower than the Angels' (above n 1), at 57 (italics omitted).

[48] Ibid at 66.

[49] Paul Marshall and Ed Vanderkloet, *Foundations of Human Rights* (1981) at 6-7.

[50] This concept, 'duty-right', is a theological one and does not approximate a neat equivalent in the Hohfeldian scheme of jural relations: see Wesley N Hohfield, *Fundamental Legal Conceptions* (1919) and R W M Dias, *Jurisprudence*, 5th edn (1985) ch 2. John Eekelaar ('What are Parental Rights?' (1973) 89 *LQR* 210 at 213) refers to 'duty-rights' as existing in law 'where Hohfield's conditions for a right are present, but where the claimant's freedom of choice has been replaced by a duty to perform the act.' In the present context, a CC would say a believer's freedom of choice is voluntarily restricted by his or her obedience to God to perform the task.

[51] Paul Marshall, *Human Rights Theories in Christian Perspective* (1983) at 20.

[52] See Mickelson, 'How Universal?' (above n 39), at 26 et seq.

[53] The International Bill of Rights consists of the UDHR, the ICCPR, the International Covenant on Economic, Social and Cultural Rights 1966, and the first Optional Protocol to the ICCPR 1966. See *Wellington District Legal Services Committee* v *Tangiora* [1998] 1 NZLR 129 at 133.

[54] See, for example, Jack Donnelly and Rhoda Howard, 'Human Dignity, Human Rights and Political Regimes' in Donnelly (ed), *Universal Human Rights in Theory and Practice* (1989) 66 at 71. See also Chris Brown, 'Universal Human Rights? An Analysis of the "Human-Rights Culture" and its Critics' in Patman (ed), *Universal Human Rights*? (2000) ch 3 at 40-41.

[55] Mutua, 'Ideology of Human Rights' (above n 36), at 592.

[56] Ibid at 607.

[57] Ibid at 592.

[58] Ibid at 605-606. The phrase in quotations is from the Preamble to the UDHR. For a rejoinder to the 'Western' charge, see Glendon, 'Foundations of Human Rights', at 37.

[59] Thomas M Franck, 'The Emerging Right to Democratic Governance' (1992) 86 *Am J Int'l L* 46 at 79.

[60] Francesca Klug, 'A Bill of Rights as Secular Ethics' in Gordon and Wilmot-Smith (eds), *Human Rights in the United Kingdom* (1996) ch 5 at 53.

[61] Mutua, 'Ideology of Human Rights' (above n 36) at 589 fn 1.

[62] Ibid at 595.

[63] Mary Ann Glendon, 'Knowing the Universal Declaration of Human Rights' (1998) 73 *Notre Dame L Rev* 1153 at 1153.

[64] Louis Henkin, *The Age of Rights* (1990) at ix: Quoted in Mutua, 'Ideology of Human Rights' at 627. For an instructive discussion, see Martin Loughlin, *Sword and Scales: An Examination of the Relationship between Law and Politics* (2000) ch 13.

[65] Mutua, 'Ideology of Human Rights' (above n 36), at 627. The same concern is expressed by Mickelson, 'How Universal?' (above n 39), at 47.

[66] Smolin, 'Church, State and International Human Rights' (above n 5), at 1537.

[67] See Glendon 'Knowing the Universal Declaration' (above n 63), at 1154.

[68] De Blois, 'Foundation of Human Rights' (above n 4), at 28-29.

[69] Marshall, 'Little Lower than the Angels' (above n 1), at 62.

[70] David M Smolin, 'Will International Human Rights be used as a Tool of Cultural Genocide? The Interaction of Human Rights Norms, Religion, Culture and Gender' (1996) 12 *J L and Religion* 143. See also Brown, 'Universal Human Rights?', at 40-41.

[71] Smolin, 'Cultural Genocide?', at 143.

[72] Ibid at 144.

[73] GA Res 180, UN GAOR, 34th Session, Supp No 46, UN Doc A/34/46 (1979). CEDAW entered into force on 3 September 1981.

[74] Smolin, 'Cultural Genocide?', at 170-171. Glendon, 'Foundations of Human Rights'(above n 40), at 3, observes the 'danger of human rights imperialism is

real.' The source is not so much the UDHR but 'the efforts of special interest groups to commandeer human rights for their own purposes . . .'

75 See Michael King (ed), *God's Law versus State Law: The Construction of an Islamic Identity in Western Europe* (1995) at 3-5; Montgomery, *Human Rights and Human Dignity*, at 116.

76 In Rushdoony's words (*Institutes of Biblical Law* (above n 9), at 5-6): 'Every law-system must maintain its existence by hostility to every other law-system and to alien religious foundations, or else it commits suicide.'

77 Malcolm D Evans, *Religious Liberty and International Law in Europe* (1997) at 260-261. See also Malcolm D Evans, 'Religion, Law and Human Rights: Locating the Debate' in Edge and Harvey (eds), *Law and Religion in Contemporary Society* (2000) ch 9.

78 Isaiah Berlin, 'Two Concepts of Liberty' in his *Four Essays on Liberty* (1969) at 122.

79 *Mendelssohn* v *Attorney-General* [1999] 2 NZLR 268 at 273 per Keith J.

80 Ibid at 275.

81 *R* v *N (No 2)* (1999) 5 HRNZ 72 at 77 per Keith J.

82 Arnold R Turner, 'The Human Rights Act 1993' in Patrick (ed), *The Vision New Zealand Congress 1997* (1997) ch 22 at 366.

83 Brian Carrell, *Moving Between Times* (1998) at 46.

84 A statement by an American CC scholar but equally applicable to New Zealand CCs: Richard F Duncan, 'Who wants to Stop the Church: Homosexual Rights Legislation, Public Policy, and Religious Freedom' (1994) 69 *Notre Dame L Rev* 393 at 415.

85 See Wayne Thompson, 'Religious practices and beliefs: A case for their accommodation in the Human Rights Act 1993' [1996] *NZLJ* 106 at 110.

86 See Oliver Barclay, 'The Nature of Christian Morality' in Kaye and Wenham (eds), *Law, Morality and the Bible* (1978) ch 1 at 130-131: 'The utilitarian ideal, the "greatest good of the greatest number", is, so long as it does not overlook the individual, a Christian concern also, and Christian ethics . . . will serve that end in society as a whole.'

87 Berlin, 'Two concepts of liberty'(above n 78), at 131.

88 Chapter 1, section 4 of *Dignitatis Humanae Personae*, 7 December 1965, in Abbott (gen ed), *The Documents of Vatican II* (1966) at 683.

89 Footnote 11 of the *Declaration*: see ibid. Fr Murray was the principal architect of the *Declaration*.

90 John Stuart Mill in his essay *On Liberty* (1859) postulated this 'one very simple principle' governing individual freedom in a liberal society: 'That principle is, that the sole end for which mankind are warranted, individually or collectively, in interfering with the liberty of action of any of their number, is self-protection. That the only purpose for which power can be rightfully exercised over any member of a civilised community, against his will, is to prevent harm to others.' Spitz (ed), *John Stuart Mill, On Liberty* (1975) at 10-11.

[91] Victor Grassian, *Moral Reasoning: Ethical Theory and Some Contemporary Moral Problems* (1981) at 220.

[92] Ibid at 221. I should note Grassian is not (to my knowledge) a CC; he simply aptly articulates the CC position. See also Berlin, 'Two concepts', at 155: 'Even Mill's strenuous efforts to mark the distinction between the spheres of private and social life breaks down under examination. Virtually all Mill's critics have pointed out that everything that I do may have results which will harm other human beings.'

[93] *Human Rights Commission* v *Eric Sides Motors Co Ltd* (1981) 2 NZAR 447.

[94] The mother, ironically, stated to the Tribunal she herself was a born again or committed Christian. Ibid at 455.

[95] The Chief Human Rights Commissioner of the time, Patrick Downey, is a Christian himself: see his essay, 'What rights do individuals have and who cares: A Christian Perspective' in Patrick J Downey, *Human Rights and New Zealand* (1983) at 53.

[96] (1981) 2 NZAR at 452.

[97] New Zealand judges, understandably, are reluctant to traverse church-state questions. See McGechan J's comment in a custody case involving parents of divergent Catholic persuasion, *K* v *K (No 1)* (1988) 5 NZFLR 257 at 279: 'Ghostly conflicts between church and state of bygone centuries in other lands have no modern place in this country.'

[98] *Eric Sides* (1981) 2 NZAR at 448.

[99] Ibid at 449.

[100] Ibid.

[101] Ibid.

[102] Ibid.

[103] Ibid at 450.

[104] Ibid at 461.

[105] Ibid. The Rev Rob Yule is quoted at the conclusion of Chapter 2.

[106] Ibid at 462.

[107] Ibid.

[108] Ibid

[109] Ibid.

[110] See ibid at 464.

[111] Ibid at 463.

[112] Ibid.

[113] Ibid.

[114] Ibid at 462-463.

[115] Ibid at 462.

[116] See Mark Jones, 'Questions of ethical and religious belief: Human Rights Commission v Eric Sides Motor Company Ltd and Others' (1983) 13 *VUWLR* 299 at 308-320.

[117] See ibid at 309.

[118] Ibid. See *CW*, 1 May 1981 (editorial), at 2.

[119] See *CW*, 24 April 1981, feature article and editorial.

[120] *The Christchurch Star*, one of the defendant newspapers, ran a critical story under the headline 'Common sense abandoned in Rights Act', *The Star*, 20 May 1981, at 4: quoted in Jones, 'Questions of ethical and religious belief' (above n 116), at 310.

[121] Jones, 'Questions of ethical and religious belief', at 312.

[122] See Jones, ibid at 314, who cites the submission by the Joint Methodist-Presbyterian Public Questions Committee.

[123] Section 2 of the Human Rights Commission Amendment Act 1981.

[124] *Proceedings Commissioner* v *Boakes*, unrep, Complaints Review Tribunal, Whangarei, EOT 14/92, 13 April 1994.

[125] Ibid at 3.

[126] Ibid at 4.

[127] A view shared by Thompson, 'Religious practices and beliefs' (above n 85), at 113 and Paul Rishworth, 'Religious Belief [section 21(c)]' in *Human Rights Act 1993 Seminar Proceedings* (18 June 1994) 12 at 15-16.

[128] *A Bill of Rights for New Zealand: A White Paper*, *AJHR* 1985, A6.

[129] 'Seminar provides good chance for careful deliberation', *CW*, 15 November 1985, at 9.

[130] 'Canadian Bill', *CW*, 15 November 1985, at 9 (quoting the Rev Bob Dobson).

[131] 'Doubts expressed over Bill', *CW*, 13 December 1985, at 3.

[132] Geoffrey Palmer and Matthew Palmer, *Bridled Power: New Zealand Government under MMP* (1997) at 268. See also Geoffrey Palmer, *New Zealand's Constitution in Crisis* (1992) at 54.

[133] See, for example, Bill Jeffries, Minister of Justice: 'Much of the opposition to the Bill was led by the looney Right; it does not have any merit.' (1989) 502 *NZPD* 13044.

[134] See *Interim Report of the Justice and Law Reform Select Committee: Inquiry into the White Paper—A Bill of Rights for New Zealand*, 9 July 1987, *AJHR* 1987, 1.8A, at 8-9. The Prime Minister, Geoffrey Palmer, acknowledged this: (1989) 502 *NZPD* 13038.

[135] See Palmer and Palmer, *Bridled Power* (above n 132), at 268 and Phillip Joseph, 'The New Zealand Bill of Rights' (1996) 7 *Pub L Rev* 162 at 164.

[136] John Allen, 'Rights Bill not needed', *Coalition Courier*, vol 4, no 1, June 1988, at 1: reproduced as a supplement in *CW*, 24 June 1988.

[137] (1989) 502 *NZPD* 13040. See also White Paper, at para 3.2.

[138] See *Interim Report* at 12. See further Paul Rishworth, 'The Birth and Rebirth of the Bill of Rights' in Huscroft and Rishworth (eds), *Rights and Freedoms* (1995) ch 1 at 18: 'While not centred on any particular provision, there was a sentiment, especially amongst some conservative churches, that the Bill of Rights was part of a conspiracy to foist a dangerous internationalist ideology upon New Zealanders.'

[139] White Paper (above n 128) at paras 4.21-4.22. See also Palmer (1989) 502 *NZPD* 13040.

[140] See White Paper at 5, para 4.19.

[141] Presumably the Reformed Church is referring to the Roman Empire prior to Emperor Constantine's conversion.

[142] The Preamble began: 'Whereas the people of New Zealand uphold principles that acknowledge the supremacy of God . . .' The 1963 Bill is reproduced in Tim McBride, *New Zealand Civil Rights Handbook* (1980) at 593-599.

[143] *Interim Report* (above n 134), at 24.

[144] White Paper (above n 128), at 81, para 10.60.

[145] Their submission was published: see Jerome B Elkind and Anthony Shaw, *A Standard for Justice: A Critical Commentary on the Proposed Bill of Rights for New Zealand* (1986) at 51-52.

[146] *Interim Report* (above n 134), at 143 and 45.

[147] Ibid at 45-46.

[148] Laury Morrison, 'Bill of Rights threatens family life', Supplement to *CW*, 23 January 1987.

[149] Graeme Lee, a CC MP, complained at the absence of family rights in the diluted 1990 Bill: (1990) 510 *NZPD* 3471.

[150] *Humanity*, December 1985. Quoted in 'Unborn child "unsafe"', *CW*, 13 December 1985, at 3.

[151] White Paper (above n 128), at para 10.85.

[152] (1989) 502 *NZPD* 13038.

[153] There were no submissions, for example, from the Coalition of Concerned Citizens, Concerned Christians, or the recently-formed Christian Heritage Party.

[154] (1990) 510 *NZPD* 3471. Richard Northey, in the third reading debate, dismissed this 'Trojan horse' thesis: (1990) 510 *NZPD* 3763.

[155] See Jane Clifton, 'Christian offended by ruling on rights', *Sunday Star-Times*, 12 November 1995, at A3.

[156] This portion of the letter is quoted in Paul Rishworth, 'Coming Conflicts over Freedom of Religion' in Huscroft and Rishworth (eds), *Rights and Freedoms* (1995) ch 6 at 249.

[157] Points made by Rishworth, ibid and Arnold Turner, 'Human Rights Act 1993' (above n 82), at 381.

[158] Clifton, 'Christian offended by ruling'.

[159] See Rishworth, 'Coming Conflicts', at 249-250 and Thompson, 'Religious practices and beliefs', at 111-112.

[160] See Clifton, 'Christian offended by ruling'.

[161] 'Rights druids need sacking' (editorial), *Dominion*, 17 November 1995, at 8. The complaint alluded to is *K* v *M*, 17 August 1994, C149/94. The HRC found a breach of s 65 of the Human Rights Act 1993 in the school's refusal to accede to the Muslim boy's request to wear long trousers. The school did not establish the 'good reason' defence (s 65) either. See Isaacus Adzoxornu, *Brooker's Human Rights Law* (1996) ch 4, at 26.

[162] See 'Agreement with New Zealand', Christian Coalition Manifesto 1996, at 8.

[163] Grant Huscroft, 'Human Rights and Electoral Politics' [1996] *NZLJ* 321.

[164] Pamela Jefferies, 'The Human Rights Commission' [1996] *NZLJ* 399.
[165] Quoted in Chris Daniels, 'Anti-hero parade ad stirs protest', *NZ Herald*, 11 February 1999, at A3.
[166] Quoted in Daniels, ibid.
[167] 'It takes real heroes to stand up to hate', *NZ Herald*, 20 February 1999, at B9.
[168] Letter by Pamela Jefferies to Arnold R Turner, 9 March 1999 (on file with author).
[169] Bruce Logan, 'Human Rights,' *Cutting Edge*, March/April 1999, 16 at 16.
[170] Ibid.

6 The Family and the Challenge of Children's Rights

The Conservative Christian Concept of the Family

The Centrality and Autonomy of the Family

The centrality of the family for conservative Christians (CCs)[1] can never be over-estimated:

> Christians can evangelize the world, but if they are neglecting their family in the process then, at least personally, their work is for nought. . . . The family should be the center of Christian life. No other institution (including the Church) or activity should get in the way of family life.[2]

Within the different Christian traditions, the family's foundational status is expressed somewhat differently.[3] In Catholic teaching, the Christian family is characterized as a 'domestic church'.[4] Its pivotal role in society is also emphasized: 'the family is the original cell of social life' and thus civil authority has a duty to honour and safeguard it.[5] In evangelicalism, the family is similarly revered as a small-scale image of the Kingdom of God.[6] It 'is a divinely-ordained guard against the ambiguities, individualism and experimentation of a modern world which has lost its way morally and religiously.'[7]

The family is 'a community of love under the authority of the parents.'[8] This loving community does not exist for the state. Likewise, a child is not (to quote the American Supreme Court) 'the mere creature of the State'.[9] The family, rather, has its own integrity, destiny, purposes and responsibilities before God.

The 'radical'[10] critique which argues there is no such thing as an antecedent, pre-political distinct entity as the family, that it is a purely political and legal construct (created, defined and regulated thoroughly by the state), is firmly rejected by CCs. 'The personal is political'[11] may be the motto for some critical theorists, but not for them. Instead, the family 'is prior to any recognition by public authority, which has an obligation to recognize it.'[12]

Families are an important type of 'intermediate' institution or 'mediating structure'[13] between the powerful state and the individual.

Such structures consist of relatively small communities (neighbourhood family, church, voluntary association and so on) which socialize individuals, enabling them to see that their self-interest is connected with the interests of others, that their actions have consequences.[14] Such entities may function as a counterweight to potential totalitarian tendencies of the modern state.[15]

How do CCs define the family? Larry Christenson defines a Christian family as 'a family that lives together with Jesus Christ.'[16] This much is incontestable, but what sort of family is it? CCs typically have the traditional nuclear family in mind when they extol the family.[17]

Apart from the core meaning of family (a monogamous married couple living with their children) CCs will often add the rider that the husband be the provider, with the wife at home as a full-time housewife and mother. While this concept of family has a strong currency among CCs—and is probably still the dominant one—there is also a wider conception increasingly held by a minority. Indeed, CCs are by no means a monolithic group on the merits of the traditional 'patriarchal' family structure.[18] Some concede that the nuclear family is neither as traditional nor biblical as most CCs believe.[19] It is pointed out that the nuclear family is 'primarily a modern, urban development of the industrial revolution, whereas the biblical tradition has to do with tribes, clans and extended families (including slaves) in ancient agrarian civilizations.'[20] Sensitive to such criticisms, a small minority of CCs adopt a broader, more relaxed, notion of family which, while it is still based upon monogamous marriage and dependent children, embraces other blood relatives (and possibly close friends). Furthermore, the rigid 'traditional' view of sex roles (working husband, housewife mother) is frequently relinquished in favour of a working couple model, albeit one where the wife's employment is secondary and sufficiently flexible to accommodate the children's needs.

Parenting and Children's Upbringing

Children are expected to obey their parents.[21] Obedience is mandated even when the parents are in the wrong.[22] Parents, under the CC view, are to raise children in 'the way they should go'[23] and thus they have a God-given mandate and responsibility to provide an intellectual and moral framework for the development of their children. *Pace* critics such as Barbara Woodhouse,[24] parents do not 'own' their children and children are not chattels. Rather, parents are 'stewards' entrusted with children by God; they hold the office of parenthood. Rights or authority are necessary to fulfil one's office and discharge one's duties. Rights, as we saw in Chapter 5, are always duty-rights.

Parents cannot of course be despots. Conservative Christians recognize that the state has a legitimate role in checking abuses of parental office. Figure 6.1 endeavours to capture the CC conception:

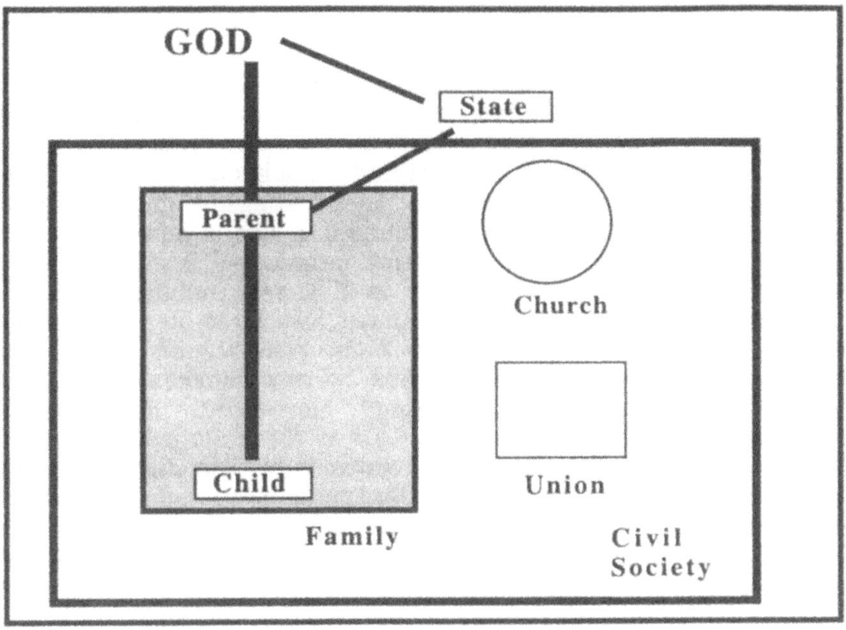

Figure 6.1 A Christian Conception of the Family

There is a direct relationship (represented by the bold vertical line) between God, through the parent, to the child. The state is to the side, and plays a secondary, 'default' role. The family, together with other mediating structures such as churches and unions, comprise civil society. The state is not coterminous with civil society.

At its broadest, the scope of the parental duty, one for which the CC is aware he or she is accountable to God, is to 'lead children into life'.[25] Christenson breaks the duty down into three: to love, discipline and teach.

Love needs no amplification, after all, to love one's own flesh and blood is only natural. In loving one's children 'excessive materialism'[26] is to be avoided; a 'child-centred parenthood'[27] whereby children are heavily indulged and spoilt is an anathema.

Discipline is an important issue for CCs. They reject the 'Rousseauist belief in the goodness of children'.[28] Sin is pervasive, tainting child as much as adult.[29] Corrective discipline thus includes 'the rod' or corporal punishment. I shall return to this topic in Chapter 8.

The third strand of parental duty is to teach one's children. According to Scripture, the primary responsibility for education rests with parents. And it is education in the widest sense—moral values and virtues, indeed 'a total world and life view'.[30] Historically, Christian parents have delegated (or abdicated) much of this responsibility to the churches. Nonetheless, the duty and ultimate accountability remain with the parents. Many CCs are suspicious of the secular public schools' abilities to teach their children in a manner which will not undermine the children's faith. Sex education is an example. Principally, this is a matter for parents, but if it is covered at school, CCs expect moral restraint and sexual abstinence to be taught alongside the technical and hygienic aspects of sexuality.[31] Evolution is also a sensitive issue for some (but not all) CCs. Concerns about 'permissive' sex instruction, the presentation of Darwinian evolution as if it were indubitable fact, and the general relativizing of moral absolutes, has led an increasing number of CCs to withdraw their children from state schools. Thus, recent developments have been the creation of the Independent Christian Schools[32] and the Home Schooling[33] movements. Both are anti-modernist reactions by Protestant CCs to the emergence of a more thoroughgoing secular state school curriculum. The diffuse Protestant flavour of the public schools of yesteryear is gone, leaving many CCs searching for alternatives. For Catholics, their minority status in New Zealand meant that a Catholic-oriented education could never be assured through the state system. The separate Catholic school system reflected a fundamental distrust of the supposed neutrality of a liberal, secular education,[34] an awareness Protestant CCs were to experience belatedly when their cultural hegemony was eroded and the tide began to turn against them.

CCs reject a certain doctrinaire liberal, 'neutral' view[35] that would suspend all religious training in the early years, waiting until the child was sufficiently mature to choose for herself. For one thing, there is always a message or religious impression being transmitted by the parents[36] (whether Christian or non-Christian) within the child's 'primary culture',[37] and by the wider institutions of society—school, neighbourhoods, and especially the popular media. Religion, as indeed with many important things, is 'caught' by the child as much as it is taught. Avoidance of all mention of religion by a child's principal role models, her parents, simply sends the message to the child that religion is unimportant to the people she is most intimately connected with.

Furthermore, prevailing Western culture militates against devout parents' best efforts at a religious upbringing. The 'playing field' is hardly 'level' these days. (It probably never was, nor will be, but the comfort for CCs was that it seemed to tilted in *their* favour in former days.)

To CCs, Christian teaching urges them not to be passive in matters of faith but to positively foster and encourage Christian virtue. The spiritual pilgrimage commences at infancy.[38] Dr James Dobson urges parents to eschew the notion that children should be allowed to decide for themselves in matters of religion. There is a crucial period in a child's life when, as he puts it, 'imprinting' or 'attachment' occurs. This opportunity must be seized when it is available. The venerable Catholic maxim, 'Give me child until he is seven . . .', rings true. Failure to seize the opportunity for fear of 'forcing religion down the children's throats' is regrettable, if not disastrous:

> The absence or misapplication of instruction throughout the prime-time period may place a severe limitation on the depth of a child's later devotion to God. When parents withhold indoctrination from their small children, allowing them to 'decide for themselves,' the adults are almost certainly guaranteeing their youngsters will 'decide' in the negative. If parents want their children to have a meaningful faith, they must give up any misguided attempts at objectivity.[39]

In the adolescent rebellious phase, children may well resent heavy-handed instruction, yet, advises Dobson, 'if the early exposure has been properly conducted, they should have an anchor to steady them.'[40]

While devout parents have the duty to guide and direct children in the faith, the regeneration and conversion of their children is not something parents can achieve by their own sincere and strenuous efforts. God alone saves.[41] Nonetheless, CC parents believe that they have a vital and foundational role in facilitating the (hoped-for) salvation of their offspring.

Here we encounter a difficulty, for it is the aim of some devout parents to so imbue the faith in their children that they will later, as adults, never depart from it. Unfortunately, as many parents lament, children do (sometimes) forgo the faith of their youth. An attempt at religious indoctrination which will carry a child through to his adult years is thus likely to be unavailing. Where it does 'succeed', the question remains whether this coerced participation is of any great merit to the church or to God. As an adult's response to God must be free, so also must a child's.[42] Christians are not, or at least ought not to be, afraid of children questioning their faith. Criticism and reflection however ought, argue CCs, to be undertaken from a base of faith first. T H McLaughlin admirably articulates the aspiration of devout parents this way:

> Their long-term, or ultimate, aim is to place their children in a position where they can autonomously choose to accept or reject their religious faith—or religious faith in general. Since, however, these parents have decided to approach the development of their child's autonomy in religion through exposing their own particular religious faith, their short-term aim is the development of faith; albeit a faith which is not closed off from future revision or rejection. So a coherent way of characterising the intention of the parents is that they are aiming at *autonomy via faith*.[43]

Threats to the Family

Most CCs are adamant the traditional nuclear family is under heavy attack. The threats to the family are legion.[44] The future of the Christian faith itself is inextricably bound up with the fate of the family.[45] It is no coincidence that the preservation and fostering of the family has become the rallying cry of conservative Christian political activists, both in the United States and here. The rise of the 'Moral Right' in New Zealand, as some dub it, first appeared under the banner 'For God, Country, and Family'. The traditional family became 'a successful articulating principle' to galvanize the Moral Right.[46] The Christian Democrats (now renamed 'Future New Zealand'), for instance, adopted the motto 'Families First' as their touchstone and the promotion of 'family values' remains their central policy plank. Likewise, the Christian Heritage Party is 'committed to the biblical concept of the family' and 'believes in promoting family values'.[47] The Rev Arthur Gunn articulates the CC unease:

> Moral absolutes are no longer applicable. Marriage is a thing of the past. Sex should be indulged in freely by all. Good people should be lampooned as being stupid; as being Victorian puritanical bags of misery. Above all, the Christian family must be destroyed. . . . Today, the family is in terrible danger. To destroy religion, the family must be destroyed. Therefore, humanistic education, especially Marxist education, is extremely hostile to the Christian family. Our answer to all these things, if we are married, is to establish a Christian family which will be a witness to all who observe it that here is the only true bulwark of a true society.[48]

The locus of much CC resentment here is often simply 'the state'. It is frequently cast as the principal underminer of parental rights (in contrast to the media or the economy). As one *Challenge Weekly* correspondent put it 'the authority of parents to make decisions regarding the training of their children . . . has been stolen from parents in New Zealand. Scripture makes it clear that God-given authority belongs to parents, not the state, no matter how benevolent it purports to be.'[49]

A Liberal Conception of the Family

It is dangerous to generalize, especially (as we saw in Chapter 3) regarding such a compendious term as 'liberalism'. Nonetheless, and at the risk of caricature, it is possible to identify a liberal concept of the family and of childrearing. Over-emphasizing the individualism inherent in liberal theory, the family is increasingly seen not as a separate entity, but rather as simply the sum of its component parts. There is a consistently reductionist tendency to view the family 'as a collection of individuals united temporarily for their mutual convenience and armed with rights against one another.'[50]

As for what constitutes a proper childrearing with respect to religion in a liberal society, the debate is still ongoing.[51] Some liberals equate any attempt at religious training with indoctrination. John White, for instance, argues:

> if the parent has an obligation to bring up his child as a morally autonomous person, he cannot at the same time have the right to indoctrinate him with any beliefs whatsoever, since some beliefs may contradict those on which his educational endeavour should be based. It is hard to see, for instance, how a desire for one's child's moral autonomy is compatible with the attempt to make him into a good Christian, Muslim or orthodox Jew. . . . The unavoidable implication seems to be that parents should not be left with this freedom to indoctrinate.[52]

What then is an acceptable liberal concept of education? For Bruce Ackerman, liberal education 'provides children with a sense of the very different lives that could be theirs—so that, as they approach maturity, they have the cultural materials available to build lives equal to their evolving conceptions of the good.'[53] Similarly, the goal of a liberal upbringing is, according to Arneson and Shapiro,

> to prepare children for lives of rational autonomy once they become adults. A 'rationally autonomous' life is one that is self-chosen in a reasonable way. Education for rational autonomy thus encompasses two requirements: (1) Upon onset of adulthood individuals should be enabled to choose from the widest possible varieties of ways of life and conceptions of the good and (2) Individuals should be trained into habits and skills of critical reflection.[54]

Parents must cooperate with the state to develop in their offspring 'critical reasoning skills that will enable their children to stand back from the values they have been taught and to subject these values to informed critical scrutiny.'[55] For liberals, it appears one should (to paraphrase the biblical exhortation): 'Train up a child in the way he should go so when he is old he may—utilizing his critical reasoning—depart from it.' As John Rawls would have it, children's education ought to 'include such things as knowledge of their consitutional and civic rights so that, for example, they know that liberty of conscience exists in their society and that apostasy is not a legal crime.'[56]

Joel Feinberg, in a classic essay, depicted a child's right to religious freedom as a sub-species of a child's 'right to an open future'.[57] Children, he argued, have 'rights-in-trust' or 'anticipatory autonomy rights'. These are rights that are preserved for the child until she is of age, but which can be violated 'in advance' before the child is in a position to exercise them. The child's right of religious freedom is a particular 'right-in-trust' which can be violated by adult conduct (by parents, teachers, the state) which effectively forecloses the child's future religious options. It would, seemingly, consist of religious indoctrination (or 'brainwashing', to use a colloquial term) of such severity so as to ensure the child has little or no chance of leaving that religion for another. In the same way an infant's right to walk down the street would be violated, before it could be exercised, by cutting off his legs (Feinberg's graphic analogy), so a child's right to seek the truth and discover God wherever, or in whomever, he finds it, can be violated now by overbearing, systematic indoctrination. Figure 6.2 captures a liberal view:

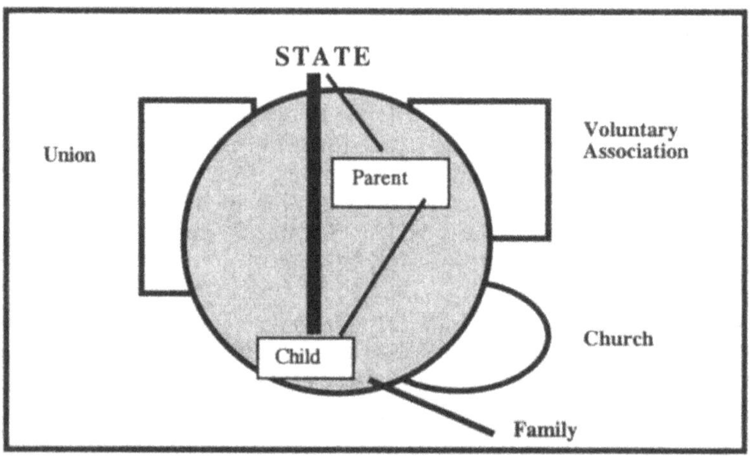

Figure 6.2 A Liberal Conception of the Family

Notice how there is a direct relationship between the state and the child. The child is a 'creature of the state'. Parents are to the side, and perform a purely facilitative role in fostering future citizens. Civil society has disappeared, for the state subsumes all secondary associations—families, churches, unions, voluntary societies—within it. God is absent.

The liberal citizen must always be able to exit, her commitment to any cause or way of life must be contingent—bridges ought never to be burned. As we saw in Chapter 3, Michael Sandel has dubbed this conception of the person, 'the unencumbered self'.

New Zealand family law scholars confirm a growing 'constitutionalization' of family law whereby individual family members are treated as rights-bearers entitled to human rights protections.[58] The root of this trend is laid at the feet of modernity by Bill Atkin and Graeme Austin. In describing modern New Zealand family law, they argue:

> The aptness of the phrase '"modern" family law' is immediately apparent when one foregrounds its modernist aspirations. . . . Much of what characterises family law in the latter part of this century is the result of a long process of debunking and rejection of principles which derive ultimately from decidedly *pre*-modern, Judaeo-Christian traditions . . . . The rules, judicial statements and procedures of modern New Zealand family law indicate, on the surface at least, just how much of a departure from these principles there has been.[59]

(Again, of course, one has to interpolate and reiterate that liberal individualist processes are, in New Zealand, countermanded, to a degree, by the recognition of pre-modern, communal-oriented, Maori influences. Maori interests and family structures are, as I noted in Chapter 3, explicitly taken into account in family legislation and the family courts.[60]) The constitutionalization of modern family law may initially seem odd. Most constitutional documents have a solely 'vertical' focus—they are there to protect the private citizen (or group) against excesses of governmental power.[61] The New Zealand Bill of Rights Act 1990 is no exception, for s. 3 states that the Act only applies to acts done by the various branches (legislative, executive or judicial) of the government and to persons performing public functions. However, the trend, or at least desire, internationally is to give such rights instruments a 'horizontal' application.[62] The state, it is argued, ought to recognize and enforce human rights norms when private individuals (or groups) clash with other private persons. Where rights legislation is invoked in private disputes between, for example, family members, the liberal, modernist model is well and truly in evidence. The courts may be—and, as we shall see in the next chapter, have been—called upon to balance one family member's rights and freedoms against another's.

There is also the well-recognized phenomenon of 'the waning of parental rights' over the course of the twentieth century. Solicitude for the most vulnerable family member, the child, grew to the point where the welfare of the child became, in law, the paramount concern. The child-centred approach was 'surely a development which must command respect; for it was in its almost brutal indifference to the child's fate that the former English law of domestic relations was so woefully defective.'[63] The ascendancy of the welfare of the child in any conflict between parents and children was, of course, to be codified in statute. In 1988 Lord Oliver of Aylmerton could confidently affirm:

> Whatever the position of the parent may be as a matter of law—and it matters not whether he or she is described as having a 'right' in law or a 'claim' by the law of nature or as a matter of common sense—it is perfectly clear that any 'right' vested in him or her must yield to the dictates of the welfare of the child.[64]

The position in New Zealand is no different. The paramountcy of the welfare of the child is expressed in all relevant child legislation.[65]

The United Nations Convention on the Rights of the Child

Parental authority is perceived by many CCs as being constantly undermined by the state. International treaties ratified by the New Zealand government are seen as principal culprits, particularly the United Nations Convention of the Rights of the Child 1989. I select it therefore as a useful case study of the clash between CC and liberal, modernist worldviews and their respective concepts of the family.

The Children's Rights Movement and the Convention

The children's rights movement has spread to New Zealand although some lament there is not yet in this country a sufficiently developed 'children's rights consciousness'.[66] The typical CC reaction to the children's rights movement is a mixture of scepticism and hostility. More rights for children necessarily signals a diminution in parental rights and greater state intrusion into the family. It is a zero-sum game. As one New Zealand CC warned: 'You don't have to be brilliant to know that you cannot give a child rights without taking away the corresponding "rights" from parents.'[67] In CCs' minds, talk of children's rights leads simply to greater state involvement in the family.

Turning to the United Nations Convention on the Rights of the Child 1989 (CRC), that convention far exceeded most child rights advocates' expectations. The CRC was adopted unanimously by the General Assembly of the United Nations without vote on 20 November 1989 and entered into force on 20 September 1990. The CRC has received widespread acceptance with 195 nations having ratified it.[68]

Of the CRC's 54 articles, 38 deal with substantive personal rights for children. (Others deal with definitions, monitoring and implementation of the Convention.) Classifications of the substantive rights vary,[69] but one convenient taxonomy is subdivision into the 'three Ps': protection, provision and participation.[70] The CRC contains extensive provisions on the *protection* of children from discrimination, cruelty, exploitation and neglect. There are, next, articles which provide for the *provision* of a child's basic needs: food, water, health care, education and so on. It is the third cluster of rights, the *participation* rights, which are most significant for present purposes. Cynthia Price Cohen explains:

> Of the thirty-eight articles . . . devoted to substantive rights, at least ten of these have never been recognized for children in any other international instrument. They are all rights of 'individual personality', and include such civil and political rights as the right to leave and return, to privacy, to freedom of expression, assembly, association and religion, among others.[71]

Cohen was puzzled by the inclusion of these autonomy articles since they were not seriously debated in earlier drafts, let alone mentioned in the earlier Declaration of the Rights of the Child. She noted:

> It is difficult to account for this peculiarity in human rights treaty-drafting. . . . the Convention on the Rights of the Child is an anomaly among human rights treaties in that an important segment of the positive law of the Convention was not preceded by rights claims based on natural law nor does it faithfully replicate the content of its related declaration.[72]

It is the advancement of these new participation rights for children which is the occasion for praise, from children's rights theorists,[73] and dismay, from many CCs.[74]

New Zealand signed the CRC in 1989 and it was ratified by the Government on 13 March 1993. In 1993 it was considered by the Court of Appeal. *Tavita* v *Minister of Immigration*[75] concerned the proposed deportation of the appellant back to Western Samoa. Tavita's permit had long since expired and he had become an overstayer. He had had a daughter whilst in New Zealand and shortly thereafter he married her mother. The Minister rejected an application to cancel Tavita's removal warrant.

Tavita's case was he would not be able to support his family in Samoa and they would not come with him. Once deported he could not return for five years, by which time he would be a stranger to his daughter. Evidence by a consultant paediatrician pointed out that the appellant was the primary caretaker of the three-year-old daughter and that his deportation now would 'certainly have a detrimental effect on the child's emotional well-being and development.' Judicial review proceedings were brought to set aside the removal order. McGechan J made an interim order for a stay of Tavita's removal pending appeal. The Associate Minister of Immigration admitted that he had not taken relevant international rights instruments (the International Covenant on Civil and Political Rights 1966 and the CRC) into account.

The Court of Appeal took a dim view of this. To the Minister's argument that the Department was entitled to ignore the international instruments, the President's rejoinder was blunt: 'This is an unattractive argument, apparently implying that New Zealand's adherence to the international instruments has been at least partly window-dressing.'[76] Cooke P referred to the duty of the judiciary to interpret and apply national constitutions, ordinary statutes and the common law in light of 'the universality of human rights.' The New Zealand Court of Appeal did not want to be a pariah in this regard. Far from it, as Sir Robin Cooke left open the possibility that, in an appropriate future case, New Zealanders may have a direct right of recourse to the UN Human Rights Commission, a body which was 'in a sense part of this country's judicial structure'.[77] He continued:

> A failure to give practical effect to international instruments to which New Zealand is a party may attract criticism. Legitimate criticism could extend to the New Zealand Courts if they were to accept the argument that, because a domestic statute giving discretionary powers in general terms does not mention international human rights norms or obligations, the executive is necessarily free to ignore them. This emerges as a case of possibly far-reaching implications.[78]

Tavita is a landmark in establishing the relevance of international rights norms for ordinary domestic jurisprudence in New Zealand.

The CRC has been taken into account many times in other courts.[79] Just three months after its ratification, the High Court in a custody dispute, *H* v *F*,[80] was referred to the Convention. Fraser J remarked, *obiter*, that there were several respects in which Exclusive Brethren beliefs were incompatible with the CRC's principles. Their 'extreme doctrine of separatism' which meant a way of life for families of 'sheltered, but blinkered, contentment'[81] contravened the Convention at several points, 'for example, freedom to seek and receive information and ideas about all kinds (art 13), freedom of association (art 15), the accessibility of higher education to all on the basis of capacity (art 28), and education being directed to the preparation of the child for responsible life in a free society in the spirit of . . . tolerance and friendship among all peoples and . . . religious groups (art 29).'[82] The CRC was easily absorbed in New Zealand family law, indeed, Fraser J ventured: 'In my view, the terms to the United Nations Convention reflect the generally accepted standards of society in this country.'[83]

Is the CRC a Threat to Parental Rights?

Many CCs perceive the CRC to be anti-family and a distinct threat to parental authority. The Christian Heritage Party in its 1999 Manifesto, for instance, promised that (if elected) it would 'protect parental rights by placing reservations against those aspects of the United Nations Convention on the Rights of the Child which undermine a parent's lawful authority.'[84] There are, however, aspects of the Convention that are supportive of the family and parental guidance.[85] Fair-minded critics of the Convention concede that 'in many respects the CRC is surely constructive.'[86] What are these 'constructive' elements?

The Preamble declares that the States Parties to the CRC are:

> *Convinced* that the family, as the fundamental group of society and the natural environment for the growth and the well-being of all its members and particularly children, should be afforded the necessary protection and assistance so that it can fully assume its responsibilities within the community.

The Preamble adds that 'the child, for the full and harmonious development of his or her personality, should grow up in a family environment, in an atmosphere of happiness, love and understanding.' The family is thus viewed as both an essential and a benign institution. Furthermore, parental rights are expressly recognized in Article 5: 'States Parties shall respect the responsibilities, rights and duties of parents . . . to provide, in a manner consistent with the evolving capacities of the child, appropriate direction and guidance in the exercise by the child of the rights recognized in the present Convention.'

Other articles stress the importance of family life. Article 7(1), for instance, stipulates that the child shall have the right 'as far as possible' to know and be cared for by her parents. Article 9(1) declares children ought not be separated from their parents against the latter's will, unless such separation is in their best interests. Children who do become separated from one or both parents have the right to 'maintain personal relations and direct contact with both parents on a regular basis.'[87] Article 18(1) leaves the reader in no doubt that the Convention considers both parents to be the best persons to raise their children: 'Parents or, as the case may be, legal guardians, have the primary responsibility for the upbringing and development of the child.'

The CRC does not ignore the spiritual dimension of life either. Article 14 addresses a child's right to freedom of conscience and religion. Article 27(1) states: 'State Parties recognize the right of every child to a standard of living adequate for the child's physical, mental, *spiritual*, moral and social development.' Again, it is the parents who have the 'primary responsibility' to secure the living conditions necessary for the child's development.[88] Placement of the child temporarily or permanently deprived of her family in any foster, adoption or similar placement is to be undertaken with due regard for, *inter alia*, the child's religious background.[89]

Finally, the Convention's Preamble provides a glimmer of hope for those CCs concerned at rising abortion levels. It states 'the child, by reason of his physical and mental immaturity, needs special safeguards and care, including appropriate legal protection, before as well as after birth'. Pro-life supporters in New Zealand have recently noticed this and used it in argument for tighter abortion controls.[90]

Conservative Christian Concerns with the Convention

CC misgivings about an international convention on children's rights go back to the mid-1980s. Madeline McGilvray, for example, writing for *Challenge Weekly* in 1985, warned readers that the proposed Convention on the Rights of the Child spelt disaster: 'If you thought you didn't have much control over your children now, just wait until this convention is ratified.'[91]

Parent's rights are recognized but in a diluted form. Article 5 refers to the rights and responsibilities of parents to provide appropriate 'direction and guidance', not the right to command obedience. Moreover, parental direction is limited to that which is 'consistent with the evolving capacities of the child', implying a diminishing degree of control as the child approaches adolescence. Furthermore, under the CRC the parental direction is direction in the exercise by the child of *its* rights, not the parents' rights. As American lawyers Hafen and Hafen speculate: 'The question remains whether the parental rights and duties recognized by article 5 extend only to the parental role in enforcing rights granted to children by the CRC.'[92] Defending the CRC against Australian CC attacks, Otlowski and Tsamenyi's explanation would simply confirm the Hafens' fears:

> although the right of parents to provide guidance and direction to their children in the exercise of their rights is unequivocally recognised under the convention, it is clearly a qualified right which is subject to external scrutiny, and which may be overridden in circumstances where, for example, the parents are not acting in the best interests of the child, or where the parents are unreasonably attempting to impose their views upon mature minors who have the capacity to make their own decisions.[93]

If Otlowski and Tsamenyi are correct and that some, perhaps many, parent-child conflicts will now be resolved by external scrutiny (read the state) operating under the vague 'best interests' standard (or even under a test of whether parental direction is 'unreasonable'), then CCs would appear to have some cause for alarm.

Some CCs apprehend that the CRC will result in greater state intrusion into family life by tilting the balance of rights in the parent-child relationship in favour of the child.[94] One New Zealand CC writing to *Challenge Weekly* typifies this concern. Mies Omen asserted: 'The UN Convention on the Rights of the Child undermines God-given parental authority.'[95] And who assumes this authority? 'The Government (not the parents) shall have the final say as to what is "in the best interests of the child" (Article 2)[sic].'[96]

Is there substance to this concern? Article 3(1) does affirm that 'the best interests of the child shall be a primary consideration' in all actions concerning children under the CRC. Article 18(1) declares the best interests of the child shall be the parents' 'basic concern'. Do these articles imply that if parental childrearing falls below some external assessment of the child's best interests, then state intervention is warranted? Could a child invoke the state's assistance against her parents if, in the child's view, her best interests are being unreasonably addressed?

The answer to this depends upon whether the best interests test applies only as a *secondary* criterion, once the family is already subject to state scrutiny, or whether the best interests test applies as a *primary* jurisdictional test.[97] The traditional approach in common law jurisdictions is the former: the welfare of the child test is only applied as a standard once the custody (or access) of the child is in dispute, or when serious neglect or abuse is established and placement is now in contemplation. In New Zealand, the legislature has consistently acknowledged that parents are the best judges of their own children's welfare. Where the welfare of the child test is applied, it has traditionally been invoked as a secondary criterion. Section 6(1) of the Guardianship Act 1968 declares that the father and mother of a child are each a 'guardian' of the child. 'Guardianship' is defined in s. 3 of that Act to mean the custody of the child which includes 'the right of control over the upbringing of a child.' In a 1994 decision, Judge Inglis observed 'unless and until ss 3 and 6 of the Guardianship Act are rewritten the fact remains that the guardians of a child have the sole legal responsibility for the child's care and upbringing.'[98] Section 13(b) of the Children Young Persons and Their Families Act 1989 (CYPFA) underscores this by requiring courts involved in child protection proceedings to be guided, *inter alia*, by: 'the principle that the primary role in caring for and protecting a child or young person lies with the child's or young person's family, whanau, hapu, iwi and family group, and that accordingly (i) A child's or young person's family . . . should be supported, assisted and protected as much as possible; and (ii) Intervention into family life should be the minimum necessary to ensure a child's or young person's safety and protection.'

Parental autonomy is not absolute and the presumption that parents will generally act in the children's best interests is just that. The presumption can be rebutted—courts retain their *parens patriae* jurisdiction. However, state intervention to protect or care for children is not lightly exercised. The threshold for state intervention has, historically, always been demanding. The parents' childrearing conduct must fall below a socially-acceptable threshold which, out of respect for family autonomy, is set at a high level. In New Zealand, the legislature has codified the traditional abuse or neglect threshold. A child is in need of care or protection under the CYPFA only if serious harm, deprivation, ill-treatment or neglect is, or is likely, to be sustained by a child or young person. The courts are mindful that a certain degree of latitude, to accommodate the unconventional, is permissible. So, in one care and protection case involving a family living in a small religious community adhering to 'fundamentalist Christian beliefs', the court reminded itself that it:

> must always be wary of imposing standards and values which are unreasonably high and which fail to recognise the width of parental style and the individuality of people and the rights of individuals to have and to nurture their children in their own religious and personal beliefs.[99]

The welfare of the child test is only a secondary criterion. The primary test for intervention in an intact or united family remains serious abuse or neglect and only when that is proven do the parents' actions fall for scrutiny under the welfare of the child standard.[100]

The real heart of CC concern is the novel introduction of 'choice'[101] rights for children. CCs have no objection to the protection or provision rights. The extension of adult participation rights to children is, however, a completely different matter.

Article 13(1) grants children 'the right to freedom of expression' which includes 'freedom to seek, receive and impart information and ideas of all kinds, regardless of frontiers . . . through any . . . media of the child's choice.' Critics of the CRC fear the breadth of this article will open the door to children being exposed to obscenity, pornography and violence without parental restriction.[102] Of the more extreme assertions is one suggesting that the article gives a teenage child the right to acquire information about devil worship, black magic or homosexuality and pass on such information to other teenagers.[103] The scope of Article 13(1) is untested. Whether restrictions upon a child's freedom of expression would be permitted under the proviso in Article 13(2) (which justifies curtailment if 'public health or morals' so require) is an open question. Given, however, that Article 34 requires states to 'protect the child from all forms of sexual exploitation and sexual abuse' and to take all measures to prevent 'the exploitative use of children in pornographic performances and materials', an unrestricted right to (for example) pornography would appear highly unlikely.

Article 14(1) recognizes a child's right of religious freedom. As I have explored in depth elsewhere, this article does not, *ipso facto*, confer an independent, enforceable right of religious liberty upon a child, but it does give impetus to the common law's incipient acknowledgement of such a right in the near future.[104]

Next, Article 15(1) requires state parties to 'recognize the rights of the child to freedom of association and to freedom of peaceful assembly.' Again, there is the proviso, in Article 15(2), allowing restrictions to be imposed where these are necessary in a democratic society so as to protect public order, safety and so on, or the rights and freedoms of others. Once more the CC verdict is pessimistic: 'Parents are NOT ALLOWED to influence or restrict in any way a child's choice of associates'[105] and 'Parents cannot stop their children from associating with friends of their choice.'[106] Whether this Article goes this far—preventing parents from stopping their children from mixing with others whom the parents deem undesirable—again, remains untested.

Article 16(1) provides: 'No child shall be subjected to arbitrary or unlawful interference with his or her privacy, family, home or correspondence.' Concerns here turn upon the uncertain scope of the child's right to 'privacy'. American case law illustrates privacy has a wide meaning, extending to a person's control over their sexual development and procreative capacities. Thus, speculate Hafen and Hafen, 'a major risk of the CRC's vague reference to privacy rights for children is that its language can be construed to support sexual freedom for children.'[107] CCs have fought many battles on this front in recent times, attempting, usually unsuccessfully, to stem state recognition of adolescents' rights to contraceptive advice, abortion and sex education literature.[108] Article 16(1) also refers to protecting the child from 'unlawful attacks on his or her honour and reputation.' Quite what is contemplated here is unclear. A parent who imposed a night-time curfew or insisted upon certain jewellery being removed might lower her child's reputation amongst her peers. Article 16(2) provides that a child has 'the right to the protection of the law against such interference or attacks' upon her reputation. The article may well be primarily directed at *state* interference with privacy and reputation, (as with the other articles) but the possibility exists, given the ambiguity of the wording, that this participation right will run against the parents.[109]

Conclusion

Conservative Christian and liberal notions of the family differ, as do their respective understandings of the desirable pattern of internal relationships within the family and the upbringing of children. The CC interpretation of the family must appear to secular liberals as antiquated, authoritarian, hierarchical and sexist. CCs are extremely sensitive to public policy concerning the family and the raising of children. For them, the family is critical to the survival of the faith; attacks upon the family, and CC parental prerogatives, elicit a typically hostile reaction.

I noted liberalism's tendency toward atomization of communities. Its emphasis upon individual autonomy has led to a growing 'constitutionalization' of family law. The individual rights of family members are increasingly recognized by the state. While hardly a negative thing *per se*, such constitutionalization carries with it dangers for the integrity and effective working of families. This, at least, is the CC belief. One facet of this incursion of 'rights culture' into family law is the children's rights movement.

While early international instruments regarding children stressed the paternalistic protection of children, the United Nations Convention on the Rights of the Child 1989 broke new ground by recognizing certain participation or autonomy rights for children. The children's rights phenomenon has provoked the same wariness from CCs that human rights theory has. It has perhaps received even greater suspicion and criticism since it impinges upon CC's most cherished institution, the family.

CCs are not opposed to protection and provision rights for children, but many are disturbed at the potential operation of participation rights for their children. In recent decades, parental authority has been undermined by myriad non-legal social and cultural factors. Hence, a potential legal undermining of their authority is hardly welcome. CC fears are exacerbated by their awareness that the 'spirit of the times' is against them. Government and legal authorities, acting in accordance with the 'Wellington worldview', are not, surmise CCs, likely to be sympathetic to them. The CC approach to family and childrearing is, they suspect, likely to be viewed as intolerant, illiberal and outdated by policy-makers and the courts. Courts in New Zealand have, however, shown more sensitivity and latitude toward 'unconventional' parenting approaches than most CCs give them credit. Furthermore, many CCs have failed to discern the positive pro-family and pro-parent elements of the Convention. As for the concern that the CRC will see greater state intrusion into the intact family (under the guise of the broad welfare standard), there are indications from the early New Zealand case law interpreting the Convention that this will not transpire. The welfare test will continue to be applied as a secondary criterion once the state has established its jurisdiction in the customary way (for example, once serious parental abuse and neglect is proven). The traditional common law deference to parental decisionmaking and the state's respect for family autonomy is unlikely to change. The strident and exaggerated concerns of some CCs appear to me to be misplaced. On the other hand, it would be unwise to totally dismiss their concerns, given that many of the CRC's participation articles are yet to be tested.

Notes

1 On the evangelical concept of the family, see James Davison Hunter, *Evangelicalism: The Coming Generation* (1987) ch 4 and James Davison Hunter, *Culture Wars* (1991) ch 7.

2 John W Whitehead, *The Stealing of America* (1983) at 116.

3 See generally Phyllis D Airhart and Margaret Lamberts Bendroth (eds), *Faith Traditions and the Family* (1996).

4 *Catechism of the Catholic Church (Liberia Editrice Vaticana)* at para 2204. For discussion, see Norbett Mette, 'The Family in the Teaching of the Magisterium' in Cahill and Mieth (eds), *The Family* [*Concilium*, 1995/4] (1995) at 74-84.

5 *Catechism*, ibid at paras 2207 and 2210.

6 Larry Christenson, *The Christian Family* (1970) at 10-11.

7 Stephen C Barton, 'Towards a Theology of the Family' in Thatcher and Stuart (eds), *Christian Perspectives on Sexuality and Gender* (1996) 451 at 458.

8 Alan Storkey, *A Christian Social Perspective* (1979) at 234.

9 *Pierce* v *Society of Sisters*, 268 US 510, 535 (1925).

10 See Laurence D Houlgate, 'What is Legal Intervention in the Family? Family Law and Family Privacy' (1998) 17 *Law and Philosophy* 141 at 143. See also Emily Jackson, 'Fractured values: law, ideology and the family' (1997) 17 *Studies in Law, Politics and Society* 99.

11 The motto means in this context 'that the family itself is political, that is, law and social policy together determine which groups of persons count as a family and which do not, and what rights and duties people have within family groups. It follows that the notion of a private sphere of family life that is immune from state intervention is "incoherent"'. Houlgate, 'What is Legal Intervention', at 143.

12 *Catholic Catechism* (above n 4), at para 2202.

13 Michael Novak (ed), Peter L Berger and Richard John Neuhaus, *To Empower People: From State to Civil Society*, 2nd edn (1996) at 158.

14 Timothy Fort, 'The First Man and The Company Man: The Common Good, Transcendence and Mediating Institutions' (1999) 36 *Am Bus L J* 391 at 428.

15 See Stephen Carter, *The Culture of Disbelief* (1993) ch 2.

[16] Christenson, *Christian Family* (above n 6), at 14.

[17] Catholic teaching, for instance, states: 'A man and a woman united in marriage, together with their children, form a family . . . It should be considered the normal reference point by which the different forms of family relationship are to be evaluated.' *Catechism*, at para 2202.

[18] One US sociologist reports 'a remarkable degree of heterogeneity' (at 400) among American conservative Protestants on the right distribution of power and decision-making in families. Traditionalist evangelicals are opposed by 'a coterie of biblical feminists and more equality-minded evangelicals' who challenge 'the hegemonic endorsement of the patriarchal family.' John P Bartkowski, 'Debating Patriarchy: Discursive Disputes over Spousal Authority among Evangelical Family Commentators' (1997) 36 *JSSR* 393 at 406.

[19] See Carolyn Osiek, 'The New Testament and the Family' in Cahill and Mieth (eds), *The Family* (1995) at 1-9.

[20] Barton, 'Towards a theology of the family' (above n 7), at 455.

[21] See Christenson, *Christian Family* (above n 6), ch 3 ('God's Order for Children').

[22] Christenson, ibid at 57.

[23] The scriptural allusion is to Proverbs 22:6. Ellison explains that 'religious conservatives grant that this [healthy psychosocial development—the cultivation of positive self-concept, confidence and social skills] as a worthy object, they stress the need to socialize moral values and to train children in submission to human and divine authority as the preeminent goals of successful parenting.' Christopher G Ellison, 'Conservative Protestantism and the Corporal Punishment of Children: Clarifying the Issues' (1996) 35 *JSSR* 1 at 6.

[24] Barbara Bennett Woodhouse, '"Who owns the child?": *Meyer* and *Pierce* and the child as property' (1992) 33 *Wm and Mary L Rev* 995. See also Jonathan Montgomery, 'Children as Property?' (1988) 51 *MLR* 323.

[25] Storkey, *Christian Social Perspective* (above n 8), at 224.

[26] James Dobson, *Dare to Discipline*, British edn (1971) at 40-41.

[27] Storkey, *Christian Social Perspective* (above n 8), at 231.

[28] Ibid at 232. See also Christenson, *Christian Family* (above n 6), at 95.

[29] See Christenson, ibid, at 98.

[30] Storkey, *Christian Social Perspective* (above n 8), at 243.

[31] See Dobson, *Dare to Discipline*, at 157-160.

[32] See Alaine Coleman, 'Christian Education in New Zealand' in Gilling (ed), *Godly Schools? Some Approaches to Christian Education in New Zealand* (1993) at 119-141.

[33] See Christina Baldwin, 'Christian Home Schooling in New Zealand' in Gilling (ed), *Godly Schools?* at 142-163.

[34] See Christopher van der Krogt, 'Good Catholics and Good Citizens' in Gilling (ed), *Godly Schools?* at 17-39.

[35] To be sure, not all liberals would take this view: see, for example, Kenneth Henley, 'The Authority to Educate' in O'Neill and Ruddick (eds), *Having Children: Philosophical and Legal Reflections upon Parenthood* (1978) 255 at 260-261.

[36] 'Parents cannot avoid revealing their vision of life, their faith, even though this may well be unconscious at times.' L Kalsbeek, *Contours of a Christian Philosophy* (1975) at 209.

[37] Ackerman's felicitous phrase: Bruce A Ackerman, *Social Justice in the Liberal State* (1980) at 159.

[38] *Catholic Catechism* (above n 4), at paras 2225-2226.

[39] James Dobson, *Solid Answers* (1997) at 216.

[40] Dobson, ibid at 217.

[41] Regeneration or 'new birth' is an act of God not man: see John 1:12-13. See further Eric Lane, *Special Children? A Theology of Childhood* (1996) at 101.

[42] See *Declaration on Religious Freedom (Dignitatis Humanae Personae)* in Abbott (gen ed), *The Documents of Vatican II* (1966). The *Declaration*, at para 10, states: 'It is one of the major tenets of Catholic doctrine that man's response to God in faith must be free.'

[43] T H McLaughlin, 'Parental Rights and the Upbringing of Children' (1984) 18 *J Phil Educ* 75 at 79 (emphasis in original).

[44] In Pope John Paul II's words, we are at 'a moment of history in which the family is the object of numerous forces that seek to destroy it or in some way to deform it.' *Familiaris Consortio* [The Role of the Christian Family in the Modern World] (1982) at 12.

[45] See Barton, 'Toward a Theology', (above n 7) at 451 and Whitehead, *Stealing of America* (above n 2), at 115.

[46] Allanah Ryan, '"For God, Country and Family": Populist Moralism and the New Zealand Moral Right' (1986) 1 *NZ Sociology* 104 at 111.

[47] Christian Heritage Party 1999 Manifesto at 5-6. The motto of the CHP is 'For Family, Values and Principles'.

[48] Gunn, 'Family life's under constant threat', *CW*, 18 October 1995, at 11.

[49] Carolyn Killick, 'Parents' authority upheld', (letter), *CW*, 13 April 1994, at 2. See also 'Children's rights law queried', *CW*, 17 November 1993, at 8.

[50] Carl E Schneider, 'Moral Discourse and the Transformation of American Family Law' (1985) 83 *Mich L Rev* 1803 at 1858. See similarly his 'Family Law in the Age of Distrust' (1999) 33 *Family L Q* 447.

[51] The *Journal of Philosophy of Education* has had a lively exchange in recent years. See, for instance, T H McLaughlin, 'Parental Rights and the Religious Upbringing of Children' (1984) 18 *J Phil Educ* 75; Eamonn Callan, 'McLaughlin on Parental Rights' (1985) 19 *J Phil Educ* 111; T H McLaughlin, 'Religion, Upbringing and Liberal Values: a rejoinder to Eamonn Callan' (1985) 19 *J Phil Educ* 119; Peter Gardner, 'Religious Upbringing and the Liberal Ideal of Religious Autonomy' (1988) 22 *J Phil Educ* 89; Eamonn Callan, 'Faith, Worship and Reason in Religious Upbringing' (1988) 22 *J Phil Educ* 183; T H McLaughlin, 'Peter Gardner on Religious Upbringing and the Liberal Ideal of Religious Autonomy' (1990) 24 *J Phil Educ* 107; Peter Gardner, 'Personal Autonomy and Religious Upbringing: the "problem"' (1991) 25 *J Phil Educ* 69; Eamonn Callan, 'The Great Sphere: Education against Servility' (1997) 31 *J Phil Educ* 221; Michael Leahy and Ronald S Laura, 'Religious "Doctrines" and the Closure of Minds' (1997) 31 *J Phil Educ* 329. See also Francis Schrag, 'Religion, Education, and the State: The Contrasting Views of James Dwyer and Warren Nord' (2000) 25 *Law & Social Inquiry* 933.

[52] John P White, *The Aims of Education Re-stated* (1982) at 166-167: quoted in McLaughlin, 'Parental Rights', (above n 43) at 77.

[53] Ackerman, *Social Justice in the Liberal State* (above n 37), at 139. See similarly, Amy Gutmann, 'Children, Paternalism and Education: A Liberal Argument' (1980) 9 *Philosophy and Public Affairs* 338 at 350.

[54] Richard J Arneson and Ian Shapiro, 'Democratic Autonomy and Religious Freedom: A Critique of *Wisconsin* v *Yoder*' in Shapiro and Hardin (eds), *Political Order: NOMOS XXXVIII* (1996) ch 14 at 388.

55 Ibid at 403.
56 John Rawls, *Political Liberalism* (1993) at 199.
57 Joel Feinberg, 'The Child's Right to an Open Future' in Aiken and LaFollette (eds), *Whose Child? Children's Rights, Parental Authority and State Power* (1980) at 124-153. See also Graham Haydon, 'Moral education and the child's right to an open future' (1993) 1 *Int J Children's Rights* 213.
58 See William Atkin and Graeme Austin, 'Family Law in Aotearoa/New Zealand: Facing Ideologies' in Eekelaar and Nhlapo (eds), *The Changing Family* (1998) ch 18 at 312-313.
59 Atkin and Austin, ibid at 306 (emphasis in original).
60 See ibid and Atkin and Austin, 'Cross-cultural Challenges to Family Law in Aotearoa/New Zealand' in Lowe and Douglas (eds), *Families Across Frontiers* (1996) ch 22.
61 On 'horizontal' and 'vertical' effects, see for example, Murray Hunt, 'The "Horizontal" Effect of the Human Rights Act' [1998] *Public Law* 423 and Ian Leigh, 'Horizontal Rights, the Human Rights Act and Privacy: Lessons from the Commonwealth?' (1999) 48 *ICLQ* 57.
62 See ibid.
63 J C Hall, 'The Waning of Parental Rights' (1972) 31 *Camb L J* 248 at 265. See also John DeWitt Gregory, 'Whose Child Is It, Anyway: The Demise of Family Autonomy and Parental Authority' (1999) 33 *Family L Q* 883.
64 *In re KD (A Minor)* [1988] 1 AC 806 at 827.
65 See, for example, s 23(1) of the Guardianship Act 1968; s 6 of the Children, Young Persons and Their Families Act 1989.
66 Graeme Austin, 'Children's Rights in New Zealand Law and Society' (1995) 25 *VUWLR* 249 at 250.
67 Madeline McGilvray, 'Political pressure on parents', *CW*, 18 October 1985, at 12.
68 At the end of 1999 only two states (Somalia and the United States) had not ratified it.
69 See, for example, Michael Freeman, 'Whither Children? Protection, Participation, Autonomy?' (1994) 22 *Manitoba L J* 307 at 317-318 (a fivefold classification).
70 Thomas Hammarberg, 'The UN Convention on the Rights of the Child—and How To Make It Work' (1990) 12 *Human Rights Q* 97 at 100.
71 Cohen, 'The Relevance of Theories of Natural Law and Legal Positivism' in Freeman and Veerman (eds), *The Ideologies of Children's Rights* (1992) ch 5 at 61.
72 Ibid at 61 and 54.
73 See, for example, Freeman, 'Whither children?', at 318: 'It is the first convention to state that children have a right to "have a say" in processes affecting their lives.'
74 See Bruce C Hafen and Jonathan O Hafen, 'Abandoning Children to Their Autonomy: The United Nations Convention on the Rights of the Child' (1996) 37 *Harv Int L J* 449 at 451.
75 [1994] 2 NZLR 257.
76 Ibid at 266.
77 Ibid. But note the Court of Appeal's rejection of the Committee as a 'judicial authority' for the purposes of legal aid under the Legal Services Act 1991 in *Wellington District Legal Services Committee* v *Tangiora* [1998] 1 NZLR 129.
78 Ibid
79 See Pauline Tapp, 'Use of the United Nations Convention on the Rights of the Child in the Family Court' in *New Zealand Law Society Family Law Conference 1998* (1998) at 267-295.

80 (1993) 10 FRNZ 486.
81 Ibid at 493.
82 Ibid at 499.
83 Ibid.
84 *Christian Heritage Party Manifesto 1999*, at 6.
85 A point made by several commentators, for example, Austin, 'Children's Rights in New Zealand' (above n 66), at 263. For a robust defence of the CRC directed at Australian CC attacks, see Margaret Otlowski and B Martin Tsamenyi, 'Parental Authority and the United Nations Convention on the Rights of the Child: Are the Fears Justified?' (1992) 6 *Aust J Fam Law* 137.
86 Hafen and Hafen, 'Abandoning Children to their Autonomy' (above n 74), at 457.
87 Article 9(3).
88 Article 27(2).
89 Article 20(3).
90 See, for example, Dennis Walker, 'Convention on the Child' (letter), *Humanity*, October 1998, at 4.
91 McGilvray, 'Political Pressure on Parents' (above n 67), at 12.
92 Hafen and Hafen, 'Abandoning Children to Their Autonomy' (above n 74), at 458.
93 Otlowski and Tsamenyi, 'Parental Authority' (above n 85), at 144.
94 See ibid at 144-145.
95 Letter (untitled), *CW*, 7 September 1994, at 7.
96 Ibid. Omen refers incorrectly to article 2 instead of article 3.
97 Hafen and Hafen, 'Abandoning Children to Their Autonomy' (above n 74), at 464.
98 *In the Matter of the S Children* [1994] NZFLR 971 at 977.
99 *DGSW* v *T*, unrep, District Court, Christchurch, CYPF 009/25-6/93, 15 July 1994, Judge Strettell, at 2-3.
100 *In the Matter of the S Children* [1994] NZFLR 971 at 977.
101 Hafen and Hafen's term: see 'Abandoning Children to Their Autonomy' (above n 74), at 450.
102 See Hafen and Hafen, ibid, at 469; Otlowski and Tsamenyi, 'Parental Authority' (above n 85), at 155.
103 Otlowski and Tsamenyi, ibid, at 155 (quoting from a paper by Australian CCs attacking the CRC submitted to the Human Rights Commission in 1990).
104 See Ahdar, 'Children's Religious Freedom, Devout Parents and the State' in Edge and Harvey (eds), *Law and Religion in Contemporary Society* (2000) ch 5.
105 Omen, Letter to *CW*, 7 September 1994, at 7 (capitals in original).
106 Goss, 'Parents choices, children's rights', *CW*, 8 February 1995, at 8.
107 Hafen and Hafen, 'Abandoning Children to Their Autonomy' (above n 74), at 474.
108 See, for example, 'Harre defends condom call', *Otago Daily Times*, 10 July 2000 (Youth Affairs Minister, Laila Harre, calls for condoms in state schools); Mayston, 'Dunedin principals uneasy about schools helping arrange abortions', *Otago Daily Times*, 4 August 2000, at 3, (a Christchurch high school arranges an abortion for a 15-year old girl without her parents' knowledge); McCurdy, 'Chastity couple amazed at criticism', *Press*, 1 October 2000, at 3 (educationalists criticize Australian 'no-sex-before-marriage' seminars being offered at state schools).
109 Hafen and Hafen, 'Abandoning Children to their Autonomy' (above n 74), at 472.

7 Religious Upbringing

This chapter examines a key conservative Christian (CC) concern with the United Nations Convention on the Rights of the Child 1989 (CRC). Some CC parents believe that they will now be hindered in their crucial obligation to teach and transmit the faith: 'Parents have the right to provide direction "consistent with the evolving capacities of the child", but cannot coerce a child to attend church or stop them attending a church they disagree with.'[1] Another feared: 'Parents are NOT ALLOWED to influence or restrict in any way a child's views on morality or religion.'[2] Perhaps the foremost parental right cherished by CCs is the right to direct their children's religious upbringing. Most CCs would, I suspect, heartily agree with Dr James Dobson:

> There is nothing more important to most Christian parents than the salvation of their children. Every other goal and achievement in life is anemic and insignificant compared to this transmission of faith to their offspring. This is the only way the two generations can be together throughout eternity. . . [3]

I shall analyze the present state of the law governing the rights of parents to control the religious upbringing of their children in the intact and united family. By 'intact' I mean the situation where the parents are married and living together; a 'united' family is one where the parents (if not the children) are of one accord on how the children should be raised.[4] The usual limitation upon parents' control of their children's religious upbringing is risk of harm to the children. The CRC appears to simply reaffirm both the traditional right of religious upbringing and its standard limitation.

The law relating to the religious upbringing of children is a large subject. Space dictates that I omit a comprehensive discussion of two further important topics: (1) the scope of the parental right to control religious upbringing in the 'fractured' family, that is, where the parents are separated or divorced, and (2) the ambit of the parental right of religious upbringing if the law should recognize an independent legal right of religious liberty for a child. These are intriguing questions that I have explored in depth elsewhere.[5]

From Paternal Supremacy to Joint Parental Control

There was a period in English legal history when the state restricted the authority of parents to rear children in the religion they deemed fit.[6] The sixteenth and seventeenth centuries witnessed various statutes preventing Roman Catholic parents from inculcating that faith in their children. The eighteenth century saw a gradual relaxation of these anti-Catholic measures explicable, it seems, because Protestantism felt itself sufficiently secure by then.[7] By Lord Eldon's time, the English courts were prepared to look with equal favour on all religions.[8]

Religio Sequitur Patrem

During the nineteenth century, the English common law embraced the doctrine of paternal supremacy in matters of religious upbringing. Control of the children's religion was for the father; thus the maxim, *religio sequitur patrem*. In the first of the *Agar-Ellis* cases, in the late 1800s,[9] Malins VC propounded the law clearly:

> The principles of this Court are the principles of common sense and the principles of propriety, that the children must be brought up in the religion of the father. The father is the head of his house, he must have the control of his family, he must say how and by whom they are to be educated, and where they are to be educated, and this Court never does interfere between a father and his children unless there be an abandonment of the parental duty . . .[10]

The Court of Appeal endorsed this summary fully. There was a strong theological flavour to the doctrine, with the *Agar-Ellis* judges constantly referring to the father's right of control within the family as 'one of the most sacred of rights'[11] and required as much by 'the laws of Christianity'[12] as by the laws of England. In the second *Agar-Ellis* case, Lord Brett MR observed: 'It seems to be that in the word "sacred" the Vice Chancellor has summed up all that I have endeavoured to express. . . . The rights of a father are sacred rights because his duties are sacred duties.'[13] Coupled with the deference to a father's divinely-ordained duty and a reluctance to 'interfere with the natural order and course of family life'[14], was a pragmatic acknowledgement of judicial incompetence in this area. Bowen LJ articulated why, palpable unfitness aside, it was better to trust paternal judgment:

> It is far better that people should be left free, and I do not believe that a Court of Law can bring up a child as successfully as a father, even if the father was exercising his discretion as regards the child in a way which critics might condemn. . . . the natural law . . . points out that the father

> knows far better as a rule what is good for his children than a Court of Justice can. . . . it is not mere disagreement with the view taken by the father of his rights and the interests of his infant that can justify the Court in interfering. If that were not so we might be interfering all day and with every family.[15]

Although the father's rights were paramount they were not impregnable. The courts would interfere where the father had been demonstrated to be gravely unfit. The cases speak of a father being deprived of his rights where he 'forfeited, abandoned or waived' his rights.[16] Immoral conduct would also disbar him. As to what precisely constituted an abandonment of parental rights, the courts frequently differed.[17] Certainly, an ante-nuptial agreement between father and mother directing that the children be raised in a particular faith (or more to the point, a faith other than the father's) was not binding.[18] A father could always change his mind. There were, even so, limits. For example, if a child was of such a stage in his religious education that a change in his religion would be 'dangerous and improper',[19] the court might thwart interference with the child's settled religious identity.

The *Agar-Ellis* cases were the apotheosis of paternal power. The outworking of the *religio sequitur patrem* principle could sometimes lead to draconian results. In *Agar-Ellis* itself, the Protestant father succeeded in effectively severing links between his daughter, aged nearly 17, and her Catholic mother. Upset at the mother's efforts at a Catholic upbringing, the father removed his daughter from her care, allowing her to visit her mother only once a month, whilst requiring all correspondence between the mother and the girl to be first vetted by him. Such a severe approach, reflecting a callous disregard for his daughter's best interests, could hardly be commended. Two of their Lordships in the landmark 1986 *Gillick* judgment vilified the Victorian judges' vindication of the father's rights in that case.

Joint Parental Authority

The father's supremacy remained intact under the common law until abrogated by statute in the 1920s. Beginning that decade, courts involved in child custody or upbringing matters were instructed to have regard, first and foremost, to the best interests of the child; any claim of paternal superiority was rejected. Section 2 of the Guardianship of Infants Act 1926 (NZ) read:

> the Court in deciding that [child custody or upbringing] question, shall regard the welfare of the infant as the first and paramount consideration whether from any other point of view the claim of the father, or any right at

> common law possessed by the father . . . is superior to that of the mother, or the claim of the mother is superior to that of the father.

Hence, both parents share an equal right to control the religious upbringing of the children. From 1926 to the present day in New Zealand, all religious upbringing questions in court proceedings are to be judged against the paramount test of the child's welfare.

The leading case on religious upbringing in the first half of the twentieth century was *In re McSweeney*, a 1943 Court of Appeal decision.[20] Myers CJ endeavoured to follow the common law approach of father's superiority, but his was a lone dissenting voice. The three judges in the majority firmly rejected the *religio sequitur patrem* approach and emphasized that the welfare of the child must be paramount in resolving disputes over religious upbringing and custody.

The case involved two children, a boy of 13, and his sister, aged eight. Both had been baptized as Roman Catholics but had, with the father's full knowledge and acquiescence, been brought up as Protestants. They had attended Sunday school under the direction of their Protestant mother and there was no evidence they had ever been inside a Catholic church or been pupils at a Catholic school. By the time of trial both parents were deceased and the children were happily living with a Mrs Prouting, a Protestant friend of the mother. She had continued to bring them up as Protestants and taken good care of them with the approval of the father while he was alive. (The father had died two years after the mother.) The present action was brought by the testamentary guardian appointed under the father's will, a Fr Fogarty. The priest, pursuant to the will, sought the custody of the children to comply with the father's wishes that they be brought up as Catholics. Fr Fogarty had been rebuffed in his attempts to give religious instruction to the children at the rural state primary school they were attending. His proposal was for the children now to be cared for by a Catholic institution. The Court of Appeal were content to quote from *Ward* v *Laverty*,[21] where the House of Lords had pronounced the distinct change in emphasis from a father's right to the child's welfare. As Smith J explained:

> The same deference is not paid today to the views of the father apart from his merits. By law, the father has now no claim which is superior to that of the mother when the custody of a child is in issue before the Court and the value of the independent personality of the child is implicit in the statutory declaration that in all questions of the custody, the Court shall regard the welfare of the child as the first and paramount consideration.[22]

It would be 'sheer caprice and a great hardship' for the children to now be uprooted from persons whom they regarded as their father and mother, and for the 'whole current of their lives' to be reversed simply to satisfy the testamentary wishes of the father.[23]

Recognition under Domestic and International Law

The parental right[24] to religious upbringing is recognized by statute in New Zealand. Section 3 of the Guardianship Act 1968 defines 'guardianship' to include 'the right of control over the upbringing of a child' and 'upbringing' is, in turn, defined (in s. 2(1)) to include 'education and religion.' This parental right is reinforced by the free exercise of religion provision in the New Zealand Bill of Rights Act 1990. Section 15 declares that: 'Every person has the right to manifest that person's religion or belief in worship, observance, practice or teaching, either individually or in community with others, and either in public or in private.' In an important case, *Re J*, the Court of Appeal affirmed that the parental right to religious upbringing fell within s. 15 (and s. 13, which deals with freedom of thought and belief): 'The right of parents to manifest religion extends to bringing up and educating children in that religion until such time as their children are able to exercise their own freedom of religion (see art 18(4) of the International Covenant [on Civil and Political Rights 1966]).'[25]

Parental control over religious upbringing is also supplemented by certain provisions in the education legislation. For example, s. 79 of the Education Act 1964 authorizes parents to withdraw their children from any religious instruction engaged in by a state primary school. Section 21 of the Education Act 1989 permits parents to conduct their own course of education for their children at their home, subject to certain curriculum guidelines. In other words, s. 21 allows 'home schooling', a form of education undertaken by parents, the vast majority of whom are religiously devout.[26]

The domestic statutory provisions on parental religious childrearing are underscored by similar rights accorded by international conventions. The International Convenant on Civil and Political Rights 1966[27] was quoted by the Court of Appeal in *Re J* to buttress the domestic provisions on parental religious childrearing. Article 18(4) reads:

> The States Parties to the present Covenant undertake to have respect for the liberty of parents and, when applicable, legal guardians to ensure the religious and moral education of their children in conformity with their own convictions.

Similarly, Article 5 of the United Nations Declaration on the Elimination of All Forms of Intolerance and of Discrimination Based on Religion or Belief 1981 sets out a detailed interlocking system of religious rights and duties within the family. This UN Declaration, while not of the same status as a Convention, nonetheless has been taken into account by the New Zealand courts.[28] Article 5(1) mirrors the language of Article 18(4) of the ICCPR in giving parents 'the right to organize the life within the family in accordance with their religion or belief. . .' Article 5(2) provides that children have a right to receive religious education in accordance with their parents' wishes and ought not to be compelled to receive any such teaching conflicting with that desired by the parents. Children not under the care of their parents are entitled, under Article 5(4), to have their parents' expressed wishes on religion taken into account in their upbringing.

The Limit of Parental Religious Child Rearing: Endangerment

> Freedom to manifest one's religion or beliefs may be subject only to such limitations as are prescribed by law and are necessary to protect public safety, order, health, or morals, or the fundamental rights and freedoms of others.

Article 18(3) of the ICCPR, quoted above, embodies the standard limitation on civil rights and freedoms found in UN instruments.[29] The Court of Appeal in *Re J* quotes it when cautioning that 'the right to manifest one's religion and belief in practice cannot be absolute. . .'[30] Drawing from Lord Scarman's speech in *Gillick*,[31] the Court of Appeal affirmed what has now become (in the last decade or so) the received wisdom on parental rights in family law. Gault J reminded that 'the scope of parental rights is reflective of parental duties towards children.'[32] The prime duty is, of course, to care for and nurture children until adulthood. The scope of the parental right of religious upbringing is limited in two broad ways.

First, there is the traditional limitation: parental upbringing practices cannot place at risk the child's life, health or welfare, what I shall call the 'endangerment' limitation for shorthand purposes:

> The parents' right to practice[sic] their religion cannot extend to imperil the life and health of the child. Before it would become necessary to embark upon a s 5 examination it would be necessary to define the scope of the right to practise religion as extending (notwithstanding the right of a child to life) to the right to refuse medical treatment for the child on religious grounds even in circumstances where it is evident death will ensue without that treatment. We are not able to do that. . . . We define the scope of the parental right under s 15 of the Bill of Rights Act to manifest their religion in practice so as to exclude doing or omitting anything likely to place at risk the life, health or welfare of their children.[33]

The courts have always retained their inherent *parens patriae* (literally 'parent of the country'[34]) jurisdiction to care for and protect children in need of such protection. The classic articulation of the boundary of the parental religious childrearing right is that of the American Supreme Court in *Prince* v *Massachusetts*:

> Parents may be free to become martyrs themselves. But it does not follow that they are free, in identical circumstances, to make martyrs of their children before they have reached the age of full and legal discretion when they can make that choice for themselves.[35]

Second, and more controversially, the right to bring up children in the religion of the parents' choosing extends 'until such time as their children are able to exercise their own freedom of religion'.[36]

Life-threatening Situations

Where a child's life is at stake, parental wishes grounded in religious beliefs are to no avail. Courts in New Zealand, as elsewhere,[37] have authorized the requisite medical treatment and overridden the parents' refusal of consent. Parents simply are not permitted to hold the power of life and death over their children and cannot elect to deny urgent life-preserving medical treatment for their children.[38]

A tragic illustration was the recent case of the devout Samoan parents convicted of failing to provide their 13-year-old son with the necessaries of life in terms of s. 152 of the Crimes Act 1961.[39] Tovia Laufau died when the cancerous tumour on his leg was left untreated. The parents (and Tovia's) fervent hope that God would provide a cure was to prove unfulfilled. The distraught parents received a 15-month suspended prison sentence.

In life-threatening situations the court will customarily intervene by placing the child under the temporary guardianship of the court, whilst authorizing suitable medical personnel to give consent on its behalf to the necessary medical procedure. The High Court draws its authority to do so from either its inherent *parens patriae* jurisdiction[40] or from its statutory power under s. 9 of the Guardianship Act 1968. The Family Court, and in limited circumstances the District Court, can make orders enabling the Director-General of Social Welfare to give consent under the Guardianship Act.[41]

Re J is itself a good illustration of the courts' approach in life-threatening situations. It is one of the many Jehovah's Witnesses blood transfusion cases where parental refusal to consent to medical treatment has been gainsaid.[42]

A three-year-old boy, J, had suffered a life-threatening nose bleed. His Jehovah's Witnesses parents declined consent for a blood transfusion, a procedure deemed necessary and urgent by the medical staff at the local hospital. Hospital, police and Social Welfare personnel obtained the relevant court order without informing the parents. The Director-General of Social Welfare was appointed guardian of the child for the purpose of authorizing the transfusion. J received the transfusion. Expert evidence was that J would have died if he had not received it. A second transfusion was also necessary due to the boy's dangerously low haemoglobin level. Subsequently, the Director-General applied to the High Court under s. 9 of the Guardianship Act for J to be placed under the guardianship of the Court, an application that was duly approved. The High Court[43] appointed a doctor as an agent of the Court for the purposes of consenting to medical treatment, whilst the parents were appointed as general agents of the Court in all other respects. J recovered and required no further transfusions. J's parents through all this were 'deeply upset.'[44] Unfortunately, J had contracted ARDS (Adult Respiratory Distress Syndrome), itself a life-threatening condition as a result, it seemed, of the blood transfusions. The Director-General attempted to have the guardianship order made by the High Court discharged, but that was opposed by J's parents so as to preserve their right of appeal.

The parents argued that the order was in breach of their fundamental rights as parents guaranteed under the New Zealand Bill of Rights Act 1990. They submitted that, pursuant to ss 13 and 15 of the Act, they were guaranteed the right to bring up children according to their (the parents') beliefs and to make decisions as to their children's medical treatment according to those beliefs. The Court of Appeal was in agreement thus far: 'The upbringing of children extends to making decisions as to health and medical treatment. That is a right long recognised under the common law in any event . . . though, as [*Gillick*] makes clear, it was never absolute.'[45]

Counsel submitted that those parental rights could only be limited to the extent justified in a free and democratic society (s. 5 of the Act). The burden, it was argued, rested upon that state to prove that the consequent limitation upon the rights was justified and that it represented the least intrusive means necessary in the circumstances. The state ought to have established (to 'a high degree of probability') that the blood transfusion was necessary, that it was not ineffective or controversial, that it would not cause substantial harm to the patient and that there was no alternative medical management (acceptable to the guardians) available.[46] (Jehovah's Witnesses have long maintained that blood transfusions are a high risk and dangerous medical procedure and have pointed to alternative procedures to accomplish the same ends.[47]) Counsel for the parents acknowledged that J had a paramount right to life under s. 8 of the Bill of Rights Act. However, his present concern was the rights of the parents.

The approach sought by J's parents was rejected. It was not a matter of deciding whether the state had justifiably restricted the parents' rights. Rather, it was a question of what were the parents' rights to begin with. Taking a child-centred approach, the Court of Appeal held that certain fundamental rights and interests *of the child* inherently circumscribed the rights of the parent. One did not need to balance the interests of the state with those of the parents, since parents' rights were inherently limited anyway, in this case by the rights of the children. The Jehovah's Witness parents' religious freedom was intrinsically limited by their three-year-old son's right to life.

The Court of Appeal's approach is, to use North American constitutional parlance, 'definitional balancing'.[48] No freedoms or rights are absolute. All are limited. The question is: *how* are they limited? Are rights intrinsically limited, such that their scope is restricted by reference to other rights and freedoms? Freedom of religion, under this view, can by its very nature never extend beyond the point at which it infringes another person's fundamental rights and freedoms. There is no religious liberty to sacrifice children since, by definition, religious liberty only extends to religious practices that do not harm others. Or, are rights widely-defined and only limited when the state succeeds, in the particular instance, in justifying the restriction as necessary?

The 'definitional' versus 'ad hoc' balancing debate is, arguably, simply the 'horizontal/vertical effect' debate from another angle. This is a large subject which cannot be pursued here, but I find myself firmly in the vertical camp. It is better, I believe, to see the issue in terms of the state's interests conflicting with the citizen's, rather than one citizen's interests conflicting with another's. Traditionally, constitutional protections are designed to safeguard the individual's (or group's) fundamental rights and freedoms against government interference. I suggest the proper approach is to first define the right broadly. Having done so, it may be discovered that some state law has the purpose or effect of substantially impeding the free exercise of the right. The next stage is to weigh the state interest in restricting the right against the individual's interest in exercising it. This final balancing is an 'ad hoc balancing', viz, is the state's interest on *this* occasion sufficiently weighty in a free and democratic society to justify *this* particular restriction upon the right? The onus lies upon the state to justify the limitation—which may, or may not, be an easy task.[49]

The majority in a 1995 Canadian Supreme Court case involving Jehovah's Witnesses children and blood transfusions, *B(R)* v *Children's Aid Society of Metropolitan Toronto*,[50] were strongly in favour of ad hoc not definitional balancing.[51] (This case was relied upon by the parents in *Re J.*) La Forest J pointed out that the Supreme Court had 'consistently refrained from formulating internal limits to the scope of freedom of religion in cases where the constitutionality of a legislative scheme was raised; it rather opted to balance the competing rights under section 1 of the Charter'.[52] In the majority's opinion it was much sounder to leave to the state the burden of justifying the restrictions it had chosen.[53] Section 1 of the Charter was specifically designed for balancing rights. That provision, like s. 5 of the NZ Bill of Rights Act 1990, permits fundamental freedoms to be limited when such limits are demonstrably justified in a free and democratic society. Applying the ad hoc balancing methodology, it found that parental religious freedom had been infringed by the Ontario Child Welfare Act's wardship procedure, insofar as it had overridden the parents' right to choose medical treatment according to their religious beliefs. Although the Act's procedure constituted a 'serious infringe[ment]'[54] on the parents' religious liberty, the restrictions were held to be 'amply justified'[55] under s. 1 of the Charter. The Ontario Child Welfare Act gave effect to the state interest in protecting children at risk, something which was 'a pressing and substantial objective.'[56] In balancing the state's interest with the parents' interest, the statute had restricted parental freedom no more than was necessary. The wardship procedure was carefully examined—something which is not required under the more abstract definitional balancing approach—and found to be acceptable in terms of accommodating parental religious convictions[57] whilst still protecting the children.

In *Re J*, the High Court had outlined a desirable protocol which had several built-in features designed to assuage the concerns of devout parents temporarily displaced as guardians under a wardship order.[58] By placing the burden of justifying restrictions of parental rights upon the state, the Court in *B(R)* ensured that the wardship procedure would remain no more invasive of parental rights than was necessary. The Court of Appeal's approach, however, obviates the need for such careful scrutiny.

Non Life-threatening Situations: Health

The position in New Zealand when the child's life is not threatened is unclear. Even the voluminous American case law on this point is unhelpful, with decisions being fairly evenly split on whether or not to intervene and override parental wishes.[59] Although each case must be dealt with on its own merits, obvious factors would seem to be: (1) the severity of the condition; (2) its curability or reversibility; and (3) the invasiveness of the proposed treatment and its prospects of success.[60] Certainly, it would be undesirable to circumscribe the *parens patriae* jurisdiction to situations where the child is at 'death's door'[61] but, on the other hand, judicial intervention to override parental religious rights where (say) a minor cosmetic improvement is at issue would seem unwarranted.

The only New Zealand case in point appears to be *Liu*. A 12 year-old Taiwanese boy had a detached retina in his right eye and was completely blind in his left eye. Expert medical opinion was that Joseph would totally lose his sight in his right eye within a few weeks if surgery did not take place. Joseph's parents opposed this. First, they disagreed with the medical diagnosis and its gloomy prediction. Second, they believed God would heal their son and indeed 'that the miracle ha[d] already begun.'[62] The parents were committed Baptists and had emigrated on the basis that God had spoken to them and promised to heal Joseph if they left their homeland (Taiwan). The parents testified that Joseph had no sight in his right eye but that recently his vision had improved (an assessment not concurred with by the attending doctor). They believed that 'what is best for Joseph is that he not have this operation. If he does, they [the parents] believe he will be subjected to terrible pain and suffering.'[63] Joseph deposed in a short affidavit:

> I do not to want to have the operation on my right eye because I believe that God is curing my right eye. I believe that this miracle has already begun. Since I was examined by Doctor Hadden on 4 July 1996, the vision in my right eye has improved. . . . I have had explained to me that the doctors say I will go blind if I do not have the operation. I understand this but believe God will cure me.[64]

Despite the sincere beliefs of the parents and Joseph, Tompkins J preferred to accept the prognosis of the two consultant ophthalmic surgeons, viz, without intervention blindness would occur in the right eye within a matter of weeks, and thus complete blindness given the blindness already in Joseph's left eye. Applying *Re J*, the High Court held that declining the operation would 'place at risk Joseph's health and welfare.' Against this were a number of considerations: the chances of success of the operation (between 70 to 80 per cent); detachment of retina again, even if the procedure was carried out; the view of parents and child, and; the emotional trauma to the family from the judicial intervention. Tompkins J was aware this was a case in the 'grey area':

> most of the other cases that have come before the courts have been blood transfusion cases which at least in most of them, involve a clear cut choice between life and death. In this case, the choice is not clear cut because success of the operation cannot be guaranteed and it is a choice between total blindness and still significantly limited vision.[65]

Weighing up all these considerations in what was 'not an easy' decision, 'the proper course for the court to take [was] to authorise the operation to be carried out.'[66] The parents were at all times to be kept fully informed of the relevant medical management and legal processes concerning Joseph.

Given the courts' adherence to the paramount principle of the welfare of the child, it may be that the majority of decisions in the grey area (of non-life threatening yet curable afflictions) will be resolved in favour of intervention. If the court believes that parental religious scruples are standing in the way of treatment that would reasonably improve the child's health and wellbeing, it is hard to see it not intervening to promote the child's best interests. American examples where the state did intervene to override parental objections to treatment include: surgery to correct a facial deformity;[67] a blood transfusion to save a child's right arm;[68] and treatment for a boy's arthritic knee condition.[69] In these situations it is likely that a New Zealand court would also intervene.

Most of the cases in the present context involve infants and pre-schoolers, but some involve adolescents of reasonable maturity. Section 11 of the Bill of Rights Act 1990 provides that: 'Everyone has the right to refuse to undergo any medical treatment.'[70] In *Liu*, Tompkins J noted:

> If Joseph were an adult, s 11 would give him the right to refuse to undergo this operation. But at the age of 12, he lacks the capacity to exercise his right under that section. . . . Whilst of course full weight should be given to Joseph's views, I do not consider that s 11 of the Bill of Rights Act can be determinative.[71]

In *Liu*, as we have seen, the boy's eloquent views, whilst weighed in the balance, did not prove determinative. Neither did Tovia Laufau's opposition to cancer treatment excuse his parents from their duty to provide the necessaries of life.[72] In *Auckland Healthcare Services Ltd* v *T*, a 12-year-old suffering from malignant lymphoma, A, was described by Paterson J as 'both mature and positive in her present situation.'[73] Despite the medical prognosis that without chemotherapy A would die, her parents 'because of genuine and sincere religious beliefs'[74] would not consent to such treatment. A herself expressed similar views but, as her counsel indicated, she was 'somewhat confused'.[75] The High Court followed *Re J* and held that A ought to be placed under the guardianship of the Court and the treatment administered. His Honour also referred to Article 6 of the CRC which recognizes that children have an inherent right to life and which requires state parties to 'ensure to the maximum extent possible the survival and development of the child.' In this life-threatening situation the state's interest in the preservation of the child's life was uppermost.

Non Life-threatening Situations: Education

Where parental religious convictions result in their children being seriously deprived of education, the line has been crossed.

In the well-known American case, *Wisconsin* v *Yoder*,[76] the Supreme Court held that a compulsory school attendance law which required parents to send their children to school until the age of 16 violated Old Order Amish parents' religious freedom and infringed their constitutional right to direct the religious upbringing of their children. Crucially, the Court found that accommodating the sincere religious convictions of the Amish by foregoing one, or at the most two, addition years of compulsory secondary education would not impair the physical or mental health of the children nor 'result in an inability to be self-supporting or to discharge the duties and responsibilities of citizenship . . .'[77] The children had, in the first eight years of schooling, acquired enough formal education 'to participate effectively and intelligently in American democratic process . . .'[78] However, as Justice White observed in a concurring opinion, it would be 'a very different case'[79] if the Amish parents had forbade their children from attending any school at any time and from complying in any way with state educational standards. It was only because the Amish children had, in the first eight years, already acquired 'the basic tools of literacy to survive in modern society'[80], together with the fact that the further year or two's compulsory education would add little to this, that the parents' claims prevailed.

The kind of religiously motivated educational deprivation alluded to by Justice White in *Yoder*, calling for state intervention, is well-illustrated in the New Zealand case, *Re The Seven P Children*.[81]

The Ps and their seven children, aged from one to 16, lived in 'spartan and primitive conditions'[82] in an isolated mountainous rural area near Levin. Their house had no mains electricity, no telephone, partly-lined interiors and unglazed windows covered with plastic. The parents were staunch Seventh Day Adventists. They were examples of separatist fundamentalists (see Chapter 2). The problem was that the parents' isolated, world-denying, lifestyle[83] had disastrous consequences for the children. Since 1982—nine years previous to the court proceedings—none of the children had received any more than minimal formal education.[84] Moreover, the evidence showed the parents had become 'expert at passive resistance'[85] to any outside attempt to provide formal education for the children. For instance, the eldest boy, R (aged 16), was found to have a reading age nearly five years behind the level expected of someone his age. The pattern repeated itself for the other children also. Summarizing the psychologists' findings, the Family Court concluded: 'There cannot be any doubt at all that the elder children have been educationally crippled and that the younger children are in danger of being educationally crippled as well.'[86]

The Department of Social Welfare in 1991 applied to the Family Court for a declaration that the children were in need of care and protection in terms of s. 14 of the Children, Young Persons and Their Families Act 1989 (CYPFA 1989).

Judge Inglis QC noted that the Ps were excellent, caring parents: 'no-one ha[d] found anything to criticise in the children's behaviour or their attitude.' 'Obviously', he continued, 'the children have been well brought up and well nurtured'.[87] The achilles heel of the parents' childrearing, however, was the almost total neglect of the children's formal education. Judge Inglis was aware that the issues raised were ones of 'great constitutional importance'.[88] The Ps had sincerely chosen, on religious grounds, a separatist lifestyle and had, to their credit, brought up children who were 'polite, courteous and "enthusiastic"'.[89] To what extent then was the state entitled to intervene in a mode of upbringing which had 'many exemplary qualities' and was 'based on sound moral values'[90] but which seriously and unacceptably neglected the children's educational development? Judge Inglis identified two legal limitations. First, education legislation imposed obligations upon parents to ensure their children received formal education. Second, the Department of Social Welfare was under the legal duty to intervene where there were grounds for believing a child needed care and protection. Here, the Department relied upon s. 14(1)(b) of the CYPFA, which states a minor is 'in need of care or protection' if the 'child's or young person's development or physical or mental or emotional wellbeing is being, or is likely to be, impaired or neglected, and that impairment or neglect is, or is likely to be, serious and avoidable'. The parents' right of religious upbringing had 'come[ ] into conflict with the right of each of the children to be educated, both academically and socially, to equip them for independence in a modern world.'[91] He concluded:

> While Mr and Mrs P may have acted with the best of intentions and motives, it is no use hiding from the fact that even on the most charitable view the elder children have for many years been seriously deprived of their rights to education and social contact, and there is a clear risk that the younger children will be similarly seriously deprived. The children have been left with no choice: their deprivation has been imposed upon them, wasting and frustrating their inherent talents and intelligence, and, perhaps of equal importance, isolating them from the experience and knowledge which they require in order to make their own informed choices as adults.[92]

The Court reminded the parents that the 'lodestone' under the CYPFA was the welfare of the children, and thus: 'On any competition for priority between the parents' rights and the rights of the children, there can be only one possible outcome.'[93] An order was made under s. 101 vesting custody of the children in the Department. The children would remain in their parents' home; school-age children would be enrolled in the Correspondence School and a registered teacher and social worker would monitor the children's progress. The children could no longer be allowed to 'drift aimlessly'.[94] Judge Inglis concluded with another bouquet regarding the parents' loving and caring efforts to raise their large family. Their neglect of education was thus 'tragic':

> the parents may not have appreciated that a loving, caring and united home with strong moral values is only one part of a child's upbringing. Each of the children is a person in his and her own right. Each of the children has a right to reach his and her full potential, educationally and socially. The parents would not deny them food when they are hungry. They must not deny them education and knowledge when they are thirsting for it.[95]

The Judge's language here resonates with Feinberg's child's 'right to an open future', discussed in the previous chapter. The state has a legitimate interest in ensuring children's future opportunities are not irrevocably foreclosed by present parental upbringing practices, whether religiously-grounded or not. The Amish children in *Yoder*, and the Seventh Day Adventist children in *Seven P Children*, may wish to continue living an isolationist, rural life, but they may also desire to become 'nuclear physicists, ballet dancers, computer programmers or historians'.[96] The state then has an interest in, to use Judge Inglis' words, ensuring that 'each [child] has a right to reach his or her full potential, educationally and socially.'

Returning to the *Seven P Children*, unfortunately there was an aftermath. Six months later the case reappeared before Judge Inglis.[97] The parents, resentful of the original Department intervention, had refused to cooperate with the educational salvage plan so carefully instituted by the Court. The original plan had proved unworkable. In December 1991, a revised plan was implemented whereby the two eldest boys were placed with relatives in Hamilton so as to enable them to attend a secondary school, whilst the three remaining school-age children were placed in a country school not far outside Levin. By now, the parents were convinced they were being 'persecuted' for their lifestyle and religious beliefs and that Department intervention was at the behest of a 'conspiracy' by their Hamilton relations to destroy their family.[98] Judge Inglis observed that the Ps, although sincere people, were 'utterly committed to a viewpoint which is impervious to any reasoned argument or suggestion.'[99] Religious conviction impervious to reason is beyond the limit of the liberal state's tolerance. The Court was blunt in its denunciation of the parents' continued placing of their religious convictions ahead of their children's education. Their conduct betrayed 'an underlying attitude that an ordinary "secular" education to the children requires no more than a token effort, that it is of far less importance than other aspects of their lifestyle, and that in any event they have the right to bring up the children in their own way.'[100]

The welfare of the children demanded decisive and urgent action lest, in the wake of parental non-cooperation, the situation continue to drift. Extensive remedial measures were put into place. Judge Inglis' final words bear quotation:

> The central issue in this case is not the parents' religious and moral beliefs. The parents have the right to the religious persuasion and beliefs of their choice. The central issue is the children's rights, which the Courts must defend. The children have a right to an education, academically and socially, which will equip them for independence and to make their own mature and responsible decisions and choices. . . . The parents have the right to choose their own lifestyle. So do the children have the right to choose *their* own future lifestyle. . . . In each case, as the experience of R and C [the two eldest] has already shown, the values and moral standards inculcated in all these children by their parents will stand all the children in good stead in confronting the evils and temptations always present in any society.[101]

Conclusion

The potential impact of the CRC upon parents' right to control the religious upbringing of their children does not appear great. In the intact and united family, CC parents still retain their rights as guardians to raise their children in the faith. Where religious upbringing practices endanger the life, health, welfare, safety or educational opportunities of children, the state, in its *parens patriae* capacity, may intervene. This paternalistic jurisdiction is reinforced by certain protection provisions of the CRC such as Articles 6 and 19.

In terms of my model of engagement (Chapter 4), the prediction of largely peaceful coexistence between CCs and the state is borne out. There have been very few cases where parental religious upbringing conduct has been scrutinized by a court. Those where the parents' behaviour was impugned have, moreover, involved religious groups at the fringe of conservative Christianity, or outside it altogether (Jehovah's Witnesses). Further, I suspect most CCs would agree with the outcome in cases such as *The Seven P Children* and *Liu*, where CC parents' wishes have been vetoed.

In the few cases of conflict resulting in litigation, the pattern has been uneven. Do illiberal religions fare badly before judges acting in accordance with the Wellington worldview? There is some limited evidence (by no means uncontradicted) that the more intolerant, unreasonable, dogmatic and indoctrinating the parents are, the less favourably a court treats them. Sometimes such parents simply lose. On the other hand, there are also instances where judges have shown sensitivity to the religious convictions of CCs (and others) and have done their best to accommodate these believers, even if the court does not agree with them.

Notes

1 Arlene Goss, 'Parents' choices, children's rights', *Challenge Weekly* ('*CW*'), 8 February 1995, at 8.

2 Mies Omen, letter to *CW*, 7 September 1994, at 7 (capitals in original).

3 James Dobson, *Solid Answers* (1997) at 221.

4 My usage accords with that by Lord Scarman in *Gillick* v *West Norfolk and Wisbech Area Health Authority* [1986] 1 AC 112 at 176.

5 I examined the former topic in Ahdar, 'Religion as a Factor in Custody and Access Disputes' (1996) 10 *IJLPF* 177 and Ahdar, 'Religion in Custody and Access: The New Zealand Experience' (1996) 17 *NZULR* 113, and the latter subject in Ahdar, 'Children's Religious Freedom, Devout Parents and the State' in Edge and Harvey (eds), *Law and Religion in Contemporary Society* (2000) ch 5 and Ahdar, 'Parental Religious Upbringing in a Children's Rights Era' in Beaumont and Wotherspoon (eds), *Christian Perspectives on Law and Relationism* (2000) 189-236.

6 See Lee M Friedman, 'The Parental Right to Control the Religious Education of a Child' (1916) 28 *Harv L Rev* 485 at 485-487 for a brief account.

7 Ibid at 487.

8 See *Lyons* v *Blenkin*, Jac 245, 37 ER 842 (1821). But the courts were not prepared to look with favour upon atheism: see the very next case in that volume of the *English Reports*, *Shelley* v *Westbrooke*, Jac 266; 37 ER 850 (1817), and also *In re Besant* (1879) 11 Ch D 508.

9 *In re Agar-Ellis* (1878) 10 Ch D 49 (*Agar-Ellis (No 1)*); *In re Agar-Ellis* (1883) 24 Ch D 317 (*Agar-Ellis (No 2)*).

10 *Agar-Ellis (No 1)* at 56-57.

11 *Agar-Ellis (No 1)* at 72 per James LJ.

12 Malins VC, ibid at 55.

13 *Agar-Ellis (No 2)* (1883) 24 Ch D 317 at 329 (CA). The reference to the Vice Chancellor is to Bacon VC in *Re Plomley*, 47 LT (NS) 284.

14 Bowen LJ in *Agar-Ellis (No 2)* at 335.

15 *Agar-Ellis (No 2)* at 335 and 338-339.

16 See Malins VC in *Agar-Ellis (No 1)*.

17 Friedman, 'Parental Right to Control Religious Education' (above n 6), at 492, commented: 'Indeed there is perhaps no situation which has betrayed the judiciary to yield to its own religious prejudices so subtly as the issue of parental abandonment in the face of rival religious claims between parents and relatives over some poor child who had been made the object of religious zeal.'

[18] See *Agar-Ellis (No 1)* at 60; *In re Browne*, 2 Ir Ch Rep 151 (1852).

[19] *Stourton* v *Stourton*, 8 De GM and G 760 at 767 (1857) per Knight Bruce LJ.

[20] *In re McSweeney and Another (Infants): Fogarty* v *Prouting* [1943] GLR 239.

[21] [1925] AC 101 at 108.

[22] *In re McSweeney* [1943] GLR at 246.

[23] Fair J, ibid at 254.

[24] I shall persist in describing it as a 'right' despite the view of some scholars that parents currently have (or, failing that, ought to have), at best, a mere 'privilege' to direct the upbringing, religious or otherwise, of their children: see, for example, James G Dwyer, 'Parents' Religion and Children's Welfare: Debunking the Doctrine of Parents' Rights' (1994) 82 *Calif L Rev* 1371.

[25] *Re J (An Infant): B and B* v *DGSW* [1996] 2 NZLR 134 at 145.

[26] See further Patrick Lynch, 'Religious Education: A Right and a Growing Societal Imperative' in Ahdar and Stenhouse (eds), *God and Government: The New Zealand Experience* (2000) ch 5.

[27] Signed by New Zealand on 12 November 1968 (999 UNTS 272); ratified on 28 December 1978 (1120 UNTS 489) and entered into force on 28 March 1979.

[28] See, for instance, the High Court in *Huakina Development Trust* v *Waikato Valley Authority* [1987] 2 NZLR 188 at 217 per Chilwell J.

[29] See also art 14(3) of the CRC and art 1(3) of the Declaration on the Elimination of All Forms of Intolerance, which repeat art 18(3) of the ICCPR.

[30] *Re J* [1996] 2 NZLR 134 at 145.

[31] *Gillick* [1986] AC 112 at 184-185.

[32] *Re J* [1996] 2 NZLR at 145.

[33] Ibid at 146.

[34] *Black's Law Dictionary*, 6th edn (1990) at 1114.

[35] *Prince* v *Massachusetts*, 321 US 158, 170 (1944) per Justice Rutledge.

[36] *Re J* [1996] 2 NZLR at 145. For discussion see my two chapters listed in fn 5 above.

[37] For overseas examples, see *B(R)* v *Children's Aid Society of Metropolitan Toronto* [1995] 1 SCR 315 (Canada); *Re S (A Minor)(Medical Treatment)* [1993] 1 FLR 376 (England); *Jehovah's Witnesses in Washington* v *King County Hospital*, 278 F Supp 488 (1967), aff'd, 390 US 598 (1968).

[38] See Jane E Probst, 'The Conflict Between Child's Medical Needs and Parents' Religious Beliefs' (1990) 4 *Am J Fam Law* 175 at 178.

[39] *R* v *Laufau [Summing Up]*, unrep, High Court, Auckland, T.000759, 23 August 2000, Potter J; *R* v *Laufau [Sentencing]*, unrep, High Court, Auckland, T.000759, 2 October 2000, Potter J. For discussion, see Joanna Manning, 'Parental Refusal of Life-prolonging Medical Treatment for Children: A Report from New Zealand' (2001) 8 *J Law & Med* 263.

[40] See *Pallin* v *DSW* [1983] NZLR 266 at 272 (CA).

[41] See s. 8 of the Guardianship Act 1968 and s. 15 of the Family Courts Act 1980. See *Re J (An Infant): Director-General of Social Welfare* v *B and B* [1995] 3 NZLR 73 at 78-79.

[42] See, for example, *Re P* [1992] NZFLR 94; *Re V* [1993] NZFLR 369; *Re CL* [1994] NZFLR 352.

[43] The High Court judgment is reported at [1995] 3 NZLR 73.

44 *Re J* [1996] 2 NZLR at 137.
45 Ibid at 145.
46 See ibid at 143-144.
47 See the literature referred to in Stephen Papps and Warren Cathcart, 'Ex parte orders for medical intervention on Jehovah's Witnesses: the risk of injustice' (1994) 1 *Butterworths Family L J* 136.
48 See Sidney R Peck, 'An Analytical Framework for the Application of the Canadian Charter of Rights and Freedoms' (1987) 25 *Osgoode Hall L J* 1 at 21-31.
49 As Bruce Hafen observes: 'the placing of the constitutional presumption essentially determines the outcome' in many cases: 'Individualism and Autonomy in Family Law: The Waning of Belonging' [1991] *Brigham Young L Rev* 1 at 17.
50 [1995] 1 SCR 315.
51 For commentary critical of definitional balancing, see Peck, 'An Analytical Framework' (above n 48), at 25 and 31; Janet November, 'Defining and Balancing Conflicting Rights' (1996) 4 *Bill of Rights Bulletin* 56; Julian Rivers, 'A Bill of Rights for the United Kingdom?' in Beaumont (ed), *Christian Perspectives on Law Reform* (1998) ch 2 at 35.
52 *B (R)* [1995] 1 SCR at 383-384.
53 Ibid at 384.
54 Ibid at 385.
55 Ibid at 386.
56 Ibid at 385.
57 For example, it made provision for notice to be given the parents, evidence to be called and for time limits on the wardship to be imposed.
58 See *Re J* [1995] 3 NZLR 73 at 88 for the High Court's protocol.
59 See Laura M Plastine, '"In God We Trust": When Parents Refuse Medical Treatment for their Children Based upon their Sincere Religious Beliefs' (1993) 3 *Seton Hall Constitutional L J* 123 at 145-147; Maureen D Manion, 'Parental Religious Freedom, the Rights of Children, and the Role of the State' (1992) 34 *JCS* 77 at 83; Probst, 'The Conflict Between Child's Medical Needs and Parents' Religious Beliefs' (above n 38), at 188; Barry Nobel, 'Religious Healing in the Courts: the Liberties and Liabilities of Patients, Parents and Healers' (1993) 16 *U Puget Sound L Rev* 599 at 643-654.
60 See Probst, ibid at 178-182 and Morag McDowell, 'Supervening parental rights: religion and the refusal of consent to a child's medical treatment' (1998) *Butterworths Family L J* 233 at 240.
61 Pennsylvania Superior Court in *In re Cabrera*, 552 A 2d 1114, 1120 (Pa Super Ct 1989).
62 *Auckland Healthcare Services Ltd* v *Liu*, unrep, High Court, Auckland, M 812/96, 11 July 1996, Tompkins J, at 5.
63 Ibid at 6.
64 Ibid.
65 Ibid at 8.
66 Ibid.
67 *In re Sampson*, 317 NYS 2d 641 (NY Fam Ct 1970), aff'd, 323 NYS 2d 253 (NY App Div 1971), aff'd, 278 NE 2d 918 (NY 1972).
68 *OG* v *Baum*, 790 SW 2d 839 (Tex Ct App 1990).

[69] *Mitchell* v *Davis*, 205 SW 2d 812 (Tex Civ App 1947).

[70] See generally Graeme Austin, 'Righting a Child's Right to Refuse Medical Treatment' (1992) 7 *Otago L R* 578; Morag McDowell, 'Medical Treatment and Children: Assessing the Scope of a Child's Capacity to Consent or Refuse Consent in New Zealand' (1997) 5 *J Law & Med* 81; Caroline Bridge, 'Religious Beliefs and Teenage Refusal of Medical Treatment' (1999) 62 *MLR* 585.

[71] *Liu*, at 7.

[72] See *R* v *Laufau [Summing Up]* (above n 39), at paras 32-33 and 47-48.

[73] [1996] NZFLR 670 at 671.

[74] Ibid.

[75] Ibid.

[76] *Wisconsin* v *Yoder*, 406 US 205 (1972).

[77] Ibid at 234 per Burger CJ (expressing the views of six members of the Court).

[78] Ibid at 225 per Burger CJ.

[79] Ibid at 238 (Brennan and Stewart JJ joining his opinion).

[80] Ibid.

[81] *Re The Seven P Children*, unrep, Family Court, Levin, CYPF 031/122-8/91, 8 October 1991, Judge Inglis QC (hereafter *P Children No (1)*).

[82] Judge Inglis' characterization in the second decision, *Re the P Children (No 2)* (1992) 9 FRNZ 93 at 95.

[83] In Judge Inglis's words (ibid): 'It is clear that their preference is to live in isolation from the influences of the outside world and that they do not wish any of their children to be contaminated by what they [the parents] see as the undesirable moral values of modern society.'

[84] The only formal education being 'a few weeks attending a school in 1984'. *P Children (No 1)* at 2.

[85] *P Children (No 2)* at 95.

[86] *P Children (No 1)* at 4.

[87] Ibid at 5.

[88] Ibid at 6.

[89] Ibid at 5 (the educational psychologists' description of them).

[90] Ibid.

[91] *P Children (No 1)* at 8.

[92] Ibid at 9.

[93] Ibid at 10.

[94] Ibid at 11.

[95] Ibid at 12.

[96] White J in *Wisconsin* v *Yoder* at 240.

[97] *P Children (No 2)* (1992) 9 FRNZ 93.

[98] Ibid at 102.

[99] Ibid.

[100] Ibid at 106.

[101] Ibid at 112-113 (emphasis in original).

8 Corporal Punishment

In this chapter I examine the present law concerning the right of parents to administer corporal punishment to their children and the movement toward abolition of that right in New Zealand. I then assess the potential impact of the United Nations Convention on the Rights of the Child 1989 (CRC) upon the parental right of corporal punishment.

Conservative Christian (CC) parents endorse corporal punishment of their children where the occasion so requires. Physical chastisement is certainly not all that discipline of children entails, but many CCs believe it is an integral part of it. Abundant scriptural support, particularly from the book of Proverbs, direct the CC in this matter.[1] If CCs needed contemporary reinforcement of the biblical endorsement of physical discipline, they need only have turned (as they indeed did, and continue to do so) to Dr James Dobson's bestsellers, *Dare to Discipline* and the like.[2] Dobson, a leading American evangelical and a qualified child psychologist, provided intellectual succour to what CCs saw as prudent parenting based on scripture and tradition.

There is a keen realization by CCs that corporal punishment may sometimes go much too far and degenerate into child abuse.[3] Abuse is condemned outright by CCs,[4] and the regrettable prospect that some foolish parents will distort the scriptural mandate into a licence for criminal violence, is not, in CCs' minds, a sufficient justification for society to jettison the practice and the benefits it brings.

Following the ratification of the CRC by the New Zealand Government in 1993, some CCs predicted the parental right to 'smack' children would come under threat.[5] One commentator even believed that the smacking debate was there and then 'effectively decided'.[6] As we shall see, the UN Committee on the Rights of the Child has consistently interpreted Article 19(1) of the CRC to include smacking with its concept of 'violence'. CCs have publicly urged the Government to remain firm in its resolve. The leader of the Christian Heritage Party, the Rev Graham Capill, warned politicians intent on banning smacking that they would be 'buying into a big fight' with Christians, and many non-Christians, one which would exceed the reaction to the Homosexual Law Reform Bill in the mid-1980s (to be discussed in the next chapter).[7]

The Present Law

The common law has long recognized the right of parental corporal punishment. Blackstone observed that a parent 'may lawfully correct the child, being under age, in a reasonable manner.'[8] Courts have understood such correction to include 'moderate' physical punishment. New Zealand codified the common law right of physical chastisement in 1893,[9] the modern encapsulation being s. 59 of the Crimes Act 1961:

> **59. Domestic discipline**—(1) Every parent of a child and, subject to subsection (3) of this section, every person in the place of the parent of a child is justified in using force by way of correction towards the child, if the force used is reasonable in the circumstances.
> (2) The reasonableness of the force used is a question of fact.
> (3) Nothing in subsection (1) of this section justifies the use of force towards a child in contravention of section 139A of the Education Act 1989.

Section 59 was amended in 1990 to remove the statutory immunity for teachers—a source of difficulty since for some small independent Christian schools[10]—and child carers.[11] (There were not unfounded criticisms that this change was 'slipped [in] . . . at the last moment' in legislation devoted to wholesale education reform with, consequently, little opportunity for public submissions.[12]) The term 'justified' is defined in s. 2 of the Crimes Act as meaning, in relation to a person, 'not guilty of an offence and not liable to any civil proceeding.' Thus, parents who come with the section's terms are protected against criminal prosecutions for child assault and also against civil liability arising from, for instance, tortious actions for trespass to the person.[13]

To be immune a parent must satisfy both limbs of the provision: proper purpose and appropriate degree of force. First, any force used upon the child by the parent must be 'by way of correction'. Any bad reason on the parent's part—revenge, spite, rage, arbitrariness, caprice or fury (some of the states of mind denounced in the case law[14])—will be fatal to the claim for immunity. The Family Court recently reminded:

> It is to be borne in mind that s 59 authorises the application of force which would otherwise be an assault and that it is the purpose for which it is used which is the principal ground of defence. . . . In inflicting punishment the parent must act in good faith, having a reasonable belief in a state of facts which would justify the application of force.[15]

Second, the use of force must be 'reasonable in the circumstances.' In deciding this question of fact, New Zealand courts have noted that the assessment takes place against prevailing social attitudes to childrearing.[16] While the Court has a broad discretion, some obvious factors that ought to be taken into account are: '[t]he age and maturity of the child'; [o]ther characteristics of the child, such as physique, sex and state of health; [t]he type of offence; [and t]he type and circumstances of punishment.'[17] So, hitting a very young child (or for that matter, an older teenager) for a minor misdemeanour would be unreasonable, as would hitting a frail child.[18] Claims that either a parent's religious or cultural background justify a greater degree of force than would otherwise be considered reasonable have not been accepted. I shall discuss religion shortly, but, as for culture, the Family Court in *Ausage* v *Ausage* stated:

> one of the prime objectives of the Convention is to protect all children, regardless of race, colour, sex or religion, by the imposition of a uniform code to apply world-wide. . . . I cannot accept that the degree of physical violence, if permitted under art 5, would differ depending on the culture of the child or parent. . . . I have formed the view that the degree of force which might be reasonable to apply for the purposes of correction under s 59 does not differ according to ethnic background or religious belief. There is to be one universal standard which applies to all families in New Zealand.[19]

The limits of the parental right of physical discipline are illustrated in two cases involving devout Christian parents. Unfortunately, in both instances the parents went much too far.

In *Director-General of Social Welfare* v *E*,[20] the Family Court considered whether three children of Mr and Mrs E were in need of care and protection in terms of s. 14 of the Children, Young Persons and Their Families Act 1989 (CYPFA). The Department of Social Welfare argued that excessive physical discipline had been administered to the children, aged nine, seven and three. The parents, described by the Judge as 'qualified intelligent professional people,'[21] belonged to a fledgling congregation, the 'New Vine Church'. At the time of trial, it comprised only four families, including that of its pastor. His doctrines relied upon 'very literal'[22] interpretations of the Bible. The crux of the problem, however, was the physical punishment regime followed by the parents at the behest of the pastor. The regime was patently excessive. Following an instance of misbehaviour Mr E admitted in evidence that his three daughters could receive up to 10 straps 10 times a day! Following discussions with their pastor, the discipline was decreased to a maximum of five smacks, five times a day. The report commissioned for the Court detailed unusual and anti-social conduct by the children at school. Serious long-term adverse effects were predicted. The Es acknowledged that their disciplining of the children had been excessive. Nevertheless, they wished to retain the right of physical chastisement in the future since it 'accords with biblical authority.'[23] Passages from the book of Proverbs were pleaded in support. The judge affirmed that the Es were entitled to form and hold their own religious beliefs in accordance with s. 15 of the New Zealand Bill of Rights Act 1990.[24] Yet they also had to accept the consequences arising from their choice of beliefs. The right of parental physical discipline was acknowledged (although s. 59 was not expressly referred to) and Judge MacCormick was aware that many conservative Christian parents strongly endorsed corporal punishment as a biblically-based part of child-rearing.

> For my part I am well aware that there are a number of parents who believe that limited physical discipline is appropriate on occasion and that there are books such as James Dobson's 'Dare to Discipline' that advocate it. But that is not with the background of excessive discipline that has occurred here.[25]

The Court was satisfied that the children were in need of care and protection. The Es were 'basically good people',[26] albeit misguided due to the 'manipulative' religious influence from their pastor. The Court ordered an end to further physical disciplining of the girls by either parent following their return. Judge MacCormick refrained from making it a condition of the children's return to the parents' care that the Es sever all links with the New Vine Church. He made his views plain nonetheless: 'To make this [severing links] a condition would be to require them [the Es] to choose between their church and the care of their children. I do not consider that to be appropriate. . . . I do, however, consider that Mr and Mrs E need to evaluate where membership of their church may have led them.'[27]

The second decision is *Ausage* v *Ausage*.[28] The applicant, aged 18, sought a final protection order against her father under the Domestic Violence Act 1995, claiming that his disciplining of her had been excessive and amounted to domestic violence. The respondent father, Mr A, was raised in Samoa but now lived in New Zealand where he was a leader in the local Samoan community and an elder in his church. He had six daughters and believed in setting a good example in terms of his family life and children's conduct. Based on his cultural upbringing and devout Christian beliefs, he believed in, and regularly practised, physical chastisement of the children. Scriptural passages from the Old and New Testaments were pleaded in support of his position. Two specific instances of the daughter's alleged misbehaviour led to the present proceedings.[29] When A was 16, some money was found missing from the household. Mr A came into A's bedroom between 1 and 3 am and dragged her out of bed. Although she denied taking the money, her father did not believe her and she was punched and hit on her arms and legs. The second incident occurred when A was 17 and employed. Mr A objected to his daughter's control (via her own bank account) of her earnings, insisting that she was not contributing enough, by way of board, to household expenses. He struck her with the back of his hand in the mouth, causing bruising and cuts to her lips and a whiplash injury to her neck.

The Court was in no doubt that the degree of force used by the father was not 'reasonable' on each occasion and constituted assault and physical abuse. Thus, the protection of s. 59 was unavailing. As noted earlier, the Court rejected the argument that the parent's (or child's) religious beliefs were a relevant factor in deciding whether physical punishment was reasonable. The CRC mandated a uniform standard be adopted; religiously devout parents have no greater freedom to smack than any other parent. His Honour, in his concluding comments, could not resist a little gratuitous sermonizing: 'the respondent believes that his views are supported by religious teaching, although in this regard I would urge him to adopt the New Testament parental model rather than continuing to follow the Old Testament model.'[30]

Impetus for Abolition

There is a groundswell of support from academics[31] and various child-oriented organizations such as the Office for the Commissioner for Children,[32] the Ministry of Youth Affairs,[33] the Youth Law Project,[34] and the New Zealand branch of EPOCH (End Physical Punishment of Children) for the abolition of the parental right of corporal punishment. This reflects international trends. Several European nations, led by Sweden in 1979, have abolished the parental right of physical chastisement of children.[35] The recent European Court of Human Rights judgment, *A* v *United Kingdom*, may give further impetus to the ban parental punishment movement in the United Kingdom.[36]

Abolition in New Zealand would, as John Caldwell pointed out,[37] require more than simply repealing s. 59 of the Crimes Act. Parents could, by virtue of s. 20 of that same Act, claim immunity from suit under the common law defence. This suggests a specific statutory prohibition upon parental physical punishment would be needed. One reform path would be for the statutory immunity in s. 59 to be repealed. The common law defence would remain during which—following the Scandinavian example—a major educational campaign would endeavour to change parental opinion. (This, as we shall see, is underway.) Finally, subject to the success of such a campaign, a specific enactment outlawing parental punishment would be passed. The scope for prosecutions of recalcitrant parents would exist but could be mitigated by (to take Caldwell's proposal) the consent of the Solicitor-General being a necessary precondition to criminal proceedings.

Whether public opinion will be swayed by an anti-smacking campaign remains an open question. 'Anglo-Saxon culture', lamented Caldwell, 'places far more emphasis on the infliction of pain on children as a means of behavioural control than do other European societies.'[38] Moreover, Maori and Pacific Island parents are strongly in favour of corporal punishment.[39] Surveys consistently show a high level of public support for corporal punishment. A 1993 survey revealed that:

> New Zealanders still approved of corporal punishment in the home, with 87% of New Zealanders believing that 'in certain circumstances it is all right for a parent to smack a child' . . . Although smacking with the hand is still both approved and used as a standard parental response to the misbehaviour of children of all ages, anything more severe is no longer part of the repertoire of most parents or the experience of most children.[40]

Certainly, severe smacking is in decline and clearly alternative methods of discipline have increased in popularity. Nonetheless, support for sparingly used, 'moderate' smacking persists. Indeed, one poll in 1997 found 56 per cent of the people polled wished that corporal punishment be reintroduced into schools for serious misbehaviour.[41] (An attempt to do this failed in the early 1990s.[42]) The 'dark stain on New Zealand child rearing'[43] of smacking, as Professors James and Jane Ritchie put it, may prove hard to eradicate.

In the face of persistent public support for the status quo, Child, Youth and Family Services (CYFS), formerly the Children, Young Persons and Their Families Service, has undertaken an extensive educational campaign in recent years. The Government amended the CYPFA in December 1994, imposing a new duty upon the Director-General of Social Welfare to 'promote, by education and publicity . . . awareness of child abuse [and] the unacceptability of child abuse . . .'[44] The 'Breaking the Cycle' campaign, which began in May 1995, is one response. Stage 4 of this 'social marketing' strategy[45] was the 'Alternatives to Smacking' campaign launched in September 1998. CYFS literature argues that smacking is outdated and ineffective. It is a form of violence imposed by larger people on smaller people which is undesirable; further, 'it can lead to emotional and physical damage' which is most regrettable as there are, according to them, effective alternatives to smacking.[46] CYFS is not trying to 'demonise smackers',[47] nor does it expressly assert that smacking *per se* is child abuse—although its language is, at times, equivocal. Its main thesis is that physical punishment is morally wrong, ineffective and can all too readily degenerate into physical abuse; better then to abolish hitting altogether. CYFS favours a change in the law and it invokes the CRC in support:

> Some people have called for smacking to be outlawed. That's of course a decision for politicians to make. However, a simple law change won't necessarily stop people smacking. What CYPFS is concentrating on is showing people there are better alternatives and that smacking can be harmful . . . Although smacking isn't illegal, New Zealand is a signatory to the United Nations Convention on the Rights of the Child. This convention aims to protect children from *all* forms of physical and mental violence. CYPFS's campaign is being conducted in this spirit.[48]

The CC reaction, or at least one section of it,[49] was as swift as it was predictable. A beleaguered Rev Graham Capill denounced the 'Alternatives' initiative as 'an attack on parenting'. It was, he believed, a part of a 'cunning Government ploy' to implement the CRC and to soften up the public for the eventual repeal of s. 59 of the Crimes Act. That section already gave children adequate protection against violence, moreover, to remove s. 59 'is to dictate to parents how they should train their children, and the Government has no right to do that.'[50] Capill urged Christians to fight every move to disempower them. One CC, a Hamilton businessman Philip Holdway-Davis, who had attracted media criticism in 1997 for defending smacking,[51] promulgated his own alternative to the CYFS campaign. The outcome was 'The Safe Smack Pyramid,' a regime which featured smacking as the final option after a number of prior disciplinary alternatives had been tried.[52] Following his safe smack methodology would, asserted its author, minimize excessive physical discipline and reduce child abuse, something he believed the CYFS approach simply exacerbated. He read the international evidence as showing no decline in child abuse in those nations that banned smacking. Perhaps, in the battle for public opinion, CCs may yet find support from libertarian-minded members of the public who resent the type of 'meddlesome busy-body' or 'ink monitor' intrusiveness represented by CYFS's attempts at social engineering.[53]

The abolition debate continues. In December 1999, Roger McLay, the Commissioner for Children, called for an end to smacking, or 'belting' as he called it. He believed it was time for New Zealand to emulate those European nations that had abolished the right of corporal punishment.[54] The Youth Affairs Minister in the recently elected Labour/Alliance Government, Laila Harre, personally supported a change in the law to this effect.[55] The Commissioner for Children repeated his call for abolition in August 2000. A spokesman for the

Minister of Social Services and Employment responded, however, that banning smacking was not a Government priority.[56]

The Impact of the Convention?

The area in which the CRC may have the most visible impact is in the abolition of corporal punishment debate. CCs quite rightly perceive the CRC as a formidable weapon against them in their battle to retain parental physical discipline.

The UN Committee on the Rights of the Child—the body established under Article 43 of the CRC to monitor states' progress in implementing the Convention's obligations—has criticized the continued retention of the right of corporal punishment of children in New Zealand legislation. New Zealand is required, pursuant to Article 44(1), to report within two years of ratification, and thereafter every five years. New Zealand's First Report to the Committee, submitted in October 1995,[57] and prepared by the Ministry of Youth Affairs, made little mention of the subject.[58] The Report noted that corporal punishment in schools had been abolished and then briefly stated that parents retained the right of physical discipline where reasonable force was used for the purpose of correction. Unreasonable force applied to children was, the Report continued, a criminal offence and there existed 'extensive measures'[59] in place for the protection of children from abuse and maltreatment. The Office of the Commissioner for Children's campaign to repeal s. 59 was alluded to, as was the International Year of the Family promotion, 'Smack-Free Week'.[60]

The Committee on the Rights of the Child has consistently maintained that corporal punishment is in violation of the Convention. In a statement issued on 15 September 1995 it observed:

> The Committee is disturbed about the reports it has received on the physical and sexual abuse of children. In this connection, the Committee is worried about the national legal provisions dealing with reasonable chastisement within the family. The imprecise nature of the expression of reasonable chastisement as contained in these legal provisions may pave the way for it to be interpreted in a subjective and arbitrary manner. Thus, the Committee is concerned that legislative and other measures relating to the physical integrity of children do not appear to be compatible with the provisions and principles of the Convention.[61]

The primary article upon which this view is based is Article 19(1):

> States Parties shall take all appropriate legislative, administrative, social and educational measures to protect the child from all forms of physical or

mental violence, injury or abuse, neglect or negligent treatment, maltreatment or exploitation, including sexual abuse, while in the care of parent(s), legal guardian(s) or any other person who has the care of the child.

Reliance is also placed upon Article 24(3) which declares: 'States Parties shall take all effective and appropriate measures with a view to abolishing traditional practices prejudicial to the health of children.'

By contrast, the Minister of Youth Affairs, at least in 1994, considered the right of parental corporal punishment to be compatible with the aims and objectives of the Convention. The then Minister, Roger McLay, argued[62] that the application of force was justifiable in certain circumstances; moreover, parental responsibilities to provide 'appropriate direction and guidance' to children were recognized by Article 5 of the CRC. Second, the Minister drew a clear distinction between physical abuse, which Article 19 is designed to address, and physical punishment. When physical discipline goes too far and becomes excessive, it becomes unreasonable force and parents lose their statutory protection. At this point (when the boundary is overstepped) Article 19 becomes relevant. Thus, he argued, s. 59 protected children from unreasonable discipline from their parents. The Minister's denial of any intention to repeal s. 59 in 1994 was important for another reason. It was made against the background of a move by the Office of the Commissioner for Children to have smacking defined as 'violence' for the purposes of the Domestic Violence Bill.[63] This move failed and Domestic Violence Act 1995 made no reference to the disciplining of children.

The Minister's interpretation of abuse is directly at odds with the UN Committee's. For the latter, moderate or 'reasonable' smacking is not a legitimate form of parental discipline but simply a species of physical violence and abuse. For the Committee all hitting of children is wrong and constitutes abuse in violation of a child's right to physical integrity. If the Committee is the authoritative interpreter of its own Convention then this raises awkward questions. Can a state place an interpretation on an article at odds with the Committee? Is the proper response in the wake of inconsistent interpretations for the state to insert a specific reservation to the Convention by way of exemption? Reservations to the Convention are, naturally enough, frowned upon by the Committee. New Zealand would likely not wish to add a fourth reservation to its current list of three, a list which the Committee has requested New Zealand consider withdrawing.[64]

The Committee on the Rights of the Child, prior to New Zealand's formal presentation of its initial report in 1997 by the Ministry of Youth Affairs, conveyed 53 questions for written answer. One question concerned corporal punishment and asked: 'Has the New Zealand

Government considered repealing section 59 of the Crimes Act which allows parents to use reasonable force in disciplining children, as recommended by the Commissioner for Children?'[65] The official response was unaltered:

> The Government does not have any plans to repeal section 59 of the Crimes Act 1961. The use of unreasonable force against a child is a criminal offence and extensive measures are in place for the protection of children from abuse and maltreatment.[66]

The response went on to mention CYFS's 'Breaking the Cycle' campaign, as well as public opinion polls reporting high levels of support for parental corporal punishment. The stance in 1997 simply echoed that in 1995. In August 1997, the then Minister of Justice, Douglas Graham, stated that he 'want[ed] to make it very clear that the National Government has no intention of changing the law'[67] on smacking of children. The Minister noted some 10 to 15 letters per day that had been sent to his office and the 27,000 signature petition which was tabled in Parliament that month. (This petition was an effort instigated by CCs to stave off any change to the law following ratification of the CRC.)

However, the New Zealand Government's written answer to the Committee's question on corporal punishment did not satisfy the Committee. In its concluding observations the Committee listed this issue in its 'principal subjects of concern', a list containing a dozen or so misgivings.[68] As for future action: 'The Committee recommends that the State party review legislation with regard to corporal punishment of children within the family in order to effectively ban all forms of physical or mental violence, injury or abuse.'[69] Again, we see the equation of corporal punishment and abuse.

To date, the judges have yet to follow the interpretation of the CRC preferred by the Committee. Judge Somerville in *Ausage* refrained from 'getting into the debate as to whether or not physical discipline applied under art 5 would amount to physical or mental violence under art 19 . . .'[70] He found it sufficient to hold that the degree of physical force permissible could not differ depending on the culture of the child or parent. Nor do counsel appear to have quoted the Committee's damning observation on the retention of s. 59 to the courts. While a ruling from the Committee is not binding on New Zealand courts, the warning of Sir Robin Cooke in *Tavita*—that New Zealand courts must not merely pay lip service to international conventions such as the CRC—still resonates.[71] The Court of Appeal in 1996 referred to 'the presumption of statutory interpretation that so far as its wording allows legislation should be read in a way which is consistent with New Zealand's international obligations.'[72] New Zealand courts may well in the future, I suggest, 'read down' the scope of parental physical discipline in light of the UN Committee's disapproval of it and a clear New Zealand Government indication that concurs with that disapproval. While New Zealand courts cannot fail to apply s. 59 on account of inconsistency with an international body's ruling, they may well treat cases of smacking in the 'grey area' as falling outside the protection afforded by the section.

Conclusion

Conservative Christians, usually identified as the principal opponents of change,[73] would seem to face a formidable array of abolitionists: Child, Youth and Family Services, the Ministry of Youth Affairs, the Office of the Commissioner for Children, the Youth Law Project, EPOCH (NZ), as well as the UN Committee on the Rights of the Child, and judges sensitive to criticism for ignoring international obligations. There is a growing 'Wellington worldview' that favours abolition. While public opinion in New Zealand still supports corporal punishment of children, that too is not beyond change.

The CRC is likely to have a much more immediate and direct impact upon the parental right of corporal punishment than upon the right of religious upbringing. The CRC is proving to be a formidable weapon in the armoury of those who seek abolition of 'smacking'.

In terms of my model of engagement in Chapter 4, we again see peaceful coexistence. Currently, the state does accommodate CC (and other) parents' desire to use corporal punishment as a form of child discipline. Parents are permitted to use moderate corporal punishment for the purpose of correction under s. 59 of the Crimes Act 1961. Parents who exceed this are violating the law. The two illustrations in this chapter of CC parents who went too far are instances which, I suggest, CCs would equally condemn. As well as accommodation by the state, many CCs have, I suspect, modified their own practice of hitting children. Consonant with the 'spirit of the times', my conjecture is that the frequency and severity of smacking is probably lower than that of a generation ago.

The prospect of conflict between CCs and the state looms in the near future in the face of mounting forces for abolition. Perhaps CCs will be able to successfully join forces with libertarian or traditionalist defenders of parental rights to resist abolition. To do so, they will need to use 'the translation strategy' (Chapter 4) and identify the 'secular', 'practical' benefits of smacking or the weaknesses in the abolitionists' case.[74]

If the parental right of corporal punishment is banned some, perhaps many, CCs might reluctantly resort to civil disobedience. It is, once more, a question of God's law being higher than human law. In good conscience some CCs will feel compelled to ignore the latter on this issue. Such CCs have a religious conviction that traditionalist, secular parents do not: it is a conscience matter for these devout parents, and an acute one given their high regard for the state. If smacking is banned, some CCs will stubbornly and publicly admit they continue to do so—they will invite a confrontation with the state in the way Eric Sides did. Overall, CCs are unlikely to win the corporal punishment debate unless they can garner support from a broader group of parental rights proponents.

Notes

1 See Proverbs 13:24; Proverbs 29:15; Proverbs 29:17; Proverbs 23:13-14; Proverbs 22:15; Proverbs 3:11-12. See also Hebrews 12:5-11. See, for example, James Dobson, *Dare to Discipline,* British edn (1971) at 205-206; Larry Christenson, *The Christian Family* (1970) at 112 and Christopher G Ellison, 'Conservative Protestantism and the Corporal Punishment of Children: Clarifying the Issues' (1996) 35 *JSSR* 1 at 3. For a vigorous critique of the CC position on this subject, see Philip Greven, *Spare the Child: The Religious Roots of Punishment and the Psychological Impact of Physical Abuse* (1992).

2 Dobson's *Dare to Discipline* is widely sold and used in New Zealand, as are his other books commending corporal punishment: see *The Strong-Willed Child* (1992) and *Solid Answers* (1997) ch 8. Dobson updated his original book in the 1990s: see *The New Dare to Discipline* (1996). Dobson's success with this book spawned an organization devoted to fostering family life called 'Focus on the Family'. The daily Focus on the Family programme is broadcast on Radio Rhema, the CC radio network throughout New Zealand.

3 See, for example, Dobson, *Dare to Discipline* (above n 1), at 55-56.

4 See, for example, Dobson, *Solid Answers* (above n 2), at 139.

5 See Arlene Goss, 'Spare the rod', *Challenge Weekly* (*CW*), 7 September 1994, at 7; Mies Omen, letter to *CW*, 7 September 1994, at 7.

6 'World wide concern', (no author listed), *CW*, 7 September 1994, at 8.

7 Mark Toomer, '"Corporal punishment", abuse link groundless', *CW*, 19 February 1997, at 3.

8 1 *Blackstone's Commentaries* 452; quoted in the leading New Zealand article on this topic: John L Caldwell, 'Parental Physical Punishment and the Law' (1989) 13 *NZULR* 370 at 371.

9 Section 68 of the Criminal Code 1893.

10 See John Steenhof, 'Corporal Punishment: Education Review Office versus Christian Schools', LLB Honours dissertation, University of Otago, 2000.

11 Section 28(1) of the Education Amendment Act 1990 inserted s 139A into the Education Act 1989, prohibiting corporal punishment in early childhood centres and registered schools. Registered schools include all state schools (primary, intermediate and secondary) as well as private schools registered pursuant to s 35A of the Act. For a detailed discussion, see Steenhof, ibid.

[12] Lockwood Smith (1990) 508 *NZPD* 2233. See also John Luxton (1990) 508 *NZPD* 2578 and Tony Steel (1992) 531 *NZPD* 12203. The Select Committee received only 20 submissions on the issue, with 13 opposed to the abolition of school corporal discipline: Anne Collins (1990) 508 *NZPD* 2237.

[13] See Caldwell, 'Physical Punishment' (above n 8), at 372.

[14] See Caldwell, ibid at 373-375, for an examination of the case law. An oft-cited passage is one by the Court of Appeal in *R* v *Drake* (1902) 22 NZLR 478 at 487 per Edwards J: 'The self-same act may be either an obviously just act of parental correction or an act of revenge . . .'

[15] *Ausage* v *Ausage* [1997] NZFLR 72 at 80.

[16] See Judge Inglis QC in *Kendall* v *DGSW* (1986) 3 FRNZ 1 at 10.

[17] *Ausage* v *Ausage* [1997] NZFLR at 79-80.

[18] The High Court recently commented: 'The use of a "smacking stick" on a young woman approaching teenage years or on younger children must be very difficult to justify': *Y* v *Y*, unrep, High Court, Auckland, HC 122/97, 27 February 1998, Baragwanath J, at 15.

[19] *Ausage* [1997] NZFLR at 79.

[20] *DGSW* v *E*, unrep, Family Court, North Shore, CYPF 4-6/96 and FP 242/96, 6 September 1996, Judge K G MacCormick.

[21] Ibid at 2.

[22] Ibid at 17.

[23] Ibid at 16.

[24] Ibid at 2.

[25] Ibid at 15.

[26] Ibid at 33, Judge MacCormick adding: 'I hope that doesn't sound condescending.'

[27] Ibid at 35.

[28] [1997] NZFLR 72.

[29] The applicant testified that minor transgressions would result in the children being told off but more serious transgressions would incur a variety of violent chastisements. These included being hit on her arms and legs with a belt, a boot, a jandal, a mop handle, a vacuum-cleaner hose, and her father's fist, leading to bruises or broken skin. Similar discipline was applied to her five younger sisters: *Ausage* at 74.

[30] Ibid at 82.

[31] See for example, Caldwell, 'Physical Punishment' (above n 8); Rochelle Urlich, 'Physical Discipline in the Home' (1994) 7 *Auck U L R* 851; Robert Ludbrook, 'Corporal Punishment: The Last Days of an Uncivilised Institution?' (1998) *Youth L Rev* 6. Perhaps the leading proponents of the abolition of child physical punishment are Waikato University psychologists (and spouses), Professors James and Jane Ritchie. Amongst their many books are *Spare the Rod* (1981) and *Violence in New Zealand*, 2nd edn (1993).

[32] See Gabrielle M Maxwell, 'Physical Punishment in the Home in New Zealand', Office of the Commissioner for Children, Occasional Paper No 2, September 1993.

[33] The Ministry of Youth Affairs funded a speaking tour by Peter Newell in November/December 1999.

[34] See Carol Parker, 'Repeal of Section 59 Crimes Act' (1994) 3 *Youth L Rev* 15.

[35] Others include Norway (1987), Finland (1984), Denmark (1986), Austria (1989) and Cyprus (1994). See Peter Newell, 'Ending physical punishment of children' (1997) 5 *Int J Children's Rights* 129 at 133. To that list can be added Latvia, Croatia and, most recently Germany. See http://www.stophitting.com.

[36] *A* v *United Kingdom (Human Rights: Punishment of Children)* [1998] 2 FLR 959.

[37] Caldwell, 'Physical Punishment' (above n 8), at 372.

[38] Ibid at 383.

[39] See James Ritchie, 'The Social Context of Child Abuse in New Zealand' in Child Abuse: Report of the National Symposium, Dunedin (1979), and other studies cited in Caldwell, 'Physical Punishment' (above n 8), at 383, fn 84.

[40] Maxwell, 'Physical Punishment in the Home in New Zealand' (above n 32), at 16 (italics omitted).

[41] 'Spare the rod, spoil the child', *Otago Daily Times,* 30 December 1997, at 1.

[42] A private member's bill was introduced by National MP, John Carter. The Education (Corporal Punishment) Bill 1992's aim was to permit individual school boards (and thus parents) to decide if corporal punishment was appropriate: (1992) 531 *NZPD* 12194-12216. See further Steenhof, 'Corporal Punishment' (above n 10), at 52 et seq. Interestingly, Roger McLay, the then Associate Minister of Health, supported this bill: (1992) 531 *NZPD* 12199.

[43] Their characterization at the 1999 national Plunket Society conference: 'Smacking a "dark stain"', *Otago Daily Times,* 26 March 1999, at 17.

[44] Section 7 (2)(ba) of the CYPFA 1989: inserted by s 4 of the CYPF Amendment Act 1994.

[45] See Susie Hall and Sue Stannard, 'Social Marketing as a tool to stop child abuse', *Social Work Now*, no 8, December 1997, at 5.

[46] 'Breaking the Cycle: Questions and Answers', Press Release, September 1998. See also 'Breaking the Cycle: Rationale—Smacking Children: Attitudes and Alternatives', Press Release, September 1988.

[47] 'Breaking the Cycle: Questions and Answers', ibid.

[48] 'Questions and Answers' (original emphasis).

[49] The Rev Capill's view, argued one writer to *Challenge Weekly*, was one not strongly held by most Christians: 'better to minimise smacking in general in an attempt to make such violent cases totally unacceptable', wrote Warwick Jones, 'Puzzled by article', *CW* (letter), 13 October 1998, at 3.

[50] 'An attack on parenting', *CW*, 29 September 1998, at 3.

[51] Holdway-Davis had personally-funded and marketed a safe-smack video: see Mary Anne Gill, 'To smack or not to smack', *Evening Post*, 18 November 1997, at 7.

[52] Philip Holdway-Davis, 'The anti-smacking campaign', *CW*, 10 November 1998, at 10.

[53] See, for instance, C H Rawle, 'Get those ink monitors out of our lives', *Otago Daily Times* (letter), 31 October 1998.

[54] 'Smacking should be illegal: Commissioner', *Otago Daily Times*, 15 December 1999, at 2.

[55] Ibid.

[56] 'No smacking ban plan', *Otago Daily Times*, 14 August 2000, at 4.

[57] Its Second Report is to be published in late 2000. A draft version of this Report was released by the Ministry of Youth Affairs in May 2000.

[58] Ministry of Youth Affairs, *United Nations Convention on the Rights of the Child: Initial Report of New Zealand* (1995).

[59] Ibid at 43, para 188.

[60] Ibid at para 189.

[61] Quoted in Joan E Durrant and Gregg M Olsen, 'Parenting and public policy: contextualizing the Swedish corporal punishment ban' (1997) 19 *J Soc Welfare & Fam Law* 443 at 457.

[62] The Minister's arguments are contained in a letter responding to a query from the Youth Law Project. The letter is reproduced in Parker, 'Repeal of Section 59 of the Crimes Act' (1994) 3 *Youth L Rev* 11 at 11. Roger McLay is currently the Commissioner for Children and he seems to have changed his view since 1994: see the text accompanying fn 54 above.

[63] See Richard P McLeod, 'The United Nations Convention on the Rights of the Child: Implications for Domestic Law', LLM research paper, Victoria University of Wellington, 1995, at 21 et seq.

[64] See Ministry of Youth Affairs, *Convention on the Rights of the Child: Presentation of the Initial Report of the Government of New Zealand* (May 1997). The withdrawal of reservations was one of the 53 questions for written answer requested. The first suggestion of the Committee in its Concluding Observations (ibid at 30, para 21) was that New Zealand be encouraged to withdraw its reservations to the CRC.

[65] *Presentation of Initial Report 1997*, ibid at 22.

[66] Ibid.

[67] 'Govt rules out ban on smacking', *Otago Daily Times*, 17 August 1997, at 1.

[68] *Presentation of Initial Report 1997*, at 29-30, paras 8-20. Concerns included, for example, the continuance of New Zealand's reservations, rises in the numbers of single-parent families, youth suicide and poor statistics for Maori children's wellbeing.

[69] Ibid at 31, para 29.

[70] [1997] NZFLR at 79.

[71] See Chapter 6, pp 171-172, for discussion.

[72] *Rajan* v *Minister of Immigration* [1996] 3 NZLR 543 at 551. See generally Law Commission, *A New Zealand Guide to International Law and its Sources*, NZLC Report 34 (May 1996) at paras 71-73 and Sir Kenneth Keith, 'The Impact of International Law on New Zealand Law' (1998) 7 *Waikato L Rev* 1.

[73] Peter Newell, UK co-founder and co-ordinator of EPOCH world-wide, complained that: 'Religious justifications for using physical punishment are particularly rife at the moment. Religious fundamentalism, with roots in America, is catching on here. . . . recently the new edition of James Dobson's, *Dare to Discipline* was published here.' Newell, 'Why we must stop hitting children' in Bainham and Pearl (eds), *Frontiers of Family Law*, 2nd edn (1995) ch 18 at 246.

[74] See further Rex Ahdar and James Allan, 'Taking Smacking Seriously: The Case for Retaining the Legality of Parental Smacking in New Zealand' [2001] *NZ L Rev* 1.

9 Church Autonomy and Gay Clergy

This chapter examines the conservative Christian (CC) concerns with homosexual conduct and gay rights. The liberal modernist state might view homosexuality as neutrally as heterosexuality, but for CCs this phenomenon is contrary to God's revealed order. Will conservative churches no longer be free to deny ordination and appointment to openly-practising homosexual or lesbian candidates for the ministry? I focus upon this paradigm incident of church autonomy, the right to select clergy, as an illustration of the clash between religious rights and gay rights.

Conservative Christian Concern with Homosexuality

Attitudes to Homosexual Practice and Gay Rights

Conservative Christians have a long history of opposition to homosexual rights and what they perceive to be a well-organized agenda to normalize what is, to them, a sinful lifestyle. Homosexual conduct is a subject that divides the CC from his or her liberal Christian counterpart. CCs are convinced that homosexual practice is never acceptable. Protestant CCs base their condemnation of homosexual acts on the various biblical prohibitions.[1] Catholic CCs buttress the scriptural proscriptions with appeals to tradition and natural law.[2] CCs draw a clear distinction between homosexual orientation or identity, on the one hand, and homosexual physical acts or practice, on the other. It is only the latter they condemn. As John Stott puts it: 'We may not blame people for what they are, though we may for what they do.'[3] The CC response to homosexuals is twofold: first, they are never to be rejected or despised but are to be shown understanding and compassion.[4] 'Homosexuals (including lesbians, transsexuals etc) are loved by God and by Christians.'[5] Second, homosexuals are urged to remain celibate and not physically express their inclinations. Same-sex liaisons or partnerships are not to be undertaken. God's grace and the spirit of self-control can be drawn upon to assist this sexual abstinence.[6]

Christian organizations such as Exodus International provide ongoing prayer, counselling and support for those seeking to abstain from a homosexual lifestyle.[7]

Whilst the majority of CCs now accept the decriminalization of homosexual conduct, the aggressive drive by the 'gay lobby' (as they term it) for acceptance of the homosexual way of life as an equally valid alternative to heterosexuality is threatening:

> With homosexual acts decriminalised only a decade ago, we are now seeing a push by the gay lobby to see homosexuality not only by society but in fact endorsed as a lifestyle as valid as any other. The church itself is being asked not only to accept homosexual behaviour as normal but to consider ordaining practising homosexuals to the ministry.[8]

Some even see gay activists at the vanguard of a 'cultural, moral and political revolution'[9] to overturn traditional Christian norms. Again, the family is the most vulnerable societal structure, with greater acceptance of homosexuality necessarily (in zero-sum fashion) undermining traditional, heterosexual-based family life. There is 'plenty of evidence of a homosexual/lesbian conspiracy which aggressively and purposefully seeks to undermine and destroy the husband-and-wife, family-centred institution of marriage.'[10]

In the 1990s, the Auckland 'Hero Parade' has been an annual locus of resentment, prompting public denunciation by CCs alarmed at this blatant affront to 'common decency'.[11] In February 1999, a visiting American CC, Mike Gabbard, Director of 'Stop Promoting Homosexuality International', mobilized a New Zealand group to carry on the world-wide counter movement.[12] This led, as we saw in Chapter 5, to the 'Real heroes' advertisement and the involvement of the Human Rights Commission. Attendance at the 1998 and 1999 parades by the Prime Minister, Jenny Shipley,[13] and several MPs, must have been a bitter blow to CC attempts to capture the high ground.

The Decriminalization Debate: the Homosexual Law Reform Act 1986

Homosexual law reform in New Zealand has, like other nations, been a controversial matter. An attempt to decriminalize private homosexual acts between consenting adult males in the mid-1970s came to naught.[14] A decade later, however, the climate, at least amongst MPs, had changed.

The Homosexual Law Reform Bill 1985 was introduced by a Labour MP, Fran Wilde. It proved to be a watershed for New Zealand CCs. The Bill became a rallying point and symbolized the drift into the permissive society and away from, as CCs perceived it, the nation's precious Christian moorings. Two CC mayors, Sir Peter Tait and Keith Hay, began a nation-wide petition to oppose the Bill.[15] The Salvation

Army offered staff to assist with the collection of signatures. Not all Christians approved. The conservative /liberal split is well illustrated here by the forming of liberal Christian coalition, Christian Action, to oppose the petition.[16] Some 835,000 signatures were collected, the largest in New Zealand's history (although there were recurring allegations of fraudulent and multiple signatures). The petition, however, proved unsuccessful. According to the Select Committee, division within the Church was a significant factor in the ultimate success of the Bill.[17] Homosexual intercourse between consenting males was duly decriminalized when the Homosexual Law Reform Act 1986 came into force.

The opponents of the legislation took advantage of the momentum created to form the Coalition of Concerned Citizens. Brett Knowles comments: 'the rejection of the Petition was perhaps the major factor which lead to the involvement of conservative Christians in the political arena.'[18] Pastor Barry Reed, a founder of the Coalition, believed: 'God has allowed the Homosexual Law Reform Bill and the petition opposing it to be the catalyst around which people who believe in a normal life can gather.'[19] The Coalition stood for 'God, Family and Country' (its motto), and while its active life was to be brief, its influence was to be lasting. CCs who had long been quietist and spurned political involvement were now galvanized into political participation. During the upheaval of the Springbok rugby tour in 1981, 'conservative Christians remained calm, pious and quick to lambaste'[20] the activist stance taken by (mainly) liberal Christians. By the late 1980s, the attitude to political involvement by most CCs had irrevocably changed. Now Christians of a liberal persuasion took umbrage and inveighed against the Coalition,[21] a move that simply stiffened the latter's resolve.

The homosexual law reform debate functioned in much the same way as the United States Supreme Court's abortion decision, *Roe* v *Wade*[22] did in provoking American CCs into action. The Coalition of Concerned Citizens withered but the seeds of CC political activism were to bear fruit in the form of the Christian Heritage Party (launched in 1989) and the Christian Democrats Party (formed in 1995).[23]

Recognition of Sexual Orientation Discrimination: the Human Rights Act 1993

The CC challenge to homosexual law reform in the mid-1980s had not been a completely futile exercise. Part II of the Homosexual Law Reform Bill 1985—amending the anti-discrimination legislation to add 'sexual orientation' as a prohibited ground of discrimination—was defeated. At the time, many MPs indicated that, while they were in favour of decriminalizing homosexual behaviour between consenting adults, they were opposed to 'legislat[ing] for public attitudes'[24] by banning discrimination on this basis. Mrs Whetu Tirikatene-Sullivan, a CC MP, articulated the concerns of CCs in forceful terms:

> I see the Bill as a radical measure. It has two revolutionary purposes. The first is to establish for the first time in New Zealand that the homosexual life-style is a legitimate option. The Bill is aimed at attesting, affirming, and enshrining that legitimacy in the laws of the country. Its second radical purpose is to attempt to redefine traditional normalcy as we have known it in our society. Its proponents are using the Bill and the debate to argue that homosexuality is a normal expression of human sexuality. The Bill seeks to make a socio-political statement that characterises the relatively recent gay liberation revolution.[25]

Success was to come, however, seven years later. Although the Human Rights Bill 1992 added five new grounds of unlawful discrimination, sexual orientation was absent. It took a belated effort by Katherine O'Regan, the Associate Minister of Health, to rectify what the then Leader of the Opposition, now Prime Minister, Helen Clarke, dubbed 'a major omission'.[26] Two new grounds of unlawful discrimination were thus included: the presence in the body of organisms capable of causing illness (addressing the HIV/AIDS issue), and 'sexual orientation'—namely, 'heterosexual, homosexual or bisexual orientation'.[27] To the concerned readers of *Challenge Weekly*, O'Regan recounted she came from a church-going family and was a member of an Anglican Church. The main lesson she had imbibed was that tolerance was a key part of Christian love. She could not see discrimination against anyone being right: 'It's about humanity', she defended.[28]

For many CCs it was a case of déja-vu. 'Ghost of '85 in new bill', ran the headline in *Challenge Weekly* as leading CC campaigners pledged to take up the battle again. A weary Pastor Barry Reed sighed: 'It seems most foolish and irresponsible to drag it [banning homosexual discrimination] up again. How many times do we have to do this?'[29] In January 1993, the Coalition, in conjunction with the Christian Heritage Party, launched a nation-wide petition to stop the two new grounds of non-discrimination being passed. Petition organizers were not convinced by assurances from O'Regan that churches would be exempt.

What was the thrust of CCs' concerns here? CCs were anxious about the proposed amendment's ramifications for, first, themselves and, thereafter, wider society.

First, some CCs foresaw a constriction in their religious freedom. Churches that condemned sodomy might be liable now to be prosecuted, argued the St Peter's Presbyterian Church, Tauranga, in its submission on the Bill. Churches would be forced to ordain practising homosexuals and Christian schools be required to hire gay teachers, predicted another. New Image Ministries believed its work—counselling homosexuals with a view to encouraging them to leave the homosexual lifestyle—would be hindered. Moreover, it perceived an inherent bias in the legislation against those with conservative religious convictions: 'religious folk will be inherently disadvantaged, and . . . the Human Rights Commission (unless its views have radically changed) will, on a clash of religious "rights" and homosexual "rights" usually judge in favour of the latter.'[30] Tirikatene-Sullivan endorsed this view in her speech on the Bill, invoking an American example:

> Research has pointed out that there is a clash between religious rights and homosexual rights. When that clash has occurred the religious rights have lost out. I give an example of the Catholic university in Georgetown, which was approached by gay groups that wanted to hold meetings on campus and to establish networks. The university authorities declined, as it went against the university's constitution as a Catholic university. However, under the human rights legislation the university was forced to go against its own constitution. So that is a very good example of religious rights missing out.[31]

Second, certain CCs foresaw disturbing consequential changes to important social institutions if the anti-discrimination measure was passed. Rob Munro MP discerned an insidious process at work:

> having taken the first step in 1985-86 [decriminalization], and having failed to take the second step at that stage [banning discrimination on the grounds of sexual orientation] . . . we should ask what the third step will be. If one takes the matter step by step, it is hard to argue that the next step will not be legal recognition of homosexual and lesbian couples and of their rights to adopt children.[32]

Michael Cullen MP aptly dubbed this phenomenon a 'kind of domino theory',[33] a characteristic belief of CCs (see Chapter 2). John Banks wondered '[w]hich moral principle [would] be next to fall victim to the permissive society?'[34] Grant Thomas was similarly exasperated: 'Where will all this end? Do we allow our moral standards and direction to continue to slide, or do we take a corrective stand and promote the decent society based on the Judeo-Christian principles that this nation was founded on?'[35] The CC MPs challenged the premise that gays were an oppressed, disadvantaged minority.[36] Quite the opposite: 'The push for the changes [was] coming from a small, active, well-organised, and very well-funded group in the community. . . '[37] The 'homosexual lobby', a group both 'powerful and sinister', had shrewdly cornered the market on rhetoric, noted John Banks: 'The lobby's rhetoric subverts language by monopolising all those good words such as "justice", "inclusive" and "tolerance", and attributes the disparaging opposites such as "unjust", "exclusive", "intolerant", and "prejudiced" to those people who sincerely think differently.'[38] Many CCs were annoyed that liberal churches had fostered this stigmatization of conservatives by their public endorsement of the Bill. For example, the submission of the Joint Methodist-Presbyterian Public Questions Committee supported the amendment, castigating those whose 'homophobia' was presented as the Christian view.[39] The editor of *Challenge Weekly* 'felt sick as [liberal] church after church' supported the Bill; he exhorted Christians to stand firm.[40]

Returning to the Parliamentiary debate, Michael Cullen discerned there had been 'a sea change in opinion'[41] since Part II of the Homosexual Law Reform Bill (containing the anti-discrimination clauses) had been voted down in the mid-1980s. The dire social consequences that CCs had prophesied should homosexuality be decriminalized had simply not occurred.[42] As Cullen mocked: 'Some members forecast that gloom and doom would descend and New Zealand would make what happened in Sodom and Gomorrah look like some sort of picnic . . . The fact is that nothing much has happened since that time, and the great majority of us have carried on with our heterosexual ways despite the legality of alternative forms of sexual expression.'[43] Before the majority of MPs there was a plain mischief of unjustifiable discrimination which the law ought to rectify. 'Can one argue', asked Cullen rhetorically, 'that if a person is engaged as a gardener or as a shorthand typist it is legitimate to refuse that person that job on the grounds that his or her sexual orientation is homosexual or bisexual?'[44] To the majority of members the answer was 'no'. The 'overwhelming weight of submissions', 497 out of 640, supported the change, as did 'the mainstream churches.'[45] It was only 'a few hysterical individuals who would give themselves the right to impose their own personal prejudices on the rest of society.'[46]

The tide had well and truly turned. Two attempts by CC MPs to preserve the religious rights of sincere CCs were unavailing. The Brethren and Pentecostal Churches sought an exemption for sincere religious employers whose convictions obliged them not to employ homosexuals.[47] Shades here of the *Eric Sides* amendment in 1981 (see Chapter 5). Some members supported the 'common-sense amendment'.[48] Richard Prebble rationalized that granting such an exemption 'would not make a huge difference to the general law but it would prevent a small group of determined people who—with the greatest respect to them, are zealots—from becoming martyrs.'[49] It would not 'help the cause of liberalism in New Zealand'[50] to make people martyrs. Liberals are tolerant. Nevertheless, the House, on a conscience vote, rejected the amendment.[51] Another CC MP supported an exemption from the employment discrimination ban to allow churches to discriminate in employment on the basis of sexual orientation. This too was defeated.[52]

Church Autonomy and Gay Ordination

Conservative Christians predicted that the Human Rights Act 1993 may force them to ordain openly-practising gay candidates for the ministry. I shall briefly outline the case for church autonomy and then traverse the debate within several mainline New Zealand churches.[53] Particularly fascinating is the role the Act played, and still plays, in the debate.

Some Justifications for Church Autonomy

Liberal Political Theory At least three arguments from liberal theory can be mounted.

First, religion can be pro-democratic where it checks the totalitarian tendencies of the large modern state. We encountered this idea earlier (Chapter 6) where families were posited as prime examples of 'mediating structures' between the individual and the state. In *The Culture of Disbelief*, Stephen Carter argues religions, at their best, may operate as a 'bulwark against government tyranny'.[54]

> Religions are in effect independent centers of power, with bona fide claims on the allegiance of their members, claims that exist alongside, are not identical to, and will sometimes trump the claims of obedience that the state makes. A religion speaks to its members in a voice different from that of the state, and when the voice moves the faithful to action, a religion may act as a counterweight to the authority of the state.[55]

As Carter colourfully puts it, 'Democracy needs its nose–thumbers'[56] and religions can—due to their allegiance to something other than, and higher than, the state—operate to resist tyranny.[57]

Not all religious communities are of the 'nose-thumbing' kind however. The conception of religion espoused by Carter is very much that of the dissenting church. There are faint echoes of Luther's remonstrance, *'Ich kan nicht anderst, hie stehe ich.'*('I cannot do otherwise, here I stand') here.[58] Some religious communities, however, may be thoroughly acculturated and see the state's policies as consistent with and furthering their religious objectives. Further, some religious groups may have such an extreme separationist attitude that they completely eschew participation in this-worldly, public affairs. They make no pretence of acting as a bulwark against tyranny.[59]

Second, man is a social being. Groups provide a context for personal growth, expression and fulfilment, and those formed on the basis of spiritual beliefs are no exception. A religious community, *par excellence*, affords its members the opportunity to interact, to find a sense of identity and meaning.[60]

Third, religious groups, among other types of association, may be a well-spring for new ideas, arguments and methods of reasoning outside the prevailing concepts and ways of thinking of liberal democracy.[61] Frederick Gedicks comments:

> In liberal society, the government has no competence to determine moral ends. In theory, at least, the goals of liberal democratic government must depend on the values held by those it governs—values that originate outside of government in churches, families, political parties, trade unions, private schools, and other voluntary associations. In the absence of these groups, government and society would be deprived of the enriching world-views that these groups contribute to . . . culture and politics.[62]

Some theorists also believe there is a crucial link between religion and the fostering of important civic virtues, such as law-abidingness, honesty, thrift and self–restraint.[63] But to speak of the virtue-enhancing propensities of religion generally is sweeping. There are religions and religions: 'To ask about religion's value-inculcating role at the close of the twentieth century one must speak not only of high-church Presbyterians, but of snake-handling fundamentalist Christians, Shiite Moslems, and Santerians, to mention only a handful of examples.'[64] Moreover, while religion may prescribe valuable moral norms and civic virtues, other institutions may also fulfil this function.[65]

Judicial Aversion to Theological or Ecclesiastical Matters The incompetence of any human authority to correctly evaluate true from false religion has been described as a 'common Protestant conviction': 'no mortal man and no human institution can be regarded as infallible.'[66] John Locke in his *Letter Concerning Toleration* argued:

> For every church is orthodox to itself; to others erroneous or heretical. . . . So that the controversy between these churches about the truth of their doctrines, and the purity of their worship, is on both sides equal; nor is there any judge, either at Constantinople, or elsewhere upon earth, by whose sentence it can be determined. The decision of that question belongs only to the Supreme Judge of all men, to whom also belongs the punishment of the erroneous.[67]

Courts in the common law world are notoriously reluctant to determine disputes of a religiously sensitive nature. There is not an absolute barrier to civil adjudication of church disputes—courts have, for example, long been called upon to resolve questions of property division following schism within a denomination—but the jurisdiction is exercised circumspectly. As the New Zealand Supreme Court observed: 'the Courts in my opinion must acknowledge that they will be chary of intervening in church matters unless there are valid and strong reasons for doing so.'[68] A generation later, the Court of Appeal endorsed the received view: 'Clearly, and reflecting the separation of church and state, Courts must be reluctant to determine what are at heart ecclesiastical disputes where matters of faith and doctrine are at issue.'[69]

Deference to church autonomy is commonplace in other common law jurisdictions. English courts, for instance, are loathe to determine matters of internal church governance. A recent example is *Wachmann*.[70] The Chief Rabbi disciplined the applicant Wachmann, an Orthodox rabbi, declaring him religiously and morally unfit to hold office. This ruling followed an internal commission of inquiry which substantiated allegations of adultery by the applicant with members of his congregation. Wachmann's employment was terminated and he sought judicial review. The High Court refused this in forthright terms. Despite judicial review extending to bodies 'which in earlier days would have surely have been thought beyond its reach'[71], further extension to this body was unwarranted. The Chief Rabbi's discharge of his religious functions was simply not of a public law character. The entanglement of church and state occasioned by permitting review added further force to this conclusion. Simon Brown J observed:

> the court would never be prepared to rule on questions of Jewish law. Mr Carus [counsel for Wachmann], recognising this prospective difficulty, says in advancing his challenge here the applicant would be prepared to rely solely upon the common law concept of natural justice. But it would not always be easy to separate out procedural complaints from consideration of substantive principles of Jewish law which may underlie them. . . . the court is hardly in a position to regulate what essentially is a religious function—the determination whether someone is morally and religiously fit to carry out the spiritual and pastoral duties of his office. The court must inevitably be wary of entering so self-evidently sensitive an area, straying across the well-recognised divide between church and state. One cannot, therefore, escape the conclusion that, if judicial review lies here, then one way or another this secular court must inevitably be drawn into adjudicating upon matters intimate to a religious community.[72]

International Human Rights Law As we have seen, New Zealand's recent rights legislation has been passed, in part, to fulfil its obligations under various United Nations treaties. Article 18(1) of the International Covenant on Civil and Political Rights 1966 makes it clear that the right of religious freedom applies 'individually or in community with others . . .' The UN's Human Rights Committee's exegesis of the Article states:

> In addition, the practice and teaching of religion or belief includes acts integral to the conduct by religious groups of their basic affairs, such as, inter alia, the freedom to choose their religious leaders, priests and teachers, the freedom to establish seminaries and religious schools and the freedom to prepare and distribute religious texts or publications.[73]

This statement is in the Committee's 1993 General Comment No 22, a pronouncement which is 'an authoritative statement'[74] of the Committee's understanding of the article. The Human Rights Committee's observation on church autonomy simply echoes the mention made in an earlier UN instrument, the Declaration on the Elimination of All Forms of Intolerance and of Discrimination Based on Religion or Belief 1981. Article 6 provides a non-exhaustive catalogue of particular freedoms within the rubric of religious freedom including, in paragraph (g), the freedom to 'train, appoint, elect, or designate by succession appropriate leaders called for by the requirements and standards of any religion or belief.'

The New Zealand Church Controversies

The ordination of openly-practising homosexual or lesbian candidates for the ministry (OPHM) has been a matter of sharp controversy within certain New Zealand denominations. Controversy has been confined primarily to two churches, the Presbyterian and Methodist Churches (with some smouldering debate in the Anglican Church as well). The gay ordination question has highlighted and, to some extent, exacerbated the liberal/conservative split documented in Chapter 2.

For some churches OPHM is not an issue. Thoroughgoing conservative denominations—the Pentecostal churches, Open Brethren, Seventh Day Adventists, Salvation Army and so on—have not, at least publicly, debated the issue. The absence of liberal theological factions within those churches means debate is unlikely to arise. However, these churches take a keen interest in the subject for it is a matter which 'affect[s] the entire church not just part of it.'[75] For the Catholic Church, the requirement of celibacy for priests and nuns officially rules out the possibility of gay clergy.[76] Bishop John Drew clarified that the celibacy requirement did not stop people with an orientation either way (heterosexual or homosexual) from seeking to train as a priest, but every effort would be made during the six years' seminary training to ensure they accepted and followed a celibate life, adding: 'We would never ordain a practising homosexual or heterosexual.'[77]

The Anglican Church has been reluctant to firmly state its position on OPHM. The *Tikanga Pakeha* (the European section of the Church) established a commission to study human sexuality issues. Bishop David Coles predicted that a diocesan-based policy would be the preferred option: 'It is up to each bishop to deal with the priests in a pastoral way, in accordance with the theological and cultural emphasis of the diocese.'[78] Some dioceses, he noted, currently had homosexual priests—some celibate, some with partners. As it transpired, the Commission's 1998 report refused to rule out gay clergy and argued instead for a case-by-case approach:

> Given that in the Anglican Church in Aotearoa, New Zealand and Polynesia, the decision to ordain a person deacon or priest lies with the Bishop after due consultation and advice from others . . . it is the view of the Commission that each application for ordination should be dealt with on an individual basis regardless of the candidate's marital status, gender, sexual orientation or sexual preference.[79]

The challenge of OPHM has been most divisive for Methodists. The catalyst for the polarizing debate between liberals and CCs in that denomination was the effort by Dr David Bromell, a self-avowed homosexual, to achieve ordination. Bromell was appointed as a supply (relieving) minister in a Dunedin parish. He applied for 'full connexion' into the ministry in 1990 but the annual Methodist Conference rejected his bid.[80] Eventually, and clearly influenced by the Human Rights Act, the 1997 Annual Conference voted to receive Bromell into full connexion.[81] The vote was not unanimous, with around a third of the Conference expressing strong disapproval. The fallout was immediate, the decision having 'ignited a flashpoint of indignation.'[82] Disgruntled evangelical Methodists—including many Pacific Island congregations—formed the 'Wesleyan Methodist Movement' with a view to breaking away from the Church.[83] The issue of OPHM was not the only concern prompting the proposed split but it was 'the straw that broke the camel's back.'[84] To avoid a wholesale schism caused by conservative Methodists breaking off to join like-minded brethren from the Presbyterian fold, the 1998 Conference agreed in principle to an 'Evangelical Synod'. Opposition by liberal elements to the creation of such a synod at the 1999 Conference left conservative Methodists frustrated and pondering their future.[85] In April 2000 the Wesleyan Methodist Movement claimed that around 1200 lay members (out of a membership of about 15,000) and 11 ministers had left because of the Church's acceptance of gay clergy.[86]

The most acrimonious and protracted debate on OPHM has been that within the Presbyterian Church of Aotearoa New Zealand (PCANZ). A series of General Assemblies since the mid-1980s has grappled with the issue. The 1985 General Assembly distinguished between homosexual orientation and practice and affirmed that 'homosexual acts [were] sinful', but added the rider that God loved and accepted homosexuals as people. The Church was urged to initiate compassionate ministry to those in a homosexual lifestyle. The 1991 Assembly passed a carefully-worded resolution: 'God's intention for sexual relationships, as affirmed by Jesus Christ, is loving, mutual and faithful marriage between a man and a woman, and that intimate sexual expressions outside of that context fall short of God's standard.'[87] While echoing the need for 'compassionate ministry, forgiveness and restoration' of those who fall short in this area, it was clear on OPHM: 'those who continue in sexual acts in any context outside of heterosexual marriage are not appropriate persons to be in the leadership of this Church.'[88]

In 1993 the Assembly deferred the vote on OPHM thereby allowing the prohibition on Presbyteries imposed by the 1991 Assembly to lapse. This was to establish 'a neutral environment'[89] and defuse deepening division until a Special Committee reported. One presbytery was impatient. In 1995 a Dunedin church attempted to license Martin Dickson, an exit student from Knox College (the national seminary) and a self-avowed practising homosexual living with a partner. A Judicial Commission of the PCANZ found that the Dunedin presbytery had failed to observe procedural fairness and had pre-empted the 1995 Assembly decision. It decided, however, that in the particular circumstances of this case, Dickson ought to be licensed. He had commenced his four-year training at Knox with the assurance from senior personnel that his homosexuality would not be an impediment to his being licensed. Although such an assurance was wrong, his legitimate expectations had now to be recognized. Invoking a regulation that gave the Church power to dispose of cases in exceptional circumstances, it approved the licensing. Dickson's lawyer was to later remark that the Human Rights Act had played a prominent role and that 'without the existence of the Act the outcome may have been different.'[90] So, on 5 November 1998, an historic first for the PCANZ took place. In a ceremony at Knox Church and attended by his parents, his partner and his partner's parents, Dickson, was 'licensed'. Licensing meant he could now accept a 'call' from a parish or act as a chaplain. Ordination would be another step again, however. Many evangelicals within the PCANZ were outraged. St Andrew's Presbyterian Church in Manurewa, for instance, described the licensing as 'unbiblical and unconstitutional'.[91]

Matters again came to a head at the 1996 General Assembly. The following resolution was adopted by 172 votes to 142:

> That Assembly, recognising the need for a clear ruling on practising homosexuals in leadership in the Church, rules that its courts shall not

> license, ordain or induct practising homosexuals. At the same time, Assembly recognises the deep diversity of convictions in the Church on issues relating to homosexuality generally and calls the Church to move ahead in a spirit of gracious respect and compassion for one another.[92]

Conservative Presbyterians were pleased but Galaxies (Gay and Lesbian Christians in Every Sphere) were dismayed. 'I'm sad', commented a homosexual elder at St Andrew's-on-the-Terrace Church, Wellington, 'at the stoney hearts of so many people in the assembly.'[93] The Rev Dr Jim Stuart of that congregation intimated that St Andrew's would flout the ruling and support the licensing of Ms Alyson Murrie-West, an ordained lesbian elder. In 1997 it made good its promise licensing Murrie-West. Presbyterian churches in Eastern Southland publicly dissociated themselves from the Wellington congregation's decision.

Hopes for a definitive verdict in 1998 were again to be frustrated. The attempt to ratify the 1996 ban on homosexual leadership failed to gain the necessary majority. The Assembly now required a 60 per cent vote for successful ratification and thus the simple majority in favour of the 1996 ruling (54.5 per cent) fell short. The Assembly voted instead to impose a one-year ban on OPHM, a similar ban on advocacy of views on the subject and for the establishment of a 'Commission on Diversity'. The latter would hear submissions and prepare plans for separate synods or streams within the PCANZ to accommodate the differing convictions of members on this vexed topic.

The Extra General Assembly in Christchurch in 1999 saw a majority of members reject proposals in favour of gay clergy. The vote (54 per cent) against each of the three motions for OPHM was interpreted as an 'impasse' by some commentators, but as a victory by Presbyterian AFFIRM, the umbrella group for evangelical Presbyterians.

Signs of battle fatigue were apparent at the 2000 Assembly in Dunedin. An attempt to reopen debate on OPHM was defeated. A challenge (by supporters of gay clergy) to the installation of the incoming Moderator, the Rt Rev Rob Yule, because of his strong public statements against the recognition of gay ministers, also failed.[94]

The Shadow of the Human Rights Act

A key premise in the church debates has been the belief that a clear ruling from the church authorities on OPHM was required. The PCANZ, for instance, took the understandably cautious approach that nothing short of a clear edict from the General Assembly would guarantee that congregations would enjoy immunity from suit under the Act. Presbyterian AFFIRM, whose affiliates had most to lose, articulated their concern thus:

> In the absence of specific regulations, the church is vulnerable to be forced to accept practising homosexuals as ministers by the provisions of the Human Rights Act, through either a ruling from the Human Rights Commission, or by a decision of the High Court in a test case. The lawyer who was acting for the practising homosexual who was licensed [Dickson] has publicly threatened that 'it ill behoves' anyone to oppose his ordination. A 'non-decision' by this Assembly would expose the PCANZ—and potentially *any* congregation—to expensive litigation.[95]

But the prospect of costly lawsuits was not the principal reason why CCs within these mainstream Protestant churches sought a definitive answer on OPHM. For them, the acceptance of homosexual or lesbian leadership was a watershed—would conservatives or liberals control the direction of the church henceforth?

Liberal Christians' response was twofold. First, they questioned what all the fuss was about. One mused, 'Some day we will look back and wonder why we struggled . . . It may be a surprise to discover the wheels do not fall off the Church when a parish appoints a homosexual minister.'[96] Another believed it 'would be wrong for us [the PCANZ] to be separated on the basis of this one rather narrow issue.'[97] The second liberal Christian tack was to strongly support OPHM as a 'matter of justice'[98] and 'the church . . . working for the human rights of all people.'[99] For them, one's sexual orientation or practice was as equally irrelevant as a test for leadership as it was for membership. God's love and mercy mandated 'inclusiveness' and 'tolerance'.

CCs replied by stressing the holiness as well as the mercy of God and reaffirming the continued relevance of the unchanging moral law. It was not an issue of justice, since no-one had an inalienable right to be a church leader, nor was it a matter of inclusiveness, for the Gospel was about repentance, grace and transformation. The distinction between membership, where inclusiveness could rightly pertain, versus leadership, which called for more exacting exclusive standards, was reiterated.[100] OPHM was not even a matter of competing interpretations since the Scripture, properly read, were 'very clear'.[101] No, it was matter of truth and a question of authority: would the Church take its lead and be subservient to the Scriptures or to man? 'The question is whether the Assembly is now willing to order the life of the Church in accordance with the will of God and the power of the Gospel, as revealed in the scriptures—or whether it wishes to slide off into uncertainty and confusion, and to put secular human opinion in the place of the Word of God as our new de facto "rule of faith and life".'[102] A defining characteristic of the CC is, as Chapter 2 explained, submission to authority. The Church was in danger of making liberal Western culture its authority. But, retorted one evangelical Methodist minister, 'Where does liberalism find its authority? Is it the Scriptures, sermons of Wesley, or somewhere else?' Liberalism was endeavouring to impose justifications for homosexuality upon the Scriptures, 'making Scripture subject to liberalism.' This was, he continued, plainly wrong.[103] Using the language of the 1990s, one CC remonstrated that 'the church needs to quickly find the courage to stand up and become BC, not PC. That is, biblically correct, not politically correct.'[104] As we saw in Chapter 2, another defining characteristic of CCs is that they are oppositional. Accepting homosexual leadership would be a graphic succumbing to the *zeitgeist*, the spirit of the times.

In the CC understanding, just as the state is under God, likewise Caesar's law is subservient to God's law. When the state exceeds its delegated authority and trespasses in spheres properly not its domain, civil disobedience may be the last resort. The belligerent streak in CCs eschews 'supine yielding to the pressures of secularisation.'[105] Presbyterian AFFIRM hinted at possible disobedience if the Human Rights Act were construed to force them to ordain practising homosexuals as ministers. It reminded its readers of its Reformation roots: 'Assembly would have ultimate responsibility not to the secular law but to the law of God.'[106] Any Christian church 'must follow its biblical conscience' in clashes between secular and divine law, 'even if obedience to a higher law brings a measure of suffering.'[107]

Liberal Christians, by contrast, harboured real reservations on flouting the law, at least on this issue. Liberals, to recapitulate, are prepared to risk breaking the law on matters of social justice such as apartheid and Springbok tour protests. But this issue was different. Liberal Christians supported the Human Rights Act. They had furnished submissions in favour of sexual orientation being added as a ground of prohibited discrimination just a few years earlier. Denominations where the liberals' sway was strong were content to comply with the Act. The Methodist Annual Conference of 1993 decided that the Methodist Church ought to 'order its life and practice within the intent of the [Human Rights] Act'.[108] The Methodist President, the Rev Mervyn Dine, said the Church 'won't be trying to find clauses in the [A]ct to get them out'[109] of abiding by the statute. For supporters of gay clergy, the Act was a valuable tool in changing church policy. It is idle to suggest that the Act was supported by liberal Christians solely to advance the cause of OPHM, but, once in place, it could nonetheless be usefully invoked. 'As minister of Christ's church I don't wish', wrote the Rev Margaret Mayman, 'to solve our deep divisions about sexuality by appealing to secular legislation. . . . But if the state can lead the Church closer to the gospel of love and compassion, then so be it.'[110] For CCs, a humanistic, post-Christian state could do nothing of the kind; rather its direction was the opposite. For them, OPHM was an issue that exposed the non-theistic grounding of contemporary human rights theory.

The experience of the churches debating in the shadow of the Human Rights Act supports the supposition of some American judges that the mere prospect of state intrusion may intrude upon a church's process of self-definition and thus entail a 'chilling effect' upon church autonomy.

Justice Brennan in *Presiding Bishop of the Church of Jesus Christ of Latter-Day Saints* v *Amos*[111] put the case for judicial deference to religious organizations' control over their internal governance in terms of the importance of self-definition. Any group, but especially a religious one, must be able to define its purpose or 'mission'. It has a 'narrative' or vision of itself.[112] It should have the ultimate say over who is a member or not, what are its core concerns. Justice Brennan explained that a religious community

> represents an ongoing tradition of shared beliefs, an organic entity not reducible to a mere aggregation of individuals. Determining that certain activities are in furtherance of an organization's religious mission, and that only those committed to that mission should conduct them, is thus a means by which a religious community defines itself. Solicitude for a church's ability to do so reflects the idea that furtherance of the autonomy of religious organizations often furthers individual religious freedom as well.[113]

Religious group self-definition may trammel upon individual rights. The organization may 'condition employment in certain activities on subscription to particular religious tenets.'[114] The process of self-definition, the control over one's own narrative, was, however, important enough for Justice Brennan to countenance the infringement of individual liberty and the thwarting of the government's interest in a societal policy of non-discrimination. Judicial determination of such matters as clergy selection may require 'a searching case-by case analysis'[115] resulting in the very sort of government 'entanglement' in religious affairs which is best avoided. As equally disturbing was the 'chilling effect' of potential state intervention upon a religious organization's internal governance.[116] A church may make its decision with as much an eye toward state standards and bureaucratic intervention as its own religious convictions: 'the community's process of self-definition would be shaped in part by the prospects of litigation.'[117]

It is difficult not to conclude that the two New Zealand denominations' process of self-definition was shaped, at least in part, by the prospects of litigation. The Methodist and Presbyterian Churches have made particular ordination decisions with an eye to avoiding litigation and bureaucratic entanglement, rather than solely on the basis of their own doctrinal assessments of who would best serve their pastoral needs. At the very least, the passing of the Act gave a heightened sense of urgency to what was already a simmering division. The influence of the Act is all the more problematic since it is by no means clear it applies to OPHM in the first place.

Does the Human Rights Act apply?

The Human Rights Bill 1992 in its original form did not cover sexual orientation discrimination. As we saw, this ground of prohibited discrimination was added at a later stage. Some CCs were concerned at their religious liberties being curtailed should sexual orientation discrimination be recognized. Katherine O'Regan endeavoured to assuage such fears: 'it is not my intention that the legislation should force churches to accept homosexual ministers. It is not my intention either that the legislation should prevent churches from preaching that homosexuality is sinful . . .'[118]

Many CCs were, nonetheless, not assured. *Challenge Weekly*, for instance, pressed the Human Rights Commission for a clear pronouncement that churches would be exempt from employing gay ministers.[119] The Chief Human Rights Commissioner, Margaret Mulgan, was quoted in *Challenge Weekly* to the effect that churches and para-church ministries were exempt from employing practising homosexuals.[120] Where a church, she was quoted two months later, could demonstrate that its doctrines, rules or customs did not allow it to appoint homosexual people, it would be immune.[121]

Section 38 of the Act stipulates that it is unlawful for a qualifying body (one empowered to confer an 'approval, authorisation or qualification' that is needed for engagement in a 'profession, trade or calling') to discriminate on any of the prohibited grounds. Section 39(1) provides an exemption for religion, but it is not a model of clarity:

> **39. Exemptions in relation to qualifying bodies —**
> (1) Nothing in section 38 of this Act shall apply where the authorisation or qualification is needed for, or facilitates engagement in, a profession or calling for the purposes of an organised religion and is limited to one sex or to persons of that religious belief so as to comply with the doctrines or rules or established customs of that religion.

Several readings of s. 39 are possible, and that has been the problem.[122]

The widest reading would afford religious organizations a complete exemption from s. 38 because of the type of qualification they confer. The section is concerned with identifying the *category* of authorization which is wholly exempt from the s. 38 ban. It is not concerned with immunizing particular determinations of the religious body based on nominated grounds. So, the Methodist Church is exempt since it ordains candidates for the purposes of Methodism and restricts candidates to those who are Methodist so as to comply with the tenets of Methodism.

This construction accords with the assurance by O'Regan in Parliament, the protection afforded clergy ordination determinations by the UN Human Rights Committee's General Comment No 22 and the immunity recognized in most common law jurisdictions. This reading does not require the church to point to a rule or custom holding that ordination of practising homosexuals is impermissible. Admittedly, it would permit churches to restrict approvals on any of the 13 prohibited grounds in s. 21(1). Thus, a denomination would be allowed, for example, to ordain only persons of one race or ethnic origin. Such a ramification is certainly unpalatable, but is, I suggest, part and parcel of recognizing a robust principle of church autonomy. Churches should be free to select leaders on bases the majority of people in society would abhor. Anti-discrimination law does not govern the life of all private associations. The Human Rights Act currently recognizes a degree of private associational freedom by exempting clubs from its coverage.[123] (For similar reasons, the majority of the US Supreme Court recently held that, pursuant to the First Amendment protection of the right of 'expressive association', the Boy Scouts of America were not required to admit an avowed homosexual assistant scoutmaster.[124]) Presumably, churches, clubs and other voluntary associations face public disapproval and evaporating patronage if their leadership and membership decisions are unpopular. A social rather than legal sanction ought to suffice.

Another construction of s. 39(1) is possible. Much denominational debate assumes that an authoritative church statement on homosexual leadership is essential. The premise has been that the s. 39(1) exemption requires churches to point to a relevant tenet. Pursuant to s. 85, the defendant institution would be required to establish, on the balance of probabilities, that there exists a 'doctrine, rule or established custom' of their church to the effect that homosexual leadership is impermissible. Evangelicals within the PCANZ have consistently sought such a ruling but it ought not to be strictly necessary, for the institution ought to be able to glean its position on such a matter from its general principles and tradition. Besides, s. 39(1) does not require a specific written rule, referring also to 'established customs'. Customs are typically unwritten and must be discerned by those following them.

If a church's national body does proffer the view that its doctrines or established customs dictate that practising homosexuals be denied (or allowed) ordination, that should be the end of the matter.[125] To go behind the assertion of the institution would be dangerous. It would risk the sort of 'entanglement' by secular tribunals with ecclesiastical affairs which has been universally decried. The tribunal ought to take at face value the authoritative statement, even amidst internal friction within the church concerned. Otherwise, it risks embarking upon a task it is ill-equipped to undertake—resolving matters of theological controversy. Of course, much turns upon what is an 'authoritative' statement.[126] The secular tribunal cannot simply take at face value any proffered statement of custom and tradition from anyone in that body.[127] The point at issue may be hotly contested, with various factions claiming to be the authentic voice of the institution. To this extent, the tribunal may be required to evaluate competing evidence from opposing 'camps'. Here, the tribunal would need to tread circumspectly and limit its assessment to determining who is the authoritative spokesperson—without becoming embroiled in the substance of the complaint or the politics of the debate. Where the denomination has a devolved structure, with autonomous local congregations and no authoritative umbrella body, it is possible that each congregation may need to be an 'organised religion' for the purpose of the section. The very fact that this inquiry can give rise to questions such as: Does a rule or custom exist? Who is in a position to state it? Do such persons speak for the institution? and so on, indicates the improbability that this construction was the one intended by Parliament.

Conclusion

Conservative Christians have lost successive battles on homosexual law reform. For them, the 'normalization' of homosexual practice and lifestyle underlines the cultural disestablishment of Christianity, reminding them that New Zealand is a post-Christian society. The Wellington worldview is marked by ethical relativism: the liberal state recognizes diverse conceptions of the good life as expressed in sexual mores and practices.

The addition of 'sexual orientation' to the prohibited grounds of discrimination under the Human Rights Act 1993 was opposed by CCs. Amongst their concerns was the possible impact of the Act upon the ordination of clergy. Would CCs' religious freedom be curtailed by the state preventing them from rejecting openly-practising gay candidates for the ministry? The answer to this is still unclear. Debates within certain denominations still rage on this issue. The uncertain application of the Human Rights Act has made the church debates more complex and urgent. From a CC perspective, the sexual orientation discrimination prohibition in the Act and the cryptic wording of the exemption for churches have played too significant a part. Uncertain application of secular law has, for CCs, had a 'chilling effect' on a critical church matter. By the same token, if the Act had unambiguously exempted churches on the issue, I have little doubt that CCs would have invoked it with the alacrity their liberal opponents have.

Returning to my model of engagement, one sees an attempt at peaceful coexistence between the two worlds. The state has sought to accommodate religious conviction by inserting exemptions for religious organizations in the Human Rights Act. The liberal state prefers liberal religions but, for those faiths which do not reflect modernist ideals, it is willing to grant exemptions. Accommodation here costs the state little: this sort of exemption, observes Mark Tushnet, 'do[es] not threaten social stability as the liberals see it.'[128] More tellingly, such exemptions for private associations do not threaten the central public institutions (rationality, neutrality, and so on) of the liberal state.

Parliament's aspiration that church autonomy and unimpeded clergy selection be preserved may be foiled due to the clumsy drafting of the Act and a Human Rights Commission determined to vindicate gay rights. If the result of a test case should go against CCs and they should lose their right to refuse openly-practising homosexual candidates for the ministry, the intolerant, totalitarian propensities of human rights laws (as predicted by some CC theorists) will have been revealed. To quote Paul Marshall from Chapter 3 again: 'in this liberal society, communities are not free: rather they are constrained to become liberal associations.' I suspect civil disobedience by many conservative churches would follow.

If churches are 'off the hook' and their exemption for training, ordination and appointment of clergy is confirmed, peaceful coexistence will have been restored. Nonetheless, CCs cannot afford to be sanguine. They will need to remind the liberal state of its own professed tenets; those such as the value of mediating institutions and their vital role in fostering moral and civic virtue. Perhaps the CC conception of the good life may no longer be one that a free and democratic society values—it is too intolerant, bigoted and disruptive of the discourse shaped by ideological pluralism. As one liberal theorist opined recently: 'The extinction of many, if not all, of the [religious] communities that pose truly radical alternatives to liberal democratic political principles is to be welcomed.'[129] CCs may need to work that much harder to remind the state of the continued merits of church autonomy.

Notes

1 John Stott notes there are four main biblical passages: the story of Sodom and Gomorrah (Genesis 19); the Levitical texts (Leviticus 18:22 and 20:13); Paul's description of a decadent pagan society (Romans 1:18-32) and Paul's catalogue of sinners (1 Corinthians 6:9-10 and 1 Timothy 1:8-11). See Stott, *New Issues Facing*

Christians Today, 3rd edn (1999) ch 16 at 385-392. See also R T France, *A Slippery Slope? The Ordination of Women and Homosexual Practice–A Case Study in Biblical Interpretation*, Grove Booklet B 16 (2000) ch 4.

2 See *Catechism of the Catholic Church* (1994) at para 2357.

3 Stott, *New Issues Facing Christians Today*, at 384. See also France, *A Slippery Slope?* at 6.

4 See, for example, Stott, ibid, at 410-418; *Catechism* (above n 2), at para 2358.

5 Julian Batchelor, 'Let's talk straight', *Challenge Weekly* ('*CW*'), 16 February 1999, at 2.

6 Stott, *New Issues Facing Christians Today* (above n 1), at 411; *Catechism* (above n 2), at para 2359.

7 See 'Exodus Ministries' in Belding and Nicholls (eds), *A Reason For Hope: Christian Perspectives on Homosexuality and Healing* (1996) at 143. This anthology is published by the Human Relationships Foundation, a CC organization.

8 'Preface', in *A Reason For Hope*.

9 'The Homosexual Movement', a response by the Ramsey Colloquium (a group comprising US conservative Christian and Jewish scholars): reproduced in *A Reason for Hope*, ibid, 1 at 2.

10 Ludwig Feiderhof, on behalf of the Public Questions Committee of St Stephen's Methodist Church, Tauranga: quoted in 'Hero parade contrary to common decency', *CW*, 12 March 1997, at 1.

11 See, for example, 'Stand for truth, decency', *CW*, 18 May 1994, at 1.

12 See Julie Belding, 'Stop Promotion of Homosexuality', *CW*, 16 February 1999, at 1 and 3.

13 The Prime Minister, a Presbyterian and daughter of a minister, defended her attendance to *Challenge Weekly*: the Hero Parade was 'not an exhibition of depravity but rather a celebration of the diversity' in modern New Zealand: 'Church is Crucial', *CW*, 24 August 1999, 1 at 5.

14 The Crimes Amendment Bill, introduced on 23 July 1974, was defeated, on a conscience vote, by 34 votes to 29: (1975) 399 *NZPD* 2829.

15 The foregoing account is drawn from John Adsett Evans, 'The New Christian Right in New Zealand' in Gilling (ed), *'Be Ye Separate': Fundamentalism and the New Zealand Experience* (1992) at 85-86; Brett Knowles, 'Some Aspects of the History of the New Life Churches of New Zealand 1960-1990', Ph D thesis, University of Otago, 1994, at 300-308 and Bruce Ansley, 'The growing might of the moral right', *NZ Listener*, 26 October 1985, at 16-18.

16 See 'Hostile attack on "fundamentalists" by pro-bill Christians', *CW*, 25 October 1985, at 16. Supporters of the bill—including a group holding a placard, 'Christians for the Bill'—were kept separate from the petitioners by police.

17 'Submissions show divided Church', *CW*, 25 October 1985, at 16.

18 Knowles, 'History of New Life Churches' (above n 15), at 308.

19 'Moral coalition to help halt decay', *CW*, 6 September 1985, at 1.

20 Evans, 'New Christian Right', at 84.

21 See, for instance, the Presbyterian Church Joint Public Questions Committee paper, 'Theology and Politics: the "Moral Right" and the 1987 General Election'.

22 410 US 113 (1973). As Carter comments: 'For many religious conservatives, *Roe*

was like a cold shower.' Stephen L Carter, *The Culture of Disbelief* (1993) at 58.

23 See generally Jonathan Boston, 'Christian Political Parties and MMP' in Ahdar and Stenhouse (eds), *God and Government: The New Zealand Experience* (2000) ch 6.

24 George Gair (1985) 466 *NZPD* 7271.

25 (1985) 466 *NZPD* 7274.

26 (1992) 532 *NZPD* 13204.

27 (1992) 532 *NZPD* 1308.

28 See Snowden, 'Shared concern for justice, health', *CW*, 20 May 1993, at 4. See also her Parliamentary speech: (1993) 537 *NZPD* 16932.

29 *CW*, 29 October 1992, at 1.

30 'Rights bill infringes Christians' rights', *CW*, 13 December 1990, at 5.

31 (1992) 532 *NZPD* 13216. The case alluded to is *Gay Rights Coalition* v *Georgetown University*, 536 A 2d 1 (DC 1987)(DC Court of Appeal). For discussion, see Shelly Wessels, 'The Collision of Religious Exercise and Governmental Nondiscrimination Policies' (1989) 41 *Stanford L Rev* 1201 at 1227-1229.

32 (1993) 537 *NZPD* 16935. The notion of an incremental extension of homosexual rights is not uncommon in literature by gay commentators: see, for example, Robert Wintemute, 'Sexual Orientation Discrimination' in McCrudden and Chambers (eds), *Individual Rights and the Law in Britain* (1994) ch 15 at 530.

33 (1993) 537 *NZPD* 16939.

34 (1993) 537 *NZPD* 16916.

35 (1993) 537 *NZPD* 16931.

36 For American judicial support, see Justice Scalia's dissent in *Romer* v *Evans*, 134 L Ed 2d 855 at 874-875 (1996) and Richard F Duncan, 'Who Wants to Stop the Church: Homosexual Rights Legislation, Public Policy, and Religious Freedom' (1994) 69 *Notre Dame L Rev* 393 at 401-411. Prior to the 1999 General Election some commentators argued the 'gay vote' was one that political parties were keen to secure: see Mark Thiele, 'Major parties branch out to swing big gay vote', *Sunday Star-Times*, 7 November 1999, at C2.

37 Rob Munro (1993) 537 *NZPD* 16935.

38 (1993) 537 *NZPD* 16916-16917. See similarly Justice Scalia in *Romer* v *Evans*, 134 L Ed 2d at 878.

39 See 'The Bill: Catholics want less, Meth's-Presb's want more', *CW*, 20 May 1993, at 4.

40 John Massam, 'Standing firm' (editorial), *CW*, 5 August 1993, at 2.

41 (1993) 537 *NZPD* 16973.

42 See Jim Anderton (1992) 532 *NZPD* 13217 and Helen Clarke (1992) 532 *NZPD* 13206-13207.

43 Ibid.

44 (1992) 532 *NZPD* 13215.

45 (1993) 537 *NZPD* 16910.

46 Lianne Dalziel MP, ibid. See also John Robertson (1993) 537 *NZPD* 16921, who referred scathingly to 'those who choose to deny basic human rights to minority groups in society', a group holding 'deep prejudices that would be a waste of time [to debate with] for they tend not to reason nor to listen.'

47 (1993) 537 *NZPD* 16934.
48 Michael Laws (1993) 537 *NZPD* 16975.
49 (1993) 537 *NZPD* 16942.
50 Ibid.
51 By 40 votes to 21: (1993) 537 *NZPD* 16957-16958.
52 By 45 votes to 20: (1993) 537 *NZPD* 16969.
53 For a fuller discussion, see Ahdar, 'Religious Group Autonomy, Gay Ordination and Human Rights Law' in O'Dair and Lewis (eds), *Law and Religion* (Current Legal Issues 4) (2001) (forthcoming).
54 Stephen L Carter, *The Culture of Disbelief* (1993) at 36. See also John H Garvey, *What Are Freedoms For?* (1996) at 153.
55 Carter, *Culture of Disbelief*, at 35.
56 Ibid.
57 'Religion makes us aware that the civil order is but part of the timeless moral order ordained by the universal sovereign, and not the mere choice of passing majorities.' Michael W McConnell, 'Establishment and Toleration in Edmund Burke's "Constitution of Freedom"' [1995] *Sup Ct Rev* 393 at 423.
58 Quoted in Scott C Idleman 'The Sacred, the Profane, and the Instrumental: Valuing Religion in the Culture of Disbelief' (1994) 142 *U Pa L Rev* 1313 at 1334.
59 See Idleman, ibid at 1348–1349.
60 Paul Horwitz, 'The Sources and Limits of Freedom of Religion in a Liberal Democracy' (1996) 54 *U Toronto Fac L Rev* 1 at 53-54.
61 Ibid at 52–53.
62 Frederick Mark Gedicks, 'Toward a Constitutional Jurisprudence of Religious Group Rights' [1989] *Wisc L Rev* 99 at 116.
63 John Locke insisted religious belief was needed to foster moral values such as law abidingness and self–restraint: see Sanford Kessler, 'John Locke's Legacy of Religious Freedom' (1984–85) 17 *Polity* 484 at 495. For a comprehensive exposition of the civic virtue rationale for religious freedom, see Timothy L Hall, 'Religion and Civic Virtue: A Justification of Free Exercise' (1992) 67 *Tulane L Rev* 87.
64 Hall, 'Religion and Civic Virtue', at 108. Steven D Smith, *Foreordained Failure: The Quest for a Constitutional Principle of Religious Freedom* (1995) at 102 comments: 'Are the social fruits of religion sweet or bitter? Upon reflection it should be plain, I think, that these questions not susceptible of any general or uniform response. The only plausible answer, rather, is "It depends . . ."
65 Schools, universities, families, service clubs, debating societies and sporting organizations are other mediating institutions which contribute to the virtues thought vital to a liberal democracy. See Hall, 'Religion and Civic Virtue', at 112–113; Smith, *Foreordained Failure*, at 103.
66 Winthrop S Hudson, 'The Theological Basis for Religious Freedom' (1961) 3 *JCS* 130 at 133.
67 John Locke, *Epistola de Tolerantia (A Letter Concerning Toleration)*, 1689, in Horton and Mendus (eds), *John Locke, A Letter Concerning Toleration—In Focus* (1991) 12 at 24.
68 *Gregory* v *Bishop of Waiapu* [1975] 1 NZLR 705 at 708 per Beattie J.

[69] *Mabon* v *Conference of the Methodist Church of New Zealand* [1998] 3 NZLR 513 at 523 per Richardson P.
[70] *R* v *Chief Rabbi, ex parte Wachmann* [1993] 2 All ER 249.
[71] Ibid at 253.
[72] Ibid at 255.
[73] General Comment No 22, at para 4. The HRC adopted the General Comment (CCPR/C/21/Rev 1/ Add 4) on 20 July 1993. It is reproduced in (1994) 15 *Human Rights L J* 233.
[74] Malcolm Evans, *Religious Liberty and International Law in Europe* (1997) at 208.
[75] Dean Comerford, 'Homosexual issues affect entire Christian church', *CW*, 21 July 1998, at 3.
[76] *Catechism* (above n 2), at para 1579.
[77] Quoted in Ian Harris, 'Sexual equality before God', *Dominion*, 23 December 1997, at 8.
[78] Quoted ibid.
[79] Tikanga Pakeha Commission on Sexuality of the Anglican Church in Aotearoa, New Zealand and Polynesia (May 1998) at 14.
[80] See Vic Francis, 'Methodist Church split over homosexuality', *CW*, 27 June 1991, at 7-8.
[81] Diane Gilliam-Weeks, 'Bromell received in to Full Connexion', *Crosslink*, December 1997, at 1.
[82] The description in the Catholic press: Norman Goreham, 'Homosexual issue causes split in Methodist Church', *NZ Catholic*, 21 December 1997, at 4.
[83] The WMM was formed by 30 evangelical Methodist leaders on 21 November 1997: 'NZ Methodism in crisis', *CW*, 27 January 1998, at 1.
[84] Frith Rayner, 'The other side', *Crosslink*, June 1999, at 8-9.
[85] See 'Real issue at stake is the authority of God's Word', *CW*, 23 November 1999, at 1 and 7.
[86] 'Members lost over division on gay clergy', *Press*, 11 April 2000.
[87] *PCANZ Minutes of the 1991 General Assembly*, at 84.
[88] Ibid (carried by 212 votes to 124).
[89] *PCANZ Minutes of the General Assembly 1993*, at 115.
[90] 'The Presbytery of Dunedin licenses gay student to the ministry', *Crosslink*, December 1995, at 1.
[91] 'Church condems licensing', *Otago Daily Times*, 17 November 1995, at 4.
[92] *PCANZ Minutes of the General Assembly 1996*, at 83.
[93] Quoting Bill Edgington in 'Church ruling opposes homosexual ministers', *Otago Daily Times*, 6 July 1996, at 2.
[94] See Mayston, 'Challenge to moderator draws little support', *Otago Daily Times*, 2 October 2000, at 3.
[95] 'Should the Presbyterian Church Ordain Practising Homosexuals? A Position Paper', Presbyterian AFFIRM, June 1996, at 8 (italics in original).
[96] The Rev Norman West in 'Te Hahi hits "the issue"', *Crosslink*, October 1997, at 5.
[97] The Rev Chris Nichol in 'Sad News', *CW*, 14 July 1998, at 5.
[98] The Rev Norman West in 'Te Hahi' hits the "issue".

[99] The Rev Chris Nichol: quoted in Mark Toomer, 'Presbyterian Church upholds historic biblical view', *CW*, 13 July 1999, at 3.

[100] See Presbyterian AFFIRM, 'Position Paper', at 1-2. See also Stuart Lange, *Homosexuality and the Church*, AFFIRM Booklet No 4 (1998) at 12 and 17.

[101] The Rev Chris Dombroski in 'Te Hahi hits "the issue"'. See also France, *A Slippery Slope?* (above n 1) at 22.

[102] *Presbyterian AFFIRM Newsletter*, 1998/2, at 4.

[103] The Rev Chris Dombroski in 'Te Hahi hits "the issue"'.

[104] Comerford, 'Homosexual issues affect entire Christian church' (above n 75).

[105] Max Lane, 'Astonishing', *CW*, 30 June, 1 at 5.

[106] *Presbyterian AFFIRM Newsletter*, 1998/2, at 7.

[107] The Rev Stuart Lange in 'A hard Act to follow' (opinion feature), *Crosslink*, June 1998, at 13.

[108] Methodist Church of New Zealand, *Reports and Resolutions of the Annual Conference 1993*, at 696.

[109] 'Methodists bow to Human Rights Act', *CW*, 24 November 1993, at 3.

[110] 'A hard Act to follow' (above n 107).

[111] 483 US 327 (1987).

[112] Gedicks, 'Religious Group Rights' (above n 62), at 108.

[113] 483 US at 342. See also Garvey, *What Are Freedoms For?* (above n 54) at 149-150.

[114] 483 US at 342.

[115] Ibid at 343 -344.

[116] Ibid.

[117] Ibid.

[118] (1992) 532 *NZPD* 13208.

[119] 'Churches' rights questioned', *CW*, 19 August 1993, at 1.

[120] 'Majority favoured discrimination', *CW*, 5 August 1993, at 1.

[121] 'Churches may be off the hook', *CW*, 17 November 1993, at 3.

[122] For a greatly condensed discussion, see Paul Rishworth, 'Bill of Rights, Human Rights' [1998] *NZ L Rev* 585 at 601-602.

[123] Section 44(4).

[124] *Boy Scouts of America* v *Dale*, 147 L Ed 2d 554 (2000).

[125] See the majority opinion in *Dale*, ibid at 564-565, where the justices were prepared to accept the Boy Scouts' assertion that homosexuality was at odds with the general mission of that organization.

[126] I am most grateful to my colleague John Dawson for this point.

[127] A point stressed by the minority in *Dale*, 147 L Ed 2d at 585-586.

[128] Mark Tushnet, *Taking the Constitution Away from the Courts* (1999) at 86.

[129] Stephen Macedo. 'Transformative Constitutionalism and the Case of Religion: Defending the Moderate Hegemony of Liberalism' (1998) 26 *Political Theory* 56 at 75.

10 Challenging Same-Sex Marriage

In post-Christian, pluralist New Zealand, are conservative Christians (CCs) hampered in influencing society and shaping public policy? Can they challenge the introduction of laws that, to them, take society down a degenerative path? Is their positive religious freedom hindered? My focus here is different from the previous chapters in this Part, which examined certain threats to CCs' negative religious liberty. I have selected the introduction of same-sex marriage (SSM) as a contemporary case study to assess the degree of CCs' positive religious liberty. I explore the legal impediments to public opposition by CCs to SSM and then briefly consider whether they can make a successful case against it under the current terms of public debate.

Concerns with Same-Sex Marriage

CCs maintain that homosexual practice is sinful and that homosexual marriage is likewise. The latter is, for them, unnatural, unbiblical and demeans the existing (and fragile) institution of marriage. SSM is a key issue for both sides of the debate, for its recognition would spell a massive and decisive victory for the thoroughgoing 'normalization' of homosexuality. It would entail, as some CCs see it, many unpalatable consequences for society, the traditional family and so on. The Rev Stuart Lange, Secretary of Presbyterian AFFIRM, articulates the concern:

> While the case for same-sex marriage is usually expressed in terms of discrimination and loss of legal rights, it would seem that the main motivation is the normalisation and full public acceptance of homosexuality. How more respectable can homosexuality get, if the law were to legitimise legally contracted homosexual partnerships as simply 'marriage'? . . . One problem with recognising homosexual marriage is that, by definition, and in every human society that has ever existed, the essence of marriage is a union of a man and a woman. A same-sex marriage is a contradiction in terms. . . . A same-sex partnership may one day be recognised in law—but whatever it is, it is not marriage. But for Christians—and for most religions—the objection to the concept of same-sex marriage goes much deeper. Marriage is something established by God,

part of the very basis of human life and society. In a word, marriage is sacred. To allow homosexual couples to marry would defile and demean marriage, and would lend to homosexuality a spiritual and moral legitimacy it can never have in its own right.[1]

For the CC, the essence of marriage ('the union of a man and woman for life'[2]) can never change. Marriage is not a human contract but a God-given institution.[3] The biblical account of creation, recorded in Genesis, establishes that marriage is innately heterosexual: 'For this reason a man will leave his father and mother and be united to his wife, and they will become one flesh.'[4] Marriage was created by God for mankind's good and reflects the way we are meant to live.[5]

Apart from being inherently contradictory and anti-normative, many CCs believe that legal recognition of SSM would entail disastrous societal consequences. The 'normative character of marriage and family life'[6] would be severely undermined, it 'would mean the end of marriage and family as they have existed since history began.'[7] Society, at its peril, undercuts the family unit (as CCs conceive it) built upon the traditional concept of marriage—permanent, monogamous and heterosexual.[8] Again, the litany of adverse consequences logically following from legal endorsement of SSM is long: the adoption of children by same-sex couples[9]; wholesale changes to public education to reflect the new equal status of homosexuality alongside heterosexuality[10]; employment quotas for gays[11]; homosexual vilification laws[12]; even homosexual television stations.[13] The principal concern is the potential disadvantage for children. Children of same-sex parents would be denied 'the obvious right of both a paternal and maternal role model.'[14] It is taken as axiomatic that children will suffer from being raised by such couples.[15]

A direct effect upon CCs and their religious liberty would be felt also: pressure upon churches to solemnize SSMs[16]; pressure not to speak out against homosexuality as a sin[17]; even, at a practical level, alterations to manses, parsonages and vicarages to accommodate homosexual couples and the introduction of pre-marriage preparation and post-nuptial 'marriage enrichment' courses catering for same-sex couples.[18] Perhaps, speculate some CCs, SSM will result in 'the stigmatization of traditional religion and morality'[19]: conservative religionists who insist upon a traditional sexual code and resist this latest phase of the sexual revolution will, in an ironic twist, be the new pariahs.[20]

Present Rejection of Same–Sex Marriage: the *Quilter* case

New Zealand law does not presently recognize SSM. The leading case is *Quilter* v *Attorney-General.*[21]

Three lesbian couples, Lindsay Quilter and Margaret Pearl and two other couples, sought to test the law in light of the Human Rights Act 1993's prohibition upon sexual orientation discrimination. They sought a declaration that they were lawfully entitled to obtain a marriage licence and marry pursuant to the Marriage Act 1955. The plaintiffs argued that following the amendment to s. 19 of the New Zealand Bill of Rights Act 1990 ('BORA') in 1993 (which incorporated, *inter alia*, the prohibition upon sexual orientation discrimination found in s. 21(1)(m) of the Human Rights Act) the courts were now required to read the Marriage Act consistently with the BORA. The BORA banned sexual orientation discrimination and, therefore, pursuant to s. 6 of the BORA,[22] the Marriage Act should be read consistently with that proscription. The latter Act, to achieve harmony with the BORA, ought now to be interpreted so as to include SSM within its concept of marriage. The word 'marriage' is not defined in the Marriage Act.

Both the High Court[23] and the Court of Appeal unanimously rejected this argument. Although the Marriage Act did not expressly mandate opposite-sex partners, it was 'clear beyond doubt',[24] indeed 'the only possible interpretation',[25] that the traditional (Christian) common law meaning of marriage was assumed. Lord Penzance promulgated this in 1866: 'I conceive that marriage, as understood in Christendom, may for this purpose be defined as the voluntary union for life of one man and one woman, to the exclusion of all others.'[26] Furthermore, Parliament had recently confirmed the traditional concept of marriage. Legislation passed since 1993 still cast marriage in traditional terms: the language in the Births, Deaths and Marriages Registration Act 1995, for instance, demonstrated that married persons have to be of opposite gender.[27]

Because the Marriage Act was so clear it was impossible for it to be interpreted, pursuant to s. 6 of the BORA, to embrace SSM. Courts might well be enjoined by s. 6 to give the BORA a 'generous interpretation'[28] in order to protect the fundamental rights and freedoms of citizens, but there were limits. Interpretation did not extend to re-writing legislation: 'The Marriage Act is clear and to give it such different meaning would not be to undertake interpretation but to assume the role of lawmaker which is for Parliament.'[29] SSM was quintessentially a matter for Parliament and not the courts. Marriage was 'one of society's fundamental institutions'[30] and the question of its transformation to embrace SSM was one 'weighted with policy considerations of the kind Parliament is both constitutionally and practically equipped to decide.'[31]

Although the combined effect of the clear meaning of the Marriage Act and the limiting operation of s. 4—which expressly prevents a court from nullifying any statutory provision because it is inconsistent with the BORA—was sufficient to dispose of the appeal, several judges explored, in lengthy *obiter* discussion, whether denial of SSM constituted 'discrimination' in contravention of s. 19 of the BORA. Here, the Court of Appeal was divided.

The majority (Richardson P, Gault and Keith JJ) held there was no discrimination. Gault J adopted a formalistic concept of discrimination. Gays were not purposely singled out for exclusion but rather fell into the class of persons who were ineligible to marry the person of their choice.[32] That class included bigamists, persons wishing to marry someone under the age of 16, persons wishing to marry a close relative, and so on. But, as Thomas J rightly rejoined, this sort of definitional argument is circular and question begging. If one begins with a definition of marriage as inherently heterosexual 'the answer is inescapable.'[33] That begs the question as to whether the definition is intrinsically biased to start with. On Gault J's logic, a definition of marriage requiring partners to be of the same race would not be discriminatory either.[34] Furthermore, Gault J's concept of discrimination is too narrow. It only embraces direct discrimination, whereas laws may indirectly discriminate due to their deleterious impact upon certain groups and not others.

Keith J took a different tack. For him it was inconceivable that Parliament would 'have effected such a major change to a fundamental institution in our society and legal system . . . in such an indirect way.'[35] Both international and domestic human rights law evidenced a 'particularistic' and 'gradualist'[36] approach. Slowly and carefully more grounds of prohibition had been added to more areas of activity. For SSM, the prudent approach might be instead of 'extending or redefining the status, the law might make a particular incident or right and duty of marital status available to a wider group.'[37] As we shall see shortly, Parliament has indeed taken this approach by providing benefits and protections to same-sex couples in certain areas.

The minority found a breach of s. 19. Tipping and Thomas JJ adopted the broader, and, I suggest, correct concept of discrimination that embraces indirect as well as direct discrimination. Laws may not purposely discriminate against an individual or group, but they may nonetheless have a 'disproportionately severe impact'[38] on a certain group. Whether by design (direct discrimination) or by effect (indirect discrimination) the injury is the same.[39] The broader view accords with the recognition of indirect discrimination in s. 65 of the Human Rights Act. It also reflects the American interpretation of religious discrimination. It has long been recognized there that deliberate restriction of religious liberty is rare, but that 'facially-neutral laws of general application' may nevertheless 'substantially burden' religious exercise.[40] This incidental burdening of religious freedom requires suitable justification by the state. The broader concept of discrimination may actually benefit CCs in any future allegations of infringement of their religious liberty. Thomas J was prepared to go beyond a bland pronouncement of discrimination and denounce the restriction in no uncertain terms:

> Based upon this personal characteristic [sexual preference], gays and lesbians are denied access to a central social institution and the resulting status of married persons. They lose the rights and privileges, including the manifold legal consequences which marriage conveys. They are denied a basic civil right in that freedom to marry is rightly regarded as a basic civil right. . . . In a real sense gays and lesbians are effectively excluded from full membership of society.[41]

Gays deserved 'much more than tolerance from the majority'[42] if they were to achieve full citizenship. Thomas J was the only judge to address the substantive merits of the present exclusion of same-sex couples from marriage and he found the case for denying SSM sorely wanting. There was simply 'no sound reason'[43] for non-recognition. The only possible objection, 'the biologic inability of gays and lesbians to procreate',[44] was unconvincing. For him, the emphasis upon procreation misconceived the real essence of marriage, which was 'to be found in the nature of the relationship, not in some biological purpose.'[45] Once marriage was apprehended as having other facets and qualities ('cohabitation, commitment, intimacy, and financial interdependence'[46]), it was plain that homosexual as much as heterosexual couples could qualify. He acknowledged that, due to the inability of judges to strike down legislation inconsistent with the BORA (s. 4), the finding of a violation of s. 19 might appear somewhat hollow. But, if it resulted in 'pressure on Parliament to change the law'[47] or 'attract[ed] the attention of the [UN] Human Rights Committee',[48] then so be it. Thomas J's judgment is in effect a 'declaration of incompatibility' (the device introduced by s. 4 of the United Kingdom's Human Rights Act 1998) that the Marriage Act derogates from a civil right recognized in the BORA.[49] This type of 'judicial indication' was endorsed recently by a full bench of the Court of Appeal in *Moonen*.[50] His judgment was no doubt solace to gay lobby groups such as 'Rights Right Now' in their battle to secure SSM.[51]

Are Christians Legally Restricted from Opposing SSM?

CCs have the usual democratic channels open to them—forming pressure groups, publishing pamphlets, lobbying MPs, writing submissions to select committees, running petitions, and so on. However, some CCs perceive that the current legal climate will prevent them preaching (in the widest sense) against gay rights and practice. For instance, the leader of the Christian Heritage Party, the Rev Graham Capill, commenting on the Human Rights Bill 1992, believed anti-discrimination could 'remove traditional freedoms' from society. He warned: 'The Church, traditionally, has always held homosexuality to be a sin. Thus, to pass anti-discrimination legislation, on the basis of sexual orientation, will remove the right of the Church to preach and teach against this wrong.'[52] Several CC MPs during the Parliamentary debate on this Bill endorsed this fear.[53] Other CCs are not so pessimistic. The editors of a 1996 CC anthology on homosexuality believed that:

> Moreover, the law does not prohibit people from speaking out against homosexuality. Indeed, the law is to opposite effect. . . . There are some particular exceptions to the right of freedom of speech. But speaking out against homosexuality is not one of them. Therefore people should not be inhibited about expressing the belief that the homosexual lifestyle is not a healthy or valid one—just as they must recognise the right of the homosexual lobby to promote their cause too.[54]

Katherine O'Regan's assurance during the Human Rights Bill's introduction (Chapter 9) is recalled: 'It is not my intention . . . that the legislation should prevent churches from preaching that homosexuality is sinful . . .'[55]

Freedom of Expression

Freedom of expression is acknowledged in s. 14 of the BORA:

> **14. Freedom of expression**—Everyone has the right to freedom of expression, including the freedom to seek, receive, and impart information and opinions of any kind in any form.

Further, s. 15 declares that the right to manifest religion or belief extends to 'teaching . . . either in public or private.' The right of Christians to teach and bear witness to the Truth in the public arena is protected. But, as with freedom of religion, free speech is not an absolute right.[56] There are limits, and ordinary legislation can abridge the right of free expression.

The High Court in *News Media*[57] made this point firmly. A paper, *News Truth*, complained of censorship when its weekly advertisements placed by providers of sexual services were found to be 'objectionable' under s. 3(2) of the Films, Videos, and Publications Classification Act 1993 (FVPCA 1993). The Court remarked that 'Bill of Rights considerations do not take matters further.'[58] The publisher did indeed have the advantage of s. 14 of the BORA, but the FVPCA was a clear Parliamentary derogation from the right of free expression, and nothing in the BORA could invalidate it. The restrictive provisions of the FVCPA 1993 were inconsistent with that freedom and took precedence by virtue of s. 4. 'Thus, despite s. 14, censorship within the law prevails and the interpretation directions of s. 6 do not arise.'[59]

The Court of Appeal in *Moonen,* however, found 'difficulties' with this passage. The High Court had erroneously downplayed the need for a censorship provision to be interpreted 'so as to adopt such tenable construction as constitutes the least possible limitation on freedom of expression.'[60] Even where ordinary legislation clearly trumps the right of free speech, there is still the need, pursuant to s. 6 of the BORA, to interpret the statute so that it 'impinges as little as possible on freedom of expression.'[61]

A very recent and significant Court of Appeal case on free speech is most apposite to the present discussion.

In *Living Word Distributors Ltd* v *Human Rights Action Group Inc (Wellington)*[62] a direct confrontation between CCs and homosexuality advocates took place. The Office of Film and Literature Classification had classified two American-made videos imported by a church, *Gay Rights/Special Rights: Inside the Homosexual Agenda* and *AIDS: What You Haven't Been Told*, as objectionable in the hands of persons under 18 years of age. As the High Court summarized:

> The two video recordings . . . discuss aspects of homosexuality in the United States context, and discuss political and social ramifications of claims made by gay, lesbian, bisexual and trans-gendered people for equal rights and the right not to be discriminated against. The videos present a point of view that opposes the granting of such claims which it regards as special rights.[63]

The Human Rights Action Group (HRAG) sought a review of the Office's decision by the Film and Literature Board of Review. The HRAG contended that the tapes—espousing, in its words, a 'strict fundamentalist Christian religious based view-point'[64]—were a misleading and dehumanizing attack upon the gay and lesbian community. Conservative Christians defended the videos as 'very effective and truthful tool[s] to help us to communicate the fact that the homosexual act is wrong and to warn people of the consequences of their behaviour.'[65] Pastor Peter Trott of the Potter's House Christian Fellowship (a Pentecostal denomination) asked: 'Would a video which showed the folly of adultery, or of extortion be considered for restriction—just in case an adulterer or extortioner was offended? I certainly hope not! Then why the double standards when it comes to the sin of homosexuality?'[66] The Classification Office in a written submission defended its decision. It believed the gay community was strong enough to withstand such a 'biased onslaught' from these

'Fundamentalist Christian message[s].'[67] Despite the bias and misinformation, an adult audience (hence its R18 classification) could cope with the material.

The Board, however, differed, imposing an outright ban on the videos. Expression of opinion, however unpopular, was permissible, but this material went further and contained outright lies: 'Advocacy of an opinion, no matter how offensive the opinion is ought not to be the subject of censorship. These videos however go beyond more advocacy of an opinion . . . They contain opinion based on misinformation . . .'[68] The video's representations, it seemed (for the public were not allowed to view the videos), contained assertions that HIV could be transmitted by casual or airborne contact, that condoms were ineffective in limiting the spread of HIV and that homosexual men were predisposed to paedophilia. These were all untrue. The videos were 'objectionable' within the meaning of s. 3(3)(e) of the FVPCA 1993:

> **(3)** In determining, for the purposes of the Act, whether or not any publication . . . is objectionable . . . particular weight shall be given to the extent and degree to which, and the manner in which, the publication—
> **(e)** Represents (whether directly or by implication) that members of any particular class of the public are inherently inferior to other members of the public by reason of any characteristic of that class, being a characteristic that is a prohibited ground of discrimination specified in section 21(1) of the Human Rights Act 1993.

The Board was in no doubt that the 'dominant effect' (s. 3 (4)(a)) of the videos as a whole was to represent that people with HIV and people of homosexual orientation were 'inherently inferior' to other members of the public by virtue of those identified characteristics.[69] The videos entailed consequential risks as well—for instance, 'confidence in public health cautions could be undermined'.[70] They drew an analogy with hate speech: 'It is no great stretch of a legal imagination to see that the principles underlying the regulation of racist speech are equally applicable to speech representing that homosexuals and people living with HIV are "inherently inferior".'[71]

What of the (perceived) clash between the freedom of expression of conservative religionists (s.14) and the right of gay citizens to be free from discrimination upon the ground of sexual orientation (s.19)? Both are 'protected' rights under the BORA. The Board's answer was that Parliament had signalled that, at least in this context, freedom from discrimination was the higher norm. It had expressly curtailed free expression by passing s. 3(3)(e) of the FVPCA. A 'definitional balancing' (see Chapter 7) had been undertaken already by Parliament. Classes of people who possessed a characteristic that was a prohibited ground of discrimination under the Human Rights Act were entitled to have their dignity preserved from demeaning publications.[72]

The High Court upheld the Board's ruling, although it was 'troubled by the inroad into the free expression of opinions which this decision represents, particularly in this area of uncertain factual assumptions and premises, and a still evolving understanding of the phenomenon of homosexuality.'[73] It was reluctant to differ from the conclusions reached by the specialist tribunal. Some CCs were alarmed: 'Freedom of expression under threat', was the front page response of *Challenge Weekly*.[74]

Living Word's perseverance was to be rewarded, however. A full bench of the Court of Appeal unanimously held that both the Board and the High Court had erred in law. The case was not decided on the basis of grand vindications of free speech, but on 'a straightforward question of [statutory] construction'.[75] Section 3(1) of the FVPCA authorizes censorship of 'objectionable' publications, items whose subject matter describes or depicts 'matters such as sex, horror, crime, cruelty, or violence in such a manner' that their dissemination would be 'likely to be injurious to the public good.' The videos simply did not fall within 'the scope of the subject matter gateway'.[76] They did not deal with sex in a manner deleterious to public welfare. The words 'such as' lent no warrant for expanding the reach of the Act to include sexual orientation. The jurisdictional litmus test in s. 3(1) could not be ignored or bypassed either by invoking s. 3(3)(e), the provision concerning portrayal of persons as inherently inferior. The latter was simply a factor in assessing the material, not a separate basis for censorship. This misinterpretation had led the Board and the High Court to make a 'fundamental error' by positing a conflict between free speech and freedom from discrimination, and in turn, treating s. 19 as prevailing over s. 14. 'But in terms of the statutory scheme there is no direct clash of rights.'[77] The Court of Appeal resisted a definitional balancing here: 'The Bill of Rights is a limitation on governmental, not private conduct.'[78] The Bill of Rights Act is designed to ensure that the free flow of opinion is duly acknowledged in any exercise of state censorship.

The videos did not contain any explicit sexual images, indeed only a minute fraction of the tapes could be said to touch on sex. Thomas J noted:

> What is emphasised in the videos is the perceived promiscuity and irresponsible sexual behaviour of male homosexuals and the fact they have chosen to pursue the 'homosexual lifestyle'. Otherwise, the videos are *essentially political tracts*.[79]

The censors had thus exceeded their jurisdiction and Court quashed the Board's decision. Thomas J thought there was little point in remitting the videos back to the Board for reconsideration, but the other four judges decided this was appropriate. They added some salutary words for the Board to ruminate upon: 'prior restraint is usually regarded as the most severe way of curtailing freedom of expression because expression that is never published cannot contribute in any way to the democratic process, to the marketplace of ideas or to personal fulfilment.'[80]

Viewpoint Discrimination American First Amendment jurisprudence recognizes the concept of 'viewpoint discrimination'.[81] The US Supreme Court has consistently held that suppression of speech simply because of the viewpoint or ideology it expresses is unconstitutional. Justice Kennedy, for the majority in *Rosenberger* v *Rector and Visitors of the University of Virginia,* stated:

> It is axiomatic that the government may not regulate speech based on its substantive content or the message it conveys. . . . When the government targets not subject matter but particular views on a subject the violation of the First Amendment is all the more blatant. . . . Viewpoint discrimination is thus an egregious form of content discrimination. The government must abstain from regulating speech when the specific motivating ideology or the opinion or perspective of the speaker is the rationale for the restriction.[82]

Thus, by way of crude summary, state restrictions, unrelated to content or viewpoint, on the 'time, place or manner' of the expression are typically upheld, whereas restrictions aimed at the content (or subject matter) of the speech or its viewpoint are not.[83] It is probably true that 'freedom of expression enjoys far greater protection in the United States than in New Zealand.'[84] And, as repeated often, the freedoms and rights in the BORA are not higher, entrenched ones like those contained in the First Amendment. Nonetheless, the doctrine of viewpoint discrimination is a useful one in the armoury of CCs.

Although not adopted or referred to as such, the concept resonates in the judgments of the Court of Appeal in *Living Word*:

> Freedom of expression constitutes one of the essential foundations of [a democratic] society. . .. it is applicable not only to 'information' or 'ideas' that are favourably received or regarded as inoffensive or as a matter of indifference, but also to those that offend, shock, or disturb the State or any sector of the population. Such are the demands of that pluralism, tolerance and broadmindedness without which there is no 'democratic society'.[85]

Thomas J re-echoed this. He wished neither to condone nor endorse the views expressed in the videos: 'In truth, my views are besides the point.'[86] The point was that the videos fell outside the scope and intent of the legislation. Unless the law insisted upon a direct link between the subject matter of the publication and the manner in which it was said to be harmful to the public good, the state's censorship powers might be unduly expanded:

> It would be open to the board to consider the question of injuriousness on a basis outside the scope of censorship legislation. Political, religious or other opinions which should have unrestricted dissemination in a free and open society would be at risk of being banned if they were expressed in a publication which also dealt, perhaps peripherally, with sex or violence. In effect, that was the position here.[87]

These were, as noted earlier, essential political tracts. The viewpoint expressed therein might be distasteful ('provocative and tendentious'[88] and 'portray[ing] the beliefs and prejudices of religious fundamentalism'[89]) but the tapes did not deserve banning on that basis alone.

Public expression of conservative religious views—such as criticism of homosexuals, *de facto* couples, atheists or 'cult' members—leavened with uncomfortable illiberal terminology of sin, hell and divine judgment, may well come to be a viewpoint, like racist speech, which is unworthy of public airing in a 'free and democratic society.' *Living Word* has, for now, forestalled that day.[90]

Homosexual Vilification Law? One response to the *Living Word* case may be a homosexual vilification law. Gay commentators condemned the decision as the failure of the law to prohibit 'hate propaganda'.[91] Tim Barnett, a gay Government MP, mentioned the possibility of banning such anti-gay hate literature.[92]

There is currently no legislation prohibiting public articulation of anti-gay sentiment. Some CC MPs during the Human Rights Bill debate forecast the likely introduction of a homosexual vilification law.[93] The Rev Stuart Lange suggested such legislation was part and parcel of the drive by gay activists to remove 'obvious obstacles' such as conservative churches, who thwart the full social acceptance of homosexuality:

> it is an established part of the agenda of the homosexual lobby to introduce legislation that would make it illegal to speak or write against the practice or ideology of homosexuality. It would be a criminal offence for anyone to criticise homosexuality. A preacher in a pulpit, or a Christian magazine, would be committing an offence to state that homosexual acts are sinful. Such legislation—even when tied in with very commendable legislation

> against racist statements—would move far beyond protecting the rights of a minority to suppressing the rights of the majority, especially the rights to freedom of belief and freedom of speech.[94]

A model for a New Zealand law is close at hand. In 1993, New South Wales enacted a homosexual vilification prohibition.[95] Section 49ZT of the Anti-Discrimination Act 1977 makes it unlawful 'for a person, by a public act, to incite hatred towards, serious contempt for, or severe ridicule of, a person or group of persons on the ground of the homosexuality of the person or members of the group.'[96] The homosexual vilification law is carefully couched. A free speech qualification in s. 497ZT(2)(c) immunizes 'a public act, done reasonably and in good faith, for academic, artistic, religious instruction . . . or for other purposes in the public interest, including discussion or debate about and expositions of any act or matter.' Christian denunciation from the pulpit, or by way of pamphlet, of the sinfulness of homosexuality might well be protected. The Rev Lange's concerns seem misplaced if this kind of provision were to be introduced in New Zealand. Christian motivation is, or at least should be, never the desire to incite hatred or breed contempt for homosexuals. Much will depend on how any such section is interpreted. If a purely subjective meaning is to be given to vilification (do the victims feel ridiculed?) much religious criticism of homosexuality would be suspect.

If a vilification law of wide sweep is introduced, or if CCs are otherwise to be lawfully restricted in arguing publicly against homosexual conduct or rights, they might well feel aggrieved. If gays are permitted to publicly advocate their cause (viz, the Hero Parade) they ought not to expect legal immunity from genuine public criticism. CCs already accept that they will be cast as intolerant and oppressive, even 'morons'[97] by the secular press and others, but a legal ban upon criticism of homosexual conduct and rights arguably goes too far.

CCs' Attitude to Freedom of Expression: Ambivalence Again

Free speech is a delicate and vulnerable one for CCs, for, on other occasions, they are all too ready to invoke the law to suppress expression which offends Christian sensibilities. As we saw in Chapter 1, CCs were horrified at the blasphemous artwork exhibited at *Te Papa* shortly after its opening. Offended Christians pressed the Solicitor General for his consent to a prosecution against the Museum for 'blasphemous libel' under s. 123 of the Crimes Act 1961. The Solicitor-General refused to give leave. The controversy was not one, he said, appropriate for resolution by the criminal courts. Furthermore, he cited the principle of freedom of expression in the Bill of Rights Act as the main factor against allowing prosecutions to proceed.[98] For all intents and purposes then, and despite s. 4 of the BORA, the blasphemous libel offence is dead and buried. In a Bill of Rights era, religious vilification (blasphemous libel by a modern name) has no place. The effective repeal of s. 123 underscores the cultural disestablishment of Christianity in New Zealand. It is no longer a Christian nation and Christian sensitivities merit no special protection.

The ambivalence of most CCs toward freedom of expression is traceable, in part, to their understanding of societal blessing and judgment (see Chapter 2). A good example is the controversy over the erection of statues of two Egyptian gods, Horus and Sobek, in Hamilton Gardens by the local city council in 1991. The Hamilton New Life Centre feared for the ill consequences to be reaped if the city sowed pagan gods in its backyard. To the mayor's irritation at this 'intolerance', its pastor replied that the 'tolerance issue',

> has been perverted and twisted around, because it is tolerance that has brought us to this place in our society we will accept Egyptian gods in our backyard, 11,000 abortions a year, practising homosexuality, an increase in all sorts of social ills round about us. We have tolerated so much that we've violated God's laws of so many aspects of living.[99]

In the minds of these CCs, erection of pagan idols in public places, indecent parades of unapologetic homosexuality, blasphemous artwork in a national museum—these and other affronts to God simply guaranteed divine judgment upon society, believers and non-believers alike. Needless to say, the Council's attempt to placate opponents of the statutes—by giving them a 'Christian blessing'—did nothing of the sort.[100] Not all CCs, however, are selective advocates of the principle of free speech. As we have seen, the editors of the 1996 homosexuality anthology acknowledged that they 'must recognise the right of the homosexual lobby to promote their cause too.' *Challenge Weekly*, moreover, did publish a defence of free speech by a Christian missionary as a follow-up to the Hamilton furore. 'All too often', chided Matt Finlay, 'we expect freedom of speech for ourselves and yet refuse it to others.'[101] Muslims may not extend free speech to non-Muslims, but that was no reason for Christians not to. St Paul, moreover, was content to preach the Gospel in Gentile cities full of idols without seeking the idols' destruction. The Christian message was sufficiently robust in the marketplace of faith to mean that state censorship of conflicting 'gods' was otiose:

> Our message in a multiracial, multireligious society must be positive, proclaiming salvation through faith in Christ, and we should not be diverted into negative attacks on things we feel unhappy about. Probably there are many 'idols' in Hamilton that will do much more harm to the city than a

> couple of curious statues from ancient Egypt. What about the 'gods' so devoutly worshipped in our country—television, videos, the bottle—which fill our homes with immorality and violence, and the mass deification of sport and materialism?[102]

The CCs' Task in Making a Case against SSM

Will SSM be recognized in the near future? If, as Thomas J argued in *Quilter*, gays and lesbians are being denied 'a basic civil right' by the state's refusal to recognize SSM, then the onus would appear to be on the state to justify its stance. The principal (perhaps only?) public supporters of the traditional (opposite-sex) concept of marriage are conservative religionists. In terms of the BORA, the restriction of marriage to heterosexuals is arguably a violation of the s. 19 right of non-discrimination and thus would need to meet the justified limitation hurdle in s. 5: is it a 'reasonable limit[] prescribed by law as can be demonstrably justified in a free and democratic society.'? A free and democratic society is, of course, synonymous with modern, liberal democracy.

There are many contemporary indications that the law sees the homosexual way of life as not just to be tolerated, but normal. If and when this process is complete, the homosexual movement will have succeeded in a 'transvaluation' of traditional values, whereby

> certain areas of conduct, traditionally conceived of as morally wrong and thus the proper object of public regulation and prohibition, are now perceived as *affirmative goods* the pursuit of which does not raise serious moral questions and which thus is no longer a proper object of public critical concern.[103]

Acceptance of Homosexuality in Family Law

The Family Court increasingly has few qualms about the normalcy of homosexuality. Thus, for example, courts have applied the equitable principles governing constructive trusts to permit homosexual partners living in a relationship in the nature of marriage to share in property following a split between the couple.[104] Further, lesbian applicants have been awarded custody and guardianship of children and, despite rejecting an adoption application, one judge nonetheless issued some favourable signals for its future acceptance. Intriguingly, several of the cases have a Christian dimension to them as well.

Re an Application by T[105] was a high-profile proceeding (featured in a television documentary) by the appellant, FT, to adopt J, the child of her lesbian partner C. The couple had lived together for over nine years during which C had had three children by artificial insemination. The appellant had assumed the role of 'breadwinner'. The youngest child, J, aged four, was to be FT's child. FT had already been appointed guardian of the two older children. She now sought to be made the legal mother of the youngest child, with C, his natural mother, being made a joint guardian with the appellant. Applying the criteria in s. 11 of the Adoption Act 1955, the High Court held that adoption would not serve J's welfare. Such advantages that existed were outweighed by the significant disadvantage to the boy of the artificial legal relationship sought here. A guardianship order in favour of FT would achieve 'virtually everything'[106] that an adoption order would.

Although the appeal was lost, the High Court affirmed the lower court's finding that FT was 'a fit and proper person to have the custody of J and was of sufficient ability to bring him up, maintain him and educate him.' Ellis J added in a clear, albeit *obiter*, statement that homosexuality *per se* is no impediment to good parenting:

> In at least one of the articles that was placed before the Court, attention was focused on the general perception that the legal system is not friendly to lesbians and gay men. In my view the decision in this case does not involve any criticism at all of the care givers. Indeed it is plain that they provide a stable and loving environment for the three children. It seems to me that the decision is gender neutral and would have been the same whatever the sex of the two care givers, be they two women, two men, or a man and woman.[107]

The fact they were not married posed another hurdle to adoption (s. 4 of the Adoption Act) and thus 'it [was] the inability to marry that is in issue in this case . . .'[108] Clearly if SSM were to be legalized, courts would be ready to grant adoption orders to partners of lesbian or homosexual parents otherwise meeting the requirements of sound parenting.

Six years later the lesbian partnership between FT and C had unravelled. C had, in 1994, publicly forsaken her lesbian lifestyle and 'became involved in Christianity.'[109] The rift was permanent between her and FT (following the latter's commencement of a lesbian relationship with a hitherto friend of C). C left, as an emergency contact address, an address of 'a Hamilton pastor at his church' and concluded her letter to FT with the words: 'I can't see any emergency that would warrant you contacting my children. If you meet Jesus then I am sure that the children would love to know that their prayers have been answered.'[110]

In 1995, C successfully sought the termination of FT's guardianship of the three children. Child support proceedings were brought by C in 1998 to secure a declaration that FT was step-parent of the children. The Family Court held that FT met the statutory criteria for being declared so. FT's conduct over the years (especially her attempt at adoption) revealed 'the most uncompromising acceptance of fiscal and other responsibility for the children possible.'[111] Such an assumption could not be 'vacated on the basis of later regret'.[112] The law could be as neutral between heterosexual and homosexual relationships in imposing burdens as well as granting benefits. The High Court agreed. The Child Support Act 1991's primary aim, the protection of children and their financial sustenance, would be advanced here if the material words were read 'in an inclusive manner'.[113] The question of SSM was 'a very controversial question', one which was 'utterly inappropriate' for the Court to discuss today.[114] Yet this issue was different: Parliament had 'clearly chosen in this statute to solidly endorse the notion that the parties to a "relationship in the nature of marriage" (however constituted) have an unequivocal obligation to materially support the children of such an enterprise.'[115]

The next case, *VP* v *PM* [116], is a fascinating decision, for it involves the clash of values explored in this study. The Family Court was confronted by a custody contest over two children following the separation of their parents. The children had stayed with their mother in the four years following the break-up, during which time the mother had commenced a lesbian relationship with another woman (also a mother of two). The same-sex couple intended to live together with their four children. The father, a Christian medical practitioner, sought custody and raised his ex-wife's sexuality as an issue. He was concerned at the absence of a masculine figure and harboured misgivings at what sort of role model all-female adult caregivers presented. He believed their mother's lifestyle would confuse them and perhaps even lead them to reject their developing Christian faith.

The Court asked the question: 'Religious values aside . . . whether lesbian mothers should be given the main custodial role towards their children, particularly where a more conventional home, based on a heterosexual relationship is available.'[117] Judge Mahony rejected the notion that the parents' sexuality of itself could disqualify them. It was a matter of their parenting ability: 'It seems to me . . . that good parenting in the particular family circumstances may be the determining factor and the reason why the Court need not be concerned in a particular case for the well-being of children living in the full-time care of a mother in a lesbian relationship. In my view that is the case here.'[118] The mother was commended for being 'very gentle, discerning and prudent [and] also very discreet.'[119] The judge was satisfied that the children were 'not going to be damaged by the relationship she plans to develop as [sic] her open and committed way of life.'[120] The father's negative, dismissive attitude to his former spouse—one he made no secret of before the children—counted against him. Placing the children in his care would psychologically harm them and 'compound [their] confusion and bewilderment' produced by the inter-parental conflict.[121] Judge Mahony's passing comments about the difficulty, if any, posed by the mother's sexuality to the children's religious upbringing are revealing:

> I am satisfied that she [the mother] has thought through an explanation which leaves intact her strong commitment to Christian values. Hers is certainly not the black and white approach of the father, which is nevertheless to be respected. . . . These parents themselves are not strong adherents to a particular religious faith where sexual orientation or the sanctity of marriage hold primary place in the religious values system of the family.[122]

The father's 'black and white approach' to homosexuality might be respected in the abstract but when acted upon (by criticizing the mother before the children) it did not attract judicial sympathy. At the risk of over-simplification, *VP* v *PM* indicates that homosexuality is no bar *per se* to good parenting: spouses who denounce it, based upon sincere religious conviction, are in danger of this rebounding against them. They are revealing intolerance towards a phenomenon that is, in a society increasingly penetrated by a liberal, modernist worldview, now regarded as neutral or benign.

Recent Legislative Initiatives

Evidence of a 'particularistic and gradualist' approach to rights, as Keith J in *Quilter* put it, is apparent in the 1990s. Instead of changing the definition of marriage, the extension of various rights, duties, and burdens of marriage to same-sex partners has been mooted. The Wellington worldview increasingly sees few problems with homosexuality. I can only very briefly canvass here some recent initiatives regarding adoption, marriage, registered partnerships and property rights.

In 1999 the Law Commission formed a 'preliminary view' that a change allowing same-sex couples to adopt was warranted.[123] Its comprehensive report in 2000 concurred. The Law Commission reaffirmed 'the value to a child of being raised within a family consisting of two parents contributing to the welfare of one another and of their children. It is, however, to be recognised that nowadays many people decide to have or raise children alone outside marriage and that the desire to parent and bring up children extends to those of homosexual orientation.'[124] A majority of public submissions (64 to 28) had argued in favour of adoption by same-sex couples. The Commission opined that there was insufficient evidence that such adoptions could not be in the best interests of the child and, in its view, a 'blanket prohibition' was unwarranted. Instead:

> applicants should be assessed on their merits. The way in which the couple intends to involve opposite gender role models in the life of the child is a matter inquiring investigation by the social worker. It is in our view desirable that Parliament make plain that applications for adoption orders by same-sex couples should be judged by the essential question as to what is in the child's best interests as a matter of *fact*, rather than by making assumptions as to the eligibility of the applicants as a matter of *law*.[125]

In 1999 the Ministry of Justice issued two discussion papers calling for public submissions on the introduction of SSM.[126] That year, the Law Commission also issued a paper in which it recommended that a Scandinavian-style registered domestic partnership law be introduced to cater for same-sex couples. To simply legalize SSM would 'cause unnecessary and understandable offence',[127] so:

> In the Commission's view the sensible choice is for New Zealand law, by a measure analogous to the Danish legislation, to provide for the registration of same-sex partnerships—such partnerships to confer the same rights and liabilities as marriage.[128]

The responses to the Ministry of Justice discussion papers were strongly opposed to such a change. Around 80 per cent of the 3546 submissions (representing 8464 individuals and groups) said they did not want SSM recognized by the law.[129] The bulk of the submissions came from church groups. The Attorney General, Margaret Wilson, rather disingenuously played down the worth of the feedback: 'There is of course no single view represented by the submissions. The sample represents the views only of those who decided to make submissions.'[130]

Whilst firmly resisting any move to redefine marriage to include SSM, many Christian organizations consider some form of registered partnership law to be a suitable compromise. The joint Public Questions Committee of the Methodist, Presbyterian, Churches of Christ and Quaker denominations also endorsed a registration system.[131] The Conference of Catholic Bishops of New Zealand's submission to the Ministry endorsed such a system of registration to enable same-sex couples to enjoy the same proprietary, tax credit, income support and similar civic rights, as married couples. But it firmly opposed SSM, as well as any registration scheme contemplating an exchange of vows for same-sex couples, their right to adopt children or their right to utilize reproductive technologies.[132]

Some CCs, such as Presbyterian AFFIRM,[133] also favoured a registered partnership regime. The path of wisdom may be to 'preserve the distinctive of marriage (as a relationship between heterosexual couples) and to support some form of legal recognition of same-sex partnerships.'[134] But others viewed it as a disastrous compromise.[135] A group of traditionalist Catholics, Catholic Action, wrote an open letter to the Pope asking for the bishops to be replaced.[136]

Finally, the De Facto Relationships (Property) Bill was introduced in March 1998 with the purpose of extending the benefits of the present Matrimonial Property Act 1976's equal-sharing regime to couples 'living in a relationship in the nature of marriage'. It did not include same-sex couples. Opposition Labour Party MPs objected to this.[137] Upon assuming office in late 1999, they set about rectifying the matter. The Government decided it was sensible to consolidate the various reforms—the Matrimonial Property Bill (also introduced in March 1998), the De Facto Relationships Bill and a possible same-sex relationship property bill—into one statute.[138] In May 2000 it introduced a massive Supplementary Order Paper (SOP) to amend the Matrimonial Property Bill 1998.[139] Henceforth, the Bill would be renamed the Property (Relationships) Bill and it would have a widened reach. The purpose was 'to extend the property division regime in [the Matrimonial Property Act 1976] so that it applies to the division of the relationship property of couples (whether heterosexual or same-sex) who have lived in a de facto relationship, when they separate or [one] of them dies.'[140] References to 'spouse' in the existing statute would be replaced with 'partner', the latter meaning someone married or in a *de facto* relationship (a relationship involving opposite or same-sex couples living together in a relationship in the nature of marriage).

Reactions were mixed. Some newspapers praised the changes as 'bringing New Zealand out of the dark ages [and] are long overdue'[141] and expressed 'astonishment [at] how far the law can lag behind social reality.'[142] Others begged to differ. There were two main objections. First, said the critics, the uniqueness of marriage would be compromised if matters pertaining to *de facto* and same-sex relationships were to be included in the same statute: 'The clear distinction between the marriage relationship and other relationships must not be blurred', warned the Catholic Bishops' Conference in a letter to the Attorney-General.[143] Second, there was widespread dismay at the manner in which this major change had been implemented. The broadening of the law had been included at the eleventh hour in a mere SOP and after the public input phase had concluded. New Zealanders 'must not be excluded from an opportunity to make comprehensive submissions to Parliament on the subject.'[144] The Government relented and reopened the matter for public comment. The Select Committee heard 91 further oral submissions—conservative church spokespeople and gay rights groups 'squaring off' before it, as one paper put it[145]—and some 1400 new written submissions flooded in.[146] The Bill is predicted to be passed by the end of 2000.[147]

If a registered partnership system for same-sex couples is passed, it is doubtful that all gay activists will be content with this, and other piecemeal reforms. Gault J in *Quilter* believed that 'the real complaint' of the plaintiffs was not their inability to lawfully marry, but simply that they were 'denied rights and privileges which are available to married persons.'[148] On that premise, he observed, their proper allegation was marital status discrimination. But for many, 'functional equality' is not the goal; societal recognition of the acceptability of homosexuality is the prize, the 'transvaluation' of homosexuality. An American commentator, Carlos Ball, explains:

> If gay rights activists and litigators were solely seeking the same practical benefits associated with marriage without having to call it 'marriage' (if they were seeking, for example, some form of comprehensive domestic partnership legislation that would guarantee the same benefits to same sex couples as are provided to married heterosexual couples), perhaps many—and maybe even most—Americans would be supportive, in the same way that a majority of Americans now believe that homosexuals should not suffer discrimination in employment and housing. But to speak of parity in the benefits associated with marriage is to speak of a functional equality that, while undoubtedly very important, is ultimately unsatisfactory because gays and lesbians currently seek not only equality in the tangible benefits associated with marriage, but also full acceptance in a *normative* sense.[149]

Some gay activists would, it seems, nonetheless settle for a registered partnership scheme.[150] For others, the registered partnership option would, commented one of the lesbian couples in *Quilter*, be 'absolutely ghettoising', simply creating legislation around a partnership that is uniquely for them.[151] It is because 'marriage is the single most significant communal ceremony of belonging'[152], 'a preferred relationship'[153] that the symbolism engendered by the state recognizing same-sex couples as *married,* not just registered, is so greatly prized. For the homosexual movement it would mark the transvaluation of homosexuality from: (i) despised, criminal, unnatural practice, past, (ii) decriminalized, tolerated conduct, through, (iii) protected human right, and finally to, (iv) approved and respected way of life. CCs equally recognize the symbolism which, for them, would mark *par excellence* the end of the Christian hegemony.

Framing Arguments

Liberal theorists insist, and CCs concede (see Chapter 4), that an 'objective', 'rational', 'secular' reason must be furnished for public policy. A purely religious reason is unlikely to persuade in a 'free and democratic society'. For many liberals, religious arguments are ruled out entirely as a species of objective, rational arguments in contemporary public discourse. To reiterate, religious justifications are, to liberals, quintessentially subjective, irrational, private, inaccessible and unscientific. While CCs would not agree—given God exists, their arguments are perfectly objective, logical and rational—nevertheless, many are prepared to translate their reasons into a form liberal secularists can digest. Pragmatically, this is the best course, for religious justifications simply do not persuade in a secular state. As the High Court pointed out:

> Neither is it appropriate in New Zealand today for the Christian concept of marriage to have an overriding sway over the legal situation. In New Zealand there is a separation between Church and State. There is no official state religion. New Zealand is home to persons who profess many faiths other than Christianity.[154]

Do 'objective', 'rational' grounds exist to thwart the introduction of SSM?[155] Some believe so. As we have seen, Thomas J believed the only possible objection—the biologic inability to procreate—was a weak one. The essence of marriage today was, for him, to be found in other things. Gay lobbyists (and others) believe the usual litany of harms associated with SSM are illusory and empirically unproven. Where is, they ask, the evidence that society will disintegrate, children will be harmed, youth will be corrupted, procreation will diminish, AIDS will spread, and so on?[156] Stephen Macedo argues that conservative moralists have 'failed badly' to advance 'a reasoned, public, secular case for legal discrimination against homosexuals'.[157] Others beg to differ. Contemporary natural law theorists, such as John Finnis, promulgate sophisticated arguments against SSM based on notions of the 'basic human good' and the like.[158] Some commentators attack specific planks in the gay argument, such as the claim that homosexual or lesbian parenting is shown not to be harmful to children[159], or that the social benefits from heterosexual marriage are matched by those of SSM.[160]

The arguments will continue.[161] The challenge for CCs is, given the belated realization they had long neglected the nurturing of 'the Christian mind' (as Blamires described it), whether they will be able to proffer the prudential, 'common-sense' arguments required to halt the recognition of SSM.

Conclusion

Same-sex marriage was chosen as a contemporary controversy to gauge the extent to which CCs' positive religious freedom (as Berlin described it) might be threatened. SSM is not lawful yet and, despite movements by Parliament to extend legal rights, privileges and duties possessed by married (opposite-sex) couples to same-sex ones, the situation may remain unchanged. The law's general acceptance of the homosexual lifestyle may instead see a registered domestic partnership law introduced. In opposing the introduction of SSM, CCs appear to enjoy the same freedom of expression as other citizens do. The right of CCs to disseminate certain anti-gay rights videotapes was recently vindicated by the Court of Appeal. There is, thus, no instance of CCs having been enjoined from genuine preaching (in the widest sense) against homosexual practice or rights.

Returning to the model of engagement in Chapter 4, peaceful coexistence again prevails. Criticism of gay practice and rights by CCs within their own milieu or sub-culture is ignored. The liberal state is indifferent to such private expression of illiberal sentiment—its major institutions are not threatened by articles in *Challenge Weekly* or talk-back programmes on *Radio Rhema*. Further, public criticism by CCs of gay conduct or rights in the secular media is unlikely to be restricted, especially if CCs adopt the liberal theorists' 'proviso'—that religious claims be first translated into 'practical', 'secular' arguments.

To date, few instances of conflict between CCs and gay advocates have reached the courts. However, conflict is likely to increase given CCs' rejection of ideological pluralism. They still seek to have their values reflected in the institutions of society. CC opposition to such matters as gay rights will continue to rankle liberal modernist sensibilities, especially if CCs express their criticism in its untranslated, biblical form, viz, homosexual conduct is 'sinful' and 'contrary to God's law'.

In the future, the 'foreign policy' problem (Chapter 3) will be revisited frequently as CCs test the limits of liberal democratic tolerance. The Wellington worldview has accepted the normality of homosexuality. Perhaps gay advocates may succeed in casting anti-gay talk as equivalent to racist speech. If a homosexual vilification law is introduced, CCs will need to secure an exemption to permit reasonable, *bona fide* criticism based upon sincere religious conviction. If the state will not grant such an exemption then a charge of 'viewpoint discrimination' would seem warranted. Yet, rather than 'make martyrs' of a few belligerent CCs, the state would probably decide it is wiser to accommodate them.

Notes

1 Stuart Lange, *Homosexuality and the Church*, Presbyterian AFFIRM Booklet No 4 (1998) at 19-20.

2 Alan Storkey, *Marriage and its Modern Crisis: Repairing Married Life* (1996) at 35. For a New Zealand account, see Bruce Logan, *Marriage: Do We Need It?* NZ Education Development Foundation Report (November 1998).

3 Storkey, ibid at 2-5 and 36-39. For a superb examination of the religious, social, legal and other dimensions of marriage, see John Witte, *From Sacrament to Contract: Marriage, Religion, and Law in the Western Tradition* (1997). Witte's magisterial survey of the various historical models of marriage cautions against unduly nostalgic, 'golden age' views of marriage.

4 Genesis 2:24.

5 Storkey, *Marriage and its Modern Crisis*, at 37.

6 Ramsey Colloquium, 'The Homosexual Movement' in Belding and Nicholls (eds), *A Reason for Hope: Christian Perspectives on Homosexuality and Healing* (1996) 1 at 6.

7 Bruce Logan, *Same Sex 'Marriage'?* Presbyterian AFFIRM Booklet No 13 (2000) at 29.

8 Bruce Logan, 'Same-sex marriages seen as threat to religious freedom', *New Zealandia*, May 1996, 14 at 15.

9 Logan, ibid.

10 Grant Thomas MP, Human Rights Bill (1993) 537 *NZPD* 16931. See further Richard F Duncan, 'Homosexual Marriage and the Myth of Tolerance: Is Cardinal O'Connor a "Homophobe"?' (1996) 10 *Notre Dame J L Ethics and Pub Policy* 587 at 599-600.

11 Grant Thomas (1993) 537 *NZPD* 16931.

12 Thomas, ibid; Graeme Lee (1993) 537 *NZPD* 16968; Whetu Tirikatene-Sullivan (1992) 532 *NZPD* 13216; Lange, *Homosexuality and the Church*, at 19.

13 Thomas, ibid.

14 Logan, 'Same-sex marriages seen as a threat' (above n 8), at 15. See also Bill Muchlengberg, 'Homosexuality and Human Rights' in Belding and Nicholls, *A Reason for Hope*, 52 at 54.

15 See Logan, *Same-sex 'Marriage'?* (above n 7), at 17-18.

16 Logan, 'Same sex marriages seen as a threat' (above n 8), at 15; Thomas (1993) 537 *NZPD* 16968.

17 Thomas (1993) 537 *NZPD* 16931.

18 Harold Turner, 'Logical Conclusions' in Belding and Nicholls (eds), *A Reason for Hope*, at 26-27.

19 Duncan, 'Homosexual Marriage and the Myth of Tolerance' (above n 10), at 600.

20 See Justice Scalia, dissenting in *Romer* v *Evans*, 134 L Ed 2d 855, 878 (1996), who criticizes the majority of the Court for 'verbally disparaging as bigotry [those displaying] adherence to traditional attitudes.'

21 [1998] 1 NZLR 523 (CA).

22 It reads: '**6. Interpretation consistent with Bill of Rights to be preferred**—Wherever an enactment can be given a meaning that is consistent with the rights and freedoms contained in this Bill of Rights, that meaning shall be preferred to any other meaning.'

23 [1996] NZFLR 523.

24 *Quilter* [1998] 1 NZLR 523 at 581 per Tipping J.

25 Keith J, ibid at 555.

26 *Hyde* v *Hyde & Woodmanse* [1861-73] All ER 175 at 177. Quoted by the High Court: [1996] NZFLR at 483-484.

27 Ibid at 580.

28 Keith J, ibid at 566.

29 Ibid at 526 per Gault J.

30 Ibid at 581 per Tipping J.

31 Ibid at 542 per Thomas J.

32 Ibid at 527. For criticism, see Andrew Butler, 'Same-sex marriage and freedom from discrimination in New Zealand' [1998] *Public Law* 396 at 397-398.

33 [1998] 1 NZLR at 546. See also at 537.

34 Thomas J, ibid at 537-538. This argument, as Thomas J notes, was demolished by the American Supreme Court in *Loving* v *Virginia*, 388 US 1 (1967).

35 Ibid at 555.

36 Ibid at 560 and 565 respectively.

37 Ibid at 568.

38 Ibid at 533 per Thomas J.

39 See ibid at 575-576.

40 See, for example, *Employment Division* v *Smith*, 494 US 872, 894 (1990) per Justice O'Connor (generally applicable laws having the effect of substantially burdening a religious practice place the onus upon the government to show a 'compelling state interest' in refusing an exemption for the religionist). The majority in *Smith*, however, refused to uphold the compelling state interest test for free exercise exemptions. This led to Congress passing the Religious Freedom Restoration Act 1993, which in turn was struck down as unconstitutional by the Supreme Court in *City of Boerne* v *Flores*, 521 US 507 (1997). See generally, Michael McConnell, 'Neutrality, Separation and Accommodation: Tensions in American First Amendment Doctrine' in Ahdar (ed), *Law and Religion* (2000) ch 4 at 67-68.

41 *Quilter* [1998] 1 NZLR at 537. Thomas J's language here is reminiscent of Justice Sandra Day O'Connor's 'endorsement test' for contravention of the establishment clause of the First Amendment: '[G]overnment cannot endorse the religious practices and beliefs of some citizens without sending a clear message to nonadherents that they are *outsiders or less than full members of the political community.*' *County of Allegheny* v *Greater Pittsburgh ACLU,* 492 US 573, 627 (1989) (emphasis added).

42 Thomas J in *Quilter* [1998] 1 NZLR at 532.

43 Ibid at 541.

44 Ibid at 547.

45 Ibid.

46 Ibid at 534.

47 Ibid at 548.

48 Ibid. One of the three lesbian couples in *Quilter*, Juliet Joslin and Jennifer Rowan, have taken their case to the Committee: see Philip Matthews, 'Partners in crime', *NZ Listener*, 18 September 1999, at 30.

49 See Paul Rishworth, 'Reflections on the Bill of Rights after *Quilter* v *Attorney-General*' [1998] *NZ L Rev* 683 at 689.

50 *Moonen* v *Film and Literature Board of Review* [2000] 2 NZLR 9 at 17.

51 See 'Lobby group vows to fight on', *Otago Daily Times*, 18 December 1997, at 3.

52 Capill is quoted in 'Ghosts of '85 in new bill', *CW*, 29 October 1992, 1 at 2.

53 See, for example, Tirikatene-Sullivan (1993) 537 *NZPD* 16927: 'If the legislation goes through I believe that the groups that will be harassed the most will be religious groups that preach honestly, according to their convictions and on the basis of scripture . . . that sodomy is unnatural.' See also Graeme Lee (1992) 532 *NZPD* 13212.

54 Belding and Nicholls (eds), *A Reason for Hope* (above n 6), Preface.

55 (1992) 532 *NZPD* 13208.

56 See *Lange* v *Atkinson* [1998] 3 NZLR 424 at 472 per Tipping J (CA).

57 *News Media Ltd* v *Film and Literature Board of Review* (1997) 4 HRNZ 410.

58 Ibid at 420.

59 Ibid.

60 *Moonen* v *Film and Literature Board of Review* [2000] 2 NZLR 9 at 18.

61 Ibid at19.

62 [2000] 3 NZLR 570 (CA).

63 Unrep, High Court, Wellington, AP 26/98, 1 March 2000, Heron and Durie JJ, at para 3. For a fuller description of the content, see Steven Price, 'Perversions of truth', *NZ Listener*, 8 July 2000, at 30-31.

64 The Board's decision is reported as *Re Gay Rights/Special Rights: Inside the Homosexual Agenda* (1997) 4 HRNZ 422 at 425.

65 Ibid at 426.

66 Ibid.

67 Ibid at 427-428.

68 Ibid at 432.

69 Ibid.

70 Ibid at 433.

71 Ibid.

72 Ibid at 434.

73 Unrep, High Court, Wellington, AP 26/98, 1 March 2000, Heron and Durie JJ, at para 31.

74 Kirk, 'Freedom of expression under threat', *CW*, 21 March 2000, at 1. See also secular criticism by Steven Price, 'Views suppressed for the good of the rest of us', *Otago Daily Times*, 20 March 2000, at 15.

75 [2000] 3 NZLR 570 at 580 per Richardson P, Gault, Keith and Tipping JJ.

76 Ibid at 581.

77 Ibid at 584.

78 Ibid.

79 Ibid at 591-592 (italics supplied).

80 *Living Word* at 585 (citing Hogg, *Constitutional Law of Canada*, 4th edn).

81 See Bede Harris, 'Viewpoint Neutrality and Freedom of Expression in New Zealand' (1996) 8 *Otago L Rev* 515.

82 132 L Ed 2d 700, 714-715 (1995).

83 See further Harris, 'Viewpoint Neutrality'.

84 Grant Huscroft, 'Defamation, Racial Disharmony and Freedom of Expression' in Huscroft and Rishworth (eds), *Rights and Freedoms* (1995) ch 5 at 172.

85 *Living Word* at 585. The Court here is quoting from the European Court of Human Rights in *Handyside* v *United Kingdom* (1976) 1 EHRR 737 at 754.

86 Ibid at 588.

87 Ibid at 593.

88 As the High Court in *Living Word* put it (above n 63), at para 3.

89 Thomas J, *Living Word* [2000] 3 NZLR at 588.

90 The case was praised in some quarters: see, for example, 'Another Victory for Free speech', (editorial), *Evening Post*, 4 September 2000; Grant Huscroft, 'Why gay video ban was unjustified', *NZ Herald*, 8 September 2000.

91 See Peter Saxton, 'Fundamentalism has no place in free speech', *NZ Herald*, 14 September 2000, at A13.

92 Quoted in Helen Robinson, 'Anti-gay video ban overturned', *Express*, 14 September 2000, at 3.

93 See, for example, Graeme Lee (1993) 537 *NZPD* 16968.

94 Lange, 'Homosexuality and the Church' (above n 1), at 19.

95 The Anti-Discrimination (Homosexual Vilification) Amendment Act 1993.

96 Prosecutions for the separate criminal offence of 'serious homosexual vilification' require the consent of the Attorney General: s 49ZTA (2).

97 Lange, 'Homosexuality and the Church', at 19: 'A prominent magazine editor recently wrote off those conservatives who object to Auckland's annual 'Hero' Parade as "morons"—so much for rational and enlightened public debate!'

98 See 'No prosecution over exhibits,' *Otago Daily Times*, 28 March 1998, at 35. See also John Burrows and Ursula Cheer, *Media Law in New Zealand*, 4th edn (1999) at 325.

99 Abigail Caspari, 'God statues cause uproar,' *CW*, 24 October 1991, at 16.

100 'Egyptian statues to be "blessed"', '*CW*, 31 October 1991, at 1. The editor of *Challenge Weekly*, ibid at 2, condemned this as 'a pathetic compromise'.

101 Matt Finlay, 'Freedom to preach—a treasure that can very easily be lost', *CW*, 5 December 1991, at 7.

102 Ibid.

103 David A J Richards, *Sex, Drugs, Death, and the Law* (1982) at 35 (original italics). Quoted in Robert P George, *Making Men Moral* (1993) at 144-145.

104 See, for example, *Hamilton* v *Jurgens* [1996] NZFLR 350 (HC); *Julian* v *McWatt* [1998] NZFLR 257 (DC).

105 [1998] NZFLR 769. The reporting of the case is tardy as the decision was delivered on 20 February 1992.

106 Ibid at 774.

107 Ibid at 775.

108 Ibid.

109 *T* v *T* [*child support*] (1998) 17 FRNZ 387 at 390 per Judge D R Brown (Fam Ct).

110 Ibid.

111 Ibid at 392.

112 Ibid.

113 *A* v *R* [1999] NZFLR 249 at 255 per Hammond J.

114 Ibid.

115 Ibid at 256.

116 (1998) 16 FRNZ 621 (Fam Ct).

117 Ibid at 629.

118 (1998) 16 FRNZ at 630.

119 Ibid.

120 Ibid.

121 Ibid at 632.

122 Ibid at 628. It is hard to imagine what form of Christianity the judge is obliquely alluding to other than a liberal kind of Christianity.

123 Law Commission, *Adoption: Options for Reform*, NZLC PP 38 (October 1999) at para 197.

124 Law Commission, *Adoption and Its Alternatives: A Different Approach and a New Framework*, NZLC R65 (September 2000) Preface.

125 Ibid at paras 359-360 (italics in original). The report was 'profoundly flawed' accused one prominent CC commentator: Bruce Logan, 'Adoption and the Law Commission', *Cutting Edge*, October/November 2000, 4 at 4.

126 Ministry of Justice, *Same Sex Couples and the Law: A Discussion Paper* (August 1999) and *Same-Sex Couples and the Law: Backgrounding the Issues* (August 1999).

127 Law Commission, *Recognising Same–Sex Relationships*, NZLC SP4 (December 1999) at para 28.

128 Ibid at para 29.

129 'Survey finds rejection of same-sex marriages', *Press*, 21 October 2000, at 8.

130 Quoted in 'Survey finds rejection', ibid.

131 See its *PQ Broadsheet*, issue 76, August 2000, at 6.

132 'Bishops back registration for couples of same sex', *NZ Catholic*, 23 April 2000, at 1-2 and 'The bishops and same-sex relationships' (editorial), *NZ Catholic*, 21 May 2000, at 9.

133 *Presbyterian AFFIRM Newsletter*, 2000/1, March 2000, at 3.

134 Arnold R Turner, 'Same–sex marriage' (letter), *Reality*, October/November 1999, at 58-59. See also Lange, *Homosexuality and the Church* (above n 1), at 20.

135 See Ewen McQueen, 'Same-sex marriage' (letter), *Reality*, December 1999/January 2000, at 58-59.

136 See Stirling, 'No reply from bishops to protest', *Otago Daily Times*, 17 May 2000, at 6.

137 The non-extension to same-sex couples was described as 'simply nonsense' by Tim Barnett MP, Labour's human rights spokesman: 'De facto couples get property rights deal', *Otago Daily Times*, 25 March 1998, at 3.

138 See 'Legal rights planned for de facto and gay couples', *Otago Daily Times*, 3 April 2000, at 1.

139 Supplementary Order Paper No 25, 16 May 2000. The SOP was 82 pages long.

140 Ibid, clause 3.

141 'Bill signals end to injustice', *Waikato Times*, 20 July 2000.

142 'Sanctity is in one law for all', *Sunday Star-Times*, 9 April 2000, at A8.

143 'Married, gay and de facto all together in new law?', *NZ Catholic*, 21 May 2000, at 1.

144 Conference of Catholic Bishops, quoted ibid at 2.

145 'Property Bill controversy grows', *Otago Daily Times*, 19 July 2000, at 3.

146 Tim Barnett MP, Chairperson of the Select Committee: (2000) *NZPD* 5113.

147 "Relationship law by Christmas', *Otago Daily Times*, 31 October 2000, at 3. The Property (Relationships) Amendment Act was eventually passed, by 65 votes to 54, on 29 March 2001.

148 *Quilter* [1998] 1 NZLR at 528.

149 Carlos A Ball, 'Moral Foundations for a Discourse on Same-Sex Marriage: Looking Beyond Political Liberalism' (1997) 85 *Georgetown L J* 1871 at 1876-1877 (emphasis in original).

150 See, for instance, Anita Jowitt, 'The Legal Recognition of Relationships Between Couples of the Same Sex: A New Zealand Perspective' (1997) 6 *Aust Gay & Lesbian L J* 30 at 47.

151 Matthews, 'Partners in crime' (above n 48).

152 Thomas J in *Quilter* [1998] 1 NZLR at 554.

153 'Marriage is the classic example of a *preferred* relationship. It is one of the most highly-preferred, historically-favoured relations in the law. Thus, the claim for same-sex marriage is not a claim for mere tolerance, but for special preference.' Lynn D Wardle, 'Same-Sex Marriage and the Limits of Legal Pluralism' in Eekelaar and Nhlapo (eds), *The Changing Family* (1998) ch 23 at 391 (original emphasis).

154 *Attorney-General* v *Family Court at Otahuhu* [1995] NZFLR 57 at 68 per Ellis J.

155 See generally Linda McClain, 'Deliberative Democracy, Overlapping Consensus, and Same-Sex Marriage' (1998) 66 *Fordham L Rev* 1241.

156 See Jowitt, 'Legal Recognition' (above n 150), at 32-34.

157 Macedo, 'Homosexuality and the Conservative Mind' (1995) 84 *Georgetown L J* 261 at 263-264 and 293.

158 See John M Finnis, 'Law, Morality and "Sexual Orientation"' (1994) 69 *Notre Dame L Rev* 1049; Robert P George and Gerald V Bradley, 'Marriage and the Liberal Imagination' (1995) 84 *Georgetown L J* 301. For a New Zealand call to find natural law arguments against SSM, see Carolyn Moynihan, 'Legal status for same-sex couples?', *Humanity*, October 1999, at 9.

159 See, for example, Lynn D Wardle, 'The Potential Impact of Homosexual Parenting on Children' [1997] *U Illinois L Rev* 833. By contrast, the Law Commission in its report (*Adoption and Its Alternatives* (above n 124), at 135, fn 419) asserted that the social science evidence did not support negative consequences for children of gay parents and expressly rejected Wardle's 'biased' article. For a further rejoinder, defending Wardle, see Logan, 'Adoption and the Law Commission' (above n 125), at 5-6.

160 See Wardle, 'Limits of Legal Pluralism', at 393.

161 For an illuminating discussion, see Julia Stronks, 'Christians, Public Policy and Same-Sex Marriage: Framing the Questions before we shout the Answers' (1996) 26 *Christian Scholar's Rev* 540 and Don Mathieson, 'Same sex relationships: ethics, Christian leadership and the law' (1999) 7 *Stimulus* 34.

PART THREE

11 Conclusion

To retrace our steps, in Chapter 1, I sketched the conservative Christian 'narrative' of New Zealand history. As conservative Christians (CCs) tell it, corrosive secularist forces have, in the last generation, eroded the nation's Christian foundations. All is not lost, however, if CCs motivate themselves to recapture the high ground. Returned to its Christian moorings, New Zealand can be blessed again. I posited a succession of 'disestablishments' of Christianity. The first disestablishment (or nonestablishment) was the *de jure* one. The Old World idea of a State Church was firmly rejected and religious equality was recognized by Parliament in the 1840s and 1850s. Although there was a formal legal nonestablishment, it was accompanied by a *de facto* cultural establishment. I argue that New Zealand was committed to a generic, non-sectarian, Protestant-influenced Christianity. About the 1960s the Christian cultural hegemony began to erode. The shift has forced CCs to re-evaluate their social priorities. Neither succumbing to the 'spirit of the age' nor withdrawing from society is favoured. Instead, many CCs increasingly stress positive cultural engagement and social transformation lest the already parlous situation deteriorates further.

Chapter 2 analyzed the subject group of this study. Conservative Christianity is an umbrella term embracing adherents from Roman Catholicism and Protestantism. Whilst they are to be found in all denominations, they are principally made up of Evangelicals, Pentecostals and Charismatics. CCs share certain core characteristics: deference to divine authority, moral absolutism, a restorationist desire and an oppositional stance towards the spirit of the age. The fundamental presuppositions and axioms of this group include, for example, belief in the supernatural realm (heaven and hell are real) and in the pervasiveness of sin in a fallen world. Truth, capital 't', has been revealed, it is written, God has spoken, His divine standards are established for everyone, not just Christians. Note the past tense; the way we are meant to live and the essential things for mankind are not contingent, ever-unfolding or mysterious. The animating spirit or *zeitgeist* of contemporary 'post-Christian' society is variously described as modernism, secularism or secular humanism. Whatever it is labelled, CCs are convinced it is antithetical to the Kingdom of God. To the extent the state usurps its delegated authority—an increasingly likely possibility in the new era—CCs must face the prospect of principled civil disobedience.

What are the basic axioms and beliefs that undergird contemporary New Zealand law and government? Chapter 3 investigated the distinctive tenets of liberal democracy in this country, what I dubbed the 'Wellington worldview' (the mindset of government, business, media, education and other leaders). The central tenets of liberalism—individualism, neutrality as to conceptions of the good life, privatization of religion, emphasis upon reason and belief in progress—are reflected in the Wellington, and I dare say, the Westminster, Washington, Canberra or Ottawa worldviews as well. For all practical purposes, the powerful operate upon naturalistic premises guided by rational, empirical, scientific knowledge. Ethical relativism also prevails. The liberal, modernist worldview is dominant, but not without rivals, as the recent incursion of Maori and postmodernist beliefs reveals. So far as CCs are concerned, the rules of public debate—secular, practical reasons for public policy must be proffered as well as (and, preferably, instead of) religious ones—are commonly observed. I suggest that the limit of liberal democratic tolerance is met when groups such as CCs challenge central tenets of that ideology. Attempts to 'impose' the Truth, as CCs perceive it, are rebuffed, as are efforts to dethrone reason as the adjudicating touchstone. Religionists who oppose the goodness of ideological pluralism are also likely to be denounced. Tolerance is meted out in proportion to conformity with liberal, pluralist values: CCs must know their place.

How do the conservative Christian and liberal, modernist 'worlds' get along? By and large, CCs and the state coexist amicably. Each mutually adjust to the other. There is, however, the real prospect of conflict given the incompatibility of worldviews at certain key junctures. CCs challenge the supposed neutrality of the liberal democratic state. Human nature abhors a vacuum and there is always, as CCs see it, a *de facto* dominant worldview. CCs believe, given their cultural disestablishment, that the range and volume of 'pressure points' between them and the state will increase. Whether this will result in CCs simply losing out, or whether their concerns will be at least partially accommodated, are possibilities explored in subsequent chapters.

In Part Two I undertook a series of case studies investigating areas of conflict between CCs and the state. The chapters all broadly concern rights and so Chapter 5 (Human Rights) commenced this section. CCs have consistently viewed talk of human rights somewhat lukewarmly. Whilst vindication of rights of the weak and powerless are proper matters for Christian energy, CCs are critical of certain aspects of modern human rights theory. The *ideology* of human rights (as opposed to the rights *per se*) is perceived as non-theistic, individualistic and potentially intolerant, even totalitarian, in its outworking. Given the liberal modernist pedigree of rights theory, CCs fear tolerance will not extend to those, such as themselves, who are not 'inclusive', 'tolerant' and 'accepting' of all ways of life. My exploration of some of the major clashes between CCs and human rights advocates and institutions in the past 20 years revealed a legacy of mutual distrust and suspicion.

The centrality of the family to CCs cannot be over-estimated. The next three chapters explored perceived threats to the family from the United Nations Convention on the Rights of the Child 1989 (CRC). The CC concept of the family (patriarchal, hierarchical, authoritarian, duty-based) is clearly at odds with liberal, modernist notions. A 'constitutionalization' of family law is underway, and with it, a greater emphasis, *inter alia*, upon the rights of children. In zero-sum fashion, greater state recognition of children's rights spells, for CCs, fewer parental rights. State intrusion in the family is, they fear, likely to increase also. CC unease at the CRC is part of a broader, longstanding antipathy to international conventions—global accords which invoke for some CCs the slippery slope of one-world government. Despite such pessimism, my assessment is that the CRC will not necessarily involve greater state intervention into the intact family. The welfare test will continue as a secondary standard, only applied after state jurisdiction has been triggered in the customary way (proven abuse or neglect). The real crux of CC anxiety with the CRC is the clutch of 'autonomy' or 'participation' rights granted children. Here the waters remain largely untested.

Next, I selected a foremost parental right for CCs—the right to control the religious upbringing of one's children. I concluded that, in the intact family, the *parens patriae* jurisdiction of the courts remains as forceful as ever, thwarting parental religious practices that might endanger the child's life, health or educational opportunities. CC's are not free to make martyrs of their children. Perhaps CC parents do face the prospect of greater state involvement in religious upbringing matters in the future. If so, I suggest it will most likely take the form of courts making pragmatic, welfare-based assessments of parental decision-making—giving due weight to the maturing minor's views—rather than a blunt judicial veto of parents' wishes. There are, in the nature of things, likely to be very few cases which ever reach the courtroom, but the symbolic effect of the few that do concern CCs. CCs would be wise here to avoid 'the wages of crying wolf'[1]: protesting too loudly, too often, and thus having a real cause for alarm going unheeded on a future occasion.

In Chapter 8, I examined another CC concern with the CRC—its role in the abolition of the present right of parents to administer moderate corporal punishment to their children. I concluded that the CRC may have a direct and significant influence. It has been regularly invoked in the ongoing debate on 'smacking' as a persuasive reason for banning the practice. The United Nations Committee on the Rights of the Child disapprove of corporal punishment, equating it with abuse. CCs face an uphill battle against a formidable array of governmental and private anti-smacking proponents to retain this practice.

The final two chapters detailed two CC concerns arising from their broader antipathy towards the 'normalization' of homosexuality. Homosexual conduct is sinful and ought not, argue CCs, to be equated with heterosexual behaviour. The Wellington worldview, however, increasingly sees such views as archaic bigotry. It is perhaps no coincidence that the watershed decade, the 1960s, which marked the beginning of the cultural disestablishment of Christianity, also witnessed the start of the 'sexual revolution'. CCs believe that the recognition of gay rights in human rights legislation will yield adverse consequences both for them and society.

I examined whether a key incident of the right of church autonomy—clergy selection—would be curtailed. Does the ban on sexual orientation discrimination in the Human Rights Act 1993 reach churches? Are churches prevented from ordaining openly practising gay candidates for the ministry? Do gay rights trump CC rights? The question is still unresolved. I traversed the significant part the uncertain prospect of litigation under the Act played in the heated church debates. A liberal modernist ethic—the equality of sexual orientations—may yet penetrate the church. Whatever the outcome—either confirmation that churches are exempt in their clergy ordination and employment decisions, or the full application of the Act to thwart non-selection of gay ministers—the 'sting' of rights ideology will have been felt by CCs.

The final case study considered the extent to which CCs' positive religious freedom might be curtailed. Following the recent acceptance of homosexuality by the powers-that-be, are CCs hampered in influencing public policy—specifically, in opposing the introduction of same-sex marriage? There is little to suggest so at present and, indeed, a recent landmark Court of Appeal decision on free speech vindicated the right of CCs to express their opposition to gay rights. Their freedom of expression might be threatened by a move to equate anti-gay speech with racist and other 'hate' speech. There is a prospect of this occurring given the political leverage of gay activists. But perhaps the bigger obstacle is the cultural and political one. Working within the rules of liberal, modernist public debate, CCs may struggle to generate cogent, secular, practical arguments why same-sex marriage, or *a fortiori*, registered domestic partnerships for same-sex couples, ought not to be recognized. The sexual revolution came and traditional moralists have (apparently) lost. The onus is upon those who resist liberalizing measures, and the further recognition of individual human rights, to make a case.

CCs find themselves an increasingly alienated minority in a land once described by Richard John Seddon, a former prime minister, as 'God's own country'.[2] A generation ago, commencing around the 1960s, a 'paradigm shift'[3], 'sea change'[4], 'architectonic transferral'[5] occurred in New Zealand, as it did in other Western societies. At the level of 'deep culture' (Harold Turner) the basic axioms, premises or worldview began to change. Judeo-Christian values and presuppositions, always admittedly mixed with secular and Hellenistic ones, began to fade. The cultural disestablishment of Christianity and the emergence of a new singular worldview is, nevertheless, not complete.

Contemporary Western Christianity is in an 'awkwardly intermediate stage of having once been culturally established but not yet clearly disestablished.'[6] Stanley Hauerwas muses: 'We are not sure whether, as Christians, we ought to or can return to times when the church at least allegedly seemed to have status if not power or whether we must seek some yet undetermined more modest stance in liberal societies.'[7] New Zealand is in 'a type of no-man's land',[8] where Christians are no longer the dominant force culturally, but Christian forms and habits remain. The new *weltanschauung*, the new society, can only be described as post-something: post-Christian, post-colonial, post-modern and so on.[9] Perhaps T S Eliot was right when he wrote: 'a society has not ceased to be Christian until it has become positively something else.'[10] Meanwhile, we are 'moving between times'.[11] In administering the last rites to the end of Christian civilization, Lloyd Geering is heartened: 'post-Christian secular society provides much more freedom for individuals to be themselves . . . not only many ways of being Christian but also many more ways of being human.'[12] Others disagree. Aidan Nichols in *Christendom Awake* urges the Church not to become a mere counter-culture, but instead, 'despite the odds, [to] press[ ] her claim to be the bearer of that revealed religion intended for all nations, and all subsequent history, and so impress on the civil community those principles which alone enable its members to encompass the society the ends for which man was made[ ].'[13]

For CCs, neither withdrawal into a defensive enclave nor meek conformity to the spirit of the age are options. Minority status may be a fact of life, but an acquiescent, subservient, privatized posture is not. To quote Lesslie Newbigin:

> true to its roots . . . [the church] could not accept relegation to a private sphere of purely inward and personal religion. . . . Christians can never seek refuge in a ghetto where their faith is not proclaimed as public truth for all. They can never agree that there is one law for themselves and another for the world. They can never admit that there are areas of life where the writ of Christ does not run. . . . the church can never cease to remind governments that they are under the rule of Christ and that he alone is the judge of all they do. The church can never accept the thesis that the central shrine of public life is empty, in other words, that there has been no public revelation before the eyes of the world of the purpose for which all things and all peoples have been created and which all governments must serve.[14]

The idea that 'the State is the only and ultimate society and that the Church is simply a limited organization for religious worship and moral instruction', may be a comforting liberal notion, but, as Christopher Dawson rejoined, 'for a Christian . . . all such ideas are blasphemy against Christ the King.'[15] Christians must continue to be 'salt' and 'light'[16], to tell their story (or counter-story), 'the old, old story'[17] of sin, judgment, creation, fall and redemption. As trustees of *the* story, CCs are obliged to tell it, to be faithful, bold witnesses. Furthermore, as Hauerwas puts it: 'Without the church the world literally has no hope of salvation since the church is necessary for the world to know it is part of a story that it cannot know without the church.'[18] As a New Zealand Catholic bishop urged recently, the Christians must 'realise how much we have to offer. We are they who have the fullest, clearest picture of what it means to be human. We who profess the Nicene Creed have the greatest reason of all for knowing the dignity of persons. What we have to offer is the very thing that needs to undergird all social, political and economic life.'[19] If the Church cannot be the triumphant 'Church of Christendom' and it scorns being merely a 'Gathered Church' (a secluded community of the faithful), it can still be the 'Witnessing Church'.[20]

Compelled to fulfil the Great Commission,[21] and desirous of recapturing the cultural reins, what is the likely pattern of engagement henceforth between CCs and the state? There will, I suggest, continue to be a variety of responses and outcomes. CCs will continue to peacefully coexist with the state and the state will turn to them (and other religionists) to advance societal goals in welfare, education and so on. In addition, conflicts will also persist. A contentious point is whether they will increase in number and severity. There is some cause for thinking they will. As the Wellington worldview becomes further de-Christianized, and its working premises and values more secular, humanistic and pluralistic, the potential for misunderstanding and disagreement widens. CCs can no longer count upon a sympathetic governmental and legal worldview. Contributing to this quandary is the growth in New Zealand of religious minorities, whether conventionally religious (Muslims, Hindus and so on) or not (atheists, agnostics, New Agers).

When conflicts do arise—for it is a question of when, not if—the traditional responses by the state will also recur. Clashes between CCs and the government will continue to see both an accommodation of CCs' religious convictions, on some occasions, and a disregarding or overruling of CC sensibilities by the law, on others. I have concentrated upon instances of overruling by the state. The *Eric Sides* and Christian bookbinder-type cases attract public notoriety, whilst the quiet adjustments and exemptions by state officials, departmental bureaucrats or judicial officers go unnoticed. Whether, on balance, CCs' interests are generally accommodated or vetoed is a difficult question to answer. I have not attempted a large scale, empirical assessment. What I have endeavoured to show is that there are two contrasting worldviews generating different conceptions of morality and law and that conflicts have arisen. There is a certain inevitable incommensurability, a *differend,* to use a postmodernist expression,[22] between the two groups. Another book could no doubt demonstrate a similar juxtaposition and mutual misunderstanding between other groups (Maori, gays, women, Buddhists) and the state. What makes CCs unique is that they are a community that largely defined the former prevailing worldview, have had the tide turn against them, and are faced with the challenge of 'where to from here'. They are now 'outsiders' and *their* story is just one of many. This puts them in a peculiar quandary. Hegemony lost is seldom regained.

A particular interest in this study is the religious freedom enjoyed by CCs. What is the prognosis? In terms of their negative religious liberty—the sphere of private religious practice wherein state interference is presumptively wrong—I predict an attenuation of this in the future. Internally, CCs will feel pressure to conform to the *zeitgeist*, the prevailing ethos and values of the age. As Mark Tushnet notes drolly: 'Fundamentalist views are unrevisable in principle, but historical experience strongly suggests they are revisable in practice.'[23] In the same way that Mormons 'reinterpreted' their faith and stance on polygamy, following the American Supreme Court's refusal to countenance that practice,[24] some CCs may revisit their views on homosexuality, religious upbringing, smacking and so on. This is nothing new. In the tradition of Luther, however, the belligerent, defiant spirit that characterizes CC will see some resist this gravitational pull. Where these CCs perceive the state to be transgressing its God-given bounds, civil disobedience, even martyrdom, remain last resorts.[25]

The positive religious liberty of CCs is also threatened. Public witness to the Truth, dogged adherence to traditional Christian mores, is disruptive of the inclusive, pluralist discourse prevalent in contemporary Western society. In the ongoing *Kulturkampf*[26] or cultural struggle—which is, at its most fundamental level, a clash of belief systems or worldviews[27]—it is possible that CC efforts to influence public policy and the direction of the nation, will diminish. Partly this may be due to internal deficiencies within CC—a plain loss of nerve, or an inability to generate intelligent, secular arguments sufficient to carry the day. But partly it may be due to political, social, and even (in the near future) legal impediments that render public expression of universal truth unacceptable in a free and democratic, multicultural, 'tolerant' society.

Overall, I suspect religious freedom is granted to CCs, and indeed the Church, to the extent it 'knows its place'. As Dr Josef Goebbels is said to have told the German churches: 'You are at liberty to seek your salvation as you understand it, provided you do nothing to change the social order.'[28] I have argued that, at any given time, there is always a *de facto* (if not *de jure*) establishment, a prevailing worldview, an ascendant hegemony. Every state 'must have its orthodoxy . . . a set of substantive beliefs and values upon which public decisions are based . . .'[29] Whether one wants to call this orthodoxy 'religious' is unimportant. (To CCs, a purely immanent, this-worldly worldview is no less religious than theirs.) The point is that an establishment or orthodoxy does, and must, exist. It may be a hybrid, incoherent, contested one, and a convenient label for it may be elusive, but it exists. If I am correct and there is always an established, prevailing orthodoxy, with its concomitant worldview, then it is more accurate to talk of religious *tolerance* rather than religious freedom.[30] The cold reality is that the state grants religion those rights and privileges that, according to the state's lights, it considers religion deserves. The concept of rights here is statist.[31] The state grants religious rights—it defines 'religion', religion's permissible forms of expression, its limits, its exemptions, and so on. It holds all the cards and it tolerates religion on *its* terms. The state does not simply acknowledge antecedent rights, ones that exist prior to the state and are superior to the claims of the state. This is, to the secular mind, a quaint understanding clung to by a few nostalgic religionists. To acknowledge higher, antecedent rights is simply to revisit the very foundation of liberal democracy and to gainsay the longstanding secular basis to the state. That debate is over, the Enlightenment happened and religion lost.[32]

Now tolerance is nothing to be sneezed at. 'In the real world', comments William Galston, 'there is nothing "mere" about toleration.'[33] Nevertheless, tolerance ought to be seen for what it is.

The ultimate security for CCs' religious liberty (apart from God) is not the state nor, given an unentrenched Bill of Rights Act, the judiciary.[34] The latter have, on occasions, been ready to treat CCs in the same unsympathetic manner as have others in society. The New Zealand Court of Appeal in *Lange* reminded us that in the present constitutional and political system: 'In substance, the people, rather than the (temporary) government, are to be seen as having ultimate power.'[35] It is, as Hauerwas argues, a temptation for Christians to believe that they are protected by legal mechanisms devised by (even) democratic states. Rather, 'states are limited by a people with the imagination and courage to challenge the inveterate temptation of the state to ask us to compromise our loyalty to God.'[36] This echoes the much-quoted observation of Judge Learned Hand a half century ago, one referred to in the 1985 Government White Paper on the Bill of Rights:

> I often wonder whether we do not rest our hopes too much upon constitutions, upon laws and upon courts. These are false hopes; believe me, these are false hopes. *Liberty lies in the hearts of men and women*; when it dies there, no constitution, no law, no court can save it; no constitution, no law, no court can even do much to help it. While it lies there it needs no constitution, no law, no court to save it.[37]

Judge Learned Hand's 1944 address on 'The Spirit of Liberty' has another passage not referred to by the White Paper. It seems an apt place to finish: 'the spirit of liberty remembers that not even a sparrow falls to earth unheeded; the spirit of liberty is the spirit of Him who, near two thousand years ago, taught mankind that lesson it has never learned, but has never quite forgotten; that there may be a kingdom where the least shall be heard and considered side by side with the greatest.'[38]

Notes

1 Here I borrow the title of a leading article on the *Roe* abortion decision: John Hart Ely, 'The Wages of Crying Wolf: A Comment on *Roe* v *Wade*' (1973) 82 *Yale L J* 920.

2 'Just returning to God's own country', wrote Seddon in 10 June 1906. See 'Richard John Seddon' in Orsman and Moore (eds), *Heineman Dictionary of New Zealand Quotations* (1988) at 573.

3 The Rev Murray Robertson, 'New Zealand as a Mission Field: The Paradigm Shift' in Patrick (ed), *The Vision New Zealand Congress* (1993) ch 3 at 46: 'A shift has occurred. There have been long-term trends, huge subterranean movements within Western culture.'

4 Daphne Hampson, *After Christianity* (1996) at v: 'In the last decade there has been a sea change. There was a time when it took much courage to say publicly in the media that one was not a Christian. Now it takes none at all.'

5 Raymond G Decker, 'The Secularization of Anglo-American Law: 1800-1970' (1974) 49 *Thought* 280 at 286-287. Architechtonic transferrals are 'the basic *Weltanschauung* of metaphysical constructs in which man and his institutions are viewed'. Decker argued that the architectonic structures, which had 'become the substratum for Anglo-American law', had 'more often than not been the prevailing Christian constructs . . .': ibid at 287.

6 George Lindbeck, *The Nature of Doctrine* (1984) at 134: quoted in Stanley Hauerwas, *After Christendom*? (1991) at 23.

7 Hauerwas, ibid.

8 John Flett, 'Unpacking Gospel and Culture' in Flett (ed), *Collision Crossroads: The Intersection of Modern Western Culture with the Christian Gospel* (1998) ch 1 at 9.

9 'The religion of progress may have been able to kill Christianity in the consciousness of many, but it has not succeeded in substituting any other lasting system in meaning.' George Grant, 'Religion and the State' (1963) 70 *Queen's Quarterly* 183 at 196.

10 T S Eliot, *The Idea of a Christian Society* (1939) at 13. 'It is my contention', he continued (ibid), 'that we have to-day a culture which is mainly negative, but which, so far as it is positive, is still Christian. . . . I believe that the choice before us is between the formation of a new Christian culture, and the acceptance of a pagan one.' See similarly Christopher Dawson, *Religion and the Modern State* (1935) at 151: 'Modern civilization is not just ceasing to be Christian; it is setting itself up as an anti-religion which will tolerate no rival...'

11 Brian Carrell, *Moving Between Times—Modernity and Postmodernity: A Christian View* (1998).

12 Lloyd Geering, *The World to Come: From Christian Past to Global Future* (2000) at 34.

13 Aidan Nichols, *Christendom Awake: On Re-energising the Church in Culture* (1999) at 6.

14 Lesslie Newbigin, *Foolishness to the Greeks* (1986) at 99-100 and 115.

15 Dawson, *Religion and the Modern State* (above n 10), at 149.

16 Matthew 5:13-16.

17 Hauerwas, *After Christendom*?, at 148, quoting lines from the old gospel hymn, 'I Love to Tell the Story'. See further Lesslie Newbigin, *Proper Confidence* (1995) at 12-14 and 76-78.

18 Ibid at 36.

19 Bishop Peter J Cullinane, 'Why is the Church not touching some people?' Paper prepared for the Mixed Commission, Wellington, March 2000. Reproduced in *The Tablet*, Issue 44, 21 May 2000, 2 at 2.

20 Thomas Shaffer's tripartite ecclesiological classification: 'Stephen Carter and Religion in America' (1994) 62 *U Cinn L Rev* 1601 at 1608 et seq.

21 Matthew 28:16-20.

22 See Jean François Lyotard, *The Differend: Phrases in Dispute*, trans Van Den Abbeele (1988) at xi: 'a differend [*différend*] would be a case of conflict between (at least) two parties, that cannot be equitably resolved for lack of a rule of judgment applicable to both arguments. One side's legitimacy does not imply the other's lack of legitimacy . . . The title of this book suggests . . . that a universal rule of judgment between heterogeneous genres is lacking in general.'

23 Mark Tushnet, *Taking the Constitution Away from the Courts* (1999) at 85.

24 Stephen Carter, 'Religious Freedom as if Religion Matters: A Tribute to Justice Brennan' (1999) 87 *Calif L Rev* 1059 at 1085. The leading Supreme Court case upholding bigamy convictions over the Mormon defendants' free exercise of religion claim is *Reynolds* v *United States*, 98 US 145 (1878).

25 '[T]hose religions that stubbornly cling to old fashioned beliefs . . . will thrive once again in the catacombs.' Richard F Duncan, 'Who wants to Stop the Church: Homosexual Rights Legislation, Public Policy, and Religious Freedom' (1994) 69 *Notre Dame L Rev* 393 at 445.

26 See Justice Scalia (dissenting) in *Romer* v *Evans*, 134 L Ed 2d 855, 868, 878 (1996) and Charles Taylor, 'Religion in a Free Society' in Hunter and Guinness (eds), *Articles of Faith, Articles of Peace* (1990) ch 6 at 108.

27 Charles Colson and Nancy Pearcey, *How Now Shall We Live?* (1999) at xii and 17.

28 Quoted in Robert Song, *Christianity and Liberal Society* (1997) at 213.

29 Steven D Smith, 'The Restoration of Tolerance' (1990) 78 *Calif L Rev* 305 at 332. See also Newbigin, *Foolishness to the Greeks* (above n 14), at 132 and Phillip E Johnson, *Reason in the Balance* (1995) ch 2.

30 See Hauerwas, *After Christendom*? (above n 6) at 179 n 27. Perhaps it is also more accurate to speak of liberal tolerance rather than liberal neutrality: see Colin MacLeod, 'Liberal Neutrality or Liberal Tolerance?' (1997) 16 *Law and Philosophy* 529.

31 See Carter, 'Religious Freedom as if Religion Matters', at 1065-1066.

[32] But see Richard John Neuhaus, 'Why We Can Get Along', *First Things*, February 1996, 27 at 32. Neuhaus argues religion did not lose but religious coercion did.

[33] William A Galston, 'Expressive Liberty, Moral Pluralism, Political Pluralism: Three Sources of Liberal Theory' (1999) 40 *Wm and Mary L Rev* 869 at 902.

[34] And some American CCs would likely say they fare little better in a constitutional system with a supreme Bill of Rights and judicial review.

[35] *Lange* v *Atkinson* [1998] 3 NZLR 424 at 463.

[36] Hauerwas, *After Christendom*? (above n 6) at 71.

[37] 'The Spirit of Liberty', a 1944 address given at Central Park, New York, in Dilliard (ed), *The Spirit of Liberty: Papers and Addresses of Learned Hand* (1952) ch 26 at 189-190 (emphasis added). The passage is quoted by the authors of the *White Paper* (*A Bill of Rights for New Zealand*), *AJHR* 1985, A6, at para 4.4.

[38] 'The Spirit of Liberty' in Dilliard, ibid, at 190. Gerald Gunther, *Learned Hand: The Man and the Judge* (1994) at 552, notes the paradoxical nature of this particular passage: 'Hand, for decades an agnostic, delivered an address with notable religious overtones, including an invocation of Jesus Christ.'

Select Bibliography

A Bill of Rights for New Zealand: A White Paper, Wellington: Government Printer, 1985

Ahdar, Rex and John Stenhouse (eds), *God and Government: The New Zealand Experience*, Dunedin: University of Otago Press, 2000

Ahdar, Rex, 'Religious Parliamentarians and Euthanasia: A Window into Church and State in New Zealand', *Journal of Church and State,* **38** (1996) 569-593

Ahdar, Rex, 'Religion as a Factor in Custody and Access Disputes', *International Journal of Law, Policy and the Family,* **10** (1996) 177-204

Ahdar, Rex, 'Religion in Custody and Access: The New Zealand Experience', *New Zealand Universities Law Review,* **17** (1996) 113-139

Ahdar, Rex, 'A Christian State?', *Journal of Law and Religion,* **13** (1998-1999) 453-482

Ahdar, Rex (ed), *Law and Religion*, Aldershot: Ashgate, 2000

Ahdar, Rex, 'Children's Religious Freedom, Devout Parents and the State', in Peter W Edge and Graham Harvey (eds), *Law and Religion in Contemporary Society: Religious Communities, Individualism and the State*, Aldershot: Ashgate, 2000, 93-114

Ahdar, Rex, 'Parental Religious Upbringing in a Children's Rights Era', in Paul R Beaumont and Keith Wotherspoon (eds), *Christian Perspectives on Law and Relationism,* Carlisle: Paternoster Press, 2000, 189-236

Ahdar, Rex, 'Religious Group Autonomy, Gay Ordination and Human Rights Law', in Richard D O'Dair and Andrew D E Lewis (eds), *Law and Religion*, Oxford: Oxford University Press, 2001

Airhart, Phyllis D and Margaret Lamberts Bendroth (eds), *Faith Traditions and the Family*, Louiseville: Westminster John Knox Press, 1996

Alexander, Larry, 'Liberalism, Religion and the Unity of Epistemology', *San Diego Law Review,* **30** (1993) 763-797

An-Na'im, Abdullah, Jerald D Gort, Henry Jansen, and Hendrik M Vroom (eds), *Human Rights and Religious Values: An Uneasy Relationship?* Grand Rapids: Eerdmans, 1995, 192-202

Arneson, Richard J and Ian Shapiro, 'Democratic Autonomy and Religious Freedom: A Critique of *Wisconsin* v *Yoder*', in Ian Shapiro and Russell Hardin (eds), *Political Order: NOMOS XXXVIII*, New York: New York University Press, 1996, 365-411

Berger, Peter L, 'Secularism in Retreat', *National Interest*, Winter 1996-97, 3-12

Blamires, Harry, *The Christian Mind: How Should a Christian Think?* London: SPCK, 1963

Brown, Harold O J, *The Sensate Culture: Western Civilisation Between Chaos and Transformation*, Dallas: Word Publishing, 1996

Campos, Paul F, 'Secular Fundamentalism', *Columbia Law Review,* **94** (1994) 1814-1827

Carrell, Brian, *Moving Between Times—Modernity and Postmodernity: A Christian View*, Auckland: DeepSight Trust, 1998

Carson, Don A, *The Gagging of God: Christianity Confronts Pluralism*, Leicester: Apollos, 1996

Carter, Stephen L, *The Culture of Disbelief: How American Law and Politics Trivialize Religious Devotion*, New York: Basic Books, 1993

Casanova, José, *Public Religions in the Modern World*, Chicago: University of Chicago Press, 1994

Christenson, Larry, *The Christian Family*, Minneapolis: Bethany Fellowship, 1970

Clouser, Roy A, *The Myth of Religious Neutrality: An Essay on the Hidden Role of Religious Belief in Theories*, Notre Dame: University of Notre Dame Press, 1991

Colson, Charles and Nancy Pearcey, *How Now Shall We Live*? Wheaton: Tyndale House, 1999

Cook, Anthony E, 'God-Talk in a Secular World', *Yale Journal of Law and the Humanities,* **6** (1994) 435-461

De Blois, Matthijs, 'The Foundation of Human Rights: A Christian Perspective', in Paul Beaumont (ed), *Christian Perspectives on Human Rights and Legal Philosophy*, Carlisle: Paternoster Press, 1998, 7-29

Decker, Raymond G, 'The Secularization of Anglo-American Law: 1800-1970', *Thought,* **49** (1974) 280-298

Dobson, James, *Solid Answers*, Wheaton, Illinois: Tyndale House, 1997

Evans, John A, 'The New Christian Right in New Zealand', in Bryan Gilling, (ed), *'Be Ye Separate': Fundamentalism and the New Zealand Experience*, Hamilton: University of Waikato Press, 1992, 69-106

Feinberg, Joel, 'The Child's Right to an Open Future', in William Aitken and Hugh LaFollette (eds), *Whose Child? Children's Rights, Parental Authority and State Power*, Totowa: Rowman & Littlefield, 1980, 124-153

Fish, Stanley, 'Liberalism Doesn't Exist', *Duke Law Journal,* **1987**, 997-1001

Fish, Stanley, 'Mission Impossible: Settling the Just Bounds Between Church and State', *Columbia Law Review,* **97** (1997) 2255-2333

Galston, William A, 'Expressive Liberty, Moral Pluralism, Political Pluralism: Three Sources of Liberal Theory', *William and Mary Law Review,* **40** (1999) 869-907

Galston, William A, *Liberal Purposes: Goods, Virtues and Diversity in the Liberal State*, Cambridge: Cambridge University Press, 1991

Gedicks, Frederick M, 'Public Life and Hostility to Religion', *Virginia Law Review,* **78** (1992) 617-696

Gedicks, Frederick M, 'Toward a Constitutional Jurisprudence of Religious Group Rights', *Wisconsin Law Review,* **1989**, 99-169

Geisler, Norman L and William D Watkins, *Worlds Apart: A Handbook on Worldviews*, 2nd edn, Grand Rapids: Baker Book House, 1989

George, Robert P, 'A Clash of Orthodoxies', *First Things*, August/September 1999, 33-40

Gray, John, *Liberalism*, 2nd edn, Buckingham: Open University Press, 1995

Greenawalt, Kent, *Religious Convictions and Political Choice*, New York, Oxford University Press, 1988

Grenz, Stanley J, *A Primer on Postmodernism*, Grand Rapids: Eerdmans, 1996

Hafen, Bruce C and Jonathan O Hafen, 'Abandoning Children to Their Autonomy: The United Nations Convention on the Rights of the Child', *Harvard International Law Journal,* **37** (1996) 449-491

Harris, Harriet A, *Fundamentalism and Evangelicals*, Oxford: Clarendon Press, 1998

Hauerwas, Stanley, 'A Christian Critique of Christian America', in J Roland Pennock and John W Chapman (eds), *Religion, Morality and the Law: NOMOS XXX*, New York: New York University Press, 1988, 110-133

Hauerwas, Stanley, *After Christendom? How the Church is to Behave If Freedom, Justice, and a Christian Nation Are Bad Ideas*, Nashville: Abingdon Press, 1991

Henry, Carl F H, *The Christian Mindset in a Secular Society: Promoting Evangelical Renewal & National Righteousness*, Portland: Multnomah Press, 1984

Holmes, Arthur F, *Contours of a World View*, Grand Rapids: Eerdmans, 1983

Hunter, James Davison, *Culture Wars: The Struggle to Define America*, New York: Basic Books, 1991

Hunter, James Davison, *Evangelicalism: The Coming Generation*, Chicago: University of Chicago Press, 1987

Jenson, Robert W, 'The God-Wars', in Carl Braaten, and Robert W Jenson, (eds), *Either/Or: The Gospel or Neopaganism*, Grand Rapids: Eerdmans, 1995, 23-36

Johnson, Phillip E, *Reason in the Balance: The Case Against Naturalism in Science, Law and Education*, Downers Grove: InterVarsity Press, 1995

Kaye, Bruce and Gordon Wenham (eds), *Law, Morality and the Bible*, Leicester: Inter-Varsity Press, 1978

Leff, Arthur Allen, 'Unspeakable Ethics, Unnatural Law', *Duke Law Journal*, **1979**, 1229-1249

Leigh, Ian, 'Towards a Christian Approach to Religious Liberty', in Paul R Beaumont (ed), *Christian Perspectives on Human Rights and Legal Philosophy*, Carlisle: Paternoster Press, 1998, 31-72

Lupu, Ira C, 'Models of Church-State Interaction and the Strategy of the Religion Clauses', *De Paul Law Review*, **42** (1992) 223-233

Marsden, George M, *Understanding Fundamentalism and Evangelicalism*, Grand Rapids: Eerdmans, 1991

Marshall, Christopher, '"A Little Lower than the Angels": Human Rights in the Biblical Tradition', in William Atkin and Katrine Evans (eds), *Human Rights and the Common Good: Christian Perspectives*, Wellington: Victoria University Press, 1999, 14-76

Marshall, Paul, 'Liberalism, Pluralism and Christianity: A Reconceptualization', *Fides et Historia*, **21** (1989) 3-17

McConnell, Michael W, '"God is Dead and We Have Killed Him!": Freedom of Religion in the Post-modern Age', *Brigham Young University Law Review*, **1993**, 163-188

McGrath, Alister, *Evangelicalism and the Future of Christianity*, London: Hodder and Stoughton, 1994

Middleton, J Richard and Brian J Walsh, *Truth is Stranger Than It Used to Be: Biblical Faith in a Postmodern Age*, Downers Grove: InterVarsity Press, 1995

Mott, Stephen Charles, *A Christian Perspective on Political Thought*, New York: Oxford University Press, 1993

Mutua, Makau wa, 'The Ideology of Human Rights', *Virginia Journal of International Law*, **36** (1996) 589-657

Newbigin, Lesslie, *Foolishness to the Greeks: The Gospel and Western Culture*, Grand Rapids: Eerdmans, 1986

Nichols, Aidan, *Christendom Awake: On Re-energising the Church in Culture*, Edinburgh: T&T Clark, 1999

Olthuis, James H, 'On Worldviews', *Christian Scholar's Review*, **14** (1985) 153-164

Otlowski, Margaret and B Martin Tsamenyi, 'Parental Autonomy and the United Nations Convention on the Rights of the Child: Are the Fears Justified?', *Australian Journal of Family Law*, **6** (1992) 137-160

Packer, James I, *'Fundamentalism' and the Word of God: Some Evangelical Principles*, London: Inter-Varsity Fellowship, 1958

Pannenberg, Wolfhart, 'How to Think About Secularism', *First Things*, June/July 1996, 27-32

Rawls, John, 'The Idea of Public Reason Revisited', *University of Chicago Law Review*, **64** (1997) 765-807

Rawls, John, *Political Liberalism*, New York: Columbia University Press, 1993

Rushdoony, Rousas John, *The Institutes of Biblical Law*, Nutley: Presbyterian and Reformed Publishing (Craig Press), 1973

Ryan, Allanah, '"For God, Country and Family": Populist Moralism and the New Zealand Moral Right', *New Zealand Sociology*, **1** (1986) 104-112

Schaeffer, Francis A, *A Christian Manifesto*, Wheaton: Crossway Books, 1982

Sire, James W, *The Universe Next Door: A Basic World View Catalog*, 2nd edn, Downers Grove: InterVarsity Press, 1988

Smith, Steven D, *Foreordained Failure: The Quest for a Constitutional Principle of Religious Freedom*, New York: Oxford University Press, 1995

Smolin, David M, 'Church, State and International Human Rights: A Theological Appraisal', *Notre Dame Law Review*, **73** (1998) 1515-1546

Smolin, David M, 'Will International Human Rights be Used as a Tool of

Cultural Genocide? The Interaction of Human Rights Norms, Religion, Culture and Gender', *Journal of Law and Religion,* **12** (1996) 143-171

Song, Robert, *Christianity and Liberal Society*, Oxford: Clarendon Press, 1997

Storkey, Alan, *A Christian Social Perspective*, Leicester: Inter-Varsity Press, 1979

Stott, John, *New Issues Facing Churches Today*, 3rd edn, London: Collins, 1999

Turner, Harold, 'Deep Mission to Deep Culture', in John Flett (ed), *Collision Crossroads: The Intersection of Modern Western Culture with the Christian Gospel*, Auckland: DeepSight Trust, 1998, 14-33

Turner, Harold, 'The Three Levels of Mission in New Zealand', in Bruce Patrick (ed), *New Vision: New Zealand*, Auckland: Vision New Zealand, 1993, 61-68

Vodanovich, Ivanica, 'Religion and Legitimation in New Zealand: Redefining the Relationship between Church and State', *British Review of New Zealand Studies,* **3** (1990) 52-64

Waldron, Jeremy, 'Theoretical Foundations of Liberalism', *Philosophical Quarterly,* **37** (1987) 127-150

Waldron, Jeremy, 'Legislation and moral neutrality', in his *Liberal Rights: Collected Papers 1981-1991*, Cambridge, Cambridge University Press, 1993, 143-167

Walsh, Brian J and J Richard Middleton, *The Transforming Vision: Shaping a Christian World View*, Downers Grove: InterVarsity Press, 1984

Wood, G Antony, 'Church and State in New Zealand in the 1850s', *Journal of Religious History,* **8** (1975) 255-270

Wuthnow, Robert, *Christianity and Civil Society: The Contemporary Debate*, Valley Forge: Trinity Press International, 1996

Index

For Product Safety Concerns and Information please contact our EU representative GPSR@taylorandfrancis.com
Taylor & Francis Verlag GmbH, Kaufingerstraße 24, 80331 München, Germany

www.ingramcontent.com/pod-product-compliance
Ingram Content Group UK Ltd.
Pitfield, Milton Keynes, MK11 3LW, UK
UKHW022218190926
475702UK00003B/430
9781138726727